HOW AMERICA
SAVED THE
WORLD

Books by Eric Hammel

76 Hours: The Invasion of Tarawa (with John E. Lane)

Chosin: Heroic Ordeal of the Korean War

The Root: The Marines in Beirut

Ace!: A Marine Night-Fighter Pilot in World War II (with R. Bruce Porter)

Duel for the Golan (with Jerry Asher)

Guadalcanal: Starvation Island

Guadalcanal: The Carrier Battles

Guadalcanal: Decision at Sea

Munda Trail: The New Georgia Campaign

The Jolly Rogers (with Tom Blackburn)

Khe Sanh: Siege in the Clouds

First Across the Rhine (with David E. Pergrin)

Lima-6: A Marine Company Commander in Vietnam
(with Richard D. Camp)

Ambush Valley

Aces Against Japan

Aces Against Japan II

Aces Against Germany

Air War Europa: Chronology

Carrier Clash

Aces at War

Air War Pacific: Chronology

Aces in Combat

Bloody Tarawa

Marines at War

Carrier Strike

Pacific Warriors: The U.S. Marines in World War II

Iwo Jima: Portrait of a Battle

Marines at Hue City: Portrait of an Urban Battle

The U.S. Marines in World War II: Guadalcanal

The U.S. Marines in World War II:
New Georgia, Bougainville, and Cape Gloucester

The U.S. Marines in World War II: Tarawa and the Marshalls

HOW AMERICA SAVED THE WORLD

THE UNTOLD STORY
OF U.S. PREPAREDNESS
BETWEEN THE WORLD WARS

ERIC HAMMEL

ZENITH PRESS

This book is respectfully dedicated to the gallant American soldiers, sailors, airmen, and marines who achieved victory in World War II, and to all the tireless workers who gave life to the arsenal of democracy.

First published in 2009 by Zenith Press, an imprint of MBI Publishing Company,
400 First Avenue North, Suite 300, Minneapolis, MN 55401 USA

Zenith Press titles are also available at discounts in bulk quantity for industrial or sales-
promotional use. For details write to Special Sales Manager at MBI Publishing Company,
400 First Avenue North, Suite 300, Minneapolis, MN 55401 USA.

To find out more about our books, join us online at www.zenithpress.com.

Library of Congress Cataloging-in-Publication Data

Hammel, Eric M.
  How America saved the world : the untold story of U.S. preparedness between the world
wars / Eric Hammel.
      p. cm.
  Includes bibliographical references and index.
  ISBN 978-0-7603-3511-6 (hb w/ jkt)
  1. United States—Armed Forces—History—20th century. 2. United States—
Armed Forces—Mobilization—History—20th century. 3. United States—Military policy—
20th century. 4. United States—History, Military—20th century. 5. United States—
Defenses—History—20th century. 6. World War, 1939-1945—United States.
7. Industrial mobilization—United States—History--20th century. I. Title.
  UA23.H363 2009
  355'.03327309041—dc22
                          2008045649

On the cover and back cover: *(background)* Foggy day. *iStockphoto.* *(main)* Marines from
Company F along with engineers patrol through the thick fog in the early morning of Nov.
18 during Operation TRIFECTA. *U.S. Marine Corps*

Designer: Diana Boger
Jacket Designer: Simon Larkin

Printed in the United States of America

Contents

Introduction

Y OU CANNOT JUST WISH a modern army into existence.

Even at the outset of the most dire national emergency, when citizens reflexively flock to the colors because the nation is under attack and about to be overrun, a military establishment cannot simply unfold into a far vaster organization than it had been on the eve of the war. It takes years to build a world-class military organization, to recruit and train the core of professional officers and noncommissioned officers that will train and lead a wartime army, to equip the recruits, to move them, to house them, to fit them into a coherent plan—and to set them toward the ultimate goal of battlefield victory followed by battlefield victory all the way unto crushing the aggressor in whatever way makes him accept that he has been crushed.

The place to begin is with a plan drawn up in peacetime by soldiers who understand all that it is possible for soldiers to understand about soldiering. It takes years and decades to create such soldiers, and years and decades more to recruit, train, and season their successors.

The army, whatever its peacetime size and condition, must be guided and supported by its national leaders over many years in setting and perfecting its full range of wartime priorities. It must be supported by some sort of reliable budgetary process as it tests, adopts, purchases, and replaces equipment over time. It must be able to spend money to maintain old equipment as newer replacement equipment is tested, adopted, purchased, and integrated. That is, it must be equipped and ready to fight a war now with whatever it has placed in the hands of the troops even as it seeks to place better weapons and equipment in their hands. It must forever look forward to what it might field at some future date, in some future war.

Even with a solid basis of seasoned troops who might oversee a sudden, rapid expansion, even with warehouses filled to capacity with adequate modern equipment ready to be issued to new recruits, the army still cannot expand more rapidly than it can assemble, house, feed, condition, and train the new recruits. No matter how dire the emergency, there are physical limitations on an expansion, even under the most serious threat. Who will build the barracks and camps that will house and train the new recruits? Who will feed them, where will the food come from, who will get it where it needs to go, and by what means will it travel? How will farmers know what to grow, and how will they be paid? How will the civilian population get what it needs to feed and clothe itself and heat its homes if the burgeoning army simply snaps everything up? If all the working-age men flock to the colors, who will run the factories and farms and trains upon which an all-out war effort perforce depends? And on and on and on.

What about a navy, too? What about an air force?

Because the United States undertook its first offensive operations in the Pacific within only eight months of Pearl Harbor, most historians and readers of history depict and perceive the quick transition in 1942 from defensive war to offensive war as a miracle: Poof; here's your army, here's your navy, here's your air force; go thrash the enemy with them. In the narrative Americans have written for themselves, the peace-loving and ill-prepared sleeping giant, the United States, is suddenly struck, out of the blue, by enemies who use her peace-loving ways against her while a mere sprinkling of gallant, dedicated soldiers, sailors, and airmen fight overwhelming odds to barely hold the line against an unremitting backdrop of tearful defeats, especially in the Pacific. Meanwhile, U.S. industry suddenly—*instantly*—gears up, becomes a magical "Arsenal of Democracy" that produces uncountable tanks and ships and guns, not to mention trained soldiers, sailors, and airmen in their legions, fleets, and air armadas that will, in less than four years, smash the wiliest and most powerful enemies yet confronted at any time in human history. The appearance of all that stuff and all those battle-ready young men so soon after the surprise attack look exactly like a miracle.

There was no miracle.

The ascension of the United States to the preeminent role in the prosecution of World War II was deliberate, orderly, and integrated. It was conceived and overseen by the best minds the nation had in place. It was a human endeavor, so mistakes were made, things didn't always go right, plans and visions had to be scrapped or transformed along the way. But there is nothing in the conduct of war that has ever run so well, so true, so straight to the heart of victory. Nothing.

A cool appraisal of the facts reveals that America's stunning, unprecedented, and overwhelming moral response to German and Japanese aggression in the mid- and late 1930s, a response that eventually brought a huge portion of the globe within its embrace, was far less a miracle than an inexorable force of nature.

America *was* a sleeping giant. But the decision to turn the entire force and will of a hard-working, innovative nation to arming for war was *not* made in the wake of Pearl Harbor. By Pearl Harbor, an alliance of the American government, American industry, and the American military community was already three-fourths the way up the road to complete preparedness, a journey that was begun in mid-November 1938, only a little late; a journey that would effectively be completed by mid-November 1942.

Once the decision to rearm was taken, the unbelievably complex, at-times-visionary work of preparing America to win a worldwide war of movement proceeded apace the necessary untangling of the bureaucratic machinery that then held government's feet to the twin fires of traditional conservative spending policies and the late- and post-Great Depression economic and social realities. Once taken, the decision the American nation made to destroy European fascism and Asian militarism never flagged, never wavered, never paused, never rested in its inexorable march to victory and world peace. In the sense that America was the sparkplug that ignited the Allied cause and the factory and warehouse from which the Allied cause sustained itself from 1940 onward, it is fair to say that America saved the world from the yoke of German-led fascism in Europe and Japanese mercantile militarism in Asia and the Pacific. Here, then, in all its glory, is the true story of how America saved the world.

Eric Hammel
Northern California
Winter 2008

Part I

DECLINE

November 12, 1918
–
November 13, 1938

Chapter 1

The Decline of the U.S. Army

What Are Armies For?

W HY DO NATIONS STAND UP and maintain armies?

Historically, armies are created to fight wars as they occur, to protect borders against invasion, and to project political will beyond their own borders. A fourth reason for a standing army is to impose internal repression within a nation. And a fifth reason is to soak up young men who face grim employment prospects and who might be induced to revolution if not for the army pay they receive and the army discipline and work they endure.

In order to accomplish any of these missions or any combination of them, the army's power must be credible. The army must be big enough, strong enough, well enough equipped, and well enough motivated and trained to be feared as it sets forth on any of its missions. And it must be backed with sufficient and credible political will by its nation or, at least, its nation's leaders.

Being credible in its mission requires that an army plan ahead and prepare adequately to carry out that mission. For a nation to *avoid* a war or to achieve any other national objective short of war through the specter of military force is to convince potential enemies that its army will win and their armies will lose a war. Doing so does not require that a nation actually be warlike, but it does require that a nation be able to credibly assert its willingness to go to war—and win.

Even in an era of universal peace, where every politician agrees that war cannot possibly trouble the land, the skies, or the seas, military professionals are, by nature and the honor of their oaths, the last people to put down the sword in order to take up the plow. In fact, while they are soldiers, they never do put down the sword. Being ready for war—at least mentally—is what they are about. There is only one thing a warrior need bother himself with in a time of peace, and that is preparation for the time of war that will eventually follow.

In the Wake of the Great War

Following the United States' immense but largely unused rearmament for the Great War, American military storehouses in 1919 were chock full of the most modern weapons and supplies of the time. Likewise, the largely unused combatant navy of the day was among the largest and most modern in the world, and it continued to commission ships well into 1922. Great War stockpiles and arrays of weapons were able to sustain the U.S. Army for approximately a decade and the U.S. Navy for even longer, so little or no replenishment took place or was needed during the early 1920s. Unfortunately, by the time new stocks and designs for modern weapons and other systems were required, the nation and the world were in the throes of the Great Depression, so there was then no money to support the growing shopping list of military necessities. Indeed, there was a strong and growing domestic political sentiment against maintaining a world-class military potential at all.

Although the United States had suffered little in the Great War, its predominant cultural inclinations were rooted in and aligned with Europe. Thus, most Americans keenly felt the terrible waste of the flower of European manhood that had taken place in the bloodletting of 1914–1918. The concept of another general world war was as unthinkable during the 1920s in the United States as it was in war-ravaged Europe. Barely submerged in 1917 and 1918, the American peace and disarmament movements reemerged and even grew in the United States during the 1920s. The coincidental interwar prominence in the United States of separate but objectively allied populist "peace" movements—pacifism and isolationism—plus the realities of the Great Depression forced the nation to undergo a de facto and nearly (but not quite) de jure disarmament and general military decline lasting for decades.

Army Mobilization Planning

The overriding concern—and goal—of America's professional soldiers in the wake of the Great War was that the army be able to mobilize, train, arm, and send to war as competent soldiers masses of men who had been civilians until called to national service in the face of a major future war. The job of the standing army, known as the Regular Army, was to prepare in every way possible, to remain prepared in every way possible, and to train and lead the mass civilian wartime army to victory.

U.S. Army planners in the immediate aftermath of the Great War determined that the nation required a Regular Army of 500,000 full-time soldiers, including medical personnel and airmen. It quickly became clear that there was no way the Congress was going to allow the Regular Army to muster more than 18,000 officers and 280,000 enlisted men at one time. The professional soldiers had a difficult time agreeing among themselves what the irreducible minimum really ought to be, but they had to agree that fewer than 300,000 was going to be what they got in the near term. Any immediate shortfalls in time of war would be made up from a well-trained National Guard, a modern extension of the traditional state militias, as well as from the army's Organized Reserve, which was composed entirely of officers. It remained to be seen, however, how large and how well trained the National Guard and Organized Reserve would be. When professional soldiers raised the issue of universal military training—a European system for training every able-bodied male, then releasing them into civilian life with an obligation to be called up in time of war—the notion was smacked down at every turn as "too militaristic."

The Regular Army was needed to fulfill the Protective Mobilization Plan, as defined in the National Defense Act of 1920. Under the plan, the Regular Army would be able, on its own, to undertake necessary overseas commitments in peacetime (defending the Panama Canal Zone and the Philippines, for example), as well as serve as the permanent framework at home around which a mass wartime army composed of fifty-four infantry divisions (nine regular, eighteen National Guard, and twenty-seven reserve) and numerous diverse ancillary units would be formed in a very short time. Specifically, in peacetime, the Regular Army was to man essential headquarters, combat units, and support units amounting to a shell for nine regionally based army corps that would be manned in time of emergency by up to four million Regular Army, Organized Reserve, and National Guard troops. Each corps headquarters was to maintain fully manned standing units, including one complete infantry division apiece that could be sent to war on short notice and cadre-manned units that could be expanded quickly and efficiently under the supervision of professionals who had been trained and equipped for the job. Subject to a call from the president, all or part of the fully manned Regular Army units and specified Organized Reserve officers could be used for military expeditions that did not require a general mobilization.

In the event of a general mobilization for a major war, the Regular Army was to both train raw recruits and form cadres around which many new units could be activated. Some Organized Reserves were to be absorbed into standing units, and the National Guard was organized into eighteen infantry divisions plus sundry independent battalions and regiments that, over time, originated in all the states and most U.S. territories. These units and unassigned reservists would be absorbed into the standing army per the mobilization plan, and then all units would be filled in as needed from the pool of wartime recruits or other available sources. Thus, in order to quickly and efficiently field a totally balanced force of up to four million men, the U.S. Army convinced itself that it required a solid professional core of, at minimum, 280,000 well-trained, full-time, regular enlisted soldiers and nearly eighteen thousand officers.

The National Defense Act of 1920 authorized a Regular Army of 175,000 to 280,000 men, a National Guard of 425,000 men organized into eighteen infantry divisions and four cavalry brigades, and an Organized Reserve of no determined size. These were goals, not numbers in hand. In reality, the postwar Regular Army had its hands full maintaining an average strength of 180,000 officers and men through 1921, and the entire National Guard mustered a high of only 150,000 that year. Moreover, the peace lobby remained hard at work to enact legislation that would set the maximum size of the Regular Army at 100,000 men. As early as 1921, it won a congressional effort to set the Regular Army at only 150,000 men. Between 1922 and 1929, the Regular Army's actual strength fell to a low of 110,000 and was never greater than 125,000. In 1923, the army had but three real and six imaginary infantry divisions on its active rolls. Of the real ones, two were hollow shells nominally guarding the coasts; only the 2d Infantry Division, stationed along the Texas-Mexico border, was anywhere near full strength.

Times were good, jobs were plentiful; there was no need for fit men to find work as full-time soldiers. On the other hand, the aspects of local politics and clubbiness that characterized the National Guard experience of the interwar period fostered growth. Ordinary workers joined the Guard in order to rub shoulders with the movers and shakers in their cities, counties, and towns; it often made good economic sense do so. From a starting number of 56,000 in 1920, the National Guard's rolls expanded to 176,000 by 1924.

The Organized Reserve was more problematical in that it was never really *organized*, beyond designating twenty-seven reserve infantry divisions on paper in 1920 and nominally assigning its forty-six thousand reserve officers to them in the event they were ever activated. The main entry point for the Organized Reserve was the Reserve Officer Training Corps (ROTC), which was set up on college and even high school campuses. While a steady flow of newly minted reserve lieutenants emerged from the ROTC, the Organized Reserve was allotted no enlisted men. There was thus absolutely no way the plan was going to yield twenty-seven of the fifty-four infantry divisions foreseen in the mobilization plan without taking in at least 475,000 raw recruits, men with *no* military experience.

As the actual number of officers and men dwindled to just 120,000 in 1932, the Regular Army was forced to abandon manning many of even the nominal core units from which the much larger wartime field force was to be formed. In time, there was no chance that an effective field force *of any size* could be forged quickly from the sickly remnant, which retained its core of three nominal rather than nine fully-manned Regular Army infantry divisions.

A Regular Army infantry battalion commanded by Lt. Col. George Marshall in 1932, on its best day, could muster barely two hundred effectives, including cooks and bakers. It was impossible to train two hundred men to do the job of the officially sanctioned, optimally sized 850-man infantry battalion, so training was largely meaningless. Indeed, putting rampant equipment shortages aside, putative combat units in the Regular Army had become so shriveled that effective training, essential tactical and operational experimentation, and even the effective testing of modern equipment and weapons became impossible. Even maintaining the equipment it had was an impossible chore for an infantry battalion standing at less than a quarter of its authorized strength. The army was so small—last in size among the major powers by a mid-1930s ranking—that there was virtually no point in having an army at all.

The new Roosevelt Administration, which took office in early 1933, provided no panacea for the army; it was a very, very long way from seeing rearmament as a tool for jump-starting the ravaged economy, and the president personally considered the army of less use in a defensive role than he did the navy. Moreover, the new administration was immediately put off by Gen. Douglas MacArthur, the army's chief of staff (November 1930 to October 1935), who had swept into office on a rather theatrical high horse that turned off many serving officers and politicians alike. In July 1932, when overseeing the breakup of so-called riots staged by Great War veterans in search of Depression relief, MacArthur had grossly exceeded President Herbert Hoover's specific instructions when he ordered his troops to demolish the so-called Bonus Army's Washington, D.C., camps rather than simply contain the demonstrations.

MacArthur's heavy-handed intervention with the Bonus Army rankled the Roosevelt people, who took office only six months later, and helped to shape an immediate move to cut the Regular Army's budget by 51 percent, the Organized Reserve's by 33 percent, and the National Guard's by 25 percent, as well as cutting the number of Regular Army officers to ten thousand. MacArthur lashed out directly at President Roosevelt when the two met: "When we lose the next war, and an American boy, lying in the mud with an enemy bayonet through his belly and an enemy foot on his dying throat, spat out his last curse, I want the name not to be MacArthur, but Roosevelt." With that, the theatrical MacArthur went outside to throw up, while the mightily offended president recovered his temper. In the end, Roosevelt backed down, but MacArthur, whose term as chief of staff was extended, had to toe the line set by Roosevelt's budgeters.

The army under MacArthur barely held its own, but at least it did not shrivel further from its 1932 low. After 1935, its enlisted strength rose steadily, but one of MacArthur's first cost-cutting measures in 1933 was to withhold ammunition from recruit training. In another cost-cutting gesture, he agreed to stand down the entire Army Air Corps if doing so would preserve the current ground-force manning levels, an eventuality that never came about.

The Army in Defense Mode

On August 27, 1928, as part of the worldwide quest for peace, U.S. Secretary of State Frank Kellogg personally signed his own labor of love, the Kellogg-Briand Treaty, which outlawed wars of aggression as national policy. Though the treaty had no mechanism to stop a war of aggression, the United States was serious enough about it to effectively place the U.S. Army in defense mode, at least as an ideal.

But even without Kellogg-Briand—which certainly had an effect on the congressional budgeters looking for an excuse to cut military spending—the interplay of three main factors—low manning, the inability to replace obsolescent equipment or even develop modern equipment (both heightened when the Great Depression took root), and the ascendant influence of the peace lobby in the Congress—defined the army's basic capabilities in the mid- to late 1930s. Beginning under the aegis of Gen. Charles Summerall during his term as chief of staff (November 1926 to November 1930), the army was forced by the stark realities of the time to turn its back on its long heritage of aggressive mobility and remake itself into a mechanism devised solely for the defense of the United States and its overseas possessions. The U.S. Army had not the power or the means to project itself into the world; it would be all it could do to man defenses along America's long coastlines and among America's modest but far-flung territories and protectorates.

Even the prospects for defending the U.S. shoreline itself diminished. In early 1930, after years of discussion and wrangling, the army and navy finally agreed that the army's Coast Artillery Corps would take the lead in defending the coastlines while the navy established a defensive perimeter farther out to sea than the range of the coastal batteries. This made little sense in the age of air power, but even as a nonstarter it was a nonstarter: the Coast Artillery Corps had for some time been woefully underfunded, was in no way up to the task, and had no prospects to get itself up to the task in any foreseeable future scenario. As if this wasn't enough, General Summerall agreed to President Hoover's request that all obsolete coast artillery batteries be shut down. How to choose? They were nearly all obsolete! One new coast artillery antiaircraft regiment—the only one so far in the continental United States—was activated in 1930, but it was assigned coverage of strategic points between Texas and the Carolinas, which obviated coherent coverage of any given point.

Summerall's successor, Douglas MacArthur, had a huge number of ideas for change—some good, some not so good. He intended to expand the Coast Artillery, for example, by ordering surplus 14-inch naval rifles salvaged from decommissioned battleships to be repurposed as mobile railroad guns that could shuttle between a hundred prepared positions along the American coasts. (This project alone would cost a nonexistent $100 million.) He also pushed a plan to replace the horse cavalry with modern armored cars. And he proposed that all fit males between the ages of eighteen and forty-five be registered for a draft in time of war. All of these projects foundered on the budgetary shoals, not to mention some internecine battles involving committed horse cavalrymen.

Bowing in the end to all the realities facing the army, MacArthur in 1933 had his War Plans Division devise a mobilization scheme of three stages that came to be called the Initial Mobilization Plan. Stage I contemplated that the Regular Army's strength would remain at the current 133,000 troops. Stage II merely hoped for an end strength of 165,000 regulars and 235,000 National Guardsmen. And Stage III looked all the way back to the 280,000 Regular Army end strength of the 1920 Protective Mobilization Plan, plus a wished-for 235,000-man National Guard. If a mobilization began in Stage I, it would take four to six months to field a defense force of but four complete infantry divisions supported by almost nothing at all. Given a Stage II start of 165,000 regulars, it would be possible to field a relatively balanced defense force built around the same four Regular Army infantry divisions plus five Regular Army brigades in the same four to six months. Also, with an end strength of 165,000 regular troops, it would be possible to expand the Army Air Corps to 14,600 officers and men, stand up four new antiaircraft artillery regiments, and modestly expand the army's nominal tank force. The basis for Stage III—a 280,000-man standing army—was so outside the realm of possibility that it remained only a planning concept, albeit an alluring one that the professionals thought of as the only realistic starting point on the table. No effort went into pressing for a 280,000-man Regular Army—it simply wasn't going to happen—but MacArthur pressed his political masters for *some* growth beyond the 1933 numbers, and so did his successor, Gen. Malin Craig (October 1935 to August 1939). Their efforts were not without fruits; by mid-1937, the Regular Army had grown to 165,000 troops, so Stage II mobilization planning could finally be equated to a real end strength. Withal, the National Guard portion of the equation *never* reached the 235,000-man threshold contemplated in any of the plans.

In terms of providing a framework for mobilization and defense, and staffs to oversee them, the 1920s mobilization plan had divided the United States into nine geographical areas and assigned a functional corps headquarters to each one. But the realities of the early-1930s budget crunch forced Chief of Staff MacArthur, in his 1933 mobilization plan, to reduce the number of military-region headquarters to a realistic four, which were dubbed armies (First through Fourth, as shown in Appendix A). During the early part of his tour, Chief of Staff Craig assigned one standing Regular Army division to each of the four army headquarters, even though not even one division could be fully manned.

All this really meant was that, per the terms of the 1928 Kellogg-Briand Treaty outlawing wars of aggression, the U.S. Army found itself, at length, of a realistic size and organization from which it *felt* it could efficiently grow *in time of national emergency* to a strength at which it *hoped* it would be able to defend the United States itself or, more likely, rush troops to defend distant territories and protectorates. And even that required enough foresight or advance notice to build up the army through emergency recruitment and training of masses of recruits and/or by calling up all or part of the National Guard as well as individual officers from the Organized Reserve. If the Regular Army itself had to rush off to war at a moment's notice, there would be no professional core around which to build the contemplated war army that was to follow on. If an expeditionary force activated under the Initial Mobilization Plan had to be dispatched in due course to wrest back a lost territory or protectorate following a successful invasion by a militarily competent foreign aggressor, there was no telling if such an expedition could achieve success.

Above all, the Regular Army of fewer than the 280,000 well-trained officers and troops that the professionals dreamed of made real the peace lobby's fondest dream: There was no way the U.S. Army could be wielded in a war of aggression, nor even in a limited preemptive military campaign. It had been turned utterly into a defensive framework—if it could even manage that.

As late as mid-1938, the army alleged an ability to field two complete corps (at least four divisions plus support units) within two days of the declaration of an emergency; that an initial protective force of 400,000 men, mostly National Guardsmen, would be ready to ship out within two months; and that 730,000 recruits and officer candidates would be undergoing training. This was highly misleading. Even though the Regular Army stood at nearly 184,000 in 1938, massive numbers were dedicated to staffs or noncombatant arms and duties that were absolutely essential for administering and supporting an army at war. And by 1938 the field force the army had in hand was still underequipped and uniformly lacking in modern weapons and equipment. On top of that, the army did not possess the facilities to house and feed 730,000 recruits, much less the equipment needed to train them, nor even the trainers.

The Army Command Structure

It is ironic, given that there was an insufficient field force to command, that one aspect of postwar modernization that went really well for the U.S. Army was a complete revamping of its command structure in the 1920s. That is, the army created an immense modern command and administrative structure to oversee the smallish field force of the day. Using the French General Staff of the Great War as its model, the General Staff of the U.S. Army, in a decisive move to streamline operations and reduce numerous crossed lines of command and responsibility, stood up major directorates dubbed Personnel and Administration (G-1), Intelligence (G-2), Plans, Operations, and Training (G-3), and Supply, Transportation, and Construction (G-4), plus a War Plans Division. Moreover, G-1 through G-4 were replicated in scaled-down form throughout the army field command structure to the battalion staff level. In addition, chiefs of the army's standing combat arms—infantry, cavalry, artillery, etc.—were included alongside the directorate chiefs. And the modernization permanently established several modern combat and support services, such as the Army Air Service, the Chemical Warfare Service, and even a new finance department, each overseen by a major general and each with a voice in relevant General Staff discussions and policy agendas. The bad news here is that manning for the new headquarters departments, directorates, and services came out of however many officers and men the Regular Army mustered in toto. At one point in the early 1920s, three infantry battalions had to be stood down at once to provide personnel spaces for the Army Air Service. Similar moves were contemplated from time to time, but not carried out, well into the 1930s.

Funding the Army

Manpower aside, the gravest of grave problems facing the army's ability to wage war competently was the miserable level of funding it faced for two full decades following the Great War. In one sense, the problem began with the massive Great War rearmament, which actually overshot the armistice by a year or two. In 1920, America's armories were bulging with some of best modern armaments of the day. There was enough for an army ground force of millions, so for years there was little the army had to carp about with respect to numbers of weapons or their place on a modern battlefield.

The problems that arose were twofold. In the first place, military goods simply wear out or break over time; the bulging warehouses were inexorably emptied, but they were not refilled. The other problem was that the United States existed in a real world of powers and would-be powers that had dynamic, ongoing weapons programs that over the course of time rendered many American weapons and much equipment obsolescent and even obsolete. Trucks, for example, evolved rapidly in the civilian world, in major part because engines providing more power at less cost evolved rapidly in the highly competitive commercial environment. A nation's access to modern, evolving motor transport affected the relative mobility of that nation's army. It is ironic that the United States, an industrial powerhouse that had a world-class army in 1918, fell behind nations like Brazil, which had relatively little in 1918. This is because the Brazilian soldiers had to fill in the many outright voids in their equipment tables, while the United States Congress saw no need to purchase—or even develop—modern military equipment until all the old, obsolete, or obsolescent stuff had been used up. It is doubly ironic that modern military goods the world over were based in very large part on American industrial advances aimed at the civilian market: aircraft design and aircraft engines, to name but two. The armies of the world eventually adopted many modern American-designed or American-inspired military equipment, but America's army did not.

Two areas of military equipment prospered: the design of aircraft and naval vessels. It appeared obvious to the budgeters and the Congress that a nation's naval and air supremacy were entirely dependent on keeping apace technological developments. Thus, as any nation—the United Kingdom, for example—made gains in naval gunnery design, the United States endeavored to keep up. This meant, at the outset, completing the conversion from coal propulsion to petroleum by scrapping old ships and replacing them with the latest models. Later, longer-range naval guns were the imperative, and that led to increasingly modern warships. This natural drive toward keeping apace creeping modernity did not always align with the ruling political outlook—President Herbert Hoover's personal pacifism, for example—but it did foster progress, even if it was grudgingly applied. Or maybe it was about panicking with respect to another navy's achieving ascendancy over the U.S. Navy's ability to protect maritime commerce, while at the same time remaining blithely sanguine over warehouses chock-a-block with army stocks that were falling behind or rotting away at an accelerating pace. It took years to build a capital ship, but only days to build a rifle or a truck, so the ship received a natural priority; a day to build a rifle did not appear to be a hurdle. But the design and testing of new, modern rifles remained moribund in the realm of ground warfare. There were too few research dollars allotted to the army's problem of keeping pace with industry's great strides.

No work was done for years and years to design new mortars or artillery pieces, or tanks or antitank weapons, or ground transport or field radios. The best example is the Congress's failure to budget a replacement for the army's basic infantry rifle, the Springfield .30-caliber bolt-action, five-shot rifle designed in 1903. The Springfield '03, as it was known, remained as lethal in, for example, 1935 as it had been in 1903 or 1918. It had the same killing power, per se. But there were modern technologies that could increase an American infantryman's rate of fire by a wide margin if only they were deployed in a new infantry rifle. The .30-caliber, eight-shot, clip-fed Garand M1 rifle, a gas-operated semiautomatic weapon—the best service rifle in the world for nearly twenty years—was produced in American arsenals from 1936 onward, but so few M1s were fabricated through 1940 because of budget constraints that the '03 went into battle with some army units when the United States entered World War II, and the Marine Corps used '03s exclusively throughout 1942.

New, modern designs for all manner of weapons and equipment were drawn up or submitted by industry, and quite often test models were fabricated, but virtually no new ground weapon or equipment was adopted or purchased. A look at what other nations were doing to modernize their armies failed to move the Congress closer to realizing that an arms race was proceeding the world around, whether the United States participated or not.

If the U.S. Army's default or even sole mission was defense, then the possibility of a successful defense became increasingly remote as the years rolled by without any progress toward maintaining a modern defensive field force.

Inadequate and at times erratic funding had a profound impact upon pay in the army, and problems with pay had an adverse impact on morale, which had an adverse impact on the ability to wage war. Very early in his new administration, President Franklin Roosevelt ordered a bank holiday—literally closed the nation's banks—as but one step toward stabilizing the economy and restoring fiscal soundness in fighting the Great Depression. Another step, passed by the Congress in 1933, was to furlough, without pay, large numbers of active-duty soldiers and sailors; freeze pay and halt promotions for others; and even roll back pay for many. Junior officers lost 20 percent of their spending power, noncommissioned officers lost as much as 23 percent, and privates lost nearly 44 percent. At some bases, local commanders sold hot "leftovers" at very low rates so soldiers eating for free in the mess halls could also feed their families, but most soldiers did not have commanders who thought to look out for such needs.

The Civilian Conservation Corps

One direct boon the army received from the Roosevelt economic recovery plan was its direct association with the Civilian Conservation Corps (CCC). The CCC was designed to throttle unemployment by putting fit young men to work on conservation projects at far-flung locations, doing jobs along the lines of planting billions of trees to overcome wilderness erosion, cutting fire breaks in wilderness forests, cleaning up lakes and streams, and generally looking after other natural resources. The CCC was designed to soak up excess manpower, an American version of a traditional role of a national army. The U.S. Army's role in the CCC was multifaceted. In the first place, most of the work was in the wilderness lands of the western United States, but most of the unemployed work force was in the East. The army's logistical expertise allowed the two to be smoothly merged as well as keep CCC camps supplied with food and other necessities. In 1933 alone, army engineers helped build 1,464 isolated CCC work camps and, for the most part, Army Reserve officers, as well as navy, marine and coast guard regulars, oversaw the facilities and trained the young workers. Senior Regular Army officers oversaw the CCC organization at a regional level. Among them was Lt. Col. George Marshall, who, concurrent with his duties as an infantry battalion commander, oversaw seventeen camps in South Carolina and Georgia that housed five hundred CCC workers. Lieutenant Colonel Henry Arnold, an army aviator and commander at March Field, California, housed three thousand CCC workers there and oversaw fifteen thousand CCC workers at project sites elsewhere in the state.

The CCC was win-win for all, but especially for the army. Its Organized Reserve officers and many noncommissioned officers got superb hands-on leadership experience overseeing an organization built along military lines (but not subject to military discipline). Also, the young workers got their first—and generally positive—taste of life in a setting very much like the army. The army, by its yeoman CCC service, received excellent publicity, which in itself forestalled a move by the Congress to cut its officer corps.

Summing Up

The U.S. Army ranked poorly in standing among world armies between 1922 and 1932. In 1933 it actually stood at seventeenth in a world ranking. Its first turn ever on the world stage, in 1917 and 1918, had been breathtaking; it stunned the world community by its power, the ability of its professional officer corps to wage modern warfare, and the breadth of the industrial infrastructure that supported it. Then the nation fell back into the isolation that had characterized the first 125 years of its history. Through the performance of its army, the Great War transmuted the United States into a preeminent world player—a role it embraced—but local politics coupled with financial distress prevented it from claiming its role as *the* ascendant world power.

Chapter 2

The Decline of the U.S. Navy

What Are Navies For?

WHY DO MARITIME NATIONS stand up and maintain navies? Historically, navies are created to guard maritime trade and, in time of war, also to attack or block an enemy's maritime trade (*guerre de course*). But as European sea-faring nation-states grew economically stronger in a condition of almost perpetual war between about 1650 and 1815, professional navies took on a life of their own. It was noted that one of the best ways to ensure the viability of maritime trade was to stand up, train, and maintain a professional navy that could take on an enemy state's professional navy in order to forestall its attacking or blockading your maritime shipping. Over time, while guarding one's own maritime trade and throttling the enemy's maritime trade remained the essential reasons for maintaining navies, most navies developed doctrine and trained to take on competing navies.

Maritime shipping is fairly vulnerable to the predations of enemy warships, but warships can more or less compete with other warships. So the nature—speed, strength, firepower, etc.—of one navy's warships was pegged at or a little higher than the nature of a competing navy's warships. To counter the superior strength of an enemy navy's warships, armed commercial shipping turned to convoying, then to requiring that convoys be escorted by naval warships capable of fending off enemy warships or sundry commerce raiders, such a privateers and pirates.

If one side developed an advantage in design of its warships, or its tactics, the other side attempted to match or exceed the new capabilities. And so forth. A perpetual arms race accompanied the rise of professional navies.

As a pure instrument of war, beyond the interests of commerce, navies undertook several additional or derivative missions. For millennia, infantry or marine detachments have served aboard ships as the core of a boarding party, to seize an enemy ship at sea, to repel enemy boarding parties, or as the core of a landing force that a ship or ships could launch against shore targets—enemy coastal batteries and watch towers, navigation markers, a shoreside warehouse district, or an enemy naval force or commercial flotilla anchored in a harbor.

Need pushed doctrine, and the development of doctrine took on the characteristics of the arms race that saw vast improvements in warships over time. Doctrine also pushed invention—better guns, capable of dueling stone coastal forts as well as wooden ships, or mechanisms capable of achieving faster or more reliable rates of fire.

By the late nineteenth century, after decades of relative naval peace and a decline of expensive navies, a new arms race broke out in Europe, primarily among the British, French, Germans, and Russians. They all overbuilt their standing armies and navies.

The Great War saw the advent of huge, modern navies that did very little direct fleet-versus-fleet fighting, even though a decisive battle between grand fleets was the center of the naval doctrine of the day. There was activity against commerce, including a searingly successful Allied blockade of Germany's access to the Baltic Sea, but the bulk of the commercial side of the naval war soon devolved into an ongoing campaign in which submarines hunted for commercial targets while relatively small naval vessels and auxiliaries hunted for submarines. To deflect these efforts, the submariners developed doctrines and systems to take on the submarine hunters, and so forth.

So, too, the attention of some of the largest warships ever to get underway on Earth's seas became fixed on similar warships. Between Germany's High Seas Fleet and Great Britain's Grand Fleet, there was really only one great battle, off Jutland in the late spring of 1916. Though in fact Jutland was the last of history's grand-fleet surface battles, it became the benchmark by which all great navies built up their surface fleets well into the 1940s. Once again, while the protection of one's own maritime commerce and attacks upon an enemy's maritime commerce remained the stated reason for which navies were built and maintained, in actual fact, the way naval vessels were built and their crews trained from about 1850 onward was to take on an enemy grand fleet in a battle involving only grand fleets. Or, if an actual grand fleet was not in the offing, then there would be battles between smaller fleets, or flotillas, or squadrons, or divisions, or between any number of surface warships versus any other groupment of surface warships. As it turned out, the Great War taught naval leaders that the best way to attack maritime trade was with submarines, and the best way to fend off submarines was with small, specialized antisubmarine surface warships.

Disarmament

The only international disarmament agreements to which the United States formally subscribed in the postwar decade were products of the Washington Naval Disarmament Conference of 1921–1922. When these lapsed, the United States signed the London Naval Disarmament Treaty of 1930. The 1922 naval disarmament agreements limited the individual and aggregate capital-ship tonnage allowed each of the world's five major navies (United States, Great Britain, Japan, France, and Italy) and four lesser powers (China, Belgium, the Netherlands, and Portugal). The ostensible objective of these naval treaties was the prevention of the world powers from reaching the same critical mass in weapons production and stockpiling that many people believed had sparked the onset of the Great War. The proportion of capital ships allowed under the treaty was 5:5:3 for the United States, Great Britain, and Japan, respectively.

In reality, from an American perspective, the central treaty was an opportunity to put the U.S. Navy on equal footing with Britain's Royal Navy, an American objective of at least a century, as well as to achieve and maintain superiority in numbers over Japan's burgeoning Imperial Navy. Moreover, a secret side deal obligated the British to forego the extension of a 1911 mutual defense treaty with Japan. Indeed, the naval disarmament conference, which actually raised Japan in the eyes of the world, served as a cover for Britain to drop the mutual defense treaty without incurring Japanese ire. France and Italy were included, each receiving a 1.75 share in the ratio, as a means to extend the cover and further raise Japan's prestige. The U.S. objectives were met because the United States had the capacity and money to build a huge, modern fleet, while the British were strapped for such funds and, indeed, heavily in debt to the U.S. Treasury. On the one hand, with respect to Britain, the United States realized a national strategic objective going back to the War of 1812, since when the Royal Navy had ruled the Atlantic. Now the U.S. Navy could rule that ocean. Getting Britain to forego extension of its mutual defense treaty with Japan was seen at the time as merely a prudent move against a nascent, distant, but worryingly energetic threat to U.S. interests in China and the Philippines in particular and East Asia and the Pacific in general. (For some years after the Great War, a wing of American "navalists" actually had Britain pegged as the next great threat to be faced by the United States. The British certainly were not happy that the Americans had wrung so many concessions from them in the 1922 treaties, but they never seriously considered squaring things by going to war with the overly energetic Anglophonic cousins across the Atlantic. Thus, the boisterous, wealthy United States replaced the war-strapped United Kingdom as the naval hegemon in the Atlantic without firing a shot, and by doing so set the conditions for *the* crucial military alliance of the 1940s.)

Oddly, except for lip service provided at the League of Nations (which the United States did not join), there were no comprehensive international agreements or conventions with respect to land armies. And even more oddly, no discussions were held between or among international heavy-weights regarding any restrictions whatsoever on the revolutionary new third dimension of modern warfare, the one on which many nations already pinned their future hopes for military supremacy: air power. The only treaty that nominally limited air power in any way was the 1922 naval disarmament treaty, which limited aircraft carrier construction. At the time, aircraft carriers, though classed as capital ships, were considered support vessels, not the important combatants they would become.

It was permissible under the 1922 treaty to bring new ships on line as long as older ships were scrapped, but only insofar as the tonnage restrictions on various types of ships were not exceeded—for example, new aircraft carriers no larger than 27,000 tons apiece, to an aggregate of 135,000 tons (that is, five 27,000-ton carriers). Other signatories openly used this device to modernize their navies, but the United States was a bit more circumspect due to the influence of the renascent peace lobby and its ardent congressional supporters.

The 1922 treaty, which was an American brainchild, caused the United States Fleet (the U.S. Navy's operational arm) to scrap or discontinue twenty-eight battleships, battlecruisers, or cruisers (i.e., "capital ships" rated at or over ten thousand tons and mounting 8-inch or larger guns). It was also agreed that the signatories would *start* no new battleships until at least 1932, a term of art that allowed the United States to complete three modern battleships already under construction—*Colorado, Maryland,* and *West Virginia.* Likewise, the U.S. Navy's first real aircraft carriers, the 33,000-ton *Lexington* and *Saratoga,* were built, per special agreement in the 1922 treaties, on the incomplete hulls of two battlecruisers that otherwise would have been scrapped; they were both commissioned in 1927.

Beginning in 1924, the Congress expressed second thoughts regarding the 1922 treaty when it authorized, under its terms, the construction of eight modern cruisers for the fleet and four light river gunboats for duty in China. As long as the United States scrapped eight cruisers built before 1907, the new cruiser construction was perfectly legal. Nevertheless, in the end, only two of the authorized cruisers were begun in 1924, and the remaining six were not started until 1927. The first of the new cruisers authorized in 1924 reached the fleet in 1935, and the last was commissioned in 1939. A single smallish aircraft carrier, *Ranger,* was authorized in the 1929 budget, laid down in 1931, and commissioned in 1934.

The United States elected a president in 1928 whose world view, as well perhaps as his Quaker roots, caused him to ban all new naval shipbuilding during his term in office. Underway projects were not discontinued, but *no* new capital ships were budgeted during the administration of Herbert Hoover, at precisely the time numerous warships had to be replaced to keep the navy competitive.

Manpower

Unlike the measure of pre- to mid-twentieth-century armies, where manpower was all, the measure of naval potency was generally linked to the number, size, and armament of the ships in the national fleet. Nevertheless, the manpower tides on which the U.S. Navy rode in the interwar period are somewhat reflective of potency. It is thus a significant measure of the strength of the U.S. Navy that in 1919, at the very top of its wartime power, its authorized strength was 215,000. In 1922 it was funded to a total of one hundred thousand enlisted sailors and nine thousand officers—down from the 122,000 men it actually had on its rolls going into that year's budget process. The actual number at the end of 1922 dropped to about ninety-one thousand as ships were withdrawn from the fleet, but also because of recruiting shortfalls. By 1933 there were only eighty-one thousand sailors on active duty. Because promotion at nearly every level became ossified as the navy contracted in size, there were so few junior-officer billets available during this period that half of the U.S. Naval Academy class of 1929 was released from its service obligation and sent home immediately upon graduation. There was no need for so many new ensigns, and no money to pay them.

Financial Constraints

While the obligations of the naval treaties were onerous to nations like Japan and Italy, which had immense maritime aspirations, the terms were in fact driven by the larger and more powerful signatories, the United States and Great Britain. The latter had immense financial problems coming out of the Great War, while the former's dominant political leaders were authentically interested in eradicating war from the face of the planet. By 1931, both nations were deep in the throes of the Great Depression, and both had powerful peace lobbies to reckon with. Japan and Italy also had immense financial woes in 1931, but neither was moved in the slightest by the peace movement's agenda; they built up their fleets and pinched pennies elsewhere.

Fleet Strength

While Great War victors squabbled over dividing up the German Grand Fleet among their own navies, German naval officers aboard German ships interned at the British naval fortress at Scapa Flow, Scotland, decided to take matters into their own hands. On June 21, 1919, the Germans scuttled nearly the entire fleet under the noses of the men guarding it. At one step, all strategic considerations regarding Germany as a naval power were swept aside. The only major fleets left in Atlantic and European waters were the U.S. Navy and the Royal Navy.

In July 1920, Secretary of the Navy Josephus Daniels reorganized the nearly monolithic United States Fleet into three unequal standing operational forces—the Atlantic, Pacific, and Asiatic fleets—each to be commanded by a full admiral. The weakest of the three was the distant Asiatic Fleet, which was composed solely of cruisers, destroyers, and smaller auxiliaries. The Atlantic Fleet, quite surprisingly, was the next weakest; it was assigned the same number of battleships as the Pacific Fleet, but it got fewer of the modern battleships.

The navy's battleship enthusiasts—the so-called Gun Club—reacted venomously to this division; they wanted all the battleships and nearly all of the rest of the fleet concentrated in a "grand fleet," which they had been taught was the best kind of fleet. Even if the Gun Club was right from a strategic perspective, plain old domestic politics held sway in Secretary Daniels' decision: West Coast residents were mildly alarmed by Japan's rise on the world stage; they wanted to see their navy from time to time. Moreover, West Coast shipyards and naval facilities were underutilized, so maintaining a strong Pacific Fleet was a good way to keep them on their toes, not to mention a way to put dollars into local economies.

This explains why Daniels formed the Pacific Fleet, but it does not explain why it had more hitting power than the Atlantic Fleet. Simply stated, Daniels foresaw Japan as the dominant emerging anti-American power in the world, a view shared by an ever-increasing number of senior military professionals.

In 1922, the new Republican secretary of the navy, Edwin Denby, bested Daniels by placing all but six of the nation's eighteen active battleships in the Pacific under the rubric of "Battle Fleet." He left in the Atlantic, as "Scouting Force," the navy's six oldest battleships, which were in fact too slow to serve as a meaningful scouting force of a fleet otherwise comprising swifter cruisers and destroyers. If feeding the workers at shipyards remained an imperative, then caring for six aged battleships did much to woo voters in East Coast ports. In due course, the modern fleet carriers *Lexington* and *Yorktown* were based in the Pacific, another sign as to where the leadership saw the gravest threat to American maritime power. It is nevertheless interesting to note that West Coast port and repair facilities were inadequate in 1920 and remained so throughout the decade.

Naval Allies

While the behind-the-scenes machinations going into the 1921–1922 naval disarmament conference were cover for America's moving up at the expense of Great Britain, the tension between the Anglophone powers dissipated quickly enough for a rational partnership to emerge. Absent a German fleet in proximity to the Atlantic, the Americans and British were united against pretty much no one in Atlantic waters. No one foresaw Italy or France as formidable naval adversaries, and the Royal Netherlands Navy, which ran near the end of the treaty pack, was certainly not expected to confront the combined Anglo-American fleet, or either one alone.

In the Pacific, the Dutch naval squadron protecting the Netherlands East Indies was fully aligned in purpose with the British Far East Fleet and American Pacific and Asiatic fleets. As Japan emerged more fully as a naval power, and especially as a super-aggressive trading power on mainland Asia, British, Dutch, and American interests became even more fully aligned.

The American plan for defense of its Pacific holdings and bases was Plan Orange, in which "orange" designated Japan. (Germany was "black," and a Plan Black remained on the navy's contingency roster even after the German fleet was scuttled.) Plan Orange was updated in the 1920s, especially in light of Japan's acquisition of German island possessions during and after the Great War. Inasmuch as a side agreement in the 1922 naval disarmament suite prohibited fortification of any bases within a huge area encompassing most of the Pacific west of Hawaii, west of the Aleutian Islands, and east of Singapore (none of which were included in the proscription), the central theme of Plan Orange—an island-hopping sweep westward from Hawaii—was not materially affected, but enough suspicion remained to justify the build-up of all the relevant Pacific and Far East fleets and squadrons as well as the eventual expansion of relevant naval bases.

Gun Club Wars

For all that the navy in general attempted to modify its ships during the 1920s, even given the treaty strictures, the aging and increasingly ossified Gun Club remained firmly in control of the navy itself. Lower-ranking hotshots of various stripes could make very little progress when promotions boards were dominated by a well-organized clique of high-ranking battleship enthusiasts. As carrier air was developing in the 1920s, the Gun Club took care to browbeat the carrier enthusiasts into cooperating in the myth that the carriers were fleet auxiliaries that might range ahead of the surface forces and use its aircraft as scouts. This was nonsense on the face of it; *Lexington* and *Saratoga* were faster than any battleship of the day and the warplanes they serviced, even in the 1920s, outranged battleship heavy guns by a factor of at least ten to one—to a distance at or near 250 miles as opposed to 22 to 25 miles for 14- and 16-inch guns. Moreover, as real experimentation got going, test after test proved that bombs delivered by dive-bombers, an American innovation and specialty, were far more accurate—by a factor of as much as ten to one—than huge shells fired over the horizon by battleships, even when the gunfire was directed by battleship- or cruiser-based spotter planes. Yet, the mix of aircraft aboard the carriers favored scout aircraft over attack aircraft, because the airmen had to keep a low profile before the turf-obsessed Gun Club.

The U.S. Navy's submariners faced the same predicament. The German navy had invented unrestricted submarine warfare—attack without warning of even unarmed vessels of all kinds. While this was authentically odious to nearly the entire world, it served as an antidote to the all-but-complete naval blockade of Germany in the Great War and as an object lesson in modern *guerre de course*. The "civilized" nations of the world took special care to outlaw unrestricted submarine warfare, and the Gun Club doubly sealed the deal in the U.S. Navy by forcing the submariners to pay public lip service to the notion that submarines were to act primarily as fleet scouts and as a forward battle line against enemy combatants. Whereas the aviators were the darlings of the Congress and had plenty of leeway to carry on experiments in offensive war with increasingly modern weapons, the submarine fiction played out in the form of arrested development that produced a truncated doctrine as well as a relative handful of short-ranged boats with very limited torpedo stowage. Where submarines took part in 1920s fleet exercises as "enemy" warships, the bold skippers who dared push aggressive attacks on surface combatants faced retaliation from Gun Club referees in the form of bad fitness reports that typically retarded promotion and retention. Through ongoing and onerous weeding out, the submarine community hewed to the necessary fictions, and the submarine service suffered accordingly across the years in that its doctrine remained limited and fixed, and bold leaders opted for aviation or left the service entirely.

✳

Cruiser Battles

The Gun Club prevailed to a lesser degree over the role and makeup of its cruiser branch. At its behest, the cruisers covered by the 1922 treaties were held to ten thousand tons and packed nothing larger than 8-inch guns. There was, however, no limit by number or aggregate tonnage of cruisers. Battleships, few in number, required cruisers and even destroyers for protection and scouting, and the more plentiful cruisers were terrific for training future battleship captains, so they were somewhat favored. Destroyers were tolerated to a lesser degree for the same reasons—they were rungs on the Gun Cub promotion ladder.

While there were no onerous treaty obligations with respect to numbers of cruisers and destroyers, President Calvin Coolidge took the view that large numbers of them the world around might embolden a dominant naval power and thus lead to war. He called a conference in Geneva, Switzerland, in 1927 to restrict cruisers and other combatant vessels. Only the United States, Great Britain, and Japan were invited. The Japanese pretty much balked; they had agreed to a lesser battleship force within the 5:5:3 strictures of the Washington treaties, but they had no intention of accepting a lesser status with respect to their cruisers. They pointed out that an Anglo-American alliance against Japan would leave Japan at a 3:10 disadvantage in battleships and that the only chance Japan had in that case lay in a large number of heavy cruisers. Indeed, the Imperial Navy in 1927 had twenty-nine cruisers in service to the U.S. Navy's twenty.

The Geneva naval conference came to nothing, and a rather hurt President Coolidge reversed himself mightily by proposing to the Congress in December 1927 an authorization for seventy-one new combatant vessels. This was overreaching by a wide margin. Alarmed pacifist and penny-pinching congressmen united to defeat the request. A chastened Coolidge Administration came back with a doable request for fifteen cruisers, which Congress pretty much ignored.

Following the Geneva debacle, the United Kingdom and France agreed to limit their fleets of 8-inch cruisers, which had the puzzling effect of riling Coolidge against both nations. In an Armistice Day speech in 1928, the lame-duck Coolidge noted that America's far-flung empire required that the navy be equipped with a large number of speedy, long-range warships—indeed, more such ships than other nations were entitled to. This led in February 1929 to the passage of Coolidge's 1927 request for fifteen cruisers: five nine-gun, 8-inch heavy cruisers and ten fifteen-gun, 6-inch light cruisers, all built on 10,000-ton platforms. Remarkably, this appropriation was passed only a few days after the Congress voted eighty-five to one to ratify the Kellogg-Briand Treaty, which renounced wars of aggression as "an instrument of national policy." Indeed, the cruiser bill contained an unusual clause that allowed the president to suspend the construction of any or all of the cruisers as well as the small aircraft carrier *Ranger* in the event another arms limitation treaty called for doing so. As it turned out, this bill was a last-gasp effort by the Coolidge Administration. Just two weeks later, Herbert Hoover was sworn in, and the new president gave fair warning in his inauguration speech that he intended to limit arms production as a means of ensuring peace.

Hoover got right to work seeking an international arms accommodation. He had pledged during his campaign to build the fifteen authorized Coolidge cruisers in the absence of a new, broader treaty, but he hoped it would not be necessary to do so. In any event, under the terms of the 1928 Kellogg-Briand Treaty, Hoover sought to limit the navy's role to defense of the coasts, and not undertake any wider-ranging missions.

As the Hoover Administration went about convening a new naval conference that would limit cruisers, destroyers, and submarines, the president made a goodwill gesture by canceling three of the five heavy cruisers, which in turn paved the way for British participation as well as setting London as the site of the conference.

Certain that Great Britain would ally itself with the United States in the event of war with Japan, the American negotiating team almost joyfully acquiesced to the British demand that the Royal Navy be allowed to build more light 6-inch cruisers than the U.S. Navy's goal of ten. Moreover, the United States agreed to limit itself to the 8-inch heavy cruisers then in service, or their replacements. Then, given the near certainty that the British and American fleets would fight on the same side, the Americans magnanimously offered Japan a slightly higher proportion of cruisers and destroyers compared to the United States and Britain—10:10:7 rather than 5:5:3. In American and British minds—and no doubt in Japanese minds as well—that added up to 20:7. By this time, France saw Fascist Italy as a threat, and it therefore declined to limit its construction of cruisers and destroyers. The tripartite London treaty of 1930 established a five-year moratorium on new battleship and carrier construction and put in place a schedule for replacing submarines and other small warships. The treaty was set to expire at the end of 1936.

Admiral William Pratt, the American chief negotiator (he had also negotiated the 1920 treaties), was immediately rewarded by elevation to the post of chief of naval operations in May 1930. Pratt personally favored light cruisers over heavies, and this had had a material effect on the proposals and agreements he had engineered with the British heavy cruiser enthusiasts in London, which limited American 8-inch cruisers. This view cut across the desires of the Gun Club and led to Pratt's status as a virtual lame duck in his own service until he retired in mid-1933. It helped Pratt not one bit that his term coincided with the first wave of serious and sobering budget woes to arise from the Great Depression.

Budget Battles

In the first round of Depression-era cuts—in reality a means to square the acquisition of new ships with the terms of the London treaty, not to mention naval manpower caps—Hoover's Department of the Navy in October 1930 ordered an old battleship, two old cruisers, fifteen old destroyers, and twenty-five submarines to be decommissioned and scrapped. President Hoover then seized upon the Great Depression as an excuse to further downsize the navy. In 1931 he personally ordered the navy to look into trimming several yards and bases from its rolls. The navy, including Admiral Pratt, pushed back ever so slightly by claiming that it could manage all the existing bases on a reduced budget but could not do without any of them. After the Imperial Japanese Army invaded Manchuria in late 1931, this issue never came up again, but the Hoover Administration demanded other cost cutting. In point of fact, given continuing alarming news of Japanese expansionist moves in the Far East, the administration's cost-cutting efforts, per se, never really got traction. Hoover would not go along with any suggestions that would make the navy ready to confront Japan—or even to counter a direct challenge from Japan—but he did stop trying to further undermine the weak navy he had.

Altogether during the Hoover Administration, which fought hard and long for naval inadequacy, the navy commissioned ten heavy cruisers begun or authorized by previous administrations. Moreover, the smallish carrier *Ranger* was laid down in September 1931, and the naval aviation order of battle was expanded to provide more combat squadrons for *Lexington* and *Saratoga*. To accomplish the latter in the face of a limit of 5,499 commissioned active-duty line officers, the navy established pilot-training programs for qualified enlisted men and Naval Reserve ensigns. The fruits of these few but significant advances in the navy's ability to wage war had no immediate or even near-term effect, but they would have a direct, positive effect on the course of the first year of America's role in World War II.

The Roosevelt Renaissance

To call the early Roosevelt years a renaissance in context of the U.S. Navy is to emphasize the dark age of the Hoover years. Even after 1933, the navy's begging bowl could not be retired.

President Franklin Roosevelt, sworn in in March 1933, had served as an assistant secretary of the navy under Josephus Daniels in the Woodrow Wilson administration. In 1939, after six years as president, he boasted to Daniels about being "my own secretary of the navy." The new president revered and romanticized the naval service.

It took several years for the Roosevelt Administration to see expansion and modernization of the military as a public works project suited to weathering a period of economic depression. Nevertheless, from the start the Roosevelt people saw the expansion and modernization of the navy as a good thing in its own right because Roosevelt himself saw it that way. It didn't hurt one bit that the Democratic chairman of the House Naval Affairs Committee, Congressman Carl Vinson, was, if anything, more enthusiastic about naval power than even Roosevelt.

Building up the military as a means to aid the national economy was a completely new and not wholly developed economic theory in 1933. (The theory was that of the contemporary British economic philosopher John Maynard Keynes, who did not really codify it for publication until 1936.) The popular notion of the day was that money spent on arms was gone: simply money denied the American people for their real needs. All sense that the money spent in American arsenals and shipyards flowed, many times over, into the pockets of American workers and merchants and large businesses, not to mention tax coffers, was not quite there yet, and even when it was there, it was at first lost on most congressional budgeters.

Whether Chairman Vinson recognized the economic implications or not, as President-elect Roosevelt prepared to take office, Vinson lobbied him to set economic recovery money aside for naval construction. Indeed, as part of an otherwise civil public-works program set forth in the "one hundred days" $3.3 billion economic package that marked the beginning of Roosevelt's economic recovery plan was the response to Vinson's request: $238 million to be used for the construction of two modern fleet aircraft carriers (*Yorktown* and *Enterprise*), four cruisers, twenty destroyers (the first to be built since 1921), four submarines, and two gunboats. (Note that no new battleships were requested; the moratorium on new battleships was still in effect.) At the same time, and thereafter, Roosevelt backed Congressman Vinson's ongoing efforts to sway the Congress toward a systematic, predictable program to upgrade or replace older ships in order to keep a modern navy at sea. This effort led to the Vinson-Trammel Act, which Roosevelt signed into law in March 1934.

The Japanese Threat

Putting all other history aside for now, Japan served notice in 1934 that it intended to withdraw in 1936 from its obligations under the 1922 and 1930 naval disarmament treaties. This meant that the Japanese, who had already occupied Manchuria, could build a fleet to match their ambitions *and* fortify Pacific islands they had acquired in the Great War. These were islands that outflanked American possessions in the Pacific that the U.S. Navy planned to use, in the event of war, as way stations for its drive from the West Coast or Hawaii toward the Japanese home islands. Moreover, in June 1935, the British made a pact with Germany that held the German fleet at 35 percent the size of the British fleet. This was interesting and alarming because Germany had no substantive fleet in June 1935.

The U.S. Congress reacted to all the alarming naval news with linked legislation that had the effect of pushing its collective head further into the sand. In August 1935 the Congress passed several bills forbidding the United States to become enmeshed in a war in Europe. In February 1936, another bill required the president to embargo the shipment of arms to any nation he certified as being a belligerent. And, in 1937, the Congress came off the brake a bit by authorizing sales of goods to belligerent nations on a "cash-and-carry" basis. Collectively, all this legislation was referred to as the Neutrality Acts. Roosevelt sat on these constraining bills until hounded by public pressure into signing all three into law in May 1937

Only weeks after the "cash-and-carry" bill was passed, Japan launched all-out war against China. Against this grim backdrop, coupled with worrisome and even intolerable acts elsewhere, President Roosevelt, on January 28, 1938, asked the Congress to mandate an across-the-board increase of the United States fleet by 20 percent, counted in tonnage. The chief of naval operations, Adm. William Leahy (January 1937 to August 1939), put this before the House Naval Affairs Committee in the form of a specific request for $1.1 billion to build three battleships of the latest design, two more *Yorktown*-class carriers, nine 6-inch light cruisers, twenty-three destroyers of the latest design, nine submarines, and a rather astonishing 950 naval aircraft of all types. On the face of it, thanks to the request for carriers that Leahy had previously told the president the navy didn't need or want, this request was as blunt a warning to Japan as the administration felt it could issue.

The Naval Affairs Committee passed out the measure with ease and even added to the $1.1 billion budget request. The president signed the resulting bill on May 7, 1938. By then, events were spinning rapidly out of control in Europe and China, and a whole new mindset had to emerge with respect to adequately arming the U.S. Navy for possible war. The 1938 naval bill was the last prewar naval legislation in which the administration thought in terms of deterrence.

Stagnation in the Surface Fleet

During the decades of postwar decline, the navy made important gains in many technical aspects, such as ship design, propulsion, and naval armament—the fruits of a period of roiling general technical advancement in all industrial arenas. But the advance of American naval tactics and even operational and strategic dicta lagged far behind those of other world-class navies.

If you train for an event in a particular way, you will almost certainly conduct yourself during the actual event in just that way. Today, this is called "behavior modification," and it is consciously employed in every sort of training, from marksmanship to typing to flying high-performance jets to pitching baseballs. In the 1920s and 1930s, the U.S. Navy imbued its officers with the need to avoid training in ways that might result in accidental damage to their precious and irreplaceable ships. It also made examples of enthusiastic officers who espoused tactics and plans that might upset the fully conceived notions and inherited wisdom of the dominant Gun Club.

The grand model of the U.S. Navy's interwar training was the Battle of Jutland, one of two major night battles in which battle fleets had engaged in the previous 150 years. (The other was the Battle of the Nile, which took place in 1798.) Even though the German High Seas Fleet was vastly outnumbered and thus was charged with the loss at Jutland, it had in fact outfought the British battle fleet ship-for-ship. But even nominal losers are ignored as nominal winners are copied. Thus, U.S. Navy surface officers of the 1920s and 1930s were trained specifically to win a victory at Jutland, in which a British battle *column* engaged a German battle *column*—a British tactical innovation of the seventeenth century.

Among the many things the British naval commanders of the Great War and their American emulators overlooked was the way the Germans employed the Morse (as distinct from the nonexistent voice) radio as a means for exchanging information and passing tactical orders. The British, who had failed to recognize the radio's potential, made poor use of the new technology during the Great War. Between the wars, the U.S. Navy failed to make adequate use of the radio, one oversight among many that was to have dire consequences in its battles of 1942.

The U.S. Navy studied Jutland and reaffirmed its guiding principle that a naval campaign would be capped by a major, decisive, fleet surface engagement. This is why, despite a moderately successful building program that brought four aircraft carriers into the United States Fleet by 1934, there was little orderly or even discernible advance in the potential wartime use of this new class of modern warship. Those in authority developed few new ways of thinking about naval warfare that made adequate use of the enormous potential of the carriers. Carriers remained relegated to the role of fleet auxiliaries; their warplanes were able to scout out the enemy, fend off attacks, or even bomb enemy vessels, but they were not given a leading role, or even an independent role.

Since Jutland had been fought by columns of ships, the U.S. Navy surface fleet practiced for war with columns of ships. Actually, this formation ideally suited the prime requirement that U.S. Navy warships avoid collisions with other U.S. Navy warships. In the U.S. Navy, where all commanders lived in mortal fear of merely damaging their irreplaceable vessels, there was no experimentation because charging about aggressively in complex battle formations was known to lead to accidents. Columns of ships spaced at long intervals, playing follow the leader, are easier to control than other types of formations, and the potential for accident is low. Thus, "battle" exercises, particularly those conducted at night, were little more than cruising or night-cruising excursions. Safety, not innovation or even education, was paramount. Moreover, thanks to the effects of behavior modification, the only formation in which American commanders felt comfortable—and to which they invariably resorted throughout 1942—was the single battle column, one ship 500 to 1,500 yards (a mile!) behind the other. Thus were trained the captains and admirals who held sway in 1942.

The melding of fast fleet surface warships and the marvel of the radio resulted in no tactical innovation whatsoever. Morse radios were installed aboard all classes of warships, but no one developed tactics that exploited the radio's enormous range-enhancing exercise of command and control, particularly at night, when signal flags could not be read. Yet it was known that America's potential enemy in East Asia was developing a thoroughly modern battle fleet and experimenting with radical new night-combat tactics that made use of the latest night-vision technologies. In fact, though Morse radios were available aboard U.S. Navy warships throughout the 1920s and 1930s, changes in course during daylight exercises were communicated solely by means of signal flags. At night, the course changes were signaled by means of blinker tube, a trigger-controlled hooded flashlight that could be aimed and narrowly focused, thus nominally concealing both the signal and the position of the ship sending the signal. Morse radios were used exclusively for long-range communication between ship and shore or between fleet units that were out of one another's sight. Brief experiments to supplement the local transmission of orders by flag hoist or blinker tube with Morse radio messages came to nothing.

The American surface navy of the mid-1930s was essentially a bureaucracy waiting for a useful enterprise. It had not fought a major fleet engagement since 1898—which means that no one then serving in the navy had ever been involved in a real naval battle. A very few officers and sailors had been involved in brief skirmishes at sea in 1917 and 1918, but at ranks so low and in ships so small as to have no credible bearing upon their later responsibilities.

A Navy Wanting in Leadership

It is in the nature of navies to seize upon technology as a way to advance war-fighting abilities. Compared to army ground officers, naval officers tend to be open to change because they are often challenged by technological change. Yet . . .

The bureaucratic aspect of the U.S. Navy's long wait for a war lay at the heart of the unpreparedness of its leadership for war. The U.S. Navy's ethos in the 1920s and 1930s simply did not prize war-fighting skills over administrative skills. Careerism was rife; many of the men who got ahead were the ones who acquired advanced skills in keeping their heads down or effusively agreeing with their superiors. All their energies went into acquiring career-survival skills. Risk-taking of any sort, even speaking up or speaking out, was totally out of vogue. By 1935, many of the officers at or approaching flag rank were masters in avoiding risk, which is to say "decisions." Inasmuch as so many such men achieved high rank, their careerist philosophies were inevitably emulated by ambitious juniors who wanted to achieve similar success. Careerists on the rise tend to bring along younger careerists because they tend to admire the way men just like them think.

The ancient adage, "He who runs his ship aground will suffer a fate worse than death," was the unspoken watchword of professional officers of the day—literally. Seven U.S. Navy destroyers ran aground on the central California coast in September 1923. The ships were unsalvageable; heads rolled. The navy radically modified its behavior, taught itself to avoid *any* risks to the hardware. Taken to its extreme, the crippling ancient tradition and the risk-abating 1923 example, set so near in time, gutted the aggressive instincts of many fine potential combat officers. It's as true today as it ever was: In order to advance to a position where war-fighting instincts and skills could have an impact, the aggressive officer has to survive. Years of mere survival take their toll; the potential warrior who cannot stomach the system leaves early, and most of the others are eventually worn down by it.

When the opportunity arose in the 1920s and 1930s, many talented professional line officers opted for flight training, where, along with physical risk and excitement, promotions were a bit easier to earn (because of frequent fatal accidents) and positions of responsibility were a bit easier to attain because military flying isn't an old man's game. In the air, at least, aggressive, innovative instincts were prized. To a lesser degree, self-reliant mavericks made their way to submarines, which typically operated alone and far from prying eyes.

In order to hone and enhance his craft, the true warrior will eventually and inevitably take risks with his life, his subordinates' lives, and the equipment in his care. Many of the surface navy's natural leaders who neither left the service nor capitulated to the system eventually "ran aground" in one form or another, their careers ruined by indelible black marks in their personnel files. That any natural, truth-telling leaders remained in the surface force late in the frustrating interwar decades is a measure both of their sense of duty and the depth of the Great Depression.

What can be said about a military service that prizes administrative and career-survival skills over war-fighting skills? Admittedly, a measure of the blame rested with a parsimonious Congress, whose unyielding grip on the purse strings prevented the navy from replacing equipment lost or damaged at the hands of both inept and combative risk-taking commanders afloat. Yet, the watchword of the era was not so much "make do" as "watch out."

Summing Up

The U.S. Navy's decline after the Great War was for the most part a phenomenon of the American political and economic scenes. It was the United States, after all, that dragged the other major maritime players to the 1921–1922 naval disarmament conference, and indeed hosted the event. On top of that, the United States declined to even keep pace with the meager allotments of new ships set by the treaty. At the end of the Hoover Administration, there were 148 combatant ships of all types on the U.S. Navy's active rolls. Great Britain had 187 warships, and Japan—which by treaty standards was of the second rank—gamed the system for all it was worth and thus had 219 active fleet combatants on its naval rolls in 1933. From almost its first day in office, the Roosevelt Administration sought to simultaneously rebuild and build up the fleet. The early positioning established a momentum that served well as economic needs gave way to alarm concerning the national defense. Sinking morale in the surface navy was not addressed, per se, in the atmosphere of declining world peace. Indeed, it would not even be recognized until the navy had been at war for most of a year, until the late summer of 1942.

Chapter 3

Army Aviation

What Are Air Forces For?

WHY DO NATIONS STAND UP and maintain air forces?
Between 1914 and 1939, a lot of people made honest guesses and nations spent immense fortunes to find out why, but no one really knew.

A Hotbed of Development

The U.S. Army Air Service ended the Great War in terrific shape. It had large stockpiles of the three main types of military aircraft of the day: bombers, pursuits, and observation planes. It had plenty of trained and even blooded pilots. It had more ideas, collectively, than it knew about, more than it could handle. Above all, the Army Air Service was the particular pet of the Congress, the one new military toy the Congress, as an institution, wanted to encourage.

Even as the darkness of budgetary constraint settled and deepened over the land-bound army at the close of the Great War, the skies in which the air service flew brightened and lengthened. There was some turbulence and even some ill winds, but the air service generally prospered.

It prospered in ways other than via the fruits of funding and manning. It prospered because it opened the gate for land-bound professional officers to become aviators, and thus it drew in some fiery, influential older men alongside the fiery but malleable lieutenants and flying cadets it generally sought. Thus, it gained stature, wisdom, and political clout.

Over time during the interwar period, army aviation learned the value of showy public demonstrations. By firing up the public in favor of military aviation, army aviation fired up individual congressmen.

Throughout the interwar period, the nation was loony about airplanes and flyers. Cheap war surplus and the demobilization of many hundreds of wartime military aviators put flying experiences within reach of average American civilians via the barnstorming circuses that offered affordable hops into the heavens. Even watching the newfangled crop-dusters doing their job fired up farm-country youths to set their sights on careers in military aviation. The popular literature of the day was all alight with flying stories, the news-papers were filled with flying news, flying seemed to be everywhere, and it was great for escapist thinking—soaring high above the ground, unbound from earthly woes.

During the 1920s, there was an aviation industry boom. There was no commercial market for tanks or antiaircraft guns, but there was a burgeoning civilian market for airplanes that spurred growth far, far beyond the needs or even the dreams of the military aviation communities. As better aircraft and aircraft engines became available in the developed world's civilian sphere, the cash-starved military naturally asked for more and better equipment to keep apace, and the requests were granted after a fashion. Civil aviation took off in the late 1920s, and that's where important money fueled important innovation. In addition to simply publicizing aviation, per se, a constant stream of cleverly engineered record-setting flights in better, more powerful airplanes consistently raised the sights of the aviation world, and often as not the new records were set by military or former military aviators. The entire wired world of 1927 held its breath over the fate of that crazy Yank, Charles Lindbergh, who dared attempt to span the Atlantic in a single solo hop. Aviation was romance itself, the stuff of instant legend.

But it wasn't about fun, and the numbers of aviators killed while attempting to "push the envelope"—not to mention in common equipment failures, weather-related crashes, and all manner of simple bonehead misjudgments—was positively grim. It is sad but true that nearly every army airfield in the nation was named for an army aviator killed in a plane crash. Fortunately, not all these lives were lost in vain; real progress was being made.

The demobilization left the Army Air Service with roughly a dozen active air groups. One air squadron was assigned to each of the nine standing army ground corps. Each of three composite groups consisting of bombardment and pursuit aircraft was assigned for air defense over the Philippines, Hawaii, and the Panama Canal Zone. And four groups were maintained just so each aircraft type and techniques for flying it could be rigorously tested and doctrinalized.

Initially there were three aircraft types—pursuit (1st Pursuit Group), bomber (2d Bombardment Group), and observation (9th Observation Group). The 3d Surveillance Group, activated in 1919, was redesignated the 3d Attack Group in 1921 to serve as a test bed for a new military aviation specialty, dedicated support of ground troops. A much larger aviation order of battle existed on paper, but for practical purposes, this was it.

As well as active groups to train to go to war and to test the limits of pursuit, bombardment, and attack aircraft, the Air Service established the Tactical School at Langley Field, Virginia, in 1920. This freewheeling, all-opinions-welcome institution had two missions: draw in the best minds in the Air Service to develop doctrine, and then teach the doctrine to Air Service pilots and commanders. Modeled on The Infantry School at Fort Benning, Georgia, the Air Service Tactical School coupled intense thought with intense practical training as it prepared future leaders for command. It was a good thing the airmen had organized their own school; as late as 1929, when Maj. Henry

Arnold, the second army officer ever to earn wings, became a student at the army's Command and General Staff School at Fort Leavenworth, Kansas, he found that the prestigious institution, attended by the best officers from every branch and service of the army, offered practically no insight into the doctrines of air power, not even as they related to the rest of the army.

An Air Force In Search of a Mission

Even though the Army Air Service came out of the Great War with a solid core of veterans and a reputation for solid, reliable service, it had no clear mission and had developed no clear doctrine beyond the support of ground troops to a distance not much farther out than the horizon of the ground battles it had supported.

Brigadier General William "Billy" Mitchell, the American Expeditionary Force Air Service's colorful combat commander in France and an industrious thinker on doctrinal topics, frankly saw the ability to perform in the aerial arena as a replacement for all manner of older, even ancient, combat arms. For example, Mitchell felt that observation planes could supplant cavalry in the reconnaissance role, or specialized attack aircraft could supplant artillery in the role of sealing off a battlefield from reinforcement or retreat and could even deliver destructive attacks against enemy artillery. He even thought that long-range bombers could supplant the navy in a coast-defense role, and he believed that air power alone, when applied at the strategic level, could supplant ground armies.

Mitchell was not alone in the spinning of many visions for a strategic air force, but he was by far the most vocal—and most senior—American airman to try his hand at adapting the Great War's lessons and examples to further the expansion of the use of combat air assets.

Pursuit

Pursuit implies defense: come to us, and we'll chase you. Today, we call planes that intentionally tangle with other planes "fighters," but throughout the interwar period, U.S. Army planes designed to combat other planes were called pursuits, and they were indeed constrained to a defensive role in concept, construction, thought, and deed. This is because the technology of the interwar period kept small, high-performance airplanes on a short tether. A small plane with a big, powerful engine carried only a little fuel, which it burned very rapidly. The pursuit was developed over the course of two entire decades to a point-defense role. That is, it defended a specific target or target area—because it couldn't chase another airplane very far or go out very far to engage incoming enemy aircraft. Nearly all the world's air forces doctrinalized this reality, and nearly all carried it into World War II. This is not to say that the pursuit mindset thwarted tactical or developmental innovation—it didn't—but it fostered it only within the world defined by "pursuit"—or even "interceptor."

For all that the concept of pursuit got concepts the wrong way around between the world wars, America's leading airman of the Great War and its most ambitious aviation thinker of the early and mid-1920s, Billy Mitchell, did perceive a strategic role for the pursuit airplane of limited range. It was Mitchell's vision that formations of aircraft were in need of the means to carve out a region of the sky—a *moveable* region of the sky—that had been neutralized of enemy aircraft. This was the starting point for the concept of air superiority, a localized and transient state in which pursuits were ascendant over other pursuits or over enemy offensive bombers.

Pursuit aircraft were developed to knock down enemy pursuits, enemy bombers, enemy observation planes—*all* enemy aircraft. They did not have the range during Mitchell's service tenure to deeply penetrate enemy air space, nor was there much recognition that they might someday be able to do so, nor any overt intellectual drive to find the means to have them do so. For the interwar years, pursuits tethered by short operational ranges sought air superiority in the point-defense role over air bases and cities as well as over the ground war's front lines and short distances into the enemy rear.

But, in Billy Mitchell's prodigious writing, the short-ranged pursuit and its potential in the at-first dimly perceived notion of air superiority occupied a place of honor. Mitchell wrote that 60 percent of all tactical warplanes should be pursuits. A large pursuit force, Mitchell felt, would sweep the skies over the battlefield of enemy aircraft and thus free a ground army supported by bombers and strafers and unfettered observation planes from all the liabilities and depredations imposed by an enemy air force.

The development of pursuit aircraft to the boundaries of technology was pretty much neglected through the first half of the 1930s, but advances in bomber development alerted the pursuit community to the oversight. The Air Corps in 1935 moved to initiate a number of design competitions from which it hoped to find the best expression of the technologies of the day. The plane to beat was the all-metal, open-cockpit, fixed-gear Boeing P-26, a revolutionary monoplane pursuit when it first flew in March 1932 but swiftly outmoded. Two rather more revolutionary designs evoked the most interest.

The first design was the Seversky (later Republic) P-35, which over several revisions featured an all-metal fuselage, an enclosed cockpit, and retractable landing gear and tail wheel. The P-35 was armed with a pair of .30-caliber wing guns and a pair of cowl-mounted .50-caliber guns, and it was equipped to haul up to 350 pounds of bombs on wing shackles. Alas, budget constraints kept the total Air Corps order to just seventy-seven airplanes, which were deployed with three pursuit squadrons. Further redesigns led in stages by 1939 to the Republic P-43, which was ordered in very small numbers before it was eclipsed by further radical improvements leading to the much larger Republic P-47 of World War II fame.

The second design winner of the 1935 competition was the Curtiss P-36, which also featured an enclosed cockpit, all-metal fuselage, and retractable landing gear. It was armed with two .30-caliber wing guns and one cowl-mounted .50-caliber machine gun, and initially it had no provision for carrying bombs. The Air Corps accepted the Seversky P-35 design, but it continued to nurture the P-36 and, in 1937, finally ordered 210 of them. An export variant saw action with the Chinese air force, but the design was obsolete by the time a few Army Air Corps P-36s got into combat in the first days of World War II. Nevertheless, further upgrades to the P-36 design, including use of an inline engine in place of the typical American radial powerplant, went on to result in the immortal Curtiss P-40 design, which was upgraded and used in combat nearly to the end of World War II.

Alas, the P-35 and P-36 were both obsolescent before they went into production. Both were utterly inferior to the Royal Air Force's Hawker Hurricane, which was first ordered in quantity in June 1936 and—far more important—to the German Bf 109 fighter, which was tested in 1935 and which the Luftwaffe began to receive in mid-1937.

Bombardment

In the environment of a postwar army that, under legal restraint, was to be used exclusively for *defensive* purposes, it became difficult for army airmen to rationalize the development of large long-range bombers. Quite obviously, a long-range bomber carrying a large payload was an offensive weapon. So, even if American industry could develop such a weapon, how could it be justified under terms of domestic laws that forbade an offensive army in any of its parts as well as international treaties that eschewed the entire notion of offense? Armies, navies, and air forces during the interwar years were for defense, and only defense.

Billy Mitchell came up with an answer long before effective long-range bombers could be built. His justification was that, given the long sea approaches to all the American coasts, large bombers capable of attacking fast warships and troop transports far out at sea could supplement, if not replace, the army's own traditional coast artillery establishment. First by proving that aerial bombs could sink a ship—tests were run on German warships and culls from the downsized U.S. Navy in the early 1920s—Mitchell and his followers methodically built a case for attacking enemy shipping far beyond sight of the U.S. coast. When confronted by the fact that the U.S. Navy's aviation program was doing the same, the long-range bomber enthusiasts countered that Army Air Corps long-range multi-engine bombers based near the coast could search farther than shore-based naval aircraft or even the longest-ranged carrier scout. Further, even in small formations, those long-range bombers could lift more bomb tonnage than a squadron or two of carrier-based light bombers or even the heaviest naval seaplane patrol bombers. Moreover, the army airmen argued that, by leaving coastal defense entirely to the army, the carriers would be free to range farther out—all the way to the enemy coast.

The battle of ideas—particularly with respect to coastal defense—raged on between the army and navy until the autumn of 1930, when Adm. William Pratt, the chief of naval operations, concluded that his service could not afford to pay for static, shore-based naval aviation units whose sole purpose it was to defend coastal cities and their own fixed bases. Pratt literally handed the task of coast-defense aviation over to the army in an agreement with Army Chief of Staff Douglas MacArthur made in January 1931. Indeed, the agreement rendered each service "free to develop within well defined limits and each with a separate and distinct mission." Pratt, an otherwise powerful naval aviation proponent, could not quite get himself to give up the naval air stations ashore, so he redesignated them as support bases for the United States Fleet's air component under the rubric "fleet air stations."

So, as things developed, the army airmen who favored the long-range bomber got their way with respect to fielding such bombers in the context of coastal defense—but only so long as they paid public lip service to a purely defensive role. Of course they did that, but they thought and thought and talked and talked about—and fully committed themselves and the bulk of the army's aviation assets to—the development of long-range, high-payload bombers. These could attack and cripple enemy war industry (which they called "unraveling the industrial fabric") as well as a variety of other *strategic* targets—rail yards, for example—deep in the enemy rear. Moreover, given that successful bombing of a fast-moving ship by a level bomber required extreme skills coupled with a superb bombsight and feather-light maneuverability, the proponents of deep, offensive strategic bombing saw that the coast-defense role, a sincere effort, could easily be redirected into a deep, offensive, *precision* bombing role. In this role, formations of large, fast bombers operating at high altitude might be immune to antiaircraft fire and beyond the ceiling of enemy pursuit aircraft as they blanketed factories, rail junctions, oil refineries, port facilities, and all manner of other strategic targets with tons and tons of bombs at a time.

By pushing the precision of the bombing system, the army aviators were able to convince themselves and their political masters that large long-range bombers were not only up to, but ideal for, the task of bombing enemy vessels within range of coastal air bases. This led to the rather convincing argument that army aviation had a role to play in defending the sea approaches to the United States. And that argument led to the acceptance of the long-range bomber as a defensive weapon.

The Self-Defending Bomber

Independent of all attempts to rationalize an offensive strategic capability masquerading as a coast-defense capability, and given the limitations of the pursuit arm's equipment, the bomber force set out to develop bombing aircraft that could fly long distances while defending themselves against attacks by enemy pursuits guarding locales along the way to and over the target. This meant arming and manning bombers for a fight for local (and moving) air superiority, which is to say for their lives.

This line of reasoning encouraged the development of big, speedy airplanes whose range, speed, and payload (carrying capacity) had to be balanced among such items as essential equipment, fuel, bombs, defensive machine guns, and people. The balancing act initially led to a type of bomber that utilized fewer guns and men and carried a smaller load of bombs because it put its faith in big engines that could carry it through enemy skies at a higher rate of speed than enemy pursuits could manage. As bigger and better engines were developed, more and more weight could be strapped onto them.

Another defensive strategy was to build bombers that could cruise at higher altitudes than pursuits could reach. But high altitude means less oxygen. In one sense, less oxygen requires breathing assistance for crewmen via heavy, bulky equipment that eats into payload, range, and altitude margins. Also, engines getting less oxygen tend to stall. The supercharger was invented to keep engines going at high, oxygen-deprived altitudes, but they burned a lot of fuel, and that also reduced range and/or speed and/or payload. Every single one of these schemes—big powerful engines and/or armor and/or protective guns and gunners and/or protective speed and/or altitude—invariably was held hostage to the fuel-payload-range formula: the more you have of one, the less you can have of the others.

James Doolittle, an army aviation reservist who was one of the world's first doctors of aeronautical engineering *and* a renowned daredevil air-racing champion, went to special effort to brief aviation leaders that his employer, the Shell Oil Company, had (at Doolittle's persistent urging) developed the richest fuel so far put on the market—100-octane aviation gasoline. Doolittle assured his service colleagues that the new fuel would conquer the supercharger's high fuel consumption at altitude and generally enhance the performance of any type or model of airplane equipped with engines that had been optimized to use it. The army tested the new fuel in 1934 and quickly reported that pursuit aircraft with optimized engines got a 7 percent boost in speed and a 40 percent boost in rate of climb. Speed and rate of climb are two of the things pursuits need the most in order to pursue other airplanes successfully. Similar gains were registered by bombers. It is very strange that few of the world's air forces switched to 100-octane fuel after the Americans proved its value; most stuck with the cheaper, easier-to-produce 91-octane formula.

If an enemy air force eventually developed pursuit aircraft that could achieve the high service ceilings the bombers could achieve, then the power-fully engined bombers could be equipped with protective machine guns that, carefully arrayed across an entire formation, could provide adequate to overwhelming self-protection.

Thus, through a judicious balancing act between speed, range, altitude, and defensive armament, was born the concept of the fast, long-range, high-altitude, *self-defending* bomber. This was, on paper and in peacetime, a self-contained offensive strategic weapons system if ever there was one. It was an article of faith, oft repeated in discussions between and among strategic bombing enthusiasts the world around, that "the bomber will always get through." Their proof for this bold assertion lay in the results of numerous mock, set-piece air battles in which no airplanes were really shot down and no one really died.

Treaty obligations and the politics of the day for nearly two decades forced the U.S. Army airmen to pretend that their bombers were defensive weapons of limited capability. But from the earliest days of American involvement in the Great War, Billy Mitchell and his acolytes referred to bombers as a "striking force" and a "strategic force." Politics and diplomacy aside, the only factor that kept an effective American offensive strategic bomber force from the world's skies was technology, and that caught up long before American aviators became embroiled in a new war.

Model 299

The ultimate expression of the prewar offensive strategic bomber fell into the U.S. Army's hands as an act of industrial desperation. As the Air Corps began taking delivery in June 1934 of the revolutionary twin-engine Martin B-10 light monoplane bomber—the first American bomber whose crew and payload rode inside the airplane's all-metal fuselage—its planners looked ahead and specified a much larger and longer-ranged airplane. At that moment, the Boeing aircraft company was hovering on the edge of failure, but its managers and designers were game for one last shot. In response to the army's request, Boeing designed and built Model 299 as a last-gasp, do-or-die effort. On July 16, 1935, only weeks ahead of a submission deadline, Boeing introduced the 15-ton, four-engine Flying Fortress, which was ultimately accepted as the B-17. The nickname, Flying Fortress, derived from one of the more powerful rationales for the design competition, army aviation's need for a long-range coast-defense airplane—a flying *coastal* fortress—and not the airplane's inherent ability to defend itself, which is something that came much later.

Coupled with the revolutionary, beautifully engineered, and remarkably compact Norden bombsight, the B-17 was capable of attacking fast-moving ships out to a prodigious eight-hundred-mile operational range at an average speed of 252 miles per hour, faster than most pursuits of the day. The army ordered thirteen test examples in 1935. These were delivered in 1937, and twelve went to the 2d Bombardment Group for operational testing of the airplane as well as the emerging doctrines the airplane made possible. A May 1938 mock attack by three B-17 test aircraft on the Italian liner *Rex* at a range of 750 miles from land nearly started a shooting war with the U.S. Navy, with the result that the most vocal army bombardment enthusiasts were dispersed and quashed, but only after the B-17's ample capabilities had been born out. The controversy and inadequate budgets impeded aircraft orders until after war broke out in Europe, but the army airmen pinned many of their hopes on the B-17, and the B-17, constantly upgraded through technological innovation, came through for them—and for Boeing, which managed to stay in business until the big orders were finally written. But even in 1935, it was plain to see that the B-17 was everything the "bomber boys" wanted: fast, high flying, heavily armed, highly maneuverable, and capable of carrying eight tons of bombs over greater distances than any bomber in the world.

Attack

The first time the Army Air Service considered a role for "attack" aircraft, per se, was in 1922, when several observation aircraft were rigged out as low-level strafers to support the infantry. This was a venture driven entirely by the persistent demands of the ground army, which thought of the aircraft as "flying artillery." The balance here was between speed, armament, and protection from enemy ground fire. All the combat performance was required at combat altitudes that hovered between "low" and "very low," with no margin whatsoever for "too low." Attack flying took immense nerve, skill, coordination, and just plain bravery. All types of aircraft fell out of the sky from time to time, for a host of reasons. Attack aircraft *fly* out of the sky mainly because of tiny misjudgments or minuscule coordination problems. The 2d Bombardment Group got the long-haul drivers, the 1st Pursuit Group tended to grab the larger-than-life personalities, and the 3d Attack Group got the really intense daredevil types.

By 1935, thanks to the primacy of the bombardment community in the Air Corps hierarchy and at the Tactical School, the army attack community was reduced to the role defined by an association with strategic bombers rather than the needs of the ground army. After 1935, with four-engine strategic bombers looming on the Air Corps event horizon, attack's prime mission was changed to assaulting enemy airfields, with an eye to clearing the skies of enemy aircraft ahead of the passage through the area of a strategic bomber force—that is, to achieve air superiority. If the ground forces requested air support, the best they were going to get was attack—not bombardment—and only if they could prove the request was a response to a dire emergency beyond the range of friendly artillery. This obviated attack's reason for existing, except as it applied to gaining local air superiority in behalf of a transiting strategic bomber force.

In 1938, the commandant of the Air Corps Tactical School responded negatively to the suggestion that attack aircraft be doctrinally teamed with fast-moving tanks on the battlefield of the future. The idea was that air and armor, working together, could achieve breakthroughs on the ground and then rapid advances for miles and miles beyond the pierced front line. The commandant noted that even attack aircraft were frail when compared to tanks, that tying them to a low-level ground-support role would ensure their destruction by small-arms fire. What the estimable Air Corps colonel in fact rejected was an American carbon copy of Germany's well-advanced blitzkrieg doctrine, which American air and armor did not effectively bring off as a doctrine until 1944—five years after the blitzkrieg technique was unveiled in Poland.

Whatever its mission, the small attack brotherhood had a difficult time coming up with the optimum airplane. A case could be made equally for a single-engine airplane manned by a pilot and perhaps one radioman-gunner or a twin-engine airplane manned by as many as three airmen. The Northrop A-17 design, which began reaching tactical units in 1935, was a single-engine all-metal monoplane manned by a pilot and a radioman-gunner housed in an enclosed "greenhouse" cockpit. It was armed with four wing-mounted

.30-caliber machine guns, two rear-facing .30-caliber dorsal machine guns on a flexible mount manned by the gunner, and up to 1,800 pounds of bombs stowed in an internal bomb bay and external racks.

The A-17 and its follow-on variant, the A-33, were adequate enough airplanes for their day, but they were totally eclipsed in October 1938 by the earliest operational version of the twin-engine Douglas A-20, whose design was in many ways guided by the enormous strides in attack aviation taken by the combatant air forces in the Spanish Civil War. Manned by a pilot, a radioman-gunner, and an optional bombardier, the A-20 was everything an attack airman could dream of. It was fast, with a maximum speed of 310 miles per hour, at high and very low altitudes. Heavily armed as a strafer, it had fixed .30-caliber machine guns in a two-gun blister on each side of the nose, four fixed .30-caliber machine guns in a replaceable nose section, plus a rear-facing defensive .30-caliber machine gun mounted on a flexible dorsal mount and another in a retractable ventral mount. Not only that, but the A-20 could be rigged out as a light tactical bomber with a replaceable nose blister for the bombardier and his sight, and it could haul an internal bomb load of up to four thousand pounds.

Other Aircraft

As well as bombers, pursuits, and attack aircraft, the army utilized numerous noncombatant types during the interwar years, such as cargo and transport aircraft, numerous types and models of training planes, liaison and communications aircraft, even a succession of amphibian aircraft. Many of these were purpose-built military models, but many others were civilian models adapted to military use with or without modification.

The halting journey to the World War II era of long-haul, high-capacity strategic cargo/transport aircraft began as the twelve-passenger Douglas civilian airliner known as the DC-2, which first flew in 1934. The navy bought a number of DC-2s that year, and the army accepted them for the first time in 1936. At least seven DC-2 variants and test models flew for the army in the mid- and late 1930s. Also in 1936, the army and navy purchased test examples of the Lockheed Electra, a ten-passenger airliner the army tested in at least three configurations. The DC-2 and Electra variants were all relatively small aircraft of no strategic potential.

Air Corps Manning

Within the army's 1920 authorization for 280,000 men and 18,000 officers, the Army Air Service stood at a strength of around 1,500 officers, 13,500 enlisted men, and 2,500 flying cadets. By 1926, the newly renamed Army Air Corps mustered around 900 officers, 8,700 enlisted men, and fewer than 150 flying cadets. Unlike other service components, the Air Corps actually grew during the lean years of the Herbert Hoover presidency to 1,300 officers and 13,400 enlisted men. Its numbers remained fairly flat for the next six years, but by restricting the active tours of many pilots, it built up a reserve component of several thousand trained officer pilots who kept up their skills as they could, often in civilian flying jobs. Through 1938, the Army Air Corps was ranked seventh in size among the world's air forces. For all that it was smaller than its proponents wanted it to be, the Army Air Service and its successor tended to attract some of the army's best minds and most aggressive personalities. It quickly became one of the major nodes of experimentation in a service that was, on average, moribund because it lacked the troops, equipment, and training dollars to keep it usefully occupied.

An Independent Air Force?

The deeply held belief by military airmen that it was necessary for airmen exclusively to shape and guide the future of military aviation was a powerful force during the interwar decades. As the airplane itself grew up as a weapons platform, army aviators became even more convinced that it was their solemn duty to wring out every possible advantage from what the bounty of technology was heaping on them. Not unreasonably, they felt it was self-evident that land-bound commanders had not the time nor the insight nor the dedication to develop air power to its full potential, that the holy mission to extend the reach and force of aerial weapons was something only professional airmen could accomplish. They felt that the constant risk of life and limb to locate the ultimate expression of air power gave them the right to oversee the destiny of their profession. And they felt that, in the twentieth century, an independent national air force was *as* critical to the national defense as an independent army or an independent navy.

In 1925, while appearing before the Morrow Board—a civilian panel looking into the state of military and civil aviation—Gen. Billy Mitchell lobbied hard for creation of an independent national air force to be formed from the army and naval aviation services and overseen by a cabinet secretary. This was something naval aviators wanted no part of, and, although a similar board of the period endorsed the idea, it did not fly in the Congress. Nevertheless, the Congress did allow the Army Air Service to be reconstituted as the Army Air Corps, an independently administered force within the army in the same way the Marine Corps was an independently administered force within the naval service. In fact, the Air Corps Act of 1926 stipulated that 90 percent of each grade of Air Corps officer be composed of qualified pilots, thus assuring an air arm run by airmen. The Army Air Corps was to be overseen by a civilian holding a newly created post, assistant secretary of war for aeronautics. The Air Corps Act of 1926 further authorized a five-year plan to build army air power back to a strength of 1,518 officers, 200 flying cadets, 16,000 enlisted personnel, and 1,800 airplanes.

The 1926 Air Corps solution, a compromise between ardently warring factions within the army, did not take firm hold in the Congress, where between 1926 and 1935 twenty-nine proposed bills argued for and against an independent national air force. None of these bills became law, but by 1933 even army airmen committed to the idea of an independent air force saw that it was not going to happen any time soon. Rather, they regrouped around the idea of the General Headquarters (GHQ) Air Force, which would bring the entire far-flung combat power of the Air Corps under one command. The GHQ Air Force scheme would replace the system whereby army tactical aviation units reported, in a combat-support role, to the regional commanders, all ground generals whose focus was in overseeing ground formations. This idea reached fruition when GHQ Air Force was activated on a trial basis by Maj. Gen. Frank Andrews on March 1, 1935. Andrews was given command of all army flying units and was made responsible for their training, operational planning, and organization. He was directly responsible to the army chief of staff, which effectively made the fighting portion of the Air Corps an autonomous combat component of the army. Administration of the entire Air Corps—chiefly training, procurement and supply, personnel assignments, and research and development—remained within the purview of the chief of the Air Corps, who also reported to the army chief of staff, but administration of army air bases, per se, remained under the control of regional ground commanders.

Under the GHQ Air Force scheme, all of the combatant air units based in the United States were deployed in three wings: the 1st Wing, headquartered at March Field, California, was allotted one attack group, two bombardment groups, and three observation squadrons; the 2d Wing, headquartered at Langley Field, Virginia, was allotted two pursuit groups, two bombardment groups, and three observation squadrons; and the 3d Wing, headquartered at Barksdale Field, Louisiana, was allotted one attack group and one attack squadron, one pursuit group and two pursuit squadrons, and two bombardment squadrons. The 1935 reorganization also redesignated the 9th Observation Group as the 9th Bombardment Group, the beginning of a trend that downgraded observation throughout the Air Corps. In 1937, the 12th Observation Group was deactivated and the 10th Transport Group was activated as the first unit of its type.

Putting aside all the organizational rationales and considerations, the purpose of carving out a GHQ Air Force composed of flying units and commands reporting to a single operational aviation commander was to provide the army with a combat air component from which it could draw support for army ground components in defense of the United States and its possessions or take part in a war almost anywhere in the world. But it also provided the Air Corps with the *means* to further the creation of an autonomous strategic air force composed of self-defending heavy bombers unbridled by the need to directly support a ground army.

Friction between the two top Air Corps command elements was felt from the get-go, but the powerful elixir of turf prevented the two air chiefs and their minions from quite reaching a consensus as to which officer ought to have ultimate responsibility for the Air Corps. In the end, it was necessary to revise the system within the context of a frightening outside threat.

The Air Corps in 1938

No one knew it as the new year got underway, but 1938 was to be a turning point for the Army Air Corps. Many of the unanswered questions that had in so many ways stunted its development throughout the 1920s and 1930s were on their way to being answered.

For all the intramural argument and maneuvering that went on during the 1930s, the Air Corps remained weak, undertrained, and in search of a galvanizing mission that might focus the many superb thinkers in its ranks. While it was hoped that GHQ Air Force might do the job of focusing on mission and raising training standards, the small number and wide dispersal of Air Corps flying units and the scarcity of training dollars all but prevented large enough multi-group, multi-type operations that might instill a unity of purpose, a unity of mission, a unity of command, a unity of vision. There were too many parts but no whole.

Major General Frank Andrews's first order of business in 1935, reorganizing the flying units based in the continental United States into three regional wings, was a boost to training and doctrinal development, as the wing commanders sought to run integrated exercises with their own disparate units. Andrews also organized exercises to test the Air Corps' coast-defense doctrine. Hundreds of bombers and pursuits at a time were shifted to coastal areas on very short notice to turn back mock invasion fleets. What little the Air Corps had in training dollars was at least—and at last—put to work in hands-on tactical exercises that honed combat skills, raised morale, produced new ideas and insights, and brought to light deficiencies that could then be fixed.

Unfortunately, the mock anti-invasion drills raised the navy's hackles. General Douglas MacArthur's private 1931 pact with Adm. William Pratt regarding aviation's coast-defense role was repudiated by Pratt's successor in 1934. More to the point, the advent of the long-legged B-17 seemed to herald a day when the navy, afloat and aloft, would have no role to play in coastal defense. Indeed, following the long-range mock B-17 attack on the Italian liner *Rex* in May 1938, an aroused and worried navy pressured MacArthur's successor, Gen. Malin Craig, until he restricted the B-17s and shorter-range army aircraft to flights of a mere hundred miles from land—as if that would be a realistic boundary in the event of a real invasion. But the deal was sealed when the first production order for B-17s—beyond the test examples the 2d Bombardment Group had in hand—was cancelled, a follow-on strategic heavy bomber design was scrapped on the drawing board, and the thoroughly inadequate twin-engine Douglas B-18 tactical bomber—a variant of the DC-2 airliner!—was ordered in quantity.

By the autumn of 1938, the future of a strategic role for the Air Corps had suddenly turned bleak. Absent the coast-defense assignment, there seemed to be no mission or outlook left that might unify the disparate ranks of army aviators.

Chapter 4

Naval Aviation

Synergy

W
HEN YOU SAY "NAVAL AVIATION" you *think* "carrier air," which is fair enough, given all the hoopla about it. But before World War II, both carrier air and seaplanes performed the navy's air efforts, and beginning very early in the war, the navy built up a force of land-based patrol bombers. While carrier air came to predominate American naval strategy, at no point was land-based or sea-based air abandoned or left out—not in the Pacific War and not in the Battle of the Atlantic. Indeed, carrier-type aircraft operating from a land base in the Pacific—Guadalcanal—had more to do with the definitive Pacific War victory than carrier aircraft operating from carrier decks. And for nearly all of 1943, carrier-based aircraft played *no* role in the Pacific War.

No one knew this future as American naval aviation developed between the wars. And no one could foretell the degree of synergy that would occur in World War II between naval aviation, Marine Corps aviation, and army aviation. The army and navy went pretty much their own ways until at least 1929, neither cooperating nor even consulting one another as they did. The Marine Corps fit in about halfway: it used mainly naval-type aircraft to eke out its own aviation doctrine, suitable for an expeditionary, force-projecting amphibious organization dependent on naval support as much as it was dependent on its own assets.

Wish List

The U.S. Navy entered the air age in 1911, but the technology of the day was not immediately adaptable to an inherently naval role. It wasn't until 1916 that the Congress authorized the Naval Flying Corps, but even then it could field only land-based units for the Great War, and these units fielded mostly army-type aircraft.

There were no aircraft carriers in 1916. By the end of the Great War, only the Royal Navy had built and operated true aircraft carriers—the type of flat-top ship we think of today. The world's first true aircraft carrier, HMS *Furious*, a converted battlecruiser, launched the world's first carrier air strike against Zeppelin sheds in northern Germany on July 19, 1918—only four months before the armistice.

The value of aircraft carriers was not self-evident in 1918. The Royal Navy developed its first carriers primarily to go after the bases of long-range dirigibles armed to bomb targets in Great Britain. In this sense, the notion of the aircraft carrier began its days as the antidote to a strategic weapon, and not *as* a strategic weapon, per se. But navies are traditionally havens for technology, and there were plenty of technically proficient dreamers in the world's major navies who wanted to tinker with the British concept as soon as the armistice gave them the time. Meanwhile, British tinkerers who had actual carriers in hand worked out all the vital systems and techniques: hangar decks for servicing aircraft, elevators to carry aircraft between the flight deck and the hangar deck, techniques and rules for the safe and orderly launch and recovery of aircraft, arresting gear, and so forth. They didn't come up with everything on their own, but they made a good start and got the fundamentals right.

The Naval Flying Corps closed out the Great War with nearly seven thousand officers and thirty-three thousand enlisted men on its rolls, and more than two thousand aircraft on its equipment roster. These numbers were cut back drastically after the armistice. Indeed, as late as mid-1919, the chief of naval operations averred that he could not "conceive of any use the fleet will ever have for aircraft," and "the navy doesn't need airplanes."

Far from following the lead of their service chief, naval aviators, in a 1919 proposal to Secretary of the Navy Josephus Daniels, called for a program to build one aircraft carrier per four battleships, which would have been a formidable undertaking with revolutionary consequences. The carrier-based aircraft—which were the real weapon—were to be used as long-range scouts, as spotters for over-the-horizon gunfire, and perhaps (pending the evolution of better aircraft) as a *supplement* to naval gunnery. The naval aviators also suggested that each cruiser and battleship be equipped with an airplane catapult from which gunfire-spotter aircraft could be launched. And while they were at it, they asked Daniels for large numbers of scout seaplanes and large rigid airships—the latter to be used both as scouts and bombers in and of themselves, but also as airborne aircraft carriers.

Far from providing the navy with one aircraft carrier per every four battleships, wiser and penny-pinching heads decided to provide the aviators with one experimental carrier to use as a test bed for carrier doctrine. Authorized by the Congress in 1919, America's first true aircraft carrier, a converted collier, was recommissioned USS *Langley* on March 20, 1922, and designated CV-1 (C for carrier and V for heavier than air, a designator for non-gas-filled flying machines).

In the same 1919 legislation that authorized *Langley*, the naval aviators were assigned a merchant ship for conversion to a seaplane tender and funds to develop two dirigibles. In the time it took to complete the construction of their new toys, and thereafter, the naval aviators worked hard to develop doctrines and weapons built around land-based aircraft, including the lighter-than-air machines.

The Naval Flying Corps had no real mission following the armistice. It had plenty of constituencies of bright young men with bright new ideas, but it lacked an over-arching vision of itself. Its chief was a civilian administrator working under the secretary of the navy. No senior naval officer was a pilot, and none served at its helm. And the Naval Flying Corps had a wily adversary in the Army Air Service's Billy Mitchell, who, along with many army aviators, wanted his own service and the Navy Flying Corps to be amalgamated into a unified, independent, national air force, along the lines of Britain's postwar Royal Air Force. While the navy had no real view of the future of air power, per se, it knew it needed its own air service under its own officers—if for no other reason than to grope toward a future in which that air service could be fully integrated into the fleet.

One of the chief naval proponents of an independent air service was Capt. William Moffett, a tough but diplomatic negotiator with a particular flare for public relations that at least matched the flare exhibited by General Mitchell. In the end, following exhaustive hearings, Moffett swung the Congress to the navy's view. In July 1921, under direction of a new law, Moffett, newly appointed rear admiral, stood up the navy's new Bureau of Aeronautics, which reported directly to the secretary of the navy, bypassing even the chief of naval operations and, thus, the inconvenience of inside politics that might have swamped it. In Moffett's small, tightly knit leadership team, naval aviation had a strong central authority and a powerful proponent to shape, nurture, and grow it to its full potential.

It is ironic that the navy won its right to its own air service at a time when most of its senior commanders were opposed to the development of that air service. The navy seniors saw the advancement of an aviation agenda as a zero-sum game that would take away limited resources from the development, maintenance, and manning of the surface force. It could be argued that the navy's fight before the Congress for a new bureau of aeronautics was really in opposition to giving naval assets over to an independent air force that was likely to be led by the army's General Mitchell and his soldier henchmen.

Fits and Starts

For a period in the 1920s, the army aviation program overlapped the navy's program. In an effort to foster army air power, Billy Mitchell set out to demonstrate that the army's force of large, land-based bombers had made the battleship obsolete. The peace lobby actually backed the Mitchell bomb tests as a means to advance naval disarmament: If you can kill ships easily with airplanes, why buy expensive ships when you can buy inexpensive airplanes? The army tests, which were an adjunct to a much broader navy quest to determine the parameters of vulnerability of warships to aerial bombs, were open to foreign observers as prelude to the 1921 naval disarmament conference, to make the point that the day of the battleship was over. Mitchell agreed with other leading air power advocates of the day that air power would dominate all battle dimensions and win wars.

Mitchell's demonstration program managed to sink an obsolete German battleship that was stationary when it was bombed—and both army and navy aircraft sank other obsolete German and American vessels, from tiny submarines to once-mighty battleships—but even Army Chief of Staff John J. "Black Jack" Pershing agreed that the battleship had not been rendered obsolete by the set-piece bombing demonstrations. Nevertheless, Mitchell continued to voice his argument, while the navy's take-away from the tests was to provide its surface ships with greater speed and maneuverability, and lots of antiaircraft weapons. As well, the navy redoubled its efforts to develop land- and carrier-based pursuit aircraft—which the navy called "fighters"—as an antidote to bombers.

While *Langley* was under construction, the commander in chief of the newly established United States Fleet, the navy's combat arm, ordered that each of his battleships be made ready to carry two small seaplanes to be used as over-the-horizon scouts and gunfire spotters, and that each cruiser be equipped with one such airplane. In practice, however, the first American capital ship to be equipped with aircraft catapults was the new battleship *Maryland*, which arrived for fleet duty in 1922.

On October 26, 1922, the diminutive (11,500 tons displacement) *Langley* launched the first airplane to take off from an American aircraft carrier deck. In due course, American naval aviators had caught up with the trailblazing Royal Navy in developing the aircraft carrier as a viable weapon of war. In 1924, the Americans passed the British when U.S. Marine Corps pilots, who were trained by the navy and designated naval aviators, became the first pilots in the world to develop dive-bombing tactics, which the carrier navy immediately embraced and which marines first used on combat ashore in Nicaragua in 1927. Dive-bombing was the pinpoint technique navy pilots required to drive home attacks against enemy ships conducting evasive maneuvers at high speed.

Despite its slow start, naval aviation, which the 1922 naval disarmament treaties had not effectively touched, was abloom with experiments and trials throughout the 1920s involving dirigibles, balloons, land-based aircraft, aircraft carriers and carrier aircraft, seaplanes, and seaplane tenders.

The Morrow Board

Putting aside the navy's modest enlisted pilot program, which had been put in place to augment the ranks of naval aviators without going over the absolute legal limit of 5,499 commissioned naval officers, there were two sources of pilots open to the interwar navy. The first and by far the largest was composed of U.S. Naval Academy graduates who applied for pilot training, and the second was through a variety of programs that came and went through the years to enlist aviation cadets, many of them Naval Reserve officers, from the civilian community.

Annapolis graduates had to serve aboard ship or ashore as commissioned officers for at least two years before they could begin flight training, but civilian college graduates who signed up for flight training generally went right to work as naval aviation cadets. As a result, the civilian cadets who earned their wings did so at lower ranks than newly minted pilots who had graduated from the Naval Academy. Often, Annapolis graduates who earned their "wings of gold" as lieutenants had less flying experience than the pilots they oversaw, but higher rank in the air was always trumped by flying experience, even between commissioned and enlisted pilots.

The two-year rule for Annapolis graduates had a benefit for the navy's aviation community in that the Annapolis experience and two years' service aboard ship assured that would-be aviators rubbed elbows and developed lifelong friendships with officers who would rise through the surface fleet or even the submarine navy. This ensured alliances and cross-pollination over the course of decades.

In September 1925, following the tragic loss of the navy dirigible *Shenandoah* in a thunderstorm, President Calvin Coolidge convened under the direction of Dwight Morrow, a prominent lawyer and diplomat, a top-to-bottom study of the state of military and commercial aviation. Among many, many other items, the Morrow Board recommended with respect to the navy in its November 1925 finding—and Rear Adm. William Moffett, the powerful head of the navy's Bureau of Aeronautics, decreed—that all naval flying units, aircraft carriers, aviation tenders, and naval air stations had to be commanded by qualified naval aviators or naval aviation observers (a rating that practically died out between the wars). This ensured that naval aviators would guide the future of the air service and that they would necessarily rise to positions of authority, right on up to the level of fleet command, because command of ships and bases at appropriate ranks and ages was the ticket to eventual promotion to flag rank. Many naval line officers with an interest in aviation were allowed to qualify as aviators or observers, and some of the most senior of these—Ernest King, William Halsey, Frederick Sherman, Aubrey Fitch, John Sidney McCain, and Richmond Kelly Turner, to name but a few—rose to high rank and national prominence during World War II.

Despite vigorous lobbying by Billy Mitchell and his confederates, the Morrow Board recommended against the creation of a unified national air force to be formed, like the Royal Air Force, by stripping the army and navy of their respective aviation services. The board members felt that the roles of army and navy aviation differed sufficiently and had diverged far enough with respect to missions, doctrine, capabilities, and equipment to warrant their remaining separate. To seal the deal, the Morrow Board recommended the creation of the post of assistant secretary of the navy for aeronautics, which would guarantee that the naval aviation program was adequately represented and nurtured within the government. This was the board's most important finding; as it turned out, a Royal Air Force dominated by army aviators devoted to land-based bombers utterly neglected naval aviation until the Fleet Air Arm was reconstituted, with not a moment to spare, in 1937.

Further, in mid-1926, as an outgrowth of Morrow Board recommendations, the Congress enacted an orderly five-year building program, via competitive bidding, aimed at bringing the number of modern aircraft in service with the navy to one thousand. Adequate reserve and replacement aircraft to maintain that number were also authorized.

Overall, the size of the naval aviation establishment was expanded, while promotion within the aviation community would take place on a track separate from the rest of the navy. This ended a longstanding and corrosive worry that had kept career surface officers united against the expansion of naval aviation.

Carrier Air as a Strategic Weapon

Right out of the box, with its first use of carrier-based aviation, the Royal Navy had found a strategic mission for the new weapons system: standing up to a newly contrived German strategic weapon, long-range dirigible bombers capable of terrorizing London even though they were based hundred of miles away, in northern Germany. The British breakthrough was only partly in operating offensive aircraft from a carrier deck; the other half of the system was the ability to move a short but functional airfield—the carrier deck itself—closer to the target and, beyond that, to sail it around as a means for shielding it from enemy counterattack. So the first British conception *and use* of the ship-plane combination wove the ultimate connection between the two—airplanes and a mobile carrier air base—as whole cloth.

Even with this solid example so close in time, the battleship-centric U.S. Navy hierarchy managed to relegate carrier air to a role subordinate to its favored weapons system, even though U.S. Navy battleships had played no substantive role in the Great War. The battleship admirals devolved the promise of carrier air to peeping over the horizon ahead of the battleship-centered surface fleet and then to spotting surface gunfire and, at most, fending off attacks against the surface fleet by enemy naval and air forces. Navy pilots saw things a little differently and did what they could to advance doctrines that seemed obvious to them, but they labored for a decade after the armistice under the weight of an orthodoxy embraced by most of the senior officers who dominated the navy.

While the *Langley* pilots and aircrewmen were developing and learning their trade, the navy set to building two new fleet carriers on battlecruiser hulls that otherwise would have been sold for scrap. The first of the new electric-powered carriers to be launched was the 33,000-ton *Saratoga* (CV-3), which was commissioned on November 16, 1927. On December 15, the *Lexington* (CV-2) joined the fleet. Both of the huge carriers were powered like the swift battlecruisers they were originally intended to be; both could run at nearly 35 knots (two and a half times *Langley's* top speed of 14 knots). Moreover, both of the new carriers were large enough to operate at least seventy-five warplanes from their 800-foot-long, 160-foot-wide armored steel flight decks, and both were capable of sailing vast distances between refuelings. Both were considered—by naval aviators, if not their battleship-enthused superiors—to be strategic weapons of the first order, and their appearance on the high seas carried the potential for U.S. naval aviation well into the late first half of the twentieth century.

The first time carrier aircraft were used in an American war-game scenario the way the carrier people wanted to use them was in January 1929's Fleet Problem IX. The so-called Black Fleet, including *Langley* and *Saratoga,* was to represent an enemy fleet attacking the Panama Canal from the Pacific side, and the Blue Fleet, including *Lexington* and all the army aircraft based in the Canal Zone, was to defend from the Atlantic side. As it happened, *Langley* was unavailable, so a small seaplane tender and one seaplane stood in to represent her and her air group.

The Black Fleet, commanded by Vice Adm. William Pratt, a prominent line officer who was quite taken with the promise of aviation, went straight for the jugular in a breathtaking plan that put carrier bombers over both ends of the canal and the Canal Zone's two army airfields at one time. The heart of the plan, fostered by the day's leading carrier-air proponent, Rear Adm. Joseph Mason Reeves, was the dispatch of *Saratoga* and several speedy escorts, including the swift scout cruiser *Omaha,* to a location remote from the Black surface fleet. Reeves, a qualified naval aviation observer and long an avid airpower proponent who had been hobbled in earlier exercises by *Langley's* slow speed, had long reasoned that aircraft controlled by battleship enthusiasts would attack opposing battleships before they bothered to look for a separate force built around a carrier. Available to Reeves for the first time in this exercise was *Saratoga,* whose high speed and long sailing endurance provided the means to create an independent and highly mobile carrier task force that might evade the inevitable opposition effort to sink battleships.

The unfolding exercise did not go entirely as Reeves had envisioned, but he more than made his point. At one swoop, Reeves's bold offensive use of carrier air power changed the way many American naval officers looked at this new strategic weapon. It decisively shaped the future of naval warfare and the manner in which vital bases vulnerable to carrier aircraft needed to be defended. Attacks by carrier aircraft on opposing carriers during Fleet Problem IX also showed vulnerabilities in the way the carrier forces were placed relative to the surface forces, and they pointed toward more complete antiaircraft defense of carriers by surface escorts organized around the carrier. This pointed the way to doctrine for a carrier-centered battle group. Indeed, taken well into the future, the common wisdom that carriers should serve as tactical escorts for surface fleets was turned on its head in January 1929; Admiral Reeves used his surface warships to protect the carriers. Further, Fleet Problem IX pointed to flaws in the system of radios used by the fleets to control the actions of detached sub-units, and along those lines it pointed to a need to integrate army and navy communications systems and protocols.

Ongoing exercises built on Admiral Reeves's stunning vision, but every single major lesson gleaned from the 1929 fleet exercise had a direct payoff during the terrible first months of the Pacific War and in turning the tide by the end of that conflagration's first year. Indeed, new situations that arose with respect to carrier air in exercises after 1929 eerily foreshadowed actual events of the Pacific War.

In 1934, Admiral Reeves was named commander in chief of the United States Fleet, a post that had been held from May 1929 to September 1930 by Adm. William Pratt, who then became chief of naval operations until June 1933. Reeves and Pratt did as much as they could during their overlapping tenures at the top of the naval hierarchy to promote naval aviation in general and wide-ranging uses for carrier air in particular.

New Carriers

Only two years after *Lexington* and *Saratoga* joined the fleet, the Congress authorized construction of a small (14,500 tons displacement) fourth carrier, the *Ranger* (CV-4), which was touted as the namesake of a class of inexpensive but numerous new constructions. Although *Ranger,* which was commissioned in 1934, was the first American carrier to be designed as such from the keel up, her marginal performance (top speed of 29 knots, deficient arresting gear, and just two elevators between the flight and hangar decks that did not quite fill the bill) forced naval strategists to opt for larger, rather more expensive carriers that could do the job required of them.

The designers amassed all the information that could be gleaned from the four previous efforts, and in 1932 the navy requested two new swift twenty-thousand-ton carriers. The Congress turned down the original request, but the 1933 naval appropriations budget contained authorization for two thoroughly modern fleet carriers, each weighing in at 19,800 tons displacement.

The new ships, *Yorktown* (CV-5) and *Enterprise* (CV-6), were to be the prototypes for most of the fleet-type aircraft carriers that eventually carried the navy through World War II. There were numerous changes made along the way, but the *Yorktown*-class carriers set the pace.

Each of the new carriers' flight decks was constructed of teak or Douglas fir laid over a steel frame (similar to *Langley*'s and *Ranger*'s, but unlike *Lexington*'s and *Saratoga*'s steel-platform flight decks). Both could get up to operational speeds of 32 knots—too fast for the battleships of the day to keep up—and both had plenty of built-in underwater anti-torpedo protection. The underwater protection was considered crucial for avoiding and defeating submarine- or air-launched torpedoes, and the high speed would aid in the launch and recovery of airplanes as well as in the avoidance of torpedoes and bombs. Each *Yorktown*-class carrier had three built-in elevators to speed the deployment of airplanes between the flight deck and hangar deck. And both were fitted out with numerous antiaircraft weapons, from .50-caliber machine guns up to 5-inch guns, mounted in gun galleries edging the flight deck. Each of the new carriers was capable of operating approximately seventy-five warplanes.

Langley was downgraded to tender status in 1934 to allow the United States to replace her within the 135,000-ton allocation provided for fleet carriers under the 1922 treaties. The lobby that had brought forth *Ranger* as a precursor to small, inexpensive carriers got another chance. Thus, at 14,700 tons displacement, the seventh U.S. carrier, *Wasp* (CV-7), was something of a throwback. She was a vastly improved three-elevator cousin to *Ranger*, capable of operating a full seventy-five-plane air group (the standard of the day) as efficiently as the *Yorktown*-class ships. Numerous delays and ongoing upgrades prevented *Wasp* from joining the fleet until 1940.

The 1922 and 1930 naval treaties lapsed at the end of 1936, but the U.S. Congress did not authorize any new carrier constructions until 1938, when a third *Yorktown*-class carrier, dubbed *Hornet* (CV-8), was more or less forced upon the navy after Chief of Naval Operations William Leahy averred that his service needed and wanted no new carriers.

Carrier Aircraft

Most of the world's carrier air groups in late 1941 were composed of three basic warplane types: fighters, scout/dive-bombers, and torpedo/light, level bombers. The mix of airplanes reflected the similar but not identical offensive and defensive doctrines the major naval powers employed.

The Carrier Fighters

The naval service's first all-metal monoplane fighter was the Brewster F2A Buffalo, a design specified in a 1936 call by the navy for a modern carrier fighter with retractable landing gear, an enclosed cockpit, and four wing-mounted .50-caliber machine guns. Following service testing in January 1938, the navy ordered fifty-four F2As. Enough were finally in hand a *year* later to go to one carrier-based squadron, but the balance of the order was sold to the Finnish air force. Several improved variants ordered in small numbers by the naval service equipped one navy carrier squadron and one marine squadron in late 1940, but shoddy workmanship and a host of other problems left only the one carrier squadron and one marine squadron in possession of F2As at the start of the Pacific War. The carrier F2As never saw action, but practically all of the Marine Corps F2As were shot down in one mission during the Battle of Midway.

The 1936 design call also brought forth the Grumman F4F Wildcat, a sturdy follow-on to the naval service's last biplane fighter, the F3F. Indeed, the F4F-1 was originally presented as a biplane, but a single monoplane version was ordered instead in July 1936. Like the F2A, the F4F-2 was an all-metal monoplane with retractable landing gear, enclosed cockpit, and four .50-caliber wing guns. Except for speed, the initial F4F-2 design was deemed inferior to the initial F2A, so Brewster won the competition, and Grumman went back to the drawing board, eventually to produce the F4F-3, which completely eclipsed the F2A when it finally flew in early 1939.

✳

The Carrier Scout-Bombers

The naval service's first monoplane scout bomber was the Vought SB2U Vindicator, a 1935 reconception of an earlier Vought biplane scout bomber. The SB2U featured an enclosed cockpit, retractable landing gear, metal frame, and fabric and metal skin. The SB2U was capable of carrying a single 500- or 1,000-pound bomb or depth charge on a centerline yoke and was also armed with a single, cowl-mounted .30-caliber machine gun fired by the pilot and a single .30-caliber machine gun fired by the rear-facing radioman-gunner. Almost as soon as the first planes from the first production order of fifty-four SB2Us reached the first navy carrier squadron in December 1937, the navy realized that advancing technology could provide a better, more capable dive-bomber/scout-bomber within a year or two, so the SB2U was seen as an interim service plane. With upgrades, a total of 194 SB2Us were delivered to navy and marine squadrons by early 1940, but only the marines were still flying them at the outbreak of the Pacific War, and the last of these flew at Midway, with disastrous results.

The Carrier Torpedo Bomber

The third U.S. carrier type at the start of the war was the Douglas TBD Devastator torpedo bomber, which, like all torpedo planes of the day, doubled as a level bomber as needed. When the TBD was introduced into the fleet in October 1937, it was briefly the world's only carrier-based monoplane bomber. It was also the first carrier plane with an all-metal fuselage, the first to have power-assisted folding wings for denser storage, and the first to feature at least semi-retractable landing gear. It was very briefly the world's best carrier bomber—even though its cruising speed was only 128 miles per hour and its top speed was 206 miles per hour. The TBD had a maximum range of 416 miles—or a combat radius of around 150 miles. In all, between 1937 and 1939, 130 TBDs were built for the six U.S. fleet carrier torpedo squadrons as well as for reserve and training squadrons.

The TBD accommodated a three-man crew: pilot, radioman-gunner, and a bomb aimer, who was left home on torpedo missions. Used offensively, the Devastator could carry one 1,000-pound aerial torpedo, or one 1,000-pound bomb, or one or two 500-pound bombs on external shackles between the main landing gear. The TBD's only reasonable defensive role was on patrol against submarines, in which case it could carry one or two 500-pound aerial depth charges on its bomb shackles. Defensive armament, such as it was, consisted of a single cowl-mounted .30-caliber machine gun and a single flexible .30-caliber machine gun fired to the rear by the radioman-gunner.

Seaplanes and Floatplanes

The navy's carrier constituency was never the only force pushing naval aviation as an ultimate, war-transforming weapon. From the earliest days of flight, years before the first aircraft carriers were built, naval aviators foresaw a vital need for seaplanes—stationed in sheltered waters anywhere in the world but especially near important naval ports, and bordering inter-coastal shipping routes—as a means to defend America's coast and coastal trade and the nation's far-flung island possessions and protectorates. When carriers came along, even the most enthusiastic carrier proponents agreed that highly mobile, tender-based, multi-engine seaplanes had a role to play in long-range reconnaissance and the occasional offensive bombing mission. The navy gave little or no thought during the interwar years to acquiring land-based combatant aircraft, per se. All the naval long-range patrol bombers were seaplanes until 1939, when an amphibian variant was intro-duced. No exclusively land-based, multi-engine patrol bomber was acquired until after the United States entered World War II, and then only because they were available.

A fourth type of naval airplane was composed of very light observation and spotter aircraft based aboard cruisers and battleships or, in rare cases, tender-based. These floatplanes were used to locate shore targets, correct naval gunfire, and, in a more limited sense, as over-the-horizon scouts. The result was that carrier-based air was developed in parallel with the tender-based force, and both were ultimately integrated via a single doctrine.

For a time in the early and mid-1930s, proponents of seaplane bombers hoped that they might eventually be developed into a powerful standalone bomber force that would overcome the proscription on carrier construction. Alas, there are technical limits on how heavy a seaplane and its payload can measure, and the seaplane bomber force never reached the stage at which it might have had a strategic impact.

The central tenet of naval aviation doctrine was that, even if carrier air was to play a pivotal role within the fleet, a limited number of carriers could not be everywhere at once. Tender-based air was designed to fend for itself, and tender-based reconnaissance units were highly maneuverable because the tender could relocate on very short notice, either to hide out or get closer to the action. To a degree, tender-based aircraft that could overlap a carrier's area of operations were designed to supplement the carrier's search capability—a dandy force multiplier and a sound, well-founded doctrine.

The most versatile of the prewar patrol airplanes was the Consolidated PBY Catalina flying boat, a 1936 upgrade of an earlier, successful design. Even in its earliest trials, the test PBY set a nonstop flight record at optimum settings of 3,443 miles, which says it all about its value as a patrol bomber. As the PBY developed, it could carry heavier payloads of bombs, depth charges, or torpedoes, which were mounted externally beneath the wings. All-around defense against enemy aircraft was provided by machine guns in the nose, at the lower rear of the fuselage, and at two waist positions.

The navy's first seaplane tender was the USS *Wright*, which was commissioned in December 1921. She bore out the concept of tender basing of patrol seaplanes, but no new purpose-built seaplane tenders joined the fleet for many years. With no new aircraft tenders coming forth via congressional appropriations, the navy had to make do for nearly two decades with a number of small vessels doing double duty. These included a minelayer, a former collier, and several partially converted minesweepers that simply did not fill the bill. When *Langley* was no longer useful as a carrier, she was converted into a tender, but she ended her days as an aircraft transport. Between 1938 and 1940, facing an urgent need, the navy took sufficient funds from its budget to pull fourteen old destroyers out of mothballs and convert them into seaplane tenders by adding magazines for bombs, torpedoes, and depth charges; accommodations for aircrew and groundcrew; shop spaces for aircraft servicing and repair; and a one-hundred-thousand-gallon aviation fuel tank and necessary fuel-transfer equipment. Also in 1938, the Congress finally appropriated funds for one large and four small purpose-built tenders to be laid down that year, a small tender to be laid down in 1939, and one large and one small tender to be laid down in 1940. In the end, five large and five small tenders emerged from this program, which—with the *Wright* and all the pre-1938 field-expedient tenders—carried the navy through World War II.

A False Trail

The navy spent many years and millions of dollars in an attempt to develop the full potential of lighter-than-air platforms during the 1920s and early 1930s. Despite the loss of the *Shenandoah* in 1925, the continuation of the airship program was made at the insistence of Rear Adm. William Moffett, who was reappointed three times as chief of the Bureau of Aeronautics after he stood it up in 1921. Thanks to Moffett's enthusiastic support, the dirigible became a so-so aircraft carrier of very limited capacity, even though it had great range.

Alas, hydrogen-filled dirigibles proved to be far too delicate and volatile for military (and even civilian) use. This was driven home to navy when the *Akron* went down in stormy weather over the New Jersey coast on April 3, 1933. Among the seventy-three fatalities was Admiral Moffett.

Moffett was replaced at the Bureau of Aeronautics by the brilliant but irascible Rear Adm. Ernest King, who had earned his wings in 1927 as a forty-eight-year-old captain and had commanded *Lexington* from 1930 to 1932. One of King's early decisions was to abridge the American dirigible program, an act sealed in sorrow when *Akron's* twin, *Macon,* went down over the Pacific in February 1935. Rigid airships disappeared from all the world's skies following the crash of the German passenger airship *Hindenberg* in 1937.

The dirigible's much lighter, non-rigid half-sister, the blimp, did turn out to be a viable (if extremely slow) long-range airship that eventually found a place in the World War II navy as a convoy escort and antisubmarine search platform far out into Atlantic waters. Nevertheless, the blimp was too slow and too fragile to serve as more than an aviation auxiliary.

Land-Based Aircraft

Through the entire interwar period, the navy's array of land-based combat aircraft virtually mirrored its array of carrier-based planes. This nurtured funds and training expenses in straitened times and served the important cause of providing backup and reinforcement for the carrier-based squadrons. Pilots of carrier-type planes who rotated to duty with land-based squadrons could keep up their skills.

Summing Up

By late 1938 all meaningful political opposition to carrier air had been quelled by good experience piled on good experience, not to mention the retirement of all the old Gun Club lions and the ascension of several late-blooming, high-ranking naval aviators to the topmost reaches of the naval service. Naval aviation was a well-integrated given within the navy's highest planning circles, and carrier air appeared to have found its niche. To a degree, the navy had remodeled itself to deal with both the threats posed by enemy aviation and the possibilities offered by its own aviation community. New ideas and new technologies hovering on and over the horizon seemed to hold promise for the future. The naval aviation community of 1938 was confident in its ability to fulfill its mission.

Chapter 5

The Navy Line of Battle

The Pressures of War

THE U.S. NAVY WENT into the Great War as a classic line-of-battle fighting navy. It was composed mainly of large, coal-powered surface combatants supported by an array of smaller warships designed and built almost solely to support the largest ships. It had trained to undertake and prevail in a classic strategic set-piece, all-or-nothing naval action along the lines of the Battle of Trafalgar (1805). But the Great War's naval component didn't play out to that script. The German battle fleet spent most of the war bottled up in Baltic ports, so the Germans resorted to an utterly new tactic for the conduct of *guerre de course*: the throttling of maritime trade across the Atlantic with submarines that could sneak past the blockade. The depredations of unrestricted submarine warfare drew the United States into the war as an ally of Britain and France, and it shaped the ways in which American naval combatants took part in the war.

American heavy naval combatants played no role whatsoever in the Great War. The burden fell on several new classes of destroyers, submarine chasers, and submarines that took part in antisubmarine warfare, mainly as convoy escorts. There was no grand strategic battle, only a number of very small tactical engagements in support of troop and supply convoys that sailed to and fro the United States and Europe.

The navy also found in the Great War a requirement to build and maintain flotillas of small surface and sub-surface combatants far out of proportion to any prewar planning. These ships, many hundreds of airplanes, and an assortment of tenders, transports, supply ships, and other noncombatants cost money the navy might otherwise have spent on new battleships and battlecruisers. In an effort to have its cake and eat it too, the navy placed orders for large combatants that would be built on extended schedules so as to allow it to develop and deploy the smaller ships and planes. No one knew how long the war would last, so it was a prudent bet. Moreover, all the new large combatants were oil-fueled exemplars of the latest naval technologies, so they would at very least arrive for fleet service in time to replace obsolescent coal-burning capital ships that were not engaged in the war anyway.

✳

The Problems of Peace

The U.S. Navy's problems came when the Great War ended abruptly before significant numbers of all types of new ships authorized in the 1916 naval spending legislation were ready for service, either because they were shaking down or had not been completed. There were too many ships to man and maintain within a normal peacetime budget. The decision was made to scrap older, outmoded ships of all types and mothball many of the smaller combatants in order to make way for supporting the many large combatants still under construction.

The 1922 naval disarmament treaties, which went into effect before many of the new ships had even been launched, put the screws to all previous naval planning. But, while the treaties retarded the growth of battle fleets and even the deployment of new technologies, they did not outlaw naval war, per se. The signatories were entitled to maintain fairly strong navies, and nothing in the treaties prevented the signatories from making belligerent use of their fleets; they only limited belligerent use by forcing navies to make do with much smaller national fleets.

The upshot of the disarmament accords was that the U.S. Navy could retain eighteen battleships as the core of its battle fleet. This included three of the four 32,600-ton *Colorado*-class battleships—each armed with eight 16-inch guns—that were still being built.

The accords also proscribed all six of the American battlecruisers under construction in 1921. (The U.S. Navy had no active battlecruisers in its inventory before, during, or after the Great War.) Four of the incomplete battlecruisers were scrapped and, in due course, two were converted into the aircraft carriers *Lexington* and *Saratoga*.

Nearly two dozen battleships commissioned between 1895 and 1910 were sold for scrap between 1920 and 1924, both because of their age and to make way for the three *Colorado*-class ships. Nevertheless, one battleship commissioned in 1910, two commissioned in 1911, and two commissioned in 1912 made the cut; the two oldest were scrapped in 1931, two were downgraded as training ships, and the last, USS *Arkansas,* served in World War II. While six modern battleships authorized in 1916 were cancelled in 1922, before they were completed, eleven battleships belonging to six classes that were commissioned between 1914 and 1921 were retained in the fleet and, indeed, served as the fleet's backbone. Two were lost at Pearl Harbor, but the rest served through World War II.

The U.S. Navy's entire complement of cruisers through the Great War consisted of two 3,769-ton protected cruisers commissioned in 1898 and 1900, five 3,200-ton protected cruisers commissioned in 1904 and 1905, and three 3,750-ton scout cruisers commissioned in 1908. These were all scrapped in 1930 and 1931.

Ten modern, 7,050-ton, oil-fueled *Omaha*-class scout cruisers, laid down in 1920 and still under construction by 1921, were allowed under the treaty and thus completed in 1923 and 1924. Conceived before anyone dreamed of employing aircraft as fleet scouts, the swift *Omaha*-class ships, which were armed with twelve 6-inch guns, provided over-the-horizon scouting and closer-in support for the battleships through a large part of their interwar service. They continued to serve, quite usefully, through World War II.

There were no cruisers queued up behind the *Omaha*-class ships that met the treaty specifications. In late 1924, the Congress authorized the construction of eight modern "treaty" cruisers. Although each of the two *Pensacola*-class and six *Northampton*-class cruisers carried ten 8-inch guns, they were very lightly armored because their displacement had to be held to ten thousand tons. Derisively referred to as "tinclads," they were originally classified as light cruisers due to their light armor but were later redesignated heavy cruisers because of their 8-inch main guns. Due to a building moratorium to await the outcome of the 1927 Geneva naval conference, which failed to produce results, the first of these ships was commissioned in late 1929, and the last was commissioned in early 1931. All served in World War II.

Next up was an authorization in 1929 for nine additional 8-inch cruisers. Two of these ships were built more or less to the 1924 specifications, six were a new design altogether but still lightly armored, and the last featured heavier armor protection.

The two battlecruiser conversions that gave the fleet *Lexington* and *Saratoga* were odd in one respect that bluntly shows the early confusion the navy experienced with respect to the deployment of aircraft carriers within the battle fleet schema. In addition to antiaircraft weapons, including 5-inch guns, rimming the flight deck, both of the huge vessels were equipped with eight 8-inch guns deployed in dual mounts directly fore and aft the island. These big guns were provided so the carriers could take part in a fleet gunnery duel, in rather more *direct* support of friendly ships than any naval aviator ever contemplated. These 8-inch guns were eventually removed.

In addition to their main armament, be it 14- or 16-inch crushers or 6- or 8-inch bruisers, all of the modern battleships and cruisers were equipped with 5-inch guns. Before the Great War, the 5-inch mounts were deployed to provide "broadside" fire against enemy warships. After the Army Air Service sank several tethered battleships and cruisers in the early 1920s, the navy raced to equip all of its ships with antiaircraft weapons, up to 5-inch guns, that could be used against both ships and planes. It was necessary to replace flat-trajectory guns with dual-purpose guns capable of high-angle fire. As well, it was necessary to place many antiaircraft guns fitted on battleships and cruisers on higher decks than the old broadside guns, so they could benefit from wider vistas and cumulatively reach targets all the way around the ship, from directly overhead on out to the horizon. Additionally, it was necessary to fit mechanical and optical gun directors and antiaircraft gunnery command posts on every ship's crowded deck and superstructure, and add new magazines and handling equipment to older ships. Also, if it was necessary to add antiaircraft crewmen to ships' companies, provisions had to be made to feed and berth them. The design of new ships took all these factors into account, but the classic dilemma of responding to the needs of being prepared to go to war immediately while preparing for a war in the future had to be factored into upgrades for older ships. So did other aspects of creeping modernity. All manner of devices and techniques led to additions and reconfigurations that were added to new ships and retrofitted to older ships, all with the war-now-versus-war-later dilemma muddying the waters. Some upgrades made life easier and were easily integrated, but others made for immense headaches even as they offered appreciable gains in the constant tail chase for the ideal war-fighting platform.

Another Set of Restrictions

In the purely naval realm, and devoid of the politics, the creation of treaty navies during the 1920s found the major naval powers bumping up against all the treaty limits and thus looking for ways to game the system. The 1930 naval conference, while mainly a political solution to a problem stemming from hurt Japanese pride—sought to rein in the major players with respect to the game they were playing at the margins of the 1922 treaties.

The 1922 treaties had focused on the largest naval combatants. When the signatories reached the imposed limits, they naturally looked for ways to gain an advantage. Even the United States overcame its self-imposed peace-questing myopia to do so.

The solution lay in more and better sub-capital ships, mainly destroyers, but also in cruisers armed with lighter guns. The U.S. Navy had sailed from 1918 to 1929 on its hundreds of Great War–vintage 1,110-ton and 1,200-ton oil-powered flush-deck four-stack destroyers. It still had many of them in mothballs. But progress had passed the four-stackers by, and it was time to build modern ships.

Once again acting against her own interests and capabilities as a means for holding back a competitor—Japan in this case—the United States agreed in the 1930 accords to limit the size of destroyers to 1,850 tons displacement and armament of 5.1-inch guns. It also extended the moratorium on new battleship construction to the treaty's 1936 term limit, set a moratorium on new aircraft carrier construction out to 1936, and reapportioned the treaty ratio on all ships somewhat more in favor of Japan.

At a practical level, the lightly armored 8-inch cruisers that had reached the fleet or were abuilding were reclassified as "heavy" cruisers, and the construction of new heavy cruisers was halted. New cruisers built to the same ten-thousand-ton displacement limit as the heavy cruisers were to be armed with long-range 6-inch guns and dubbed light cruisers. This last was hardly a concession, however; the new light cruisers could be armed with *fifteen* 6-inch guns to the nine or ten 8-inchers carried by the heavies, and because these guns could be fired at a greater rate, a 6-inch cruiser could actually place more "steel on target" more quickly than an 8-inch cruiser.

Last Call

The first naval construction bill submitted by the Roosevelt Administration passed the Congress in mid-1933. It authorized construction of two 19,800-ton aircraft carriers *(Yorktown* and *Enterprise)*, one heavy cruiser, three light cruisers, eighteen destroyers, and four submarines. It paid for the ships in part by holding the line on naval end strength at one hundred thousand men as well as by reducing pay for officers and sailors by 15 percent, discontinuing reenlistment bonuses, and subjecting naval personnel to other onerous pay and benefits cutbacks. It is a tribute to the depth of the Great Depression that more than 93 percent of sailors up for reenlistment in 1934 did so despite the pay cuts.

Another tribute to the depths of the Great Depression was the Congress's acceptance of an argument that building up the navy would help fight the prevailing economic trends. It was agreed that enough money would be authorized to build the navy up to various treaty limits, but no more. The Naval Parity Act, passed in March 1934, authorized the construction of more than a hundred ships out to 1939 and specified the immediate construction of two modern 35,000-ton, 14-inch battleships *(North Carolina* and *Washington,* which were not actually laid down until 1937, by which time each was to be equipped with nine 16-inch guns); one small 14,700-ton carrier *(Wasp)*, an improvement on the 14,500-ton *Ranger* design; sixty-five destroyers of various designs; and nine modern submarines. The bill also authorized construction, out to 1939, of one thousand naval aircraft.

If the Congress was feeling good about itself, the new chief of naval operations, Adm. William Standley (June 1934 to December 1936), spoiled the celebration when he noted that seven of the navy's fifteen active battleships would be considered obsolete by the end of 1936, as would numerous destroyers and submarines. Standley further noted that maintenance and modernization of the obsolete ships would cost more than outright replacement. With a bow to the navy's needs in the event of a war now, Standley relented on sending the *S* class of submarines to the scrapyards until a modern class, the so-called "fleet" submarines, had been built up, but it was necessary to strike from the rolls and replace eighty-one Great War–vintage four-stack destroyers as soon as possible.

The United States routinely informed its treaty partners of the decision to build combatant vessels up to the limits of the disarmament agreements. Japan replied with a threat to abandon the treaty when it lapsed in 1936 if it was not given absolute parity with the United States and Britain. As soon as the treaty nations reconvened in London in December 1935, the Japanese chief delegate announced that his nation had no interest in being bound by the 1922 or 1930 treaties, nor by a new naval treaty. The Americans and British attempted to woo a reversal of the Japanese decision, but the negotiations played out to a fait accompli. The proffered treaty was never signed, and the Japanese went their own way.

Of course the United States decided to race Japan to the finish line—or, at least, to attempt to deter Japan. America's interests in East Asia and the Pacific required it to take heed of the threat implicit in Japan's withdrawal from the treaty regimes. Besides, by the time the naval treaties lapsed, it was reasonably clear that building up a navy was indeed a good way to help dig out of the Depression, and Admiral Standley's admonition that it cost more to maintain and modernize obsolete vessels than to replace them gained significant traction as time passed and events unfolded.

Eight destroyers and four submarines were routinely ordered in 1937. There was no sign so far that the Congress had even noted Japan's withdrawal from the arms-limitation accords. But the Naval Expansion Act signed into law on May 7, 1938, spurred in part by the sinking of the gunboat *Panay* by Japanese aircraft in December 1937, authorized the navy to increase its size by 20 percent above the overall limit implied in the 1934 Naval Parity Act, including authorization to recruit twenty-one thousand additional officers and sailors to man the expanded fleet. This translated to two newly designed thirty-five-thousand-ton, 16-inch battleships *(South Dakota* and *Indiana)*, one *Yorktown*-class aircraft carrier *(Hornet)*, and the first of a new class of 27,100-ton carriers *(Essex,* which had not yet been designed and thus was not laid down until 1941), nine light cruisers, twenty-three destroyers, nine submarines, numerous auxiliaries, and an increase in naval aircraft to a new high of three thousand.

The new *North Carolina-* and *South Dakota*-class battleships would be called "fast" battleships because their modern propulsion systems would allow them to sail in formation with the so-called "fast" carriers. It was yet to be determined which would support which. Along that line, the navy also designed during this period a class of 6,000-ton light antiaircraft cruisers, each armed with *sixteen* 5-inch guns deployed in eight dual mounts, as well as numerous lighter antiaircraft weapons. The four nimble *Atlanta*-class ships were designed specifically to provide antiaircraft protection for the fast aircraft carriers, though they turned out to be very good bombardment vessels because they could fire up to fourteen 5-inch guns per broadside at a very fast rate.

The various naval authorization bills focused heavily on combatants, and not on the literally scores of smaller types that would be needed to support the fighting fleets. Even though the navy's strategic growth was authorized because of the threat posed by Japan, the U.S. Navy was in no position to fight its way across the wide Pacific without enough transports to haul the ground troops it needed to capture and defend successive forward bases. Nor were there enough minesweepers to clear harbors the fleet required to rest and revictual, nor enough minelayers to parry Japanese surface and sub-surface raiders. There were not enough tenders for seaplanes, submarines, and destroyers; nor enough fleet oilers to fuel the fleet at sea. There were not enough repair ships or floating dry docks needed to keep the advance guard of the fleet in fighting trim following bruising naval actions, nor an organization to build airfields on newly claimed islands—and on and on and on. It wasn't that the navy didn't possess any of these types of vessels and units, but that it didn't possess enough of them to sustain a years-long offensive. A fighting navy is not measured by its key combatants alone, but in its ability to keep itself moving across Earth's wide oceans.

Several naval construction bills and supplementals followed on the May 1938 Naval Expansion Act. Thus, in August 1939, as most of the world was about to be plunged into six dark years of relentless global warfare, the U.S. Navy had 105 new ships at various stages of construction. Eight were fast battleships (*Alabama, Indiana, Iowa, Massachusetts, New Jersey, North Carolina, South Dakota,* and *Washington*), two were fast carriers (*Wasp* and *Hornet*), one was a light gun cruiser equipped with fifteen 6-inch guns, four were light antiaircraft cruisers equipped with sixteen 5-inch guns, forty-two were fleet destroyers of several modern classes, and twenty were modern long-range fleet submarines. Noncombatant and auxiliary types included one minelayer, six seaplane tenders, and two destroyer tenders. Moreover, the Maritime Commission, which had already developed and delivered a high-speed fleet oiler (*Cimarron*), had two of her sister ships under construction. These last three ships, and others not yet started, would put the U.S. Navy at the forefront of at-sea refueling technology, a long-sought solution to a nagging problem that was destined to play a major role in winning the looming war in the Pacific. The *Wasp* would be commissioned on April 25, 1940; on June 1, 1940, the *Washington* would become the first American battleship to be launched since *West Virginia* was commissioned in 1923; and the *North Carolina* would be launched on June 13. On July 25, 1940, the navy would commission the USS *Benson,* the first and namesake of just one modern class of destroyer that would, with her ninety-five sisters, bear a large part of the burden for naval operations in the coming two-ocean war.

The U.S. Navy wasn't nearly ready to go to war in 1939. It had not the requisite ships, sailors, doctrine, training, or experience for bearing its part of the burden for waging a global two-ocean war, but it was well along in preparing for what would nevertheless be America's terribly hard first year of total immersion in war, 1942. Better equipment and more men were to reach the navy through legislation enacted before December 1941, but few ships, except many of those (but by no means all) that were abuilding in August 1939, would reach the fleet before the U.S. Navy was finally pulled into the new world war.

Chapter 6

War Now Versus War in the Future

War in Manchuria

THE IMPERIAL JAPANESE ARMY'S INVASION of Manchuria on September 18, 1931, led to the first test of America's preparedness for war after 1918. The nearest American combat units to the trouble spot were the Asiatic Fleet and army ground units based in the Philippines. There was no immediate danger that the United States would be drawn into the conflict, but the nation had commercial interests in the region and was more or less obligated to take a principled political stand on what appeared to be outright Japanese aggression. (It would not come out for years that local Japanese commanders engineered the initial steps of the invasion without the permission or even the knowledge of the Japanese government, or of their own military superiors. Also, there was a large faction of Japanese officers that saw war with the United States as inevitable and, as events unfolded, that hoped to go to war right then.)

Secretary of State Henry Stimson, upon receiving his first briefing on the crisis, advised President Hoover to challenge the Japanese moves. But Hoover well knew that that United States was utterly incapable of waging war so far from home in the event Japan reacted to a threat with military force. Stimson then publicly protested the invasion and, on January 7, 1932, issued notice that the United States refused to recognize the Japanese conquest. The toothless League of Nations invoked the Kellogg-Briand Treaty and established a commission to look into the matter. Nothing of substance was done.

The Japanese next established a puppet regime in Manchuria and formally recognized the newly named state of Manchukuo. When the government of China protested the creation of Manchukuo by calling for an anti-Japanese trade boycott, the Japanese reinforced their garrison in Shanghai—an internationally administered trading enclave—and sent their troops on a murderous rampage against civilians until they felt their honor had been avenged.

These were sobering events for the Hoover Administration, which learned firsthand how easy it was for wars to ignite. The United States had long since espoused an "Open Door" policy for international trade in China and it had troops stationed in various places, not to mention hundreds if not thousands of U.S. citizens roaming China in search of trade or converts to Christianity. The Hoover Administration could not abandon American citizens or American interests in the face of Japanese adventurism, but it lacked the muscle, will, and allies to confront Japan overtly.

In early February 1932, as a soft, middle-ground demonstration meant to send a message (whatever that means) without provoking an attack, a U.S. Army infantry regiment and four hundred Marines based in the Philippines were ordered to Shanghai along with a heavy cruiser and six destroyers drawn from the small Manila-based Asiatic Fleet. Their mission was to help "keep order." In fact, the commander of the Asiatic Fleet took his cruiser flagship and *ten* destroyers, thus leaving the Philippines nearly defenseless. Seven U.S. Navy river gunboats, reinforced by three destroyers, took to patrolling the Yangtze River with a smidgen more purpose than they routinely displayed.

In March 1932, at the conclusion of scheduled annual fleet maneuvers in the Pacific, the Atlantic Fleet's Scouting Force, including its aged battleships, was ordered to remain in Pacific waters rather than return to home ports on the East Coast. This was seen as a sign of strength and will. Following a set of maneuvers off Panama in the spring of 1932, one of the naval force commanders, whose eyes must have been on Japan, recommended that two, or even four, new aircraft carriers be laid down immediately, so great was the need for fleet-based air power at the tactical and strategic levels.

The navy's prayers were incompletely answered when both the House and Senate passed measures to build new carriers and cruisers, but even then President Hoover refused to sign the bill into law. Rather, he actively promoted world peace and general disarmament at the Geneva Disarmament Conference of 1932. The conference failed to achieve a result. By October, weeks before the presidential election, Hoover finally agreed to build the fleet up to the limits of the 1922 and 1930 naval treaties.

In 1932, if the United States were forced into a war, it was by no remote gleanings of the imagination prepared to defend its holdings abroad and probably couldn't defend the beaches of the continental United States.

War Now Versus War in the Future

In their ongoing straitened financial circumstances after 1930, the U.S. Army and U.S. Navy always had to balance two competing yet inseparable imperatives: they both were compelled to arm for war that might begin right now *and* to develop and build better arms and equipment for war in the future. Clearly, the Manchuria-Shanghai crisis of 1931–1932 demonstrated that the United States was incapable of fighting a war now.

The requirements for a war that might erupt at any moment could not be held hostage to the promise of better weapons and equipment at some ideal future date, but neither could the military services afford to mortgage their ability to fight a war in the future for the sake of being ready to fight a war in the immediate term. That is, they couldn't put off buying bullets to train marksmen now in order to save money to buy new rifles of a more effective caliber later, or vice versa. This might seem like a moot argument in light of ongoing personnel and materiel issues throughout the two decades following the Great War: there were never enough soldiers or sailors or equipment or ships to fight a major war. But it had always been far easier to recruit a vastly expanded war army and war navy than it had been to equip them to train for and fight the war for which the precipitous expansion was required.

As the needs of modern warfare became more technical and specialized, armies needed more time to train even their cannon fodder, and more time to keep apace technical advances among its potential adversaries. It *had* been easy to train masses of common line infantry, even for the Great War, but a future war would require higher technical proficiency for new infantry sub-specialties as common as machine gunners and mortar gunners.

Not only more time, but more money was needed to train even common infantrymen—it was necessary to expend more bullets to train a machine gunner than a rifleman—and *way* more money was needed to develop new weapons and equipment for a battlefield of the near future, not to mention for a battlefield of even a decade out. If American industry could produce the world's best cargo truck of 1930, then what lay in the future of American cargo trucks by, say, 1935? When should the research and development cycle begin for the 1935 truck, and how much money was it necessary to commit to that single endeavor, not to mention countless other endeavors that competed for urgent attention in the immediate, near, and farther terms?

The U.S. Navy found itself in even worse straits from the perspective of training a preponderance of specialists and gazing into the future. All enlisted sailors started as unrated seamen, but as their time aboard ships or bases lengthened, they became specialists under the guidance of older, rated sailors. Most sailors learned their specialties on the job, aboard naval bases and ships. In due course, they achieved the rank of petty officer and were rated in a specialty, say as machinist's mate third class, from which one could advance in stages to chief machinist's mate and, in rare cases, to warrant officer rank as a machinist. Scores of specialties were memorialized in a large and growing array of petty officer rates, such as radioman, water tender, motor machinist's mate, pharmacist's mate, electrician's mate, gunner's mate, torpedoman, aviation machinist's mate, carpenter's mate, and so forth. As the navy modernized, it had to establish new ratings, such as radar technician, which would first appear in the fleet in 1942. It took years to train a specialist to the point at which he could reliably train younger specialists. To make up for years of experience, sailors selected for newly created ratings had to be intensively school trained, often on rare and expensive equipment that had to be devoted to training only and thus kept back from the fleet. This was expensive and time-consuming for the navy, and it became even more so as technological horizons broadened.

The idea of it all was to fight a war at least on the same footing as the enemy, but preferably with more and better equipment and more and better-trained war fighters. The central argument that soldiers, sailors, and airmen wielded was that there was no point fielding an army, navy, or air force that was designed to emerge second best in a two-way fight. It was a persuasive argument, but it fell on the ears of politicians who shared a dream of no war at all—and thus no need to win wars. The contingent viewpoint from which the interwar army and navy sprang called into question the entire enterprise: Defend against whom with what? Morale, even among committed professionals, was never all that high due to the budgetary and practical straitjackets imposed by the dominant national political agenda with respect to the military. The military professionals dreamed of a perfect world, but they were more than prepared to accept an adequate world backed by policies that approached practical and realistic. Taking rifle bullets away from recruits was neither practical nor realistic, but when Chief of Staff Douglas MacArthur did so in 1933, he felt he had no choice, because the alternative use for the money thus saved, whatever it was, seemed to him to be more important than training infantrymen to hit targets with live ammunition.

On a larger scale, the navy was not allowed to practice with live torpedoes, because they were too unimaginably expensive to be blown up against anything but an enemy ship. The result, well into 1943, was that the navy had no way of knowing that the torpedoes its sailors launched at grave risk to their lives from surface ships, submarines, and torpedo planes were fatally flawed.

It is sheer lunacy to train riflemen without bullets and to spend a decade training men to maintain and deliver torpedoes that most likely would not blow up. Alas, most dogma produces only lunacy, and the American political dogma of the day prevented an army and a navy from being warlike. The professionals recognized the lunacy and dogma for what they were. Some of the best of them hung on in the hope that their political leaders would come to their senses.

Buy Now Versus Buy Later

For the army, the war-now-versus-war-later dilemma came to the fore in September 1932 when the chief of staff's office warned the chiefs of the supply arms and branches that, based on years of experience, their wish lists and budgets for fiscal year 1934 would probably be truncated yet again. Nevertheless, the memorandum went on to ask the supply people to formulate a realistic six-year plan (1935 to 1940) that established realistic priorities for all the foreseeable purchasing and development projects that were or would be required. The initial objective was to give support to the million-man mobilization plan Chief of Staff MacArthur was preparing for release in 1933; what would it take to have *modern* weapons and equipment in hand to support the influx? This was seen as the "rearmament and reequipment" phase, and it would be followed by a "research and development phase." Simply put, how would the army prepare for war now, then for war in the future, out to 1940?

The two-step modernization effort was more theoretical than real, but it got the army supply people thinking about future needs as an extension of current needs; it made for more realistic forecasts. In 1933, the current-needs list was followed by a "Policy for Mechanization and Motorization," which achieved a reality-grounded wish list for fielding a thoroughly modern combat force in the relatively near future.

An oft-used example, one among hundreds, beautifully highlights the balancing of current and future needs and illuminates the plight of the services during what amounted to the planning stage for World War II. As late in the game as the first half of 1940—months after the actual outbreak of war in western Europe—the House Committee on Appropriations was apprised of the state of the army's field artillery component. At that time, a typical army infantry division's principal artillery type was a 75mm field gun of late nineteenth-century French design, the so-called French 75. The U.S. Army had designed and tested a thoroughly modern 105mm field howitzer in 1934, but it had received no production budget in the intervening term. Meantime, high-angle fire had become the vogue in world-class artillery arms—that is, field howitzers ascended over field guns. The 105 was superbly designed to deliver high-angle fire, but the French 75 was a field gun that could not provide high-angle fire for a modern battlefield unless the weapon was retooled for wider traverse and higher elevation of the gun tube. Without adequate funds, the obsolescent 75mm gun could not be made less obsolescent. Alteration to enhance both traverse and elevation was approved but budgeted at a very slow rate. By mid-1940, only 140 of the army's several thousand French 75s had been so modified. Nevertheless, it remained the army's intention to eventually scrap the French 75 in favor of the 1934 105mm howitzer that was similar to and even a cut above the 105mm weapons favored by modern European armies. In service of the requirements for a war now, scarce funds were expended to upgrade the French 75s, because there was not nearly enough money to procure enough of the new 105mm howitzers. At one point, the army felt it needed to know whether it should stop modifying French 75s, since the effort seemed pointless if money would soon be forthcoming for purchase of the newer, larger, longer-ranged, and more destructive 105mm howitzers. Asked by the Congress in February 1940 what it would take to purchase enough of the 105mm howitzers to replace the French 75s, the army replied that it needed $36 million. That seemed a low enough figure, given the stakes, but the army representative added that in order to replace the ready stockpile of 6 million rounds of 75mm ammunition with the same number of 105mm rounds required an additional $192 million. And, of course, in the event of war, six million rounds was barely an adequate starting point; it was just enough to allow the munitions factories to catch up with actual needs and expenditures. In sum, the army thought it best to continue to upgrade the older weapons at the same time it was replacing them with the newer. That might *seem* wasteful, but it was the only way to meet both current and future requirements.

Another dilemma arrived with a significant American breakthrough in small arms technology, the new semiautomatic M1 Garand rifle, which had first been conceived in 1924. As with automatic pistols adopted early in the century, the M1 rifle harnessed violently expanding gas from the previous explosive combustion of a bullet cartridge to charge the chamber with a new round and reset the firing mechanism, thus obviating the use of a hand-operated bolt to do the same job. This allowed a faster rate of fire as well as greater accuracy. Getting the right balance between explosive force and stress on the parts suggested use of a smaller round than the standard American .30-06-caliber round, so a .276-caliber round was recommended and backed up with voluminous engineering evidence when the M1 was first presented in 1932. General Douglas MacArthur, who worried about not having enough .30-06 rounds in hand to fight a war *right now* and who, within a year, curtailed the use of .30-06 rounds even for training, rejected the visionary weapon simply because he felt he could not waste precious resources—old bullets in hand or dollars for new bullets—on an obviously superior weapon that would nevertheless require the fabrication of billions of new bullets and the casting off of billions of perfectly good bullets of a putatively less-efficient caliber. This sent weapons designer John Garand quietly back to the drawing board, pretty much in his spare time, until in 1935 he had rebalanced the equation to accommodate the powerful .30-06 round. The result, accepted in January 1936, was a standard 9.5-pound, 8-round infantry rifle that could fire a decisively lethal bullet 2.5 times faster than the fastest bolt-action rifle in service with any army in the world.

Overall, from 1933 onward, the army did apply more effort—and funds—to research and development of weapons and equipment. This is not to say the new devices were purchased, but more prototypes were built and tested against the time when needs became so great that the budget gates would open wider. The aviation arms were highly favored throughout this period because their success in combat so obviously hinged on technological superiority in an era of burgeoning technological advances. They also fell heir to the Depression-wracked aircraft industry's willingness to expend resources on speculative designs and prototypes in the hope of having those designs turn into production orders. The development of Boeing's Model 299 into the B-17 is a sterling example of that process, even though it took years for the Air Corps to agree to a fair price for each B-17 and issue a production order.

For all that research and development had a resurgence after 1934, the army never requested an annual research budget as high as $10 million through 1938. Between 1924 and 1933, the average annual research expenditure had been $4.6 million. Between 1934 and 1938, proposals made to Congress—much less actual expenditures—did not exceed $9 million.

Where they could, the armed services got around the research strictures by going abroad to purchase proven weapons from other nations. There had been no antitank weapons devised during the Great War, so there were none in U.S. Army postwar warehouses, much less in the hands of troops. In 1936, when the army could no longer blind itself to the need for antitank weapons—when the requirements for a war now overwhelmed the ordnance department's long-held desire to design its own antitank weapon for a war in the future—the German army's 37mm antitank gun was built under license in American arsenals. As late as 1942, the navy first licensed for use aboard ships a 20mm light antiaircraft cannon of Swiss design and a 40mm medium antiaircraft gun of Swedish design. The former replaced thoroughly inadequate water-cooled .50-caliber heavy machine guns in use as late as June 1942, while the latter, in late 1942, replaced a home-grown 1.1-inch gun whose faulty ammunition was never adequately tested until it was fired in combat. And even though the aviation arms were favored to some degree, they went shopping abroad to cut through research red tape and budget constraints (which actually played out as time constraints). Not surprisingly, the American armed services hit the cost-effective motherlode after September 1939, when the British conceived, built, and tested numerous weapons and systems in real combat. As well, the full range of hard-won British war experience from September 1939 onward accrued to the benefit of the American armed services as they raced to prepare for war in the *immediate* future. But this gets ahead of the story. In the mid-1930s, the British experience was not so different from the American experience of constraint, constraint, and more constraint.

Army-Navy Cooperation

Forced by its size and its political masters to depict itself as a defensive enterprise, the U.S. Army nonetheless sought to push the so-called defensive sector as far out from the United States as possible. The reality the army faced was that it could not mount a decisive defense until it had mobilized, trained, equipped, and integrated hundreds of thousands—perhaps millions—of conscripts, Organized Reserve officers, and National Guardsmen. At minimum, that required months and months under all the mobilization scenarios extant throughout the 1930s.

In order to gain time to stand up an effective wartime army in defense of the continental United States, army planners reasoned that the early defense would have to take place at some peripheral location or locations, and that the forces deployed there might have to be sacrificed while holding up an enemy advance upon the continental United States. This is known as a passive defense—getting the enemy to attack you as far from his strategic objective as possible to give you time to build up defenses around that strategic locale.

Given the geography in play, the army required the active cooperation of the navy to ship troops, weapons, and supplies to distant strategic locales, and to take part in the actual defense by holding enemy sea convoys at bay or even providing direct air or gunfire support. These are missions the U.S. Navy knew something about through its doctrinal joint planning with the Marine Corps. Nevertheless, the navy needed to upscale its planning and capabilities massively if it was to support a forward-deployed land force large enough to defeat or significantly retard the advance of an enemy army.

In due course, thanks in large measure to the alarmingly swift rise of aggressive fascist states in Europe and the first inroads by Italy and Germany to woo political support among Italian and German expatriates in Latin America, the army found real cause for concern in the effort it might take to force useful political attention to be turned to what came to be called "hemispheric defense." As Italy and Germany acted more openly and aggressively in Latin America from about 1935 onward, Secretary of State Cordell Hull grew more and more alarmed that the United States might in due course be outflanked from the south.

Events in Europe were of infinitely more interest and importance to most Americans than events in far-off Asia, which in the mid-1930s was *very* far from the minds and cares of most Americans. Yet, from then until World War II actually started, the Japanese were more overtly hostile to Americans and American interests in Asia and the Pacific than the Germans and Italians were to American interests in Europe. If a reasonably aware but detached observer had looked ahead in 1935 or even early 1938 to possible American involvement in a war by, say, 1941, the choice of an adversary would have been Japan, hands down. And the probability of such a war rose steeply as the months and years ticked by. To the insiders, Japan was certainly a major concern, but even if Japan went to war with the United States, the war would be fought "over there." German and Italian machinations in Latin America, however, were of infinitely greater concern, even though Germany and Italy were infinitely more focused on Europe than on the United States. This is because the nearest relatively unstable Latin state open to German and Italian subversion was "right here," opposite Texas, New Mexico, Arizona, and California.

Secretary Hull's growing concerns—those of the savvy insider—led to informal joint meetings, roughly once a month, between the army and navy service chiefs and Under Secretary of State Sumner Welles from January 1938 onward. The navy was initially resistant to—or at least blasé toward—the concept of working on political topics at this level with the army and the State Department, but the fruits of an April 1938 letter from Secretary Hull to President Roosevelt resulted in the meetings being elevated to a higher plane that obligated the navy to buckle down. Besides, the exercise could not be downplayed once the topic turned to defense of the Panama Canal, the navy's strategically vital interoceanic link that played an essential role in the nation's most pressing war scenarios. Once formalized by presidential order, the service chiefs and Under Secretary Welles convened monthly as the Standing Liaison Committee.

The moment of truth, with respect to hemispheric defense, finally came for Secretary Hull when Italy and Germany offered numerous Latin armies the loan of training missions. Taken to its logical conclusions, a German- or Italian-trained Latin American army might be induced to undertake the replacement of a neutral or pro-American national government with one of a pro-German or pro-Italian stripe. Given the weakness of the American military services—no great gains had yet been made in the wake of the 1931 Manchuria invasion and 1932 Shanghai incident—even one hostile Latin state militarily allied with Germany and Italy was something the United States could not tolerate. So, while they groped in other arenas toward joint defensive strategies, the army and navy got into the business of dispatching training missions to Latin America, to establishing spaces at West Point and Annapolis for Latin American military and naval officer cadets (often the scions of influential families), and for training Latin American officers at various service schools, such as the Army Command and General Staff College at Fort Leavenworth, Kansas, and the Naval War College at Newport, Rhode Island. But, mainly, the services looked to building up the Canal Zone defenses and drawing up plans to defend the Caribbean region. In due course, combined planning with British counterparts regarding issues impacting the defense of the Western Hemisphere also started up.

Planning for the defense of the Pacific coast and American possessions and bases in the Pacific also heated up during the late 1930s, as Japanese aggression in China heated up. While the Standing Liaison Committee was pretty much a State Department–supervised political tool aimed at hemispheric defense, the much older Joint Army and Navy Board—the so-called "Joint Board"—predated the Great War as the *only* formal means for the army and navy to even take a stab at coordinating their many strategic contingency plans. The Joint Board did not meet regularly, but it did serve as a useful coordinating body that more or less prevented the services from spinning too far out of one another's orbit at the strategic planning level. The Joint Board's brief was worldwide; it was the formal means by which the services shared insights and planning that spanned the globe.

With respect to Japan, the Joint Board met in March 1937 to study Joint Army and Navy Basic War Plan Orange, the strategic plan for a war with Japan that had last been modified in 1928. It took until November 16, 1937, for the Joint Board, at the urging of Army Chief of Staff Malin Craig, to rescind Plan Orange as entirely unworkable under current army and navy capabilities.

On December 12, 1937, Imperial Japanese Navy land-based aircraft attacked the clearly marked and neutral U.S. Navy gunboat *Panay* in the Yangtze River near Nanking. Three oil barges under escort by *Panay* were attacked at the same time. The gunboat and two of the barges were sunk, and three lives were lost.

It was not known at the time that this overtly hostile act by Japanese airmen against the United States was precipitated by an Imperial Army colonel who expressly wanted to drag his own nation and the United States to war. What the colonel and his cohorts failed to reckon on was that the United States was incapable of going to war with Japan. Rather, in public, the U.S. government accepted the lame excuses and weak apology offered by the Japanese government. But in private, certain elements of the American political and military establishments marked it down as high time to build up the power required to convincingly intimidate Japan, or defeat it in war.

On January 19, 1938, War Plan Orange was turned over to a joint committee to be redrafted, and a new and realistic plan was passed out to the secretaries of war and the navy, who approved it in late February. Key to the planning was a call to raise the navy's warship tonnage by 20 percent, which required an expenditure of $1.1 billion to build three battleships, two aircraft carriers, nine light cruisers, twenty-three destroyers, nine submarines, and 950 naval aircraft. This the Congress agreed to, and President Roosevelt signed the bill on May 7, 1938, as soon as it reached his desk.

The British Factor

Key among American strategic planning assumptions during the mid- and late 1930s was that the United States and the British Commonwealth would make common cause in a war against European fascism and Japanese militarism. Certainly this was a working assumption among British and American military professionals.

The assumption began to achieve substance on December 24, 1937, when navy Capt. Royal Ingersoll, the head of the navy War Plans Division, undertook a "purely exploratory" and "private" trip to London to sound out prominent figures in the Admiralty over their desires to cooperate with the U.S. Navy, especially with respect to War Plan Orange. In reality, Ingersoll had received his marching order from Adm. William Leahy, the chief of naval operations, who was acting on behalf of President Roosevelt. The timing is significant: Ingersoll left Washington only twelve days after the *Panay* was sunk in China and on the very same day that Secretary of State Hull was forced to tacitly admit his nation's military impotence by publicly accepting Japan's apology, which no one in the world believed to be authentic.

On January 12, 1938, Captain Ingersoll came away from the Admiralty with an "agreed record" in which the British granted the U.S. Navy rights in British waters, and vice versa, in the event their fleets were required to work together against Japan. In Ingersoll's own words, "We had to make preliminary arrangements to explore what could be done—for communicating with each other, for establishing liaison, intelligence, and other things, so that if war did come we would not be floundering for months until we got together." That is as close as you can get to a naval alliance without diplomats. It was the first step in the coordination of Anglo-American military planning since the end of the Great War, and it held within it the implied prospect of greater and closer cooperation well beyond naval matters.

The significance of naval cooperation between the U.S. and Royal navies at this juncture was that both nations considered themselves to be maritime powers, first and foremost; both navies considered themselves ascendant in national importance over their respective armies; and the cooperation was contemplated for littoral regions far from the home countries, where a naval force was the main force. This was correct in terms of American and British worldviews and in the actual physical strength each navy possessed over its national army. In other words, the dominant American and British national military arms had made themselves a pact against Japan that stood a good chance of being expanded with respect to their armies and air forces to other threats, and ultimately to binding agreements and perhaps formal mutual-defense treaties between the two nations themselves.

No Magic Moment

By mid-1938, certain elements within the government of the United States and the military branches had taken the first important steps toward facing the threats of fascism and militarism across all of America's protecting seas—across the Pacific with respect to Japan, across the Atlantic with respect to Italy and Germany, and across the Caribbean with respect to potential German and Italian allies in Latin America. The concept was firmly emplaced among several of the key players, and even the Congress was acting rationally, if fitfully so, with respect to the most alarming threats. But even after the *Panay* sinking of December 1937, there remained a yawning gap between America's ability to wage war and the looming *probability* that war would soon engulf large parts of the world, including the United States. The first halting steps had been taken, both conceptually and materially, but reality had not yet set all the way in. The great leaps of imagination and political fortitude that needed to be made had not yet been made. The moment, the *magic* moment, had not yet arrived.

Part II

FIRST
THINGS FIRST

November 14, 1938
–
April 7, 1940

Chapter 7

The March of Events

I T IS A LARGELY POLITICAL STORY that explains how the U.S. military services came to be permitted to bootstrap themselves from the low ebb in the mid-1930s to become, in several rather broad stages, the premier all-around, globally significant military force of the mid- and late twentieth century. A number of related factors, crystal clear in hindsight but perhaps not all that evident at the time, ruled the massive growth—first in awareness, then in determination, next in conceiving solutions, and finally in action.

It was in September 1931 that the Japanese fired what many believe to be the first shots of World War II. As they told it, they reacted to Nationalist Chinese "provocations" by invading and subsequently occupying the northern Chinese province of Manchuria, an event culminating in a war between Japan and China that lasted until 1945. In September 1932, Germany's National Socialist Workers Party received in national elections more votes than any other German party, and in November of that year, Franklin Delano Roosevelt was elected president of the United States. On February 27, 1933, the German Reichstag was gutted by fire, the Nazis blamed the Communists, and civil liberties were suspended in Germany. On March 28, enabling legislation gave Adolph Hitler dictatorial powers.

From an American vantage point, events in Europe and East Asia seemed to be spinning out of control, but even more threatening events were to follow. On October 14, 1933, Germany left the League of Nations, and a year later, on October 1, 1934, Hitler ordered the expansion of the German army and navy and the creation of an air force, the Luftwaffe. On March 16, 1935, Germany repudiated the disarmament clauses of the Versailles Treaty, which had ended the Great War. Thus, German rearmament began. On October 3, 1935, Italy invaded Ethiopia. The United States' response to these portentous events overseas was the passage by the Congress of the three Neutrality Acts, which limited the expansion and use of American military or industrial power on the world stage.

The spiral continued. On January 15, 1936, Japan abrogated the naval disarmament treaties of 1922 and 1930 and announced plans to massively expand the Imperial Navy. Shortly, in Europe, despite protests and even threats from the United Kingdom and France, on March 7, 1936, Hitler's revitalized army reoccupied the Rhineland, which had been set aside as a demilitarized buffer zone under terms of the Versailles Treaty. Italy, Hungary, and Austria signed a military alliance on March 23. On July 18, 1936, the Spanish Civil War began with an effort by fascist-led army units to overthrow the popularly elected socialist government.

As concerns deepened in the United States, President Roosevelt, on May 1, 1937, was finally hounded by public opinion into signing the Neutrality Acts, the earliest of which had been languishing on his desk since 1935. Next, not to be outdone by German and Italian depredations in Spain and Ethiopia, Japan unleashed its bombers against three Chinese cities on July 7, 1937, and thus started in earnest the Sino-Japanese War, which China's Premier Chiang Kai-shek had declared but not actually initiated the previous December. On July 28, 1937, Japanese forces seized Peking, and by November 9, Shanghai came firmly under Japanese control. The Chinese city of Nanking was beset by a Japanese military riot on December 12 and 13, 1937, in which many thousands of civilians were slain. Also on December 12, the USS *Panay* was sunk on the Yangtze River by Japanese naval aircraft.

On January 28, 1938, in his first public discussion on the topic of war, President Roosevelt noted in his State of the Union speech that America's defenses were inadequate in the face of preparations for war that were obviously speeding up overseas, in Europe and Asia, which he called "a threat to world peace and security." Roosevelt asked the Congress to appropriate funds for the navy and, in general, to improve America's security, mainly in the form of adequate antiaircraft defenses.

On March 28, 1938, the Japanese established a puppet Chinese government in Nanking. Meanwhile, in Europe, the Austrian government fell over the question of "reunification" with Germany, and German troops entered Austria on March 12, 1938, effectively joining the two nations.

And, finally, there occurred several events in Europe that for President Franklin Roosevelt would amount to the last straw: Hitler ordered a general mobilization throughout Germany and Austria on August 12, 1938, and German troops occupied the Sudeten region of Czechoslovakia on October 1, following the resignation of the Czech government on September 22, the resignation of the Czech president on September 25, and the complete and humiliating collapse of British and French political will on September 30.

Five weeks later, on the night of November 9, 1938, following nearly five years of steadily rising oppression and violence directed toward Germany's Jewish citizens, Nazi street thugs staged a bloody pogrom throughout Germany, an event history has dubbed *Kristallnacht*, the night of broken glass, an allusion to the windows of Jewish-owned businesses that were shattered that night.

Adding to information provided on September 22 by Joseph Kennedy, the U.S. ambassador to the Court of St. James, on October 13 William Bullitt, the U.S. ambassador to France, provided President Roosevelt with crucial, inside knowledge pertaining to the British and French capitulation over

Czechoslovakia: Hitler had simply, bluntly, and quite credibly threatened his British and French counterparts with unleashing the Luftwaffe on London and Paris in the event they stood up to him over the fate of the Czechs and Slovaks. Bullitt further explained that British and French leaders felt their weak position vis–à-vis Hitler's bluntly stated willingness to unleash the powerful Luftwaffe could be countered in the short term only through the acquisition of combat aircraft from the United States.

The German mobilization, the destruction of Czechoslovakia, the regional threat posed by the Luftwaffe and a resurgent German army, and perhaps even the open humiliation and even murder of Jews in the streets of Germany proved to be too much for Franklin Roosevelt. At last, the American president decided to act decisively in behalf of his own nation and, as it turned out, in behalf of humanity. The "magic moment" had come at last.

Chapter 8
The Aircraft Meeting

The Magic Moment

ALL OF THE WARS and warlike events in the world from 1931 onward did not go unnoticed or uncommented on in the halls of the War and Navy departments in Washington, D.C. Military professionals blanched anew each time a hostile act was committed in Europe, Asia, or Africa, and new efforts were laid on, albeit within the limited budgetary means authorized by the president and allotted by the Congress. These, as everyone except the peace lobbyists and the swelling ranks of their followers realized, were inadequate and potentially suicidal. Yet, given the legal strictures, there was nothing even the most prescient of the military professionals could do beyond waiting and plotting for the hoped-for recovery of will among the national leaders.

The change came, more or less out of the blue, six weeks after Czechoslovakia was destroyed and in the week after *Kristallnacht*. There is no way of telling whether the change came as a direct result of the open and arrogant Nazi depredations against Germany's own Jewish citizens, or whether *the* key American player just happened to arrive at his decision following a much longer period of introspection. Whatever the case, on Monday, November 14, 1938, President Franklin Roosevelt summoned a number of his key military and political advisers to the White House for what might have been *the single most-important meeting in modern American history,* maybe in modern world history.

The Context

President Roosevelt called this most important of White House meetings on a day on which the U.S. military was weak beyond imagination. The modern fleet was not yet built, nor even convincingly conceived. The Air Corps had in its possession only thirteen strategic bombers and several hundred tactical bombers of dubious utility. It had no base in the world from which any of its aircraft could reach German, Italian, or Japanese territory and return. It had no strategic airlift capability whatsoever, and its two best pursuit models had been obsolete before they were even built. In all of 1938, the Army Air Corps trained only three hundred new pilots. The army ground force was in laughable condition, neither with the ability to fight a protracted skirmish with a minor enemy (even if it could get within range), nor capable of managing, training, housing, feeding, clothing, nor even arming an influx of wartime conscripts. There was no American armored force, not even an American anti-armor force. And there were not enough serviceable infantry rifles in the nation's armories to equip the Regular Army and National Guard, much less a mass army of conscripts.

The navy was in scarcely better shape. Its surface fleet was midway through a transition that left its emerging modern doctrine halfway operational and dependent on ships from an old era that were held in service to gap the shortfall in modern vessels that had not yet been delivered and, in many cases, had not even been laid down. The combined navy-marine air fleet was built on interim and stopgap aircraft models that could not compare to aircraft already fielded by its two main potential adversaries, not to mention the hundreds of fighter and bomber pilots who had been or were going to be seasoned in combat in Spain or China.

To call the American armed forces of the day "forces" is to extend the meaning of the word beyond all meaning.

The Meeting

In attendance at the November 14 meeting were President Roosevelt and, representing his administration, Secretary of the Treasury Henry Morganthau Jr.; General Counsel of the Treasury Herman Oliphant; Harry Hopkins, the head of the Works Progress Administration but more importantly, one of the president's key personal advisers; Solicitor General Robert Jackson, who had already been named to the post of attorney general; and Assistant Secretary of War Louis Johnson, who had been a leading industrial figure before he joined the Roosevelt Administration to oversee the modernization of the army and whose staff acted as the statutory clearinghouse for purchases of the army's weapons and equipment; Gen. Malin Craig, the U.S. Army chief of staff; Brig. Gen. George Marshall, Craig's newly appointed deputy (in office since mid-October), who, among other duties, oversaw the army's budget; Maj. Gen. Henry Arnold, the new chief of the Army Air Corps (in office since October 28); and Col. James Burns, executive assistant to Assistant Secretary of War Johnson and the army's leading authority on industrial mobilization. The only naval officer in attendance was the president's senior military aide, Capt. Daniel Callaghan. Significant by his absence was Secretary of War Harry Woodring, a stalwart isolationist President Roosevelt had named to the post in 1936 to allay suspicions that the administration was secretly rearming. The atmospherics between the president and Woodring were tense, and there is no doubt that Woodring's absence this day was his way of registering an emphatic no vote against any proposal to expand the nation's ability to wage war.

The president's remarks and the articulation of his ideas were obviously hastily contrived and largely unshaped. Nevertheless, it appeared to several of the men in the room that Roosevelt had made his mind up, perhaps by earlier discussion with individuals who were present and no doubt with other advisers who were not.

President Roosevelt started off by observing that the national defenses were patently weak. He stated categorically that the first imperative was the rapid development of a large force of *offensive* army airplanes, which directly flew in the face of everything the flying services had heard from presidents for the past twenty years. He also mentioned in passing that the navy needed to increase its holding of fewer than 2,000 airplanes by arranging for a factory output of at least 350 and as many as 500 new airplanes per year.

This was late 1938; the production figures were *prodigious* in that place and at that time. By way of comparison, the president noted that France, which was considered to have a large air force, could boast only 600 modern warplanes overall but had an annual production potential of 3,600 airplanes. Great Britain, he noted, had 1,500 to 2,200 aircraft in service and a production potential of 4,800 per year. And then Roosevelt got to the nub of the matter: Germany, he averred, already had built at least 5,000 and as many as 10,000 modern warplanes and could build as many as 12,000 per year with its current but growing production capacity. (Roosevelt did not reveal that these numbers had recently been supplied in secret by the legendary American aviator Charles Lindbergh, for whom the admiring Germans had thrown open the whole of their air force and aircraft-production facilities in an effort to win him over to their cause, or to channel through him news that would intimidate the American president.) Roosevelt added that Germany's ally, Italy, already possessed a 3,000-plane inventory and a 2,400-plane annual production capacity.

Given the degree to which air power had come to the fore in the civil war in Spain, where Germany was blatantly and brutally testing its modern tactics and weapons, President Roosevelt put it to the gathering that America's first priority lay in building up the Army Air Corps. He also stated, again in passing, that it was essential to build large numbers of antiaircraft guns and deploy them in new units. The president next said that he *wished* in a few years to reach an objective of 20,000 aircraft in service and an annual production capacity of 24,000. Nevertheless, after wryly referring to the congressional penchant for halving reasonable requests for the military, he directed the War Department representatives to draw up a plan to actually build 10,000 airplanes. Of that number, 2,500 were to be training models, 3,750 were to be first-line combat models, and 3,750 additional combat models were to be built and warehoused against future need. Moreover, all of the Army Air Corps' new airplanes were to be produced in two years' time—8,000 in existing factories and 2,000 in new, government-owned plants yet to be constructed. Indeed, Roosevelt directed Harry Hopkins to upgrade plant construction to the point where the *unused* capacity would be sufficient to produce an additional 10,000 airplanes per year. The president specifically ordered Hopkins to contract for the construction of seven new government-owned airplane factories, of which two would be utilized to produce the 2,000 new airplanes mentioned earlier and the rest would be set aside for later use. This was a portentous request if ever one was made!

Interestingly, except for some very fleeting allusions to them, the president made no mention of the entire web of support the gathering knew would be needed to keep all the new airplanes flying: the new airfields, depots, maintenance organizations, and communications and navigation systems; the stockpiles of spare parts, bombs, and bullets; the new supply systems; the new fueler trucks; the new pilot, crew, and support training facilities; and on and on and on. Indeed, the president made no mention whatsoever of a program to *train* pilots for all the new warplanes. He said he wanted 2,500 new training aircraft, but he did not say he wanted pilots to be trained on them. He seemed to imply that such was his desire, but he did not say so.

It seemed strange to a number of the men who attended the meeting that there were no flag-rank naval officers or senior Department of the Navy officials in attendance, and that no mention of the navy was made beyond a few opening remarks about modestly increasing production capacity of naval aircraft. And what were they to make of the president's failure to request all the things that would make ten thousand warplanes a real air force and not just a bunch of inanimate objects? For the moment, they kept silent. Perhaps they chalked it up to oversights by a novice.

Whatever the president left out, his proposals, when they were at last put into action, were the first giant step in the American rearmament process. In the end, the Army Air Corps received a crucial early and massive opportunity to outnumber and outbuild all the air forces of the Axis nations, combined. So did the rest of the army, as pertained to its assets for fighting a ground war.

Aim for the Stars

On Tuesday, November 15, 1938, Assistant Secretary of War Louis Johnson directed Army Chief of Staff Craig to develop and submit a budget that, over the next two years, would provide the Army Air Corps with the ten thousand new airplanes the president had requested the day before and develop the seven new government aircraft factories the president had also requested. Then, doing what a well-trained and highly motivated overseer of the army's material needs would feel obligated to do, Johnson embellished on the president's explicit order. He directed Craig to provide for the necessary materiel and services required to support an Air Corps that would end up being ten thousand airplanes larger than it already was. Though the last part in itself went far beyond the president's explicit brief, Johnson further directed General Craig to include in his budget proposal all of the items the *entire* U.S. Army would require in order to upgrade its ability to serve as the basis for a massive national mobilization—a budget to oversee the conversion of domestic factories to the production of military items; to provide modern machinery for existing government arsenals; to complete plans, long on hold, for the output of critical supplies; to complete all current surveys and specifications with an eye on accelerating a long-nascent industrial mobilization program similar to but better and larger than the Great War model; to provide a *reserve* of machinery required to produce munitions; and to stockpile critical raw materials. Implicit in Johnson's directive was an offer for army budgeters to completely ignore a supplementary spending limit of $500 million that the president thought he could arrange with the Congress.

Louis Johnson was literally going for broke to begin the long, hard job of building out the entire army. But Johnson was not acting on his own. He was merely one leading member of a cabal that had never met or even acknowledged its own existence. The unstated goal of this unacknowledged cabal was, by November 15, 1938, to use the president's push for a much larger Air Corps as the means to develop a much larger and much better equipped Air Corps *and* ground army—a *balanced* and *integrated* army in which each branch, service, and corps was scaled to a vision of the whole. One other member of this cabal-in-waiting was Works Progress Administrator Harry Hopkins, President Roosevelt's staunchest inside enabler, a man who usually supported the president to the hilt but who was in such a favored position that he had no fear of telling Roosevelt things Roosevelt didn't want to hear. A third member was Gen. Malin Craig, who had been pushing mightily for an expansion of the ground forces but was in no way averse to giving the Air Corps its share of the pie. A fourth member, a man so new to the scene that he had no idea there were other important men in agreement with *his* quest for a balanced army, was Deputy Chief of Staff George Marshall, who revealed himself to Johnson and Hopkins by being the only man inside the Aircraft Meeting (as it came to be called) who actually had had the courage to tell the president that he thought so much emphasis on aviation was a bad idea.

General Craig ordered his staff heads to do all they could to help develop the new budget in time for President Roosevelt's New Year's message to the Congress. It was necessary to beef up the entire U.S. Army General Staff, and most especially the staff of the chief of the Air Corps, Major General Arnold. Many of the best and brightest officers in the army were systematically drawn into these humming centers of power and influence.

And not only the Air Corps or the staffs in general prospered as a result of the new budget process. As these things often occur—as was occurring already in Assistant Secretary Johnson's budget directive—General Craig, a thoroughgoing professional with a clear understanding of the big picture, ordered his expanding staff to see to it that the entire force structure of the army was balanced—on paper, at least—in all essential areas, such as budget, procurement, manpower, organization, supplies and munitions, equipment, and so forth.

Among the items on the army's own supplementary wish list, as articulated in the new budget proposal, were the creation of a fully manned, fully equipped, fully armed three-division expeditionary force to mount a forward hemispheric defense in certain Latin American and Caribbean states; enlargement and improvement of defensive establishments in the Panama Canal

Zone, Puerto Rico, Hawaii, and Alaska; and upgrading the National Guard through recruitment of twenty-seven thousand additional men for nine new antiaircraft regiments and other units, including several engineer companies and battalions.

When the army's draft budget proposal was sent up to Assistant Secretary Johnson, it included the president's ten thousand new airplanes and his seven new government aircraft factories as well as a request for money to recruit, train, and maintain for the then-twenty-thousand-man Army Air Corps 7,900 new officers, 1,200 new flying cadets, and 73,000 new aircrew and support personnel. And it proposed an increase by 58,000 officers and men of the army's ground forces and by 36,000 officers and men of the National Guard. And, to top everything off, the army's budget stipulated a standing reserve of materiel adequate to equip and see into battle a mobilized force initially comprising 730,000 men, plus a reserve factory capacity capable of equipping an additional 270,000 men within five months of the initial date of mobilization.

President Roosevelt reacted rather sharply when the army's budget requests reached his desk. In late December, he summoned several key players to the Oval Office and reminded them that he had asked for a $500 million budget *for airplanes alone*, with no extras. It eventually dawned on the servicemen that the president wanted all along to bluff the Germans and Japanese into believing that the Army Air Corps was huge, which he could accomplish by bandying about in public mere numbers of combat aircraft in hand—even if there was no one to fly them. Also, it appeared that Roosevelt wanted to massively equip the British and French air forces so those nations could stand up to Hitler's threats to unleash the Luftwaffe. But the American military planners and leaders remained fixated on their own perceived needs, which were real enough to embolden them to stand up to the president.

After much wrangling, Roosevelt finally signed off on the army's much broader budget proposal. He even agreed to request an additional $100 million for naval aviation. This appeared to the airmen to be a victory of the first magnitude, but even then it appears that the president allowed himself to be won over because he realized that a powerful American air force sitting on the sidelines—an American *deus ex machina*—might have a powerful deterrent effect on German, Italian, and Japanese predations in their respective regions.

The eye of the needle Roosevelt had to thread, then, became the speed with which a credible deterrence could be built up in all arenas—in the air, at sea, and on the ground. It had to be well along before possible adversaries were moved to mount preemptive war ahead of being outbuilt or outclassed by a re-emergent United States. Once embarked on such a dangerous path, the United States would have to pull out all the stops, and it would have to be seen by potential enemies as pulling out all the stops.

If this is what Roosevelt and those around him saw, it was not what the American people or the Congress saw in late 1938. Before any sort of aviation modernization and expansion program—much less outright, across-the-board rearmament—could even begin to get off the ground, it would be necessary to win over the people and their elected representatives. Nothing could happen without them being on board.

To start the ball rolling, and as an act of good faith, the president used the occasion of his State of the Union Address, on January 12, 1939, to request of the Congress a $300 million appropriation to develop and purchase new aircraft for the Air Corps. He gave as his reason the "increased range, increased speed, increased capacity of airplanes abroad" as having "changed our requirements for defensive aviation."

Fueling the Recovery

The dollar figures the army tabulated seem puny by today's standard, but in late 1938 it was money that had to be squeezed from stone. There were no end of cross purposes and constituencies and agendas and requirements in play at the outset, and that morass was certain to be eclipsed as the process gained momentum.

As the process matured, it was found that old wish lists no longer matched the real world, and it was necessary to correct many false starts, often in reaction to events and developments overseas, in the political arena. Thanks to the direct, energetic, and ongoing personal involvement of President Roosevelt, the maturing war-readiness plans were matched by budget requests realistic for the time, the requisite executive orders directing the expenditure of the new money, and the ability of the anorexic military services to pack on sustenance, which required deliberate ramping up and not a gorging on goodies the military could not metabolize in one sitting.

There can be no doubt that Roosevelt's pump-priming ruminations and then his almost total acquiescence to the army's immense wish list were motivated by the endless progression of alarming developments abroad. But John Maynard Keynes' revolutionary treatise on modern economics, *The General Theory of Employment, Interest, and Money,* published in 1936, also must have had a profound impact upon Roosevelt. Regard that Secretary of the Treasury Henry Morganthau Jr. and General Counsel of the Treasury Herman Oliphant attended the November 14 Aircraft Meeting. Why were they there to listen to the president ruminate on military aircraft production if Roosevelt didn't have the final stages of national economic recovery intertwined with his perception of deeply alarming news in the world? One of Keynes' major tenets was that government spending could be used as a throttle on the economy of a nation. There is no better way to open the spending throttle than to let loose a military expansion and modernization program in a time when the prospects for peace seem to be dimming. It is a time-tested theory in use today.

Chapter 9

The Indispensable Man

Marshall the Soldier

GEORGE CATLETT MARSHALL was the greatest American military man of his age. If the U.S. Army had kicked off the twentieth century with the specific intent of constructing a chief of staff to lead it to victory in World War II, it could not have done a better job than what chance provided in the triumphs and travails over forty years that molded George Marshall.

Marshall was born in Uniontown, Pennsylvania, on December 31, 1880. He entered the Virginia Military Institute (VMI) with the class of 1901, with which he graduated as first captain. His first posting as an infantry lieutenant was to a unit in the Philippines a year after the insurrection there had been put down. Following a two-year tour in Oklahoma, Marshall was selected (at the urging of his mentor, Brig. Gen. John J. Pershing) to study at one of the early service schools, the School of the Line, at Fort Leavenworth, Kansas. He excelled academically, passed an exam for promotion to first lieutenant, and was assigned as a student to the Army Staff College, and then for two more years as an instructor. In the remaining years before the Great War, Marshall undertook routine assignments, but he took extended leave twice, first to watch the British army train in the United Kingdom and later to tour Russo-Japanese War battlefields in Asia and discuss tactics with Japanese officers. He came away from these interactions with a list of things he wanted to see fixed in the U.S. Army, among them a paucity of night battle doctrine, a technique he drove home throughout his career. Well regarded by his peers and his superiors as a comer, but without any firsthand experience in war, Marshall was finally promoted captain in mid-1916.

With a temporary promotion to lieutenant colonel, Marshall arrived aboard the first American troop transport to reach France as an assistant operations officer with the 1st Infantry Division. The arrival was more symbolic than anything, for it became Marshall's job to train the division to take part in actual war. This he did with great success. Alas, Marshall was considered too valuable to command troops in battle; he ended the war as an unblooded temporary colonel serving as operations officer of the First Army.

Marshall's brilliant work in France brought him an assignment to his old mentor, General of the Armies John Pershing, whom he served for five years right after the war as aide-de-camp. This was as career-boosting a friendship as could befall any Regular Army officer.

From an office in Washington, Lieutenant Colonel Marshall was transferred to an office in China, where he served as executive officer of an infantry regiment based in Tientsin. It was here that he rekindled a friendship with Maj. Joseph Stilwell, who had served on the 1st Infantry Division staff with Marshall in France. Marshall's relationship with the fiery but intellectual Stilwell is emblematic of the relationships, forged over a long career, that served the World War II army so well when Marshall was able to reach back, so to speak, to elevate officers who had made an especially good impression on him, whose work ethic and thought processes he particularly admired.

Marshall at The Infantry School

In 1927, Marshall was an instructor at the Army War College, a heady assignment he might have relished had it not coincided with the death of his beloved wife. Seen by friends and interested superiors as a man who might need to bury his grief in hard work, Lieutenant Colonel Marshall was reassigned as assistant commandant of The Infantry School at Fort Benning, Georgia, which placed him in charge of the instructional staff and the curriculum.

Marshall's posting to Benning was the assignment from which the U.S. Army derived its victory in World War II. A listing of students and instructors at The Infantry School during Marshall's five-year tour as assistant commandant and then commandant is tantamount to a list of the best army, corps, and division commanders the U.S. Army—which is to say George Catlett Marshall—put into play during World War II. The comprehensive changes, the instructional innovation, and the sheer amount of training to think on their feet engineered by Marshall during his Benning tour set these younger officers up for the battlefield victories they would one day win. Approximately two hundred future generals transited Benning as students or instructors during Marshall's tenure, and he had a direct hand in elevating nearly every single one of them to flag rank. Officers who served on Marshall's school staff and prospered later included Lt. Col. Joseph Stilwell, Maj. Omar Bradley, Maj. Gilbert Cook, and Capt. J. Lawton Collins. Also, Lt. Col. Courtney Hodges served on the Infantry Board with Marshall. A few of the more celebrated future generals who passed through The Infantry School as students during Marshall's tenure included Terry Allen, Clarence Huebner, James Van Fleet, Walter Bedell Smith, Matthew Ridgway (who had served with Marshall in China), Manton Eddy, and Norman Cota.

The Infantry School itself, which was dedicated to training mid-career officers who were ticketed to move up, underwent a renaissance under Marshall, who encouraged—in fact, demanded—original thinking and inspired experimentation on the part of everyone with whom he came in contact there. At Marshall's urging, basic infantry tactics, all the way to squad level, were stripped down, studied, rejiggered, and finally updated for the modern battlefield and its modern weapons. At The Infantry School, Marshall quite literally changed the way American infantrymen at all levels conducted war and, in so doing, he personally gave rise to the intellectual renaissance that swept the U.S. Army ground establishment in the lean 1930s.

Marshall built upon the work of his immediate predecessor, Col. Frank Cocheau, who put into play a new teaching principle when he arrived at Benning in mid-1925: demonstration-explanation-performance. All of the students had to go through each lesson. First, the instructor demonstrated to the students what they had to learn, usually by employing crack infantry units assigned to The Infantry School for that purpose. Next, the students were expected to explain the lesson to the instructor. And finally, the students had to prove to the school staff that they had learned the lesson. This evolution revolutionized military training in the United States, and it was significantly bolstered when Cocheau dispatched an instructor for a year at the University of Minnesota to study educational psychology. When this officer returned to Benning, Marshall asked him to run a seminar for the school staff to enhance the overall approach to the mission of educating intelligent men years away from college and at the edge of a phase of life in which many adults literally close their minds.

It was Marshall's mission in life when he arrived at Benning to not so much remake The Infantry School, per se, as to remake The Infantry School in such a way as to eventually transform the entire army by changing the way army officers thought about war. It was Marshall's observation from numerous field exercises and the experience of developing operational plans for an infantry division and ultimately a field army in France that to plan a battle is an effort in controlling chaos: it couldn't be done. Marshall's key insight and innovation, which alone would have earned him a secure spot in military history, was that battlefield commanders could be systematically reconditioned to accept the chaos as inevitable and to factor it into both advance planning *and* the actual way they would undertake their quest to dominate any battlefield of any size.

As much to train officers to be flexible thinkers, Marshall's new syllabus proved to be an excellent tool for weeding out officers who could not be weaned from an unbridgeable tendency to freeze up when their plans inevitably went awry.

Marshall backed his theory with ample training examples: a last-minute change in objectives just as a fully briefed infantry force was about to set out; the appearance out of the blue of a flanking movement by enemy tanks that had never been briefed into the exercise; or orders for moves that did not match up to any maps any of the students had in hand. Marshall and his instructors were positively diabolical in the ways they screwed up the best-laid plans of their students, all with the intention of forcing them to rely on and hone their native ability to think on their feet under intense pressure. Marshall also demonstrated in a hundred different ways how even the smartest students had not sufficiently honed their powers of observation. And he forced his students to think, observe, and act as much in the dark of night as in the light of day, for the night attack, which was underappreciated and therefore underutilized by the U.S. Army, was a chaos-inducing tool embraced by many potential adversaries. Indeed, the night attack had become Marshall's favorite tool after he heard Japanese officers extol it during his tour of Russo-Japanese War battlefields before the Great War.

Another ironclad idea Marshall taught was economy of thought. He constantly harped on the instructors to tighten up their written and verbal lessons, and for the students to explain things in the fewest possible words, oral and written. He wanted the essence, the heart of the matter, to be delivered clearly in the least possible time. As with all of Marshall's practical lessons, this revolution in brevity eventually permeated the army, for instructors and students alike were released back into the army's many nooks and crannies when their time at Benning ended, all unabashedly enthusiastic to train their fellows.

Marshall's influence reached well beyond the classroom during his tour at Benning. The Infantry School was as much a laboratory as it was an educational institution. By employing the demonstration infantry regiment resident at Benning, Marshall and the various geniuses he commanded played with the size and internal organization of the infantry battalion to find an *optimal* size and organization. The battalion was the smallest organization in the army that could conduct independent, self-contained operations. Mirroring the army general staff setup, the infantry battalion had a complete staff with slots for personnel and administration (S-1); intelligence and scouting (S-2); training, planning, and operations (S-3); and logistics and supply (S-4). The battalion comprised three infantry companies and a weapons company armed with mortars and machine guns. The questions Marshall posed was how big could a battalion be if it was to be easily controlled in battle by its commander, and what was the smallest it could be to accomplish its missions while freeing up troops and officers to man a larger number of battalions? Where was the balance? Working with battalions ranging in size from 300 to 3,000 men, Marshall's team arrived at 850 as being the optimal manning requirement for an infantry battalion of the day. This was so accurate an analysis that many of the world's armies field infantry battalions roughly 850-strong to the present day.

As soon as The Infantry School had designed the ideal infantry battalion, Marshall went to work to design the ideal infantry regiment and division— indeed, the ideal infantry squad, infantry platoon, and infantry company. He and his men made a lasting mark on all these levels except at the divisional level. In a report Marshall had probably written over the signature of General Pershing, the chief of staff had attempted to make a case for a smaller infantry division than the four-regiment behemoth the army fielded in France. Riding on his other successes at The Infantry School, Marshall attempted to get the generals to sign off on a plan to triangularize the entire infantry, from platoon to division. The seniors agreed to do so from platoon to regiment (three squads per platoon, three rifle platoons and a weapons platoon per company, three infantry companies and a weapons company per battalion, three infantry battalions and a heavy weapons company per regiment). But the attempt to change the shape of the infantry division (from *four* infantry regiments and *two* artillery regiments) was quashed. The division was, after all, the purview of generals. Marshall and his acolytes proposed providing so much firepower to the smaller, triangular division that it could throw twice the old weight in steel but tie up only half as many men. The generals quashed this recommendation as well, but Marshall and his subordinates filed it all away, certain that at least one of them would one day cast the deciding vote.

Once the infantry organization was triangularized from platoon to regiment, The Infantry School focused on the optimum tactic for such an organization: the holding attack. Even at squad level, a fire element that included at least one automatic weapon could establish a base of fire and engage the enemy on his front—hold the enemy in place—while the rest of the unit attempted to skirt the beaten zone to deliver a flank or rear assault. One element *holding* the enemy under fire and a maneuver element delivering an *attack* from outside the ring of fire equals a holding attack.

It takes fewer troops to hold than to attack. Thus, one squad and perhaps an attached machine gun could establish and hold the base of fire while the other two squads in a platoon maneuvered to mount a flank attack. With the aid of light mortars and one or two machine guns, one platoon could hold and two platoons could attack. Even better, to hedge against inevitable chaos, one element could hold, one element could attack, and one element could be held in reserve to perhaps bolster the attack, reinforce a base of fire, exploit a breakthrough, or repel an enemy counterattack. Companies, battalions, regiments, divisions, corps, field armies, and even army groups could exploit the utter simplicity of the holding attack. And, of course, the holding attack Marshall favored was ideally served by a triangular organization.

In 1930 Capt. J. Lawton Collins, a particular favorite of Marshall's, came up with a simplified scheme for close-order drill that finally took into account the fire-and-move small-unit tactics of every American battlefield since Gettysburg, or even First Bull Run. The objective of drill prior to the Great War's trench warfare was to move an infantry unit across a battlefield in a solid, protective block that could put out massive, coordinated volleys of fire as well as reload behind a protective screen of bullets or bayonets. Repeating rifles and machine guns, when they appeared, shredded the old battle formations and led to fire-and-move tactics. These allowed individuals and small groups of infantrymen to make use of cover and terrain as they advanced on the enemy in small rushes, putting out suppressive fire as they went or with suppressive support from a stationary base of fire. The first real use of fire-and-move tactics was posited by Confederate Gen. James Longstreet of the Army of Northern Virginia in around 1863, a response to rapid-fire breech-loading rifles in the hands of Union common infantry. In any case, 1930 seemed about time to alter the very old close-order drill regulations, and Captain Collins had a very simple drill all worked out. Marshall agreed; he endorsed it and sent it up the chain. It was dead on arrival. Both the chief of the infantry branch and the chief of staff, Gen. Charles Summerall, rejected it out of hand, claiming its very simplicity would hurt army morale. This speaks volumes about the usefulness of the drill; it was no longer about battlefield evolutions, it was about the discipline many officers thought could be derived from mind-numbing, time-eating, make-work projects aimed solely at keeping idle hands and feet moving in some regimented way. The Collins drill endorsed by Marshall was aimed at building confidence, enhancing teamwork, and developing unit esprit. Marshall was unwilling to go to the mat with General Summerall, whom he had served under in the 1st Infantry Division in France, but he kept Collins and his modern drill in mind for some future opening.

Under Marshall's influence, The Infantry School professional library was massively built up, and everyone who passed through the school was expected to read voraciously—to make time to read within an impossibly busy schedule.

Even without the crucible of World War II, Marshall and the hundreds of officers he influenced during his tour at The Infantry School changed the U.S. Army forever. They learned and tested and nurtured truths about making war—and about teaching and learning and running organizations, about working cooperatively, and on, and on. Their efforts stood their nation in good stead for nearly as long as the youngest of them drew breath. They infected the army and a nation of wartime soldiers with their virus for getting things done, with their patented American can-do spirit. And in doing so, they changed the world.

If George Catlett Marshall had accomplished in life *only* what he accomplished at Fort Benning between 1928 and the fall of 1932, he would have been accorded a place of honor in American military history.

Marshall in Command

When the Benning tour ended, Marshall, who had remarried in 1930, was posted to Georgia to command a rag-tag battalion of infantry. It was a unit so small and so poorly equipped that it could not realistically train. Morale was extremely low because the poorly paid troops could not buy enough food for their families, a problem Marshall fixed on the sly by selling the needy troops "leftovers" from the battalion kitchens for pennies on the dollar.

During his tour in Georgia, and from May 1933 as commanding officer of an infantry regiment in South Carolina, Marshall had his first experience with the Civilian Conservation Corps (CCC), for which he oversaw the construction and administration of thirty-four camps, staffed in part by Regular Army officers and noncommissioned and Organized Reserve officers. This experience, and a later one in the Pacific Northwest, gave Marshall a refresher course in dealing with the induction and training of masses of people who, to an army officer, looked an awful lot like raw recruits. This is what he had done for the 1st

Infantry Division in 1917 and part of 1918, and it helped prepare him for what he would have to do beginning again in 1940.

In October 1933, after only five months in command of his regiment, the crown jewel of many a career, Colonel Marshall was abruptly reassigned as senior instructor to the staff of the 33d Infantry Division, the Illinois National Guard command based in Chicago. The move came as a blow to Marshall. Had he done something wrong? Was he being shown the door?

None of that. The 33d Division had been called out in 1932 to dampen the effects of forecasted labor unrest in an urban area facing 50 percent unemployment. The Guardsmen had performed less efficiently than expected. It was Marshall's brief to train the division to a level the army required in the event the National Guard was called to war.

Yet again, a playwright could not have done a better job than Chance really did when it came to scripting the details of the career of the man who would be the nation's number-one soldier when, indeed, the entire National Guard was called to the colors. It would be Marshall's lot to oversee the training and equipping, even the streamlining and a massive change in management for the entire Guard. The insights he gained into Guard methods, shortcomings, and politics while he served in Illinois, not to mention new ways to apply The Infantry School experience, were legion.

Up or Out

The promotion clock nearly ticked out on Marshall. If he didn't get a star soon, he would be mandatorily retired as a colonel. And even if he won one star, could he earn two before the unofficial cutoff, at age sixty-one, after which tradition forbade generals from being considered for the post of army chief of staff? It is true that by the mid-1930s, Marshall wanted to be chief of staff, and he even felt he had an outside chance to get there.

Several senior officers who knew Marshall well took it on themselves to extol his merits as a means to getting him a star. Marshall, on the other hand, made only one request of only one man. General Pershing, who had been Marshall's best man at the second wedding, agreed to lay out Marshall's career in writing, via efficiency reports dating back to 1915, to the secretary of war. Pershing, however, had a better card to play: he spoke in Marshall's behalf directly to Franklin Roosevelt. And Roosevelt, in May 1935, took care of the secretary of war in a brief note:

> General Pershing asks very strongly that Colonel George C. Marshall (Infantry) be promoted to Brigadier.
>
> Can we put him on list of next promotions? He is fifty-four years old.
>
> F.D.R.

The 1935 promotion list was issued without reference to Marshall. Someone high up was willing to defy the president. But defy Pershing? Even in old age and long retirement, Black Jack would not take it. The old general of the armies went to work behind the scenes. Chief of Staff MacArthur was set to swing into action, but the other player whose wishes had been defied set another mechanism in motion. On October 2, 1935, the president announced that MacArthur was to nominally retire in order to travel to Manila to advise the new defense force of the Commonwealth of the Philippines, which was only a few years away from being granted independence as a sovereign nation. Named in MacArthur's place as chief of staff was Maj. Gen. Malin Craig, who was elevated to four stars.

Craig and Marshall were friends going back thirty years. The new chief backed Marshall's advancement, but he could not move the promotions board. Rather, the commanding general of VI Corps, who was based in Chicago, who lived across the hall from the Marshalls and was another of Marshall's old friends and admirers, arranged for Marshall to pay a visit to Secretary of War George Dern in April 1936. The colonel came away from the meeting with a verbal commitment that Dern would see to the promotion no later than September.

On October 1, 1936, George Catlett Marshall was promoted to brigadier general and elevated to command the 3d Division's 5th Brigade in Washington State. Ironically, all the political pull on the Marshall promotion got him his star no more than a matter of weeks before seniority alone would have done the job. But chalk up another lesson for the future chief of staff: mere seniority would not play a decisive role in moving good men ahead in an army he might ever run.

Marshall in the Pacific Northwest put in much of his time overseeing the regional CCC program and camps. He was particularly caught up in educating and training the young CCC men for work and life in the real economy. Marshall did his best, also, to nurture professional education for his officers, especially the young ones. The list he maintained of especially promising young men grew and grew.

Near the end of 1937, Marshall had a one-on-one conversation with President Roosevelt when the latter toured the Pacific Northwest. Nothing came of it; it was probably as forgettable to Roosevelt as a brief encounter the two had shared in 1928.

Washington

The call came in June 1938. Beginning on July 7, Brigadier General Marshall was to prepare himself to run the army's War Plans Division, as soon as he could get up to speed in a place where reading material was yards thick. Chief of Staff Craig greeted him thusly: "Thank God, George, you have come to hold my trembling hands."

The War Plans job lasted only three months. As the true meaning of the Munich Crisis and the destruction of Czechoslovakia settled upon the world, planning in Washington for a war in Europe broke down when Assistant Secretary of War Louis Johnson refused to attend a vital meeting called by General Craig on the excuse that a two-week-old vacancy of the deputy chief of staff had to be filled first, because the deputy oversaw the army's budget process. On a personal level, Craig was all for filling the vacancy with Marshall, but Marshall was a very junior one-star general. What would that do to protocol and the morale of most of the army's generals? But Assistant Secretary Johnson, who was pretty much running the Department of War in place of a largely absent Secretary of War Harry Woodring, wanted Marshall for the job. To break the stalemate, Johnson issued Craig a direct order. This was the cover Craig needed. The deed was done during the third week of October 1938. Even though he would wear only one star, Marshall became the number-two man in an army that appeared to be headed for war. It didn't hurt one bit that the voracious information-gathering vessel that was George Marshall had just undergone a three-month crash reading course on just about everything the army needed and wanted to do to win a war almost anywhere in the world.

Marshall Speaks Out

Weeks after he became Craig's deputy, Marshall finally made a lasting impression on President Roosevelt. At the November 14, 1938, Aircraft Meeting, as the assembled honorables listened mutely and nodded appreciatively to the president's ruminations on the singular virtues of air power, only Marshall spoke up, but only after the president asked his opinion: "Don't you think so, George?" Marshall was not ready to be addressed so familiarly by a man he barely knew, not even *this* man. "Mr. President," Marshall responded in a rather chilly tone, "I am sorry, but I don't agree with that at all." And then Roosevelt ended the meeting.

It didn't matter whether or not George Marshall agreed with the president; the planning Roosevelt set in motion on November 14, 1938, would move forward because Assistant Secretary Johnson and General Craig—not to mention Roosevelt himself—wanted it to. Marshall could content himself with simply overseeing the budget, or he could advance his case with Johnson and Craig while there was hope that the planning and spending would not so favor the Air Corps that the entire rest of the army would shrivel up and blow away. Marshall was not against building airplanes, but he could not fathom who would fly tens of thousands of them, nor how they might win a war—maybe two wars, simultaneously—without a little help from a ground army, or even a navy.

When Marshall spoke out at the Aircraft Meeting, he instantly but unknowingly cemented his relationship with two men in the room whom he barely knew. One, Assistant Secretary of War Louis Johnson, had been the man who had had the most to do with Marshall's appointment as deputy chief of staff, but the two had not done much to exchange views. Equipping and arming the *entire* army was not just a job to Johnson, it was a mission. Johnson expected to be elevated to secretary of war when the president finally tired of having Harry Woodring, an uncooperative, moralizing isolationist, around. Thus, Johnson's backing for Marshall's elevation was probably an omen that he was building up his own following within the War Department.

The surprise relationship was with Works Progress Administration (WPA) chief Harry Hopkins, a key personal advisor to the president, who, like Marshall, was unafraid to say "no" to the great man. So unafraid and so committed to rearmament was Hopkins that he had taken several blatantly illegal actions to benefit the army. In the first instance, he had cunningly reallocated $2 million in funds earmarked for the WPA to purchase machine tools army arsenals needed but could not get from the Congress, in order to manufacture small-arms ammunition. In the second case, Hopkins saw to it that $250 million in Civilian Conservation Corps funding was used to build permanent housing and other facilities for CCC workers on army posts. If the army ever got around to expanding—and Hopkins was betting it would—a significant start in needed barracks and other buildings had been made.

Marshall knew Hopkins had engineered these windfalls, but he did not speak directly with the man until the last week of 1938, when Hopkins phoned Marshall to set up a meeting at his Department of Commerce office. At that meeting the two spoke frankly of their shared views with regard to a balanced army. This was the beginning of a great friendship and strategic partnership. When Hopkins urged Marshall to make his case for a balanced force directly to the president, Marshall said he felt his earlier candor might have made his opinions moot. Marshall then asked Hopkins to speak up, and Hopkins agreed to do so.

At the Oval Office followup to the Aircraft Meeting, which took place at the close of December 1938, Roosevelt complained that his November 14 request for airplanes had resulted in the army's asking him for a few planes and everything else in the world it felt it needed in the near term. True to his word, Hopkins spoke first in an effort to realign the president's thinking. Then Assistant Secretary Johnson piled on. General Craig spoke up too, somewhat more diffidently than the civilians. And in the end Marshall quietly and methodically aired his views in some detail.

Speaking out twice in a row transformed Brigadier General Marshall into an inside player—not because of his titular power, but by the power of his character. Far from experiencing an ignominious transfer from his post, he virtually cemented himself in many powerful minds as the leading contender to replace Craig whenever Craig retired. As Douglas MacArthur had learned from his 1933 temper tantrum at his first meeting with the new president, Roosevelt favored one character trait above all others, and that was the courage of conviction that obligated a man to speak truth to power. In the harrowing years ahead, it was perhaps through his powerful trait of unflinching candor that Marshall best served his nation, and perhaps humanity as a whole.

Marshall and Hopkins

Following their candid and friendly get-together in the immediate aftermath of the November 1938 Aircraft Meeting, Deputy Chief of Staff Marshall and WPA Administrator Hopkins met whenever they could during the first quarter of 1939. In the main, Marshall educated Hopkins on the ways and needs of the army, because Hopkins was the one person in the Roosevelt inner circle who felt the president urgently needed educating. Roosevelt favored the navy virtually to the extent of ignoring the army, and that, Hopkins and Marshall agreed, needed to be corrected. So, as a deep and genuine friendship blossomed between men who were polar opposites in all things except their passion to build a balanced army (which had become a catch phrase in army circles), Marshall filled out Hopkins's feelings with facts and insights, and these typically found their way to the president's ear, which became increasingly willing to listen.

Chief of Staff

Overworked and in faltering health, General Craig gave notice to President Roosevelt in March or April 1939 that he intended to go on terminal leave in late June and formally retire from the army on August 31. Though Craig favored Marshall to replace him, this was entirely the president's call.

Marshall was junior to thirty-three other generals, but when age was factored in, only four could serve out a four-year term before mandatory retirement at age sixty-four. The competition was going to be fierce, but the front-runner from the army's perspective was a little too ardent in his request for the taste of his fellow generals, and he quite possibly offended the president.

Marshall was extremely circumspect in spite of attracting many influential supporters, not least being old General Pershing. But the voice that swayed the president to a man he barely knew and had not yet fully sized up was that of Marshall's new friend, Harry Hopkins. On April 23, 1939, Marshall was called to the White House.

When they met in private, once the offer was made but before it was accepted, Marshall asked the President of the United States if he would be allowed to always speak his mind, even if his was an answer or issue Roosevelt didn't want to hear. The president said, "Yes" and then "Yes" again when Marshall requested a confirmation. The deal was thus sealed.

Chapter 10

Arnold's Air Corps: Part 1

Hap Arnold

HENRY HARLEY ARNOLD was born in Gladwyn, Pennsylvania, on June 25, 1886, and attended the U.S. Military Academy with the class of 1907. Arnold's classmates called him Hap, after an enigmatic smile that seemed to be glued permanently to his face. It was an effort at irony, for there was no sign that the jolly-looking Arnold had a sense of humor or was even happy. He was a plodding, hard worker who set his sights on a commission in the cavalry but ended up in the infantry after blurting out an inappropriate response to West Point's senior cavalry instructor only four days before he graduated somewhat below the middle of the class standings.

Lieutenant Arnold spent his first four years of service at Governor's Island, New York, pining for more excitement, or at least a chance for promotion. After he had seen early airplanes fly from the small airfield at Governor's Island at the hands of aviation pioneers Wilbur Wright and Glenn Curtiss, Arnold requested a transfer to the Signal Corps and parlayed that into assignment to the U.S. Army's first venture into flight training, a class of two from which he graduated as army aviator No. 2 with less than four hours of actual flight time to his credit. Getting aloft and then getting down safely was the extent of the U.S. military's aviation event horizon in 1911. Thereafter, for two years, everything Arnold accomplished in the air was considered pioneering: the first strafing attack and the first reconnaissance flight over friendly ground troops, among many others. Nearly everything he did in the air was a first. In 1912, Arnold nearly died when his airplane went into a sudden dive as he was trying to figure out how to adjust artillery fire from aloft. He was so shaken that he refused to fly for four years.

Arnold met Col. Billy Mitchell in 1914 and was so taken by the prophet of American airpower that he allowed Mitchell to cajole him back into the air in 1916. By then he had been bypassed by numerous aviators, younger and older, who received higher consideration for key commands as army aviation geared up for the Great War.

Arnold served out the war as executive officer to the commander of the Signal Corps Aviation Section and only received a posting to France as the guns were about to go silent. But his time in Washington turned out to be crucial to the future of army aviation, because it gave Arnold a front-row seat and hands-on experience with the immense difficulties American industry faced in building thousands of combat-worthy airplanes in a very short time. Indeed, in this venture, the vaunted American industrial base came as close to failure as possible without flat-out failing.

In 1924, Arnold was tapped for an assignment that, many years later, seemed to be a matter of destiny: he attended the inaugural class of the Army Industrial College, which the War Department was standing up to grapple with the horrors Arnold and others like him had faced in turning American industry into a world-class arsenal. The whole purpose of the enterprise was to think of ways to efficiently mobilize industry for a future war.

In 1925, as Billy Mitchell was being drummed out the army for being overly aggressive in his campaign to make aviation ascendant over all the other combat arms, Arnold was serving on the staff of the commanding general of the Army Air Service, an engineering officer who backed the creation of an autonomous Air Corps within the army structure but was not a backer of Mitchell's vision for an independent air force. Arnold, a Mitchell man all the way, launched a campaign to support Mitchell right from the commanding general's office, an indiscretion that left him exiled far from the center of power in much the same way he had been banned from his beloved cavalry in the wake of a previous indiscretion.

In 1929, following a great deal of lobbying, Major Arnold attended the Army Command and General Staff School. And, from there, he punched an important ticket with an assignment to command Fairfield Depot in Dayton, Ohio. Fairfield, which became Wright Field in due course, was part of the Air Corps' materiel hub; it was built over the Wright brothers' airfield, on which Arnold had learned to fly, and served as army aviation's iconic center of gravity.

In 1931, with an assist from his close friend, Maj. Carl Spaatz, Arnold was given command of March Field, California, which he was to transform into the Air Corps' West Coast tactical aviation center. Along with this coveted assignment, Arnold was promoted to lieutenant colonel. Although a committed bomber man, Arnold's work with dashing pursuit and attack pilots at March exposed to him a side of military flying he came to love and respect. Also, Arnold's preeminent position west of the Rockies put him in touch with western aircraft moguls, especially an admiring Donald Douglas, and allowed him to play an important role in organizing the Civilian Conservation Corps in his area, an experience that left him with sound ideas regarding a future expansion of the Air Corps in time of war. He also played a pivotal role in getting emergency supplies to the city of Long Beach following the massive March 1933 earthquake, an important lesson in innovative on-the-fly crisis management. Arnold's decision to break into civilian warehouses to get at supplies put him crosswise with the IX Corps commander, Maj. Gen. Malin Craig, but the two sorted out their differences, and Craig ultimately supported Arnold's actions as necessary when higher command probed the incident.

In May 1934, as part of a public relations effort to put right the Air Corps' poor showing in delivering the mail during a railroad strike, Arnold led a mass flight of modern B-10 all-metal bombers on an eighteen-thousand-mile, goodwill expedition. Returning from the Alaska leg of the journey, Arnold rather willfully led the formation across a thousand miles of open water between Juneau and Seattle. This put him crosswise with Army Chief of Staff Douglas MacArthur, whose 1931 pact with the navy had banned the Air Corps from such displays over the sea. For all that MacArthur was incensed at Arnold, the notoriety the airman gained from leading the flight boosted him into the public's mind as one of America's leading airmen. In 1936, under the GHQ Air Corps reorganization scheme, Arnold was given command of the 1st Wing and a temporary two-grade promotion to brigadier general.

After he had commanded 1st Wing for only nine months, Arnold was called to Washington to serve as assistant Air Corps chief with permanent rank of brigadier general. The chief of the Air Corps was killed in a plane crash on October 21, 1938, and Army Chief of Staff Malin Craig immediately offered Arnold as the replacement. President Roosevelt was disinclined to agree, but Arnold's friend, Donald Douglas, a lion of the Democratic Party in the West, interceded, and the die was cast. Arnold was sworn in as Air Corps chief and promoted to major general on October 28, 1938, two weeks before the Aircraft Meeting.

Arnold Goes to Work

America's rearmament for World War II began with the somewhat mistaken belief among those attending the November 14, 1938, White House meeting that President Roosevelt had asked that the Army Air Corps be built up to a much higher world stature than it enjoyed at the end of 1938. Hap Arnold emerged from the Aircraft Meeting a very happy man; he called the event the Air Corps' "Magna Carta."

It was April 1939 before a budget request for new Air Corps airplanes finally went to the Congress. By then, President Roosevelt had pared back his November rumination on 10,000 (or was it 20,000?) Air Corps airplanes of all types to a manageable 3,300, for a grand total of 5,500 aircraft allotted to the Air Corps. The president's temperate request and personal appeal carried the day; the Congress authorized the new aircraft to a budget limit of $180 million. The same bill revised upward the personnel strength of the Air Corps to 3,203 officers and 45,000 enlisted men, which represented near-term growth rates of 200 and 150 percent, respectively.

Despite the early setback with respect to numbers of aircraft promised versus numbers of aircraft requested and authorized, Hap Arnold placed his faith in Roosevelt's word; he continued to plan for a 10,000-plane Air Corps to be up and running by late 1940. By Arnold's reckoning, the front-line end strength would be 3,750 combatant aircraft of all types, plus 3,750 reserve combatants, and 2,500 trainers of various types.

No one counted on President Roosevelt's next move, which was to offer the British and French governments the opportunity to purchase American-designed and -built aircraft from the excess capacity of new aircraft factories whose construction was being overseen by Harry Hopkins. When the War Department, with Arnold's backing, protested the overseas sales at a time the Air Corps was scrambling to upgrade itself—that there was no *excess* capacity—the president, who was rather miffed, asked Secretary of the Treasury Henry Morganthau Jr. to mediate the conflicting needs. Morganthau elected to split production down the middle—half to be divided equally between the Air Corps and naval aviation, and half to the British and French. The War Department chiefs and Air Corps senior commanders protested the decision for varying reasons: The civilians were pushing absolute neutrality—which was the law of the land—in European affairs, and the aviators wanted to avoid the dilution of industrial capacity, which had not even begun to ramp up. On the other hand, the Department of the Navy and naval aviation acceded because they understood that the American aviation industry needed the foreign revenues just to stay in business, much less to build up its production and design capacities. Matters went from bad to worse; the army, especially the unsubtle Arnold himself, ended up alienating the White House over the issue.

The only up side the Air Corps saw in the ongoing debate around overseas sales was General Arnold's adamant refusal to equip French or British export aircraft with the latest American technologies, such as turbochargers and the Norden bombsight. This might have been a wise choice, given the fate of the French air force in mid-1940, but withholding the best stuff might also have been spectacularly dumb, because use in combat by the British and French against the Germans in mid-1940 might have forestalled the fate awaiting those armies and air forces, might have obviated America's entry into the war in Europe altogether, or might have contributed to an easier, cheaper ultimate victory. Who could know? Such spectacularly altered outcomes from tiny factors are the stuff of all wars.

To go along with the new aircraft production, and modulated to it, Arnold raised the 1939 pilot-training goal to 1,200, a 50 percent increase over the 1938 training goal of 800 new pilots. Further, he projected the 1940 goal to an unprecedented 4,500 new pilots—men whose recruitment had yet to be authorized by anyone in the civilian chain of command, much less by the Congress. This would require an intensive recruitment and screening effort, many new training facilities in temperate climates, lots of training aircraft, thousands of competent instructors, thousands of trained mechanics, and a host of other things.

Arnold and the men close to him knew what was needed, and they had a pretty good idea about how to get there. They spent every waking moment thinking or talking through plans and preparations for the immediate growth as well as for projected growth. They set a manageable goal in the spring of 1939 to build out the Air Corps by June 30, 1941, to a strength of twenty-four combat-ready tactical groups.

Training

Given the Air Corps' extremely limited pilot-training infrastructure, it would be difficult to train 1,200 new pilots in 1939 and extremely difficult to train 4,500 new pilots in 1940 and who-knew-how-many thereafter. The experts decided that it would take two years to expand existing facilities, build up the needed additional facilities, and train the instructors, many of whom would have to fill training billets upon graduation from flight school in order to meet demand. That wasn't going to cut it; waiting two years would cause a severe shortfall in both 1939 and 1940 quotas of both trainees and future instructors.

One idea was to contract civilian flying schools to train new pilots, at least through the primary phase, the first of three phases of training that led to a pilot rating. In the fall of 1938, twenty-three Civil Aeronautics Authority (CAA)–approved private pilot-training schools operated across the United States. Air Corps officers visited each of them and, by the spring of 1939, nine had been asked to undertake primary flight training on an experimental basis. Contracts followed a few months later.

The Civil Aeronautics Authority was both a regulatory agency and a booster for the civilian aviation community. It ran a moderately successful pilot-training program of its own, known as the Civilian Pilot Training Program (CPTP), which was designed to train civilians for pilot certification, from the ground up. The idea was to build a pool of qualified pilots for the civil aviation industry, but a trained and certified pilot is a trained and certified pilot. Indeed, young men who had undergone CPTP training and certification on their own initiative and at their own expense before the expansion got underway were already flying for the army and the navy. As well as training for civilian jobs, the CPTP became a proving ground for hundreds and then thousands of college-age men who, upon earning civilian licenses, would constitute a pool of future military aviation trainees who had at least the rudiments of flight to call upon. As well as young pilots who might be called to service as aviation cadets, the CPTP produced civilian primary-level instructors and, once the war overtook the United States, contract ferry pilots whose service would free up the young military hotshots for duty at the front rather than tedious chores that could be handled by older pilots. In due course, CPTP-trained female pilots followed the men into ferry service. Physically fit CPTP graduates entering military service gained no time in the training cycle—everyone in both aviation services had to start from scratch—but they were pretty much assured a crack at pilot training.

At the same time the CPTP program ramped up to take on the military's needs, ridiculously high physical fitness standards were ramped down. Under the nonemergency interwar entrance requirements, the military services demanded perfect physical specimens, including no history of broken bones and perfect teeth. These largely unnecessary standards of perfection were established to help winnow down the tens of thousands of applications for pilot training to fit the hundreds of available openings. Once the needs became greater, it was necessary to pare back the otherwise exclusionary standards closer to norms for average young American men.

Pilots (and copilots) were not the only people needed to man airplanes. Among the four officer-level spots aboard a B-17 were a navigator and a bombardier. Many candidates for these billets were recruited directly, while others were selected from among pilot-training washouts, especially if they had completed most of their pilot training. This policy provided a fair chance that, during a dire emergency, especially in combat, there might be one or two additional knowledgeable pilots aboard a heavy bomber. Also, two enlisted technicians had to be arduously trained for duty aboard each heavy bomber: the flight engineer and the radioman. The four remaining enlisted aircrewmen were machine gunners, who also required rigorous training.

It was necessary to establish or expand schools for each flying specialty and for dozens and scores of the ground-service specialties required to keep the airplanes and the airmen flying. Early on in the expansion, the more technical specialties also required the contracting of civilian schools.

Unity of Command

It wasn't until March 1939 that Army Chief of Staff Craig had an opportunity to deal with the Air Corps' split command, an issue Arnold had placed before him almost as soon as he was named chief of the Air Corps in October 1938. As Arnold and others noted, the Air Corps chief could deal with GHQ Air Force only by way of the army chief of staff; there was no direct legal means for the two halves of the Air Corps to communicate, much less cooperate. Major General Frank Andrews' tour as commander of GHQ Air Force ended in March 1939, and it was then that General Craig named Arnold as Andrews' successor. This united the entire Air Corps under one command, but Arnold's duties as chief in these turbulent times required that he delegate the running of GHQ Air Force to other men—who could at least speak with him.

Craig's solution to the GHQ Air Force conundrum probably had less to do with streamlining the Air Corps decision-making mechanism than with silencing Andrews, who had become a wearying presence who used his position to preach inexorably on the virtues of the heavy strategic bomber. The general staff of the army, which was composed almost entirely of ground officers, was sick to death of hearing from Andrews, not least of them being Chief of Staff Craig. The expiration of the order establishing GHQ Air Force on a provisional basis was the perfect antidote: Andrews was reduced to his substantive rank—colonel— and banished from Washington, and most of his bombardment-minded staff was spread to the winds. Arnold was himself a bomber enthusiast, but he had commanded pursuit and attack pilots at March Field, understood them as well as a bomber man could, and at least worked within the system without preaching bombers, bombers, bombers to every ground officer with breath in him.

The smashing of the Andrews brain trust saw the expulsion of several of Andrews' associates to irrelevant jobs across the country. Indeed, the mood was so vituperative that Andrews' hand-selected chief of staff was forcibly retired on the pretext that he had become mentally unstable, as evidenced by obsessive talk about the importance of bombers.

In the larger scheme of a radically expanding Air Corps that would eventually have a war to fight, the Craig solution for placing GHQ Air Corps under the chief of the Air Corps merely traded one set of problems for another. Andrews and his people were exiled beyond carping range, but the solution was as inefficient in running the Air Corps day to day as the original problem had been. The tinkering would recommence in due course.

Lindbergh Lends a Hand

In April 1939, Arnold met secretly with Charles Lindbergh, with whom he had been corresponding for about a year regarding the qualitative advances of the Luftwaffe, which had opened its heart and its doors to Lindbergh in an attempt to woo him to the German point of view. In fact, the Germans scared the hell out of Lindbergh, who came away with the certainty that war was about to engulf the whole of Europe. Though the German airmen failed to make an ally of Lindbergh, they did scare him into becoming a vocal supporter of the isolationist camp. Nevertheless, Lindbergh was a patriot, if a misguided one, and his correspondence and meeting with Hap Arnold truly spurred the Air Corps chief to seek higher goals with respect to matching the Luftwaffe in strength and power, then overtaking it, and in the end accumulating the strength and power to crush it.

Before removing himself from the Air Corps scene in September 1939, to devote all his time and considerable energy to the isolationist cause, Lindbergh served on an informal board established by Arnold to develop a five-year Air Corps modernization and development program. The senior military member of this board was the chief of the Air War Plans Division, Col. Carl Spaatz, a renowned, technically gifted pursuit pilot who had trained hundreds of American pilots in France as well as having shot down three German planes during a brief front-line tour in the Great War. Among this board's many recommendations was the impetus to develop better liquid-cooled inline engines than were currently available for Air Corps pursuits. It also recommended that the Air Corps get right to work on a strategic bomber that could fly twice as far as the B-17. Both of these recommendations bore fruit; the Air Corps veered away from equipping all of its future pursuits and fighters with air-cooled radial engines, and it set out the design specifications for what eventually became the B-29.

A World Gone to Hell

The crises of late 1938 that led to the Aircraft Meeting ramped up following a brief respite. As they did, immense portions of the world became less stable.

In China, a massive, continuous Japanese offensive swallowed up the lower Yangtze River valley. Then the Japanese foreign ministry suggested that China,

Manchukuo, and Japan be tied together into a single economic entity that might one day include the East Indies (properly known at the time as the Netherlands East Indies, a qualifier the Japanese failed to mention), the Philippines (an American protectorate on its way to independence), and Indochina (which French colonists and administrators tended to call French Indochina).

In Europe, on March 15, 1939, German troops crossed from occupied Czechoslovakia to annex the tiny remaining rump of that dissolved state. And on March 19, Germany annexed Memel, a city governed by her helpless northern neighbor, Lithuania. The Nazi government also demanded the annexation of the Danzig Free State, a former German city that had been ceded to Poland as Gdansk following the Great War. At the same time, Italy picked a rather bombastic scrap with France centered on an old border dispute. Also, on March 25, 1939, Italy demanded that Albania accede to Italian occupation. When the Albanian king refused to accept a bribe to do so, Italy invaded on April 7, and on April 12 the Albanian parliament voted to unite with Italy as a protectorate.

These bold moves, which were carried out with utter impunity, finally moved the French foreign minister to utter, "It is five minutes to midnight." They also moved British Prime Minister Neville Chamberlain, on April 26, to ask Parliament to allow conscription for the military to begin. By their taking action so late, and in a fairly lame manner to boot, the British and French governments, which had raised "appeasement" and "apaisement" to terms of art, now guaranteed the onset of war, because Hitler and Mussolini could not be bluffed.

There was little a militarily impotent United States could do about anything the Japanese, Germans, or even the Italians wanted to do. But early in the spring, President Roosevelt privately told a member of the Senate Foreign Relations Committee, "If Germany invades a country and declares war, we'll be on the side of Hitler by invoking the [Neutrality Acts, which would revoke all arms sales to all combatant nations, such as England and France]. If we could get rid of the arms embargo, it wouldn't be so bad."

Unbeknownst to the senator, the things the president wanted to accomplish after getting around the arms embargo spelled out in the Neutrality Acts had been at the root of the Aircraft Meeting: getting modern aircraft to the British and French in the event of war in Europe. It is even likely that the senator did not yet know of the massive staff work the services were attending to in aid of that goal as well as in transforming the United States into a competitive potential combatant with teeth to go with its bark.

As a gesture to isolationists and pacifists that turned into a practical demonstration of American military weakness, Roosevelt broadcast an appeal to the Axis nations—Germany, Japan, Italy, and Hungary—to guarantee the borders of neighboring nations for ten years. Hitler and Mussolini both rejected the call for peace, which many offended senators and congressmen took as an affront to the United States. (Perhaps this is what Roosevelt had in mind when he went on the air to hold back the whirlwind with his pinky.) Other esteemed elected national officials felt Roosevelt had been given a comeuppance he deserved.

Using a phony border incident as pretext, the German war machine invaded Poland on September 1, 1939. The invasion itself was not the surprise that shocked the world; what did that was the *efficiency* of the German forces in the field. Poland's military never could be a match against the German war machine of 1939, but the Germans were so superior at every level—equipment, organization, planning, speed, firepower, coordination between air and ground units, and so forth—that the world's leaders and the world's armies and air forces expressed a common thought: Oh. Wow. How can we stand up to *that?*

When the war in Europe began, the United States actually had to halt sales of war goods to the British and French in the face of the Neutrality Acts. At the urging of the Roosevelt Administration as early as July 1939 and once again on September 21, and guided by overwhelming support for those nations by the American public, the Congress passed legislation on November 4 that restored such sales under the rubric "Cash and Carry." This opened the whole of American industry, such as it was on that date and in the months thereafter, to British and French purchasing missions. (Technically, it also opened U.S. industrial output to German and Japanese orders, but that wasn't going to happen as long as Franklin Roosevelt was the ultimate arbiter.)

There were many congressional isolationists and pacifists who helped to overturn the laws preventing sales of strategic goods and military hardware to nations allied against the aggressors. Nevertheless, many who voted to rescind the arms embargo did so in the hope that Britain and France would be able to stem the Axis tide without the intervention of the United States as a combatant. These were the men who continued to oppose or pare back spending increases for the U.S. Army.

War Spurs Production

The German invasion of Poland spurred Hap Arnold to appoint a team of his best and brightest officers to grapple with an orderly progression toward an optimally sized and balanced Air Corps combat component, a leap into what was seen then as the *distant* future. This group was headed by Canadian-born Lt. Col. George Kenney, who had dropped out of his senior year at the Massachusetts Institute of Technology to fly U.S. Army Air Service pursuits in France. Kenney, who had been Frank Andrews' GHQ Air Force G-3 when Andrews was ousted, became a vital player in Arnold's own inner circle, but only after Arnold rescued him from a meaningless, penance-serving exile at The Infantry School, where Kenney taught infantry officers the intricacies of machine gun tactics.

Kenney, who was probably the best natural engineer among army aviators of his generation, became Arnold's go-to guy on technical issues, and he served as Arnold's lead troubleshooter for the industrial expansion attending the Air Corps' early growth phase. He and a small, hand-picked cadre of fellow geniuses were dispatched to Wright Field, Ohio, the technical hub of the Air Corps, to come up with a plan to expand the service in phases, as aircraft, warm bodies, and a host of supplies and gear became available. Indeed, Kenney's team was to have a hand in deciding which aircraft, which warm bodies, and which supplies and gear the Air Corps needed, and in what order they would be needed. Major Kenneth Wolfe, a particularly talented engineering specialist, was delegated to hash out the details and come up with the schedule and a budget.

It was Wolfe's effort that came first to amaze the Air Corps seniors as to the practical breadth of the task at hand. Asked to quantify the near-term, foundational expansion in terms of dollars, Wolfe's leading financial whiz handed Kenney a detailed estimate that, line by inexorable line, topped out near $4 billion. In the whole time between the end of the Great War and this prognostication, the Air Corps had not spent as much as $1 billion on everything it had owned and everyone it had paid.

Kenney's team also foresaw a looming shortage of the metal that aircraft builders needed most, aluminum. And then there was President Roosevelt's issue about creating enough aircraft-building capacity to meet the needs of army and navy aviation as well as the British and French air forces. The Aircraft Meeting's ambitious order for more plants was not going to cut it; many more factories, and larger ones at that, were going to be needed just for the Air Corps expansion.

Caught up in the spirit of the moment, Kenney's team decided to bypass the cumbersome, time-wasting protocols the government expected its minions to cleave to. The need was urgent, and the path ahead was clear. In direct violation of a mind-boggling array of laws, Kenney, Wolfe, and other members of the team went directly to the nation's three leading aluminum manufacturers and told them they better all put their heads and resources together to build up capacity to meet the onrushing tidal wave of demand. And then the Air Corps planners went to the aircraft manufacturers and associated industry groups to *order* them to upgrade their cumulative capacity to build previously unimagined numbers of military airplanes.

This is a magic moment too. When Kenney's team slipped its leash, the military was not yet in an open dialog with American industry, and American industry was not yet caught up in the movement toward wartime production. The government agencies responsible for mobilizing industry had not yet come into being or were slow off the mark. And the Roosevelt Administration was not yet fully and morally committed to the military's burgeoning effort to effect a massive but measured movement to a realistic and credible war footing. All the time between the Aircraft Meeting and the Kenney team's well-meaning but illegal call to action was spent in rumination and on business done as usual, albeit with an eye toward immense possibilities.

The moment was magic, but it was not yet officially sanctioned. Thankfully for Kenney and his action-oriented deep thinkers, their moment was not yet really noted.

Yet, even the small steps taken by industry to live up to the military's—especially the Air Corps'—new demands almost immediately taxed America's crippled Depression-era industrial base. In very short order, Major Wolfe's concern that the nation's three aluminum producers would be unable to provide the needed product was proven correct, and only shortly after that the American machine-tool manufacturers just about threw in the towel. The skilled workers needed to build the tools, expand the factories, and, ultimately, produce the weapons and equipment had long since been driven from the workplace. It would take immense effort to find the skilled workers who could still work, to put them to work, and to train tens and hundreds of thousands of new skilled workers.

Secretary of the Treasury Henry Morganthau Jr. was first into the breach. The wealthy son of a German-Jewish immigrant (Henry Sr. had been the U.S. ambassador to Turkey during the Great War), Morganthau had trained to be a farmer, but he took a crash course in industry when he pulled together an ad hoc team of experts to help him puzzle out the needs and priorities of industry if it was to gear up efficiently to manage all that the Air Corps and naval aviation needed of it.

The Morganthau team was only getting started in tackling its stupendous task when President Roosevelt, in May 1940, called for the construction of an even more stupendous fifty thousand new airplanes. A week after this call, Roosevelt created the National Defense Advisory Commission under William Knudsen, the chairman of General Motors. This new entity co-opted Morganthau's team of experts, and the treasury secretary was relieved of his command.

The American press loved the Swedish-born Knudsen, and that notoriety sparked the effort into high gear. It was under Knudsen, with Hap Arnold laboring mightily over his part of the equation, that American industry finally found common cause with the American military *and* the imagination to grapple with what had suddenly become *the* national priority—preparing for war. Once industry, government, and the military were all on the same page, reading the same specifications, there was no holding back. The American Colossus was back in business.

The military did whatever it could to ease the pressure on industry, to erase bottlenecks and smooth the flow from drawing board to airplanes in the air. Through the mechanism of the Joint Army and Navy Board's cooperative procurement planning arm, the Army and Navy Munitions Board, the services' aviation planners had, since 1922, routinely put their heads and experience together to agree on standardized components common to the aircraft both were buying through independent contracts. These decisions pretty much involved the parts manufacturers who supplied Boeing, Curtiss, Douglas, Grumman, and other aircraft companies with such items as generators or pumps or even just screws and nuts—but also engine manufacturers. This way, a small manufacturer could devote itself to producing many more units of a smaller range of products that ended up doing exactly the same thing in every type of airplane produced across a range of aircraft manufacturers. Standardization also kept costs down, and it ended up reducing development time for upgrades. As things turned out, the British were brought into the standardization scheme, which got them what they needed sooner as well as providing a shortened and less noisy feedback loop with respect to how common components—and entire aircraft— stood up to the rigors of combat.

Also in 1939, as a result of the new war in Europe and its clear implications to the West, the Roosevelt Administration asked the Congress to authorize the construction of ten thousand additional planes for the Air Corps. This the Congress did with alacrity. And, of course, it was up to Arnold and his growing brain trust to figure out exactly how to usefully absorb so many airplanes.

Mass Production

The aircraft industry didn't yet have the hang of mass production at the time the Air Corps and naval aviation began gearing up in earnest for war. There is an impulse to assume that the fabrication methods employed by the huge and hugely successful automobile industry were wholly transferable to a ramped-up airplane industry, but they were not. In the first place, any airplane under construction took up more space than any automotive product under construction; the automobile industry changed designs no more than once a year; and those changes were often cosmetic rather than substantive. Aircraft designs, which were infinitely more complex and required infinitely more parts and subassemblies, were constantly upgraded, even as construction was underway. For example, as early as February 1940, the British reported that they perceived— through actual experience at war—that self-sealing fuel tanks and better crewspace armor were vital to the survival of bombers and the men who flew them through even light antiaircraft fire. Critical upgrades like these, which had to be made on the run, as information became available, obviated the economies of scale that made automobile manufacture as profitable as it was. Of course, profits were not the driving force behind the manufacture of military aircraft, except to the companies building them, but there were budgetary limits and the threat of government oversight if there was even a hint of profiteering at the expense of the brave American eagles whose lives depended on exacting construction values.

The advent of the reasonably all-metal warplane made life much harder for the manufacturers. In the days of fabric-covered airplanes, aircraft plants were located in sunny climes with predictable weather patterns and little rainfall. This was because most airplanes were assembled outdoors from subassemblies constructed indoors or delivered from afar. The heat of the sun expands metal by day, but the same metal contracts by night—and it does both unevenly, depending on how high the temperature rises or how much shade can be provided in tented construction areas. The result was that individual components of each airplane, such as engine cowlings and even windshields, had to be more or less hand-crafted—individually hammered and filed into unique shapes to fit into weather-altered spaces. As a result, the parts of one airplane were not identical to—and thus not interchangeable with—the same parts of another airplane, even though they appeared to be the same. A tiny difference in the size or shape of an engine cowling or its frame over the engine prevented a clean fit. This is the sort of headache that inevitably drove maintenance and repair technicians nuts because it was necessary to modify or duplicate a damaged or lost part by hand as a one-off, in the field, perhaps under combat conditions, and no doubt on a rush basis.

The initial production run of Boeing B-17 in-service test models was thirteen. The next B-17 deliveries began in June 1939, and a total in hand from this order reached thirty-eight in March 1940. That's fifty-one B-17s so far, six months after Germany and the Soviet Union invaded Poland beneath massive air umbrellas. Meanwhile, in 1939, the B-17's engines and armaments were upgraded, thirty-eight of the new B-17 model were ordered, and the first of these flew in July 1940. The RAF ordered twenty other B-17s.

So far, in the years that had passed since the Army Air Corps had adopted on a test basis the B-17—the biggest, most complex airplane by far in U.S. service—109 had been ordered and 89 had been built. This was not a strain on Boeing's ability to produce B-17s from parts provided by a dizzying array of vendors.

It was no big deal—indeed, it was business as usual—to build a few dozen heavy bombers per year under the old conditions of financial constraint. That pretty much matched deliveries of civilian airliners. It wasn't even a particularly big deal for Air Corps maintenance and technical crews to keep track of custom-made fittings such as engine cowls, or to customize or fabricate replacements. That is, it was no big deal in a peacetime military aviation service that craved extra work to keep its enlisted hands from going idle. But there was a war looming.

If America's stock of aircraft factories had to be radically expanded to meet the radically expanded needs of the military services, the manufacturers had to tap into the large skilled labor pools and compact infrastructure of the northeastern and midwestern industrial belts, where extremes in weather absolutely required that the manufacturing process move entirely indoors—a double seal on the absolute requirement that every part in every airplane of the same type, and every replacement part, be 100 percent identical and interchangeable.

At first, it seemed like a darn good idea to expand the aircraft industry directly *into* the existing automobile industry, but that caused or brought to the fore numerous problems. Auto plants were smaller and had confined work spaces compared to aircraft plants, and automobile assembly lines were built at the scale of cars and trucks, not airplanes. Also, the automobile industry was swamped with orders for military vehicles of every imaginable configuration, many to fill the needs of military aviation. Automobile manufacture need not be and was not held to the much more precise tolerances of aircraft manufacture, even though the military eventually backed off its mindless obsession for perfectly built weapons and support systems that were pretty surely going to be damaged or destroyed in combat. But it was necessary to build even ruggedized aircraft built from ruggedized components to higher standards and tolerances than cars or trucks, or even tanks, because a broken tank, truck, or car does not inevitably fall out of the sky with from one to ten humans aboard.

Exports Pay the Bills

In the eighteen months after the Aircraft Meeting, the Air Corps purchased no operational heavy bombers except B-17s, but there was pressure on the aircraft manufacturers to develop a second-generation strategic bomber with a wider operational radius and a higher payload capacity. Likewise, several new pursuit types were in development, but only two were actually in production by mid-1940. Also, there was a push for either a better medium-range bomber than the 1935-vintage Douglas B-18, or at least a larger attack airplane than the Douglas A-20. For all the talk and planning as American industry tried its darndest to gear up toward wartime production capacity, foreign orders did more to fund the expansion than did Air Corps spending.

The French and the British were more interested in twin-engine bombers than the Army Air Corps, and the French were urgently interested in packing in pursuits to supplement the output of their own aircraft industry, especially following the jaw-dropping German invasion of Poland. American manufacturers were happy to accommodate because European and other foreign air services had to pay for American-made warplanes in cold, hard cash. The Nationalist Chinese air force purchased American aircraft, chiefly the Hawk 75 export version of the Curtiss P-36 pursuit, which the French air force ordered in quantity. The French also ordered a relatively large number of the DB-7 export version of the Douglas A-20. Only around sixty of these DB-7s were operational in France by May 1940, but the RAF ultimately purchased the undelivered French DB-7s, as well as a succession of A-20 variants known to the RAF as Boston. The Lockheed Hudson, a derivative of a civil airliner, served with the RAF as a light maritime bomber from February 1939 onward. Hudson variants were considered by the Air Corps under the designations A-28, A-29, and C-67, and by the U.S. Navy as the PBO, but few of any of these types were ever ordered or deployed (even though PBOs sank the first two German U-boats credited to the U.S. Navy in World War II). The Air Corps did purchase three hundred Hudson variants as advanced navigational trainers under the designation AT-18. A total of 140 Martin Model 167 light reconnaissance bombers, derived from an entry the Air Corps rejected, were delivered to the French by May 1940, and the remainder of the French order, 75 Model 167s, was delivered to the RAF under the designation Maryland, as were follow-on orders.

New Air Corps Pursuits

The first of two new pursuit types to reach Air Corps operational units by May 1940 was the innovative Bell P-39 Airacobra, which the manufacturer designed on speculation in 1937 around a nose-mounted 37mm cannon that fired through the propeller hub. The notion was that rounds as large as 37mm could down a bomber in only a few hits. With the cannon forward of the cockpit, it was necessary to place a powerful inline engine behind the cockpit and link it to the propeller via an extension shaft. It was a tricky design, but the Air Corps took it seriously, with the result that the first American pursuit equipped with tricycle landing gear (nose wheel rather than tail wheel) was put into production in August 1939 following many modifications. In addition to the 37mm cannon (replaced by a 20mm cannon in exports to the RAF), the earliest production P-39s (P-39Bs), of which eighty were ordered, were equipped with two nose-mounted .30-caliber machine guns and two wing-mounted .30-caliber machine guns. After twenty P-39Bs had been built, the remaining sixty, redesignated P-39C, were equipped with the two .30-caliber nose guns and four wing-mounted .30-caliber guns. The next P-39 upgrades, which were based in large part on reports of French and British combat experience, would include standard self-sealing fuel tanks and more cockpit armor, even though both of these heavy upgrades actually negatively impacted performance.

In the spring of 1938, as Curtiss began its first production run of P-36s for the Air Corps, the tenth airplane was pulled from the line to have its radial engine replaced with a liquid-cooled inline engine as well as to undergo related modifications. This airplane first flew on October 14, 1938, some changes were made, and it was redesignated P-40. Following competition against other candidates, the P-40 was accepted by the Air Corps, which entered into a contract in April 1939 for 524 aircraft—the largest single order for pursuit aircraft by the U.S Army to that time. The Air Corps accepted the first of the production P-40s, each armed with a pair of cowl-mounted .50-caliber machine guns, in May 1940, following numerous design upgrades. By then, the French had ordered 140 Hawk 81 export variants, but none of these was even started by June 1940.

Summing Up

The Army Air Corps was given a huge opening by President Roosevelt at his November 1938 Aircraft Meeting. The new chief of the Air Corps, Maj. Gen. Hap Arnold, made a literal and moral beeline for that opening, taking many of the best and brightest Air Corps officers along to support the unfolding program. Industry opened its shuttered doors for business, and war-plagued France and the United Kingdom provided cash—and a test bed—for the expansion. New vistas broadened at more frequent intervals, often before recent vistas could take shape. For all that everyone involved worked unto and beyond mere exhaustion, no one knew if the Air Corps would be ready when war overtook it.

Chapter 11

The Army Prepares to Prepare

A Slow Start

As THE ARMY AIR CORPS GEARED UP in early 1939 for an intense expansion whose scope even its own leaders vastly undercalculated at the outset, nearly the whole rest of the army remained functionally moribund. Even as the Congress went along with the Roosevelt Administration in voting funds for the Air Corps, its old habit of short-changing the rest of the army proceeded along well-worn ruts.

Out of a $646 million appropriation for fiscal year 1939 for the entire Department of War, less the Air Corps, $192 million was for routine defense of the Panama Canal and the Corps of Engineers' traditional civic work of dredging and otherwise maintaining ports and river navigation; and $267 million was the aggregate for pay, clothing, and subsistence, which is to say the least an army can offer its officers and troops. For new equipment, including replacement of outmoded as well as broken equipment, $84 million was set aside; maintenance of existing arms was allocated $25 million. Maintenance of bases and other plant items was also $25 million, while new base construction or expansion of existing bases received $10 million. Seacoast defense was allocated $5 million; "miscellaneous" received $21 million. All training was funded with $12 million, and research and development was allocated $5 million.

This is hardly the fiscal signature of an army gearing up for a war in a world in which only more war seemed inevitable. Many budget categories were statutory in nature—they could not be drawn down for other purposes—so the work of reconstituting an adequate field force could be funded only by dipping into just three budget categories: training, new equipment, and research and development, which totaled $101 million, or 15.6 percent of the annual $646 million budget. This was itself a record-high aggregate for these three categories for the years following the Great War mobilization.

Perhaps the most depressing number to be taken from the fiscal 1939 budget was the miserable and absolutely inadequate $5 million allocation for research and development, just 0.8 percent of the total. East Asia was awash in war, east Africa had been the object of an Italian invasion as early as 1935, and there was virtually no question that the Germans were very close to achieving critical mass in their rearmament program, a tidal wave so powerful by 1938 that

Hitler had been able to credibly bluff Great Britain and France into throwing in the towel with respect to Czechoslovakia. But even as that was happening, the Congress puttered around with its inadequate Department of War budget, ultimately presenting it as a singular achievement from which the ground army was bound to prosper. This was because the budget was grossly inadequate at a higher rate of spending than at any time in fifteen years.

As the budget went into effect, the army had not yet done more about armor, the vaunted weapons system of the future, than a few trials undertaken by its fading cavalry arm. In the face of a widely publicized German armor force, the army had settled in 1936 on an outclassed German-designed 37mm antitank gun with no plans for an upgrade. The American service rifle of the day was a 1903 model, though a 1936 improvement was being manufactured at the trivial rate of several hundred units per year. All of the army's automatic weapons had been developed and first issued between 1917 and 1919, though they would ultimately meet the test of 1940s (and even 1950s) warfare. Modern infantry mortars remained on the drawing board in fiscal 1939, part of the to-do list funded within the $5 million research and development allocation.

At least the ground army found scant hope in the groups of bright officers gathered in the wake of the Aircraft Meeting to draw up the many and varied plans and wish lists for a vastly expanded army of, well, maybe, several years hence.

The Army Industrial College

The mobilization of American industry to support the immense growth spurt of 1916–1919 had been an unrelieved disappointment; it had been very late off the mark, muddled in its approach, lacking in a clear central vision, and unbelievably and embarrassingly slow in reaching its stride. So late and so slowly had the army-industry partnership become functional that, in the main, soldiers and airmen of the American Expeditionary Force in France were outfitted with arms, equipment, and even ammunition of British and French design *and* manufacture.

Only after the war was concluded did modern thinkers dwelling on solutions realize that the Great War was humanity's first "total" war, in the sense that the creation and dispatch of a field army into battle required the attention and unremitting backing of a nation's entire economic base, from industry to banking to science to education to farming, and so forth. The failure of the American economic base in 1916–1919 was more one of imagination and experience than of an impulse for cooperation that ran between and among all sectors of the economy.

To obviate an out-and-out disaster in the event of the rapid onset of a future war, the Department of War and the Congress got together in the National Defense Act of 1920 to centralize and oversee the procurement authority of eight competing army supply bureaus through the creation of the post of assistant secretary of war, who would be "charged with the supervision of procurement of all military supplies and other business of the War Department pertaining thereto and the assurance of adequate provision for mobilization of materiel and industrial organizations essential to wartime needs."

Most telling was that the 1920 legislation provided the assistant secretary of war with the authority to plan the nation's *entire* wartime economy, from top to bottom. But it was quite obvious that neither the office of the assistant secretary of war nor the army chief of staff, nor indeed the army as a whole, could plan a complete wartime economy, much less efficiently run it in wartime, without first knowing what the peacetime economy looked like and how it might be wielded, as a sum of all its parts, in time of war.

The actual work of getting a handle on the American economic base began in March 1921, under the new Harding Administration. Former Senator John Weeks was appointed secretary of war, John Wainwright became the first assistant secretary of war, and Wainwright appointed an army engineer, Col. Harley Ferguson, as his executive officer. It was Ferguson who established what, by October 1921, had become the nascent procurement division, the planning branch, and the current supply branch to which the lean starting personnel allotment would be assigned. The work began with the leavings of the more-or-less failed attempt to organize data for the Great War mobilization, and it advanced slowly under the crushing weight of the data and the small number of officers assigned to master and organize it. Slowly, however, the officers under Colonel Ferguson's enlightened leadership fanned out to industrial conferences and the like, where they met the men who were at the forefront of shaping and leading the booming American postwar economy. Of particular importance in shaping the work was Bernard Baruch, a strong-willed capitalist who had had an overt hand in the 1916–1919 military industrialization as well as in the creation of the Office of the Assistant Secretary of War.

Unconnected to the developments in army economic mobilization planning was a renaissance in advanced education for senior army officers. The Army War College, shut down during the Great War so its best and brightest instructors and students could take part in the hostilities, was reestablished as such in 1921. In 1923, following the navy's lead, eight senior army supply officers were sent to the Harvard Business School. The climate for the professionalization of the army's senior leaders was becoming more and more favorable.

President Harding, a strong supporter of business, passed away in San Francisco in August 1923. He was replaced by Vice President Calvin Coolidge, an even more ardent pro-business national leader.

In March 1923, Dwight Davis replaced John Wainwright as assistant secretary of war. Davis, who had served as an army colonel in France, where he was awarded a Distinguished Service Cross, the army's second-highest valor medal, was a strong supporter of military preparedness. He wanted to bolster the hard-working officers who were attempting to get a grip on American industry, but he felt he couldn't just throw warm bodies at the task. It was

Davis's conviction that select officers, regular and reserve, needed to be trained up to a standard equal to the daunting but vital task.

Davis's first step was to ask his office's planning branch to prepare a reading list for regular officers and a set of instructions on procurement planning for reserve officers. By then, on their own initiative, Colonel Ferguson and others had developed or were working on training aids of various types for a range of problems. The upshot was that the two senior officers who were given lead positions in the development of training schemes came up with a proposal to establish a school they called the Institute of Economic Preparedness. Under tried-and-true military experience, army officers assigned to staff the institute would train the students selected to attend. At around the same time, a pair of Ordnance Corps majors working and living in the San Francisco Bay Area drafted a letter to the Office of the Chief of Ordnance in which they proposed the establishment of *two* new schools: one to provide professional training within the Ordnance Corps and the other within the Office of the Assistant Secretary of War to train officers from the whole rest of the army so the army itself would be able to direct and oversee a future industrial mobilization without being subsumed by a wartime agency of civilians lacking real knowledge of the army's needs or the army's systems.

The memorandum outlining the two schools reached the chief of ordnance in due course. In July 1923, Maj. James Burns, one of the letter's authors, was ordered to Washington from San Francisco to work for Colonel Ferguson and Assistant Secretary Davis. Within a month Burns petitioned the chief of ordnance to establish the school for senior ordnance officers. This was done under the chief of ordnance's own authority in mid-September 1923, under the name Ordnance Staff College.

In the meantime, Colonel Ferguson and Major Burns worked at getting Assistant Secretary Davis to approve their in-house school, but Davis wasn't ready to act. As this process played out, Secretary of War Weeks visited with Ferguson and Burns, who showed off their training materials. They also noted that only six of their fellow officers could be considered well versed in the task of getting a grip on and preparing for industrial mobilization, but their estimates indicated that they needed to fully train—each year!—about forty regular and a whopping four hundred reserve officers. Ferguson boldly suggested that he wanted to open the necessary school, and Weeks immediately, on the spot, said he supported the idea.

Things were moving quickly. At around the same time Colonel Ferguson was trying to land Secretary Weeks, the chief of ordnance had a private conversation with Assistant Secretary Davis that finally motivated Davis to press for an army-wide school dedicated to training select officers to take charge of industrial mobilization in their own corps and branches. In mid-October 1923, Davis formally petitioned Secretary Weeks to open such a school, and in January 1924 Colonel Ferguson traveled to Fort Leavenworth, Kansas, to deliver a lecture at which he announced his staff plan to recruit to the Office of the Assistant Secretary of War knowledgeable officers who would oversee industrial mobilization planning.

Climaxing all the effort and intellectual energy expenditure, the Army Industrial College, into which the months-old Ordnance Staff College was fully subsumed, was formally established at the Munitions Building in Washington, D.C., on February 25, 1924, with Col. Harley Ferguson as its first director. The stated mission of the new professional school was "the training of army officers in useful knowledge pertaining to the supervision of procurement of all military supplies in time of war and to the assurance of adequate provision for the mobilization of materiel and industrial organization of essential wartime needs." At a practical level, the Army Industrial College's main purposes were to train future leaders to appreciate the benefits and limitations of industry, to maximize the benefits and overcome the limitations, *and* to catalog the possible uses to which virtually every factory and industrial business in the United States might be put into support of the army's procurement needs.

In establishing its brilliantly conceived industrial college, the U.S. Army took the last big leap into the world of modern armies, for in 1914 it had been hardly more than a frontier constabulary with little to keep it occupied. Now it had a finger on the pulse of the mightiest industrial behemoth the world had ever seen, and the other hand was on a throttle that had the power behind it to send itself and that behemoth racing into the pages of world history. (Major James Burns himself graduated from the school he helped found in 1926. Much later, as a colonel, he attended the pivotal Aircraft Meeting, and much more.)

By the 1929–1930 academic year, the Army Industrial College's brief had expanded to incorporate "the study of the broad aspects of governmental control of national resources." This is as sweeping an assignment as one can imagine in the event of an *economic* mobilization, for, far beyond controlling industrial output, it contemplates control of the allocation of raw materials dug out of the earth and of the human capital that undergirds all business. The incumbent director of the college referred to the place as "an institution of research," a mission embodied in uncountable index cards containing data on every aspect of the American economy. Moreover, under its expanded brief, the college was to investigate "the efficacy of present solutions and plans initially formatted by the [Office of the Assistant Secretary of War's] Planning Branch" and the supply branches of the army and its components. What this, along with later expansions of its role, meant was that the Army Industrial College and its practical output—trained officers and immense stores of data—were contemplated as being perhaps the most essential factor in a future wartime economy. And that is a singular mission in the history of armies and of nations.

The first class of nine officers graduated in June 1924. One of the members of this class, its only airman, was Maj. Henry "Hap" Arnold. It is impossible to overstate the benefits the nation gained from that one classroom experience. Scores of others—including growing proportions of naval officers and marines—followed Arnold and his classmates through the Army

Industrial College, in times of bounty and in times of ruin. The legacy was a solid core of officers, including some who would rise to very high rank, who had taught or learned the expanding lessons of military industrialization and economic mobilization as well as which businesses could do what to speed the necessary processes to meaningful ends. The immense gaps rendered by the Great Depression were disheartening, but college staff stoically maintained and updated the massive card catalogs as class after class amassed and assessed newly sought data. So, too, the Army Industrial College staff and students worked ceaselessly through the many political ups and downs of the era, during which the military was generally vilified by large segments of the public and ignored or shortchanged as shifting weather fronts of hot air billowed through the Congress.

Dubbed "merchants of death" for large tracts of the interwar period, the industries that catered most or most frequently to the needs of the military services had a hard sell before the Congress, which tended to overreact in the face of public outcry. Wartime profiteering had indeed been rife during the 1916–1919 rearmament period, and to ensure that it was curbed, the Congress considered more than two hundred remedial bills, some of them quite silly with respect to how effectively they removed all semblance of profit from transactions with the military. Bernard Baruch, who was not without insight or experience in this realm, in 1931 published "Taking the Profits Out of War," which set forth reasonable safeguards to quash profiteering in the event of a future emergency economic mobilization. The army chief of staff, Gen. Douglas MacArthur, that very year quieted public concern when he pointed out that the army had knowledge of these matters and would not allow them to get out of hand. What we have here, then, is the creation of an ethos among trained military officers rising to positions of influence and prominence to use their training as much in behalf of the public good as in behalf of the legitimate interests of the military to guide and take from the economic base what it needed to mobilize for a war, and win it.

In but one example of what military spending could do to legitimately maintain the economic base it needed—for how could the services order what they urgently required from factories that had been boarded up?—a 1934 board headed by former Secretary of War Newton Baker noted that the commercial airline industry could not generate the orders for new airplanes the airplane manufacturers and their numerous suppliers needed to stay in business. As a result of the Baker Board's recommendations, the Congress budgeted more money for army and naval aviation, and both services began to push into the modern aviation era by incorporating all the modern advances into their specifications. In only two years, two-thirds of the aircraft produced by the domestic airplane industry were for the military. A similar modest naval building program kept private shipyards in business. Likewise, beginning in fiscal year 1939, on a scale that was much smaller than the aircraft program, other industries not usually associated with military spending—a washing-machine manufacturer that could switch over to the manufacture of power turrets for bombers is but one example—benefited from small "educational" orders for all manner of military hardware. The army was allotted a measly $2 million, to be plundered from elsewhere in its small budget, for this seed program, but at least it was allowed to proceed. With an educational order in hand, the washing-machine manufacturer could safely invest in whatever tools and supplies it needed to build power turrets, including training its workers, and it would thus have the experience and the means to do so directly in hand as the economy switched over to responding mainly to urgent military needs. And via the educational orders, to the small extent a tight-fisted Congress allowed them, the military purchasing community and select contractors and suppliers had an opportunity to develop long-term relationships with the army that could only have benefited both when the crunch finally enveloped them. Even better, students and staff at the slowly expanding Army Industrial College gained live, hands-on experience to complement the theoretical phases of the curriculum.

Under the Roosevelt Administration, Secretary of War Harry Woodring and Army Chief of Staff Malin Craig in 1935 and 1936 collaborated to support the first actual war plan based on the Army Industrial College's data on America's real industrial potential. Dubbed the Protective Industrial Mobilization Plan, the document was first drafted in 1936 and ultimately revised in 1939. This emphasis on modulating expressed war needs to economic and industrial capacity was entirely new in its expression, but it was the very measuring tool the Army Industrial College had been working toward since its inception. Mirroring that approach was the ability of the plan to suggest areas where economic or industrial power could be tweaked, reallocated, or even massively redirected, to meet the nation's wartime needs.

In his 1938 annual report to the assistant secretary of war, the director of the college took pains to note, "It is clear as a result of recent national experience in economic adjustments and readjustments that industrial activity must be thoroughly understood to accomplish national aims in peacetime." That word, *peacetime*, is an interesting word to use at the end of a report written in 1938, at the last possible juncture before *all* rational military thought in the United States turned to war.

In addition to providing trained staff for the Office of the Assistant Secretary of War, and its important research and outreach to industry via the Army and Navy Munitions Board, the Army Industrial College was used as a resource by various agencies that developed plans and resources for the military. One of these was the Joint Army and Navy Board, which had a hand in developing and selling the oft-revised Protective Industrial Mobilization Plan from when it was drafted in 1936 until it was rejected, as such, by President Roosevelt in 1939 because, according to some presidential advisers, it too closely resembled the Great War's approach to industrial mobilization. Nevertheless, the work the Joint Army and Navy Board did and to which the Army Industrial College contributed was recycled into the far-reaching economic mobilization plans that were adopted when, in August 1939, the president created the War Resources Board under the chairmanship of Edward Stettinius and appointed an Army Industrial College graduate and former faculty member as the board's secretary.

The success of the college can be amply illustrated in one statistic: Of twenty-seven officers working at the Office of the Assistant Secretary of War's vital Planning Branch in 1939, twenty-three were Army Industrial College graduates. One of them, an early graduate who served a tour on the college faculty, eventually directed the Planning Branch. In all, following the graduation of the 1940 class, the Army Industrial College had trained 804 army, navy, and marine officers, including Hap Arnold, Dwight Eisenhower, and J. Lawton Collins. Indeed, it was Eisenhower who, at a later date—after he had studied and taught at the college and served in the Planning Branch—succinctly summed up the college's visionary mandate: "No matter how much we spend on arms, there's no safety in arms alone. Our security is the total product of our economic, intellectual, moral, and military strengths."

As events heated up in Europe in 1938 and 1939, leading to war between Germany and Poland on September 1, 1939, the sense of urgency pervading the college and the Office of the Assistant Secretary of War ramped up. The Army Industrial College class of 1940, which started work in mid-September 1939, was especially focused on how all the planning and research might be put to use within a very short time. Indeed, in response to cataclysmic events in Europe in May and June 1940, the class of 1940 would be sent into the real world of economic mobilization before the official end of the school year.

As multiple crises deepened in both Europe and Asia, the Army Industrial College, in April 1940, stood up the Economic Warfare Information Center, which was to monitor and evaluate the economies of the potential near-term enemies of the United States. When the Roosevelt Administration established the Export Control Agency later in the year under command of an early Army Industrial College graduate, the Economic Warfare Information Center was transferred to it to carry out its vital work.

It is something of a miracle that an institution as important and influential as the Army Industrial College turned out to be was ever even set up. It is a testament to the handful of visionary officers and civilian leaders who were there at the inception that it was the only military institution of its type, in the world, when it accomplished its most important business. When the time came for the U.S. military to mesh gears with U.S. industry and the U.S. economy as a whole, America was ready. And that moment was pivotal in the long slog to clear the dark clouds of fascism from the world's skies.

Development Woes

It's all very well to be on top of a list of new weapons and to understand how and where to make them, but being on top of these things serves no purpose if the process for ordering and paying for the weapons imposes challenges that prevent new weapons from being developed and orders from going out. In the case of the U.S. Army in the long run-up to World War II, the budgeting process alone accounted for two full years of the development cycle that carried new weapons and all other gear and equipment from concept to the hands of the troops who would use them. After Marshall became chief of staff and congressional constraints on spending began to loosen up, the army's own internal processes remained as damnably slow as ever. Marshall thus ordered a staff study to determine the average time required to get a new weapon through the entire process, from concept to research to development to tooling to prototyping to testing to further development, and so forth unto placing the weapon in the hands of front-line troops, who would rapidly figure out on their own how to abuse and break them. The answer that came back was an incredible six years. It took less time for the navy to design and build a new type of battleship. So, on top of the myriad claims on his time, Marshall took a personal interest in shortening the process to the point where a new weapon requested by troops at the front could be delivered to troops at the front in something like near-real time. It was a daunting process that took on entrenched army bureaucracies and the Congress, but as the war in Europe heated up and Japan loomed larger as a near-term menace, the magnificent force of Marshall's desire to build an army second to none slowly tore down all barriers that could be torn down, and then went to work on all the remaining barriers. It took every bit as much time, and then some, as the United States had between the Aircraft Meeting and Pearl Harbor to put a dent in the system—and it would take a year or so of global war to build an efficient and, above all, responsive system that included and foreshortened all the necessary feedback loops—but the counterattack on the development and acquisition dead space that Marshall and a cast of trusted subordinates started made the then-looming world war much easier to win.

There were other bottlenecks within the army planning cycles that would be uncovered and addressed as they were encountered, and requirements that the army and navy work together on some projects forced one service to wait while the other sorted out its internal processes. But after the Aircraft Meeting, and especially after Germany invaded Poland and made real everyone's worst fears, there was a new *will* to get things done, to race to the heart of the matter, and to resolve issues that would never have been resolved by entrenched bureaucracies not faced with the impetus of an onrushing war no one believed would spare the United States.

It took the American military services much time to shake off old habits and overcome or reshape many draconian statutes and policies that limited all the horizons, but the will to do so tore down the barriers at an accelerating rate. If anything, there arose too many good and urgent ideas and requirements, but all that could be overcome were ultimately overcome by a universal willingness by all the stakeholders to cooperate on solutions. Those who clung to the old ways, those who interfered or defended turf at the expense of progress, fell or were pushed to the wayside. The services became filled with boundless optimists feeding on good will and suffused with a sense of purpose born of the challenge of saving America and, in due course, rescuing the world.

Army Manpower Expansion

Real planning for the army's expansion to its World War II end strength actually began on April 17, 1939, when General Craig directed his War Plans Division to comment on the steps the army would need to take in the event the United States was drawn into the looming war in Europe. Based on the resulting war-plans study, Craig directed G-1 to make a plan to convert the Civilian Conservation Corps into a "semimilitary" organization; G-3 to plan an accelerated training program for National Guard and Organized Reserve officers; G-4 to plan for the accelerated delivery of supplies and materiel; and War Plans to create on paper an expeditionary force that could be deployed to protect hemispheric interests or even wrest control of a Latin American nation that might fall under fascist domination. These plans, delivered in a matter of weeks, presented daunting challenges to an army that was in no way up to executing any of them. Nevertheless, they served as a beacon that pointed the army down the road to recovery.

In the meantime, the army's budget for enlisted pay was lifted from a limit sufficient for 165,000 men to 180,000 men—but only after some fiscal sleight of hand. Additional appropriations for pay allowed the army to set as its next plateau an authorized enlisted strength of 210,000 men, which led that summer to a recruiting campaign for Air Corps enlisted men and the augmentation of the Panama Canal Zone garrison.

The next statutory army troop increase came as something of a shock to General Marshall when it was enacted in September 1939, shortly after his ascension to the post of chief of staff. It had been his understanding that the Roosevelt Administration favored the army's plan to expand to the full 280,000 spaces enumerated in the Protective Mobilization Plan outlined in the National Defense Act of 1920. This was the least tenable number lying at the root of the army's plan to shift to a wartime footing. But the civilian leadership was not quite ready to challenge the Congress, even though the new and ruthless German lightning war in Poland had an unsettling effect upon many if not most members of Congress, not to mention the American public. The entire new authorization was for just 17,000 new spaces, up to a total of 227,000 active spaces—plus 35,000 new National Guard spaces, bringing the Guard's total to 235,000 (or 215,000 fewer troops than envisioned in the National Defense Act of 1920).

Marshall's use of the seventeen thousand new Regular Army spaces is instructive of his will and adroitness. Nearly all of the spaces were allotted to the infantry. Under General Craig, the infantry branch had adopted the triangular organization that had come to the fore of thinking during Marshall's inestimably fruitful tour at The Infantry School. The old square division of two brigades, each composed of two large infantry regiments, required far more soldiers than a triangular infantry division, which was deemed the epitome of flexibility and efficiency for a mid-twentieth-century battlefield. Going back to the long-held plan to field one Regular Army infantry division for each of the army's nine regional corps headquarters, Marshall was able to more substantially fill in the troop levels of five triangular infantry divisions to a moderately suitable operational state, which was up from just three half-strength square divisions considered moderately suitable for combat operations. Troop spaces left over after most of the seventeen thousand new troops were allotted to the five triangular infantry divisions allowed Marshall's personnel planners to build up or create shells for the engineer units, medical units, quartermaster trains, and even heavy artillery units that were typically assigned directly to a corps headquarters for discretionary battlefield use by the corps commander. There were even troops left over to form or expand the service units assigned directly to a field army headquarters. Skeletal though some of these units were, they literally framed out the higher echelons of an army in the field and led very soon to the U.S. Army's ability to conduct its first real corps- and army-level maneuvers in modern history.

As to the National Guard, which gained only thirty-five thousand new troop billets in September 1939, its training obligation was raised from forty-eight armory drills per year to sixty, and training days in the field went up from fifteen to twenty-one. At the same time, 1,306 reserve officers were called to active duty for a one-year term to serve in the field forces, and 283 reserve officers and 591 National Guard officers were called to active duty for a year to attend professional schools and courses.

And then matters glided along for more than six months without much progress or change. The fact that the German armed forces went idle after the conquest of Poland caused public and congressional sentiment toward building up to a robust national defense to dissipate, and the public discourse once again became dominated by the old isolationist cant.

Chapter 12

The War Before the War

Assertive Neutrality

O N THE DAY THE NEW WAR BEGAN in Europe, September 1, 1939, the brand-new chief of naval operations, Admiral Harold Stark, declared that German submarines were already in position to interdict shipping lanes tying North America and South America to Europe, and that they would soon be joined by several surface warships and a dozen armed merchant ships serving as auxiliary cruisers, which is to say commerce raiders. Stark also noted that the Royal Navy was preparing to stop neutral ships on the high seas and seize cargoes bound for nations hostile to the United Kingdom. The navy chief finally asserted that it was the duty of the United States and other neutral nations to make sure that no such interdictions, searches, or seizures take place in neutral waters.

The official position of the United States at the moment the war began in Poland was set forth in the Neutrality Act of 1935 and a 1937 amendment to it. These laws forbade direct or even indirect arms exports to any warring nation.

On September 4, Admiral Stark dispatched orders to the commander of the U.S. Navy's Atlantic Squadron to establish air and sea patrols well out to sea and to observe and report—in code—the passage of warships of any of the belligerent European states. An amendment the next day required naval vessels to provide detailed information as to identity, nationality, tonnage, markings, course, and speed of such vessels.

On September 5, President Roosevelt proclaimed that the United States was a neutral nation and that U.S. territorial waters were closed to hostile operations, which would be regarded as violations of her neutrality. The commander of the Atlantic Squadron reported back to Admiral Stark on September 6 that air and surface units under his command were on patrol in the neutral zone as it was defined at the time.

The stakes went up on September 8 and September 11 when, respectively, the French and British announced a long-range blockade of Germany and the Germans announced a counterblockade of France and Great Britain. This placed both sides on record as participants in a global *guerre de course* that could easily spill over into U.S. territorial waters unless forcibly dealt with. The Roosevelt Administration favored Britain and France over Germany, but it was in no way going to allow the United States to be pushed around by the Royal Navy.

The assertiveness implicit in the rapid configuration and implementation of the American neutrality regime, formally named the Neutrality Patrol, was significantly bolstered over the course of mere days and weeks after the German invasion of Poland. In addition to proclaiming a limited national emergency on September 8, President Roosevelt that day asked the Congress to raise the caps on military enlisted end strength from 110,325 sailors to 145,000, and from 18,325 marines to 25,000. As well, he asked the Congress to authorize the recall of select retired naval and marine officers, enlisted men, and navy nurses.

By September 20, air and surface components of the Atlantic Squadron were working tirelessly to cover pretty much all of a vast area reaching as far north as Nova Scotia and as far south as the Lesser Antilles. This area was the core of a much larger patrol area that eventually became known as the Pan-American Safety Zone. Most of the actual searches were conducted by fifty-four twin-engine seaplanes organized into five patrol squadrons overseen by two patrol-wing headquarters and supported by four seaplane tenders. Further, light, single-engine observation and scout floatplanes from the Atlantic Squadron's four battleships and four cruisers, as well as from one shore-based observation squadron and one cruiser scoutplane squadron were assigned to the effort, as were the aircraft carrier *Ranger,* her air group, and the new air group preparing to operate from the new fleet carrier *Wasp* once she was commissioned. To date, this was the largest operation of any kind ever mounted by U.S. naval aviation.

Surface forces dedicated to the inaugural period consisted of forty destroyers deployed in eight regional groupments. Fifteen oldish submarines were also assigned. An order was also promulgated on September 13 to build up the surface force by rehabilitating, upgrading, and recommissioning forty older destroyers and numerous minelayers that had been mothballed over the previous two decades. The first of these ships rejoined the fleet in early October and trained their crews even as they undertook operational assignments with the Neutrality Patrol. Larger warships assigned to the Atlantic Squadron would undertake patrolling and response to hostile action as and when they were needed and available.

The U.S. Navy was in no way prepared for so huge an undertaking as covering so vast an area. The neat billets of peacetime air patrol squadrons were partially abandoned as sub-units spread to the winds between Rhode Island and the Panama Canal Zone, coming down in several sleepy, backwater coastal stations, one run by the U.S. Coast Guard, with only the crudest of amenities to offer. But the airmen assigned to these underdeveloped backwaters were made content enough by the fact that they had a real mission to perform after years and decades of mere practice, practice, practice. In due course, as experience mounted, base assignments were rejiggered for efficiency in reaching and fully covering patrol sectors, and living conditions were set right.

In the main, within the Pan-American Neutrality Zone, foreign warships and commercial vessels (which came under scrutiny after October 16, 1939) were located by scheduled air patrols, and all available information was passed up the chain of command for analysis and disposition. (After October 20, such sighting reports were made in plain-language broadcasts.) If a particular ship required closer or more protracted scrutiny than an airplane could provide, the closest available surface ship, typically a destroyer, was dispatched to check the target visually at close range, and perhaps even to track it for some time or distance.

On September 21, the president asked the Congress to repeal the arms-embargo provisions of the 1937 Neutrality Act.

While German commerce raiders and surface warships presented a nettlesome and at times dangerous throttle on ocean trade, the main enemies Allied and even neutral merchant ships plying Atlantic routes faced were German submarines, known as U-boats (where *U* stands for *Untersee*). On September 1, 1939, the German fleet had fifty-seven U-boats in commission, of which thirty were tiny, short-range models of 250 tons displacement and the balance were larger, better-armed, long-range models of 500 and 750 tons. The puniness of the German U-boat fleet amply demonstrates Germany's—which is to say Adolph Hitler's—mindset as to Germany's role, first and foremost, as a continental power. The submarine fleet commander of the period, Kommodore Karl Doenitz, reported at war's end that Hitler's early, negligent attitude toward his Kriegsmarine (navy) in general and his U-boat fleet in particular made the war impossible to win over the long haul. For all that, the nation that chose the time and place for war, had only a fraction of a fraction of the fighting ships its adversaries had, and could build only two to four modern submarines a month at the outset was nonetheless going to wreak havoc on a worldwide sea transit system that was totally unprepared for a war that plainly had been brewing for at least three years.

The Atlantic maritime scorecard for the first month of World War II was twenty Allied and neutral merchant ships, aggregating 110,000 tons, and one British fleet carrier sunk against two U-boats sunk. During that first month, the Kriegsmarine, with Hitler's assent, went ahead full throttle to up the construction of new long-range submarines from a high of four per month to twenty to twenty-five per month, for starters. The goals were thus three hundred new submarines commissioned by the end of 1941 and another six hundred commissioned by the end of 1943.

The legitimacy of the United States' Neutrality Patrol was immeasurably bolstered on October 2, 1939, when the Conference of Foreign Ministers of American Republics, meeting in Panama City, agreed to the Act of Panama. This hemisphere-wide agreement established a uniform neutrality zone from all sovereign shores to a distance of three hundred miles.

Also on October 2, Germany announced that U.S.-flag merchant vessels were obligated to submit to visits and searches by German authorities, including naval vessels, on the high seas. This announcement was backed up in fact on October 9, when the freighter *City of Flint* was declared a contraband carrier and seized by the German pocket battleship *Deutschland* in the sea lanes between New York and the United Kingdom.

In October 1939, the *Ranger,* her air group, and the observation planes assigned to one Atlantic Squadron cruiser division were teamed up to create an aviation strike force with an enhanced search capability.

The first more-or-less partisan act to arise from the neutrality patrols came on October 16, 1939, when the *Ranger* and the heavy cruiser *San Francisco* were dispatched to locate a tanker that had departed Tampico, Mexico, to service the German pocket battleship *Admiral Graf Spee.* The German warship was quite effectively raiding commercial lanes in the South Atlantic and was thus the object of a vigorous search by the Royal Navy. By tracking the tanker and reporting its progress in clear language, the Americans were acting in aid of the British search for the *Graf Spee.* Nothing came of this foray, but it was the inaugural action in a long line of *nearly* hostile acts against Germany that benefited the Royal Navy through late 1941. (The *Graf Spee* was ultimately damaged in a naval battle on December 13, 1939, then scuttled off Montevideo, Uruguay, on December 17.)

A small number of U.S. Navy destroyers was deployed during October 1939 to patrol the Gulf of Mexico, and that month a large part of the Coast Guard's strength on the East and Gulf coasts, including aviation assets, began to devote a large part of its time to neutrality compliance in inshore areas. Among other benefits, the navy and Coast Guard learned how to seamlessly operate together under warlike conditions, and they could thus discover any operational or equipment mismatches and alleviate them in due course. Indeed, even the early and quite tame Neutrality Patrol work prepared a significant portion of the sea services for war through the experience of a wartime operational tempo backed by vigorous training and even more vigorous candid assessment of and adjustment to the realities that came clear from something approaching real combat experience.

During October 1939, German U-boats and commerce raiders sank twenty-two Allied and neutral merchantmen aggregating 133,000 tons, and the Royal Navy sank two U-boats off Ireland.

The U.S. Congress passed the Neutrality Act of 1939 on November 4. This law repealed the arms embargo of the 1937 act, replacing it with a "cash-and-carry" clause that allowed military sales to be completed as long as they were paid for on the spot. The statute also prohibited U.S.-flag vessels and U.S. citizens from entering combat zones, and it established the National Munitions Control Board under the secretaries of state, treasury, war, navy, and commerce. As the name implies, this board controlled the sale of U.S.-manufactured munitions to foreign governments. Immediately upon passage, the president declared the area around the British Isles to be a combat zone.

During November 1939, German warships accounted for the sinking of six Allied and neutral merchant ships aggregating 18,000 tons, and the Royal Navy sank one U-boat north of Scotland. That same month, U-boats and aircraft began to deploy magnetic mines around the British Isles. In November 1939, mines sank twenty-seven merchant vessels aggregating 121,000 tons, plus two British destroyers sunk and a cruiser seriously damaged. This potentially disastrous threat was somewhat abated after the British recovered an intact mine, from the study of which they developed degaussing and other countermeasures. Of course, mines cannot take note of a vessel's registry, so American and other neutral merchant ships calling on British ports had to undertake mine countermeasures or face grave risks.

Beginning December 14, 1939, the Neutrality Patrol took part in the destruction of a German ship and the internment of another. That day, the thirty-two-thousand-ton passenger liner *Columbus*, rated as the third-largest ship in the German merchant fleet and thirteenth largest in the world commercial fleet, departed Vera Cruz, Mexico, for an Atlantic crossing to Germany. At around the same time, the German freighter *Arauca* also sailed from Vera Cruz. The two ships were trailed separately by a pair of U.S. Navy destroyers, then by a succession of U.S. Navy surface ships operating in relays. Per established policy, all reports concerning the German ships were passed along in plain language. Guided by the American reports, a British destroyer located the *Columbus* 450 miles east of Cape May, New Jersey, which prompted the liner's captain to scuttle his ship to prevent capture. (The action took place within view of the American heavy cruiser *Tuscaloosa*, which rescued the *Columbus'* crew.) That same day, a British light cruiser followed American voice traffic to the *Arauca* off Miami, Florida. This ship ran into Port Everglades to avoid capture, but she was interned by the United States and turned over to the navy, eventually to be converted to a refrigerated storeship. Lost in the Atlantic in December 1939 were seven Allied and neutral merchantmen aggregating 38,000 tons, the *Graf Spee*, and a U-boat sunk by a Royal Navy submarine in the North Sea.

Help provided to the Royal Navy was not always graciously reciprocated. On December 27, the United States was forced to lodge a formal protest with the British government over the seizure of U.S. mail from ships that were stopped and searched while en route to Europe. On January 20, 1940, the United States was forced to make another formal protest to the British, this time because of delays experienced by U.S.-flag commercial ships at Gibraltar. Three days later, the British and French undermined the authority of the helpful Americans when they announced their intention to attack any German ships their navies located within the Pan-American Safety Zone.

A new dimension of antisubmarine warfare reached fruition on January 30, when an RAF patrol bomber sank a U-boat off the southwest coast of Britain. This submarine, which had been commissioned little more than two months earlier, was the first of 290 U-boat kills by Allied airmen in World War II. Other ships lost in January 1940 amounted to nine Allied and neutral merchantmen aggregating 36,000 tons.

Perhaps because it was winter, or very likely because of an increasingly effective British program to halt submarine infiltration of the Atlantic from Germany's Baltic Sea ports, the battle for the Atlantic waxed and waned through the first quarter of 1940 within moderate limits. Seventeen Allied and neutral merchant vessels aggregating seventy-five thousand tons were sent to the bottom in February, but only two ships aggregating eleven thousand tons were lost in March. German losses in February were two U-boats, and one U-boat was lost in March. The sudden downturn in shipping losses, however, was in no way determined by countermeasures. Rather, the Atlantic U-boat fleet was being recalled to take part in the long-anticipated German offensive in the West.

Part III

THE MOMENT OF TRUTH

April 8, 1940
—
January 31, 1941

Chapter 13

Hitler Moves West

Norway

ALTHOUGH THE ALLIES, chiefly France and Great Britain, went on a war footing as soon as they declared war against Germany right after the September 1, 1939, invasion of Poland, nothing much happened in western Europe. What little warfare there was took place in the air at a desultory rate or at sea at an alarming but not yet crippling rate. Neither side was ready to take on the other: The entire Wehrmacht (German armed forces, collectively) was tied up in Poland, and the Allies needed time to mobilize and modernize. When Poland was defeated—a foregone conclusion that none-theless left the world gasping over Germany's new blitzkrieg (lightning war) combined-arms doctrine—the bulk of the German land armies withdrew into their national heartland to reequip and modernize. Millions of reservists were sent back to the factories to build new and better equipment, and then reabsorbed into the reequipped Wehrmacht to take part in the next phase of Hitler's wars of aggression.

The Allies were not prepared in even one way when Hitler's war machine next went into action. The victim this time was Norway, which Germany coveted mainly as an antidote to a repeat of the all-but-total naval blockade of the Baltic Sea during the Great War; Norwegian ports along the very long Atlantic coast could not be bottled up as readily as German ports on the wrong side of the narrow passages from the Baltic to the Atlantic. The German occupation of Norway would also seal the outer flank of Sweden, which Hitler would allow to remain neutral as long as the Swedes docilely provided Germany with unlimited raw materials and finished products to use in the war.

The main port for Swedish iron ore mined at Kiruna, in far northern Sweden, was Norway's Narvik. The war in the west started there on April 8, 1940, when German surface warships sweeping ahead of an invasion convoy ran into Royal Navy warships as the British prepared to mine Narvik Harbor. Although the British were unable to assess German intentions because of bad weather, it was obvious that nothing good lay behind the German naval foray into far-northern waters. Nevertheless, the Norwegian government clung stolidly to its neutrality and utterly failed to prepare for defense of the nation.

Early on April 9, German warships landed light, lightly equipped German army forces at Oslo, Bergen, Trondheim, Narvik, and Kristiansand, and German paratroopers seized Stavanger and the airfield at Sola—the first airborne assaults in history. Also on April 9, German ground forces with heavy armored units in the vanguard and airborne units committed well to the north invaded neutral Denmark, which was swiftly overrun. As soon as Denmark fell, the Germans turned it into an advance base supporting the Norwegian campaign.

Once their homeland was invaded, the Norwegians fought tenaciously, but the outcome was foreordained. The last Norwegian troops in southern Norway were overcome by April 16 and, by that date, Royal Navy warships operating out of southern Norwegian ports were forced to pull north beyond Trondheim.

Thanks to the infusion of British ground forces, the German schedule went temporarily awry in the north. Narvik was recaptured, but it fell permanently in early June, when the bulk of the British force and some Norwegian fighters were evacuated, thus ending the campaign. In the end, the Germans gained supply routes for iron ore from far-northern Sweden as well as air and submarine bases from which they could wage a much more vigorous and widespread *guerre de course* across the North Atlantic.

The Netherlands, Belgium, and France

For all that they finally located their moral backbone when Hitler invaded Poland on September 1, 1939, the British and French governments—not to mention the Belgians or the neutral but highly vulnerable Danes and Dutch—did very little during nine months of virtual peace to prepare to defend western Europe, much less take the war to a German nation fully engaged in the east and thus reasonably vulnerable to invasion from across its western borders. Indeed, the Allies did nothing to even harry or attrit the German ground forces in adjacent sectors. During the nine-month respite, Britain and France, both great nations capable of recruiting huge armies, mobilized at a rate that did nothing to cause Hitler to alter his view that they would be easy pickings when their turn came. And neither Allied government did much to awaken its industries for wartime service, nor harmonize the potential of their modern industrial bases with the needs of their slowly burgeoning armies, navies, and air forces. They spent like sailors to procure aircraft from the United States, and they built what their own industries could produce without raising an unseemly sweat, but they never fundamentally prepared to fight the Germans in the type of face-off that might stand up to the blitzkrieg warfare that Germans had amply and quite openly demonstrated in Poland.

The German generals were against a drive into western Europe. What they saw was an Allied defensive force roughly equal in strength—ground troops, aircraft, even tanks—to the most complete invasion force they could muster. They cautioned Hitler to simply defend Germany's western frontier against an Allied invasion.

Hitler saw things a little bit differently. To him, the Netherlands and Belgium were pivotal to an effective defense of the Reich, especially because German occupation of the Dutch ports would overstretch or even break the Allied naval blockade simply by being there. Further, Hitler felt that the Allies were themselves planning to occupy Belgium and the Netherlands as a means to outflank most of northern Germany and to preemptively deny Germany the Dutch ports. (In late March, Britain and France had decided to preemptively disrupt the transport of Swedish iron ore by mining Narvik and other Norwegian ports; there was nothing to say they wouldn't mine Dutch ports as well.)

At some point, the inexorable calculus of war took hold. If Germany was to break the uneasy peace in the west by preemptively invading the Netherlands and Belgium, the slowly burgeoning Allied armies in France would surely strike back, either by driving north to directly counter the German moves, or driving east, straight into German homeland defenses that would have to be thinned out to provide forces to invade Belgium and the Netherlands. So, why not go the whole route and keep moving south from Belgium into France? Doing so would bypass the static forts comprising the French Maginot Line, in which a huge proportion of the French army was voluntarily immobilized, with no real means to come out to take part in defending northern France. Bypassing so large a portion of the French army thusly would turn the long-running stalemate endured by equal forces into a romp by a locally superior and highly mobile German invasion force.

A little after midnight on May 9–10, 1940, the Luftwaffe opened the war in the west with devastating strikes against the principal Allied airfields. At dawn, the German land forces took off into the largely unprepared Dutch nation behind a screen of disabling airborne assaults. The Netherlands caved in in only five days to a German force composed of nine infantry divisions, small airborne units, and just one armored division. The invasion was amply covered by German tactical air units at and behind the front and a terror-bombing campaign against civilian targets. The only help the Allies provided the Dutch was the brief commitment of a French field army that retreated in short order to avoid being cut off.

Once again making brilliant use of airborne vanguards to seize key points and sow confusion and demoralization, a German field army composed of twenty-one infantry divisions and two panzer divisions swept into eastern Belgium. After only a day's fighting, the Belgian army abandoned the eastern third of the country to establish a defensive line behind the Dyle River. The British and French filled in behind the Dyle with thirty-five of their best divisions, but the main German attack went in well to the south, in the Ardennes Forest, where two rather weak French field armies were surprised and swiftly overrun. With that, the Allied armies withdrew behind the Escaut River, two-thirds of the way across Belgium from the German frontier. This tragic farce followed nine months of preparation time unhindered by anything except utter lack of imagination.

Following a month of battle in which German forces beat the Allies to a pulp without any help, Italy saw an easy land grab in its future and thus declared war on France (and Britain) on June 10, and then immediately launched an incompetent ground campaign along its border with France.

The huge French army died in the field, and the bulk of surviving British units escaped without their equipment in the brave but depressing rescue at Dunkirk. On June 17, a thoroughly beaten France asked Germany for terms, and war between the nations ended on June 22. The French were allowed to retain control of a rump state in the south with its seat at Vichy, hence the name Vichy France. German forces had opened their blitzkrieg in the west only a month and a week earlier.

Chapter 14

"All You Have To Do Is Ask."

Beyond Shock

THERE IS NO SINGLE WORD in *any* language to describe the level and quality of shock felt throughout the American political and military communities as Hitler's legions gobbled up the great French nation in less than six weeks. Poland had faced the German onslaught with a huge army but also a backward army that had fielded the world's bravest (and most delusional) mounted cavalry as its best antidote to tanks. The small Dutch army had served a nation everyone had thought was going to be protected by its long standing as a neutral. The Belgian army alone was never going to be a match against the Germans, but even French and British reinforcements on a massive scale had done nothing to stem the tide in Belgium. That was troubling but not exactly shocking or even surprising.

But France? How had the vast, modern army of a modern industrial nation succumbed so quickly, so completely, so irrevocably? French tanks were bigger, stronger, and better armed than German tanks. There had been as many of them as the lighter tanks the Germans fielded. But they had been tied to French infantry formations, deployed in penny packets along the meandering front rather than held in large, operationally meaningful formations deployed to react to a German propensity to push their armor ahead without adequate infantry support at its flanks. This much was known from Poland. There had been time to respond to the lessons of Poland, to rethink and to retool a land army, but there had not been the will.

So France was gone, and the savaged British army had narrowly escaped, trading its equipment on Dunkirk's beaches for toothless exile upon its vulnerable isle. What were Americans preparing for simultaneous wars in the Pacific, in Asia, in Europe, and even in the Western Hemisphere to make of this?

The Moment of Truth

The military sector's dealings with the Congress through most of the first half of 1940 had been cordial, and the Congress had generally attempted to be helpful. Nevertheless, the president, the Congress, and the military all realized that the war in eastern Europe had heightened the public's sentiments *against* American involvement. Americans were afraid of being dragged into the European war, and the Congress was especially sensitive to the public sentiment, though at the same time it was mindful of its duty to at least set the stage for a general mobilization and rearmament if they were required.

Everything abruptly changed when, after the long lull known as the Phony War, the German army and Luftwaffe suddenly and mercilessly attacked the Low Countries. It was evident to all but the most diehard isolationist that the United States *could very well* be dragged into the war at an early date. Beyond the political reality, however, it was the German terror bombing campaign against European cities, such as Rotterdam, that simply scared many Americans into demanding protection in the form of increased air patrols and more anti-aircraft guns around major U.S. cities.

This was the moment of truth. As many millions of formerly disinterested or isolationist-leaning Americans suddenly faced up to the threat of experiencing aerial bombardment at first hand, the vast sea of public sentiment that had prevailed against merely being prepared for war changed precipitously.

The change in attitudes—public and congressional—was evident at once. The first expression of a changed worldview arrived in the form of mass public demand that American cities be defended by massive antiaircraft coverage, something the army could in no way provide without first overseeing the massive induction of new recruits and the manufacture of thousands of anti-aircraft guns and millions of antiaircraft shells. Likewise, the Air Corps had not enough pursuit aircraft or pursuit pilots to defend American cities against the feared onslaught of German bombers. To this, the public pretty much responded, "What's holding you up?"

At routine Senate hearings in 1940 for the Military Establishment Appropriations Bill for 1941, Senator Henry Cabot Lodge Jr. got into a discussion with the Air Corps chief Arnold about the training of pilots to man all the new airplanes that Arnold had just testified his service required. It had been Senator Lodge, in fact, who broached the subject of the pilots, and he eventually explained his shift to that line of questioning by observing, "I am just asking that because I think everyone recognizes that it is the general feeling of Congress, and as far as I can gather, among public opinion throughout the country, to provide all of the money necessary for the National Defense, and so all you have to do is ask for it."

All you have to do is ask for it.

There it was. Senator Lodge certainly was speaking to the new public sentiment. Literally, in one sentence, the Congress, through the mouth of one leading senator, shifted from the age-old posture of asking "How much can we save?" to asking "How much do you need, and how quickly can you spend it on what you need?"

The total change of attitude on the part of the Congress and the electorate was a direct reflection of the American view of German battlefield successes in Europe. The fall of France was beyond shocking. After that, Germany was expected to invade the British Isles. Throwing off a national historical tradition of *never once* having been prepared for a war at the outset of that war, the national will—at first nearly hysterical, but soon rather coldly pragmatic—demanded that the United States make itself as prepared as it could be for the onset of what everyone considered to be the inevitable war to come. It was never publicly contemplated that the United States would join in the war voluntarily. The American outlook, as Senator Lodge posed it to General Arnold, was entirely and authentically in the interests of the national defense. Nevertheless, as history would soon prove, the wheels that had finally begun to turn in the interest of defense would carry the American military down the road that led to the greatest military offensives in human history.

"The Whole Thing is Interwoven"

The U.S. Army and Department of War had been planning for the creation of a war army since 1920, the very year the army had in fact begun to shrink. Over the course of two decades, staff plan after staff plan had carried forward many cogent arguments for a war army of this size and that shape, but nothing much had been done to the army throughout twenty years except make it smaller and weaker. Nevertheless, the evolutionary planning processes—for there were many of them in play at any given moment—had brought to hand intelligent, conservative, and orderly ideas with respect to creating a robust, world-class army from the wreckage of nearly two decades of willful neglect. Also, the mechanisms for modulating the needs of the army to the capabilities of industry and finance had been laid down and to some degree tested before September 1939. At the very least, the army had pretty much completed its work on the *idea* of full mobilization for a modern ground and air war, and it was this idea, with all the planning and meditating, that in fact was pressed into action after the November 14, 1938, Aircraft Meeting.

All well and true, but a more relevant immediate truth was that the general staff of 1939, including G-4, was modulated to the peacetime woes of making a little money go as far as possible. An avalanche of funds and a complete opening of possibilities were not immediately matched by an influx of officers to the general staff who could work through the processes then in place. And, yes, it was as much a problem of process as it was a function of manpower, for a generation of army planners had become used to thinking too much and too long about where to put its meager budget. This changed in due course; the average age and rank of the planners dipped lower, and the senior officers who were used to and inclined toward long deliberation simply went away to perform the necessary administrative functions that kept their burgeoning offices humming. Whenever the planning staffs needed to be expanded, the smart men on those staffs recommended their equally smart comrades from West Point, VMI, the Citadel, professional schools, or service with field units. At times senior officers far from the planning centers simply dispatched young officers whose unbidden opinions on this or that seemed too good to pass up, or because those unbidden ideas were unbidden far too frequently for the senior officers' taste. As well, the eventual adoption of an integrated national war strategy provided the planners with a narrower scope of contingencies than they had previously had to take into account; it focused the planning on real objectives rather than every possible use to which the army might be put. Yet, even then, a firm strategy was a way off, and there was almost too much to do in the interim to get much of anything done.

The combined wisdom of the late-1930s Congress of the United States had very little to offer in the way of useful ideas, but after the defeat of France in mid-1940, it was able to offer cold cash as its share of the solution, and this it did in abundance. But it was the role of the army chiefs and their civilian superiors to make the flow of cash do the things they needed it to do, in the order they needed it to be done. This last was demonstrated in May 1940 in a lesson General Marshall visited upon several senators regarding a demand by nearly every city in the nation that it be guarded by ample antiaircraft defenses in order to stand off the same German bombers that had torched many of Poland's urban areas and had just torched Rotterdam in the Netherlands. The specific subject of the discussion was a budget request that asked for 138 90mm antiaircraft guns.

> *Senator Henry Cabot Lodge Jr.:* . . . they have five thousand [antiaircraft guns] around London alone, and the War Department will be accused of being negligent.
>
> *Marshall:* . . . facilities for the manufacture of antiaircraft equipment are . . . limited. What is necessary for the defense of London is not necessary for the defense of New York, Boston, or Washington. Those cities could be raided . . . but . . . continuous attack . . . would not be practicable unless we permitted the establishment of air bases in close proximity to the United States.
>
> *Senator Alva Adams:* What we need is anti-air-base forces rather than antiaircraft forces.
>
> *Marshall:* You might put it that way, sir.
>
> *Senator Dennis Chavez:* Do they not go together, general?
>
> *Marshall:* The whole thing is interwoven. . . . I have referred to the matter of the practicability of placing larger orders at the moment . . . [and] the necessity of having trained, seasoned enlisted personnel. . . All these matters have to be given proper weight to get a well integrated and balanced whole. . . . Frankly, I should be embarrassed at the moment by more money for materiel alone. . . . It is much wiser to advance step by step, provided these steps are balanced and are not influenced by enthusiasm rather than by reason.

Is that not a philosophy to cling to within an avalanche of money tied in most cases to an avalanche of advice "influenced by enthusiasm rather than reason?"

A four-stack flush-deck destroyer, the *Clemson*-class USS *Edsall* (DD-219) was launched in 1920. The *Edsall* would be sunk by the Japanese during the Battle of the Java Sea, March 1, 1942. *U.S. Naval Historical Center*

Brigadier General William "Billy" Mitchell in Washington, D.C., March 31, 1922. *Library of Congress*

General John J. Pershing, 1920s. *Library of Congress*

Members of the U.S. delegation to the 1930 London naval conference aboard the passenger liner *George Washington*. Left to right: Admiral William V. Pratt, USN; Secretary of State Henry L. Stimson; Senator David A. Reed; *George Washington*'s Master; and Secretary of the Navy Charles Francis Adams. *U.S. Naval Historical Center*

Lieutenant Colonel Henry H. "Hap" Arnold, October 30, 1932. *U.S. Air Force*

Rear Admiral Arthur J. Hepburn, circa 1932. *U.S. Naval Historical Center*

Franklin Delano Roosevelt and
Herbert Hoover ride in a convertible
on the way to Roosevelt's inauguration,
March 4, 1933. *Library of Congress*

General Douglas MacArthur,
U.S. Army chief of staff,
1930–1935. *U.S. Army*

The USS *Arizona* (BB-39) off San Pedro, California, in 1935.
History Division, USMC

A Douglas TBD-1 torpedo plane of Torpedo Squadron 6 from the USS *Enterprise* (CV-6) with a formation of nine other TBD-1s in the background, 1938. *U.S. Naval Historical Center*

Major General Frank M. Andrews, late 1930s. *U.S. Air Force*

General Malin C. Craig, late 1930s. *U.S. Army*

First Army maneuvers, August 1939. New M3A1 scout cars (foreground) with M1A1 combat cars (background). *Signal Corps*

USS *Yorktown* (CV-5), circa 1938. *U.S. Navy*

F4F-3A Wildcats, circa 1941. *U.S. Navy*

M-3 light tanks on the assembly line at Chrysler's Detroit plant. The first M-3s rolled off the line on April 24, 1941. *Library of Congress*

Wings of U.S. Army P-39 fighter aircraft in the plant of Bell Aircraft
Company, New York, 1941. *Library of Congress*

The Atlantic Conference, HMS *Prince of Wales*, Placentia Bay, Newfoundland,
August 10–12, 1941. President Franklin D. Roosevelt (left) and Prime Minister
Winston Churchill are seated. Standing (left to right) are Harry Hopkins,
W. Averell Harriman, Adm. Ernest J. King, USN; Gen. George C. Marshall,
U.S. Army; Gen. Sir John Dill, British Army; Adm. Harold R. Stark, USN;
and Adm. Sir Dudley Pound, RN. *U.S. Naval Historical Center*

Boeing B-17Bs at Marshall Field, California, circa 1941. *U.S. Air Force*

New P-40 fighters, bearing only their stars (with the red circle that would disappear in early 1942) and "U.S. Army" on the underside of their wings, on Biggs Field, El Paso, Texas, circa late 1941. *U.S. Air Force*

Chapter 15

Groping Toward a National Strategy

The Nazis Are Coming! The Nazis Are Coming!

As Americans stared in open-mouthed shock upon the mortifying cascade of catastrophic events unfolding in western Europe across the spring of 1940, army and navy planners quietly, and quite calmly, put the finishing touches on a years-long planning cycle aimed at preserving a political and military status quo in the Western Hemisphere. While they were at it, through the force multiplier of serendipity, these planners did much to jump-start the efforts of the services toward joint preparation for the global war that happened.

The future was not cast in stone. It was as likely in the period from 1937 to 1941 that the United States would become embroiled in a war or wars in Latin America as it did in fact become embroiled in wars in the Pacific and Europe.

Fearful that the European fascist states might, through decades-long migration of their citizens to Latin American states, support or lead coups that would threaten American hegemony—or, at very least, American security—in the Western Hemisphere, the Standing Liaison Committee (made up of the second-ranking civilian secretaries of the State, War, and Navy departments) and the Joint Army and Navy Board (composed of the army chief of staff, the deputy chief of staff, the chief of the army War Plans Division, the chief of naval operations, the assistant chief of naval operations, and the director of the navy War Plans Division) aired their concerns to the Congress in late 1938 as an impetus to establishing at least a contingency military focus on the region. A small group of planners at the elite Army War College was thus sworn to secrecy and tasked in early 1939 with drawing up two secret plans, one for dealing with a fascist-leaning coup in Brazil, and the other for a similar event in Venezuela. Following ten weeks' work, the planners produced a report that called for the creation of a permanent hemispheric defense force of 112,000 soldiers that would be activated as an integrated command, trained and equipped for either task. The plan also noted the need for transport, which is to say naval transport, from U.S. bases to the objective.

The Army War College plan was pretty much shelved until the fall of France, which in an incandescent moment created a very real fear that the French fleet and French colonies in the Western Hemisphere would be turned into the means for creating fascist footholds within range of U.S. shores. Indeed, the contemplated Nazi defeat of Great Britain, the capture of her fleet, and enslavement of her many Western Hemisphere colonies made those fears even more palpable. One effect of these fears was a redoubling of military and economic support to Britain as a means for staving off so grave a calamity. Another effect was renewed and redoubled interest in hemispheric defense, especially with respect to the Panama Canal, whose secure retention in American hands was utterly vital to American conduct of war in Latin America, against Japan in the Pacific, or against the European Axis and its client states in the Atlantic and Europe—or all three at the same time.

An Event-Driven Strategy

Farther removed from the concerns of countering an immediate threat of Axis incursions near at home were the infrequent, decades-long discussions between and among the services and the national command authority regarding various strategic threats to the United States and its interests, and possible responses to them. Such discussions, and attendant planning, had been ongoing for decades and were embodied in the so-called "color" plans (such as Plan Black with respect to Germany, Plan Red with respect to the United Kingdom and the British Commonwealth, and Plan Orange with respect to Japan).

Going back to the end of the Great War, American strategic planning had been heavily focused on a possible future war with Japan in the Pacific. And the chief foci of Plan Orange, which defined the American military strategy with respect to Japan, had been the defense or relief of the Philippines, Guam, Hawaii, and smaller Pacific outposts, with contingencies built in with respect to Alaska and even the three West Coast states.

As world events heated up in Asia, Europe, and Latin America, it became part of the active American war-planning discussion to moot simultaneous multiple emergencies that might militate for the dispatch of American troops and ships to several foreign shores at the same time. In mid-1940, Japan was becoming a larger threat in east Asia, Germany and Italy were active threats in Europe and the Atlantic, and there remained at least a nascent danger of European fascism infiltrating into the Caribbean through French possessions.

The services had not been blind to these threats, nor to the proposition that any or all might combine in one way or another, even if not intentionally. Plan Orange was updated in 1937, and as early as November 1938, the Joint Army and Navy Board commendably anticipated actual events by several years when it asked its Joint Planning Committee (the two service war plans chiefs and their first assistants) "to make exploratory studies and estimates as to the various practicable courses of action open to the military and naval forces of the United States in the event of (a) violation of the Monroe Doctrine by one or more of the fascist powers, and (b) a simultaneous attempt to expand Japanese influence in the Philippines." Yet more visionary was the instruction that planners assume that Germany, Japan, and Italy were bound together by a formal military alliance. As well, the plan was to factor in neutrality among non-fascist and non-totalitarian European states as long as their own colonies in the Western Hemisphere were not molested or threatened.

A draft of the study that was circulated in late January 1939 expressed doubt that Great Britain would come to the aid of the United States in the event of fascist incursions into American possessions and clients in the hemisphere—unless, of course, British possessions were likewise threatened. And the estimate made a complete and utterly surprising break with past estimates by asserting that the defense or relief of Guam and/or the Philippines was *not* in America's vital interests:

> If the American government and people had so considered [Guam and the Philippines to be vital], they would never have consented in the Washington [Naval] Conference to put the security of those possessions in pawn to the mere good faith of Japan, which even in 1922 was not on an irreproachable plane. If they had so considered, the Japanese denunciation of the Washington treaties would have instantly been followed by the impregnable fortification and garrisoning of the Philippines and Guam. If they had been so considered, the Philippine Independence Act [of March 1934] would never have been passed. . . . Whether right or wrong, they have successively undermined the possibility of successful defense by the Army and Navy of these possessions.

The draft study, after making these assertions, allowed that public opinion would require the army and navy to make an effort to relieve the small garrison at Guam and the much larger defense forces in the Philippines via a naval campaign across the central Pacific. But the study also noted, inasmuch as it was to focus as much on the Caribbean and the Atlantic as it focused on the Pacific, that America's interests to the east and southeast were by far more vital and pressing than were her interests so far out in the western ocean.

Then the study turned prophetic:

> In the event of such a concerted aggression [by multiple powers in both oceans], there can be no doubt that the vital interests of the United States would require offensive measures in the Atlantic against Germany and Italy to preserve the vital security of the Caribbean and the Panama Canal. If this is done it will be necessary to assume a defensive attitude in the Eastern Pacific. . . .
>
> Active aggression by Germany and Italy would appear to be possible only if the United States naval forces are inextricably committed in the Western Pacific. . . .
>
> If following an initial Japanese aggression, the United States should remain in a strategic state of readiness, refraining from an advance into the Western Pacific, the fascist powers could not and would not undertake active aggression against South America. . . .

If the United States on the other hand should decide to undertake offensive operations by a Western Pacific advance, she must take due cognizance at all times of the situation and its potentialities in the Western Atlantic in regard to German and Italian activities. . . .

Keep in mind that this is an early 1939 view. The Aircraft Meeting had just taken place and its implications had not begun to sink in, nor had senior officials and commanders, including President Roosevelt, signed off on anything of such an ambitious nature as to allow the military services, through a massive increase of forces and arms, to undertake multiple, simultaneous operations in two oceans. This study effectively foretold what could *not* be done in early 1939, before the events to which it refers unfolded. But it also predicted a future that more or less overlaid the reality of December 1941, and it certainly laid out the reality of mid-1940 more than a year before that reality unfolded. The antidote to such sobering analysis was to build up the military services to the point at which they could manage credible, simultaneous campaigns in both oceans, and that indeed became the aim of the U.S. military, even if an incremental approach to expansion was required as a political or fiscal gesture. Even so, this seminal study proposed an Atlantic-first strategy in place of the Japan-alone outlook that had pervaded American military thinking for at least four decades, and it did so before a shot was fired in Europe.

The study further concluded that future German and Italian actions in the Caribbean and Latin America might mask a Japanese preemptive strike against American ships and bases in Hawaii that would facilitate the swift and complete seizure of the Philippines as well as obviate any near-term effort by the United States to mount a relief expedition.

In an accompanying report compiled entirely by army War Plans Division officers, it was recommended that the president make a policy decision vis-à-vis proactively garnering support for military operations in the Western Hemisphere by the European democracies. The president made no such decision at the time, but in May 1939 a worried British Admiralty dispatched a senior naval planning officer to discuss the disposition of British and American naval units in the event both nations became involved in a war or wars with Germany, Japan, and Italy. The chief of naval operations at the time, Adm. William Leahy, seemed to suggest that Americans should take charge in the Pacific as well as a willingness to share responsibility in the Atlantic with the British cousins.

The release of the completed Joint Planning Committee study in May 1939 ignited a flurry of memoranda between and among the service chiefs and the senior war planners. As a result, once they had digested and discussed the contents, they made a further round of requests that the Joint Planning Committee undertake actual planning for a panel of five possible scenarios arising from the conditions that had been set forth for the study. The notion here was to come up with a fully integrated plan by which the United States could deal simultaneously with two or more enemy nations in two or more parts of the world. Inasmuch as this would blend major aspects of two or more of the various "color" plans—chiefly Plan Orange, Plan Silver (Italy), and Plan Black—there was agreement to dub the new plan Joint War Plan Rainbow. Five contingencies, numbered Joint War Plan Rainbow No. 1 through Joint War Plan Rainbow No. 5, were then contemplated. In due course, Rainbow 1, 2, 3, and 4 were overtaken by events in Europe, so a constantly revised, expanded, and updated Rainbow 5 plan became the primary roadmap by which the United States prepared—recruited, built, trained, equipped, and fielded forces—for a war very much like the one it found itself in by the end of the second week of December 1941. Portions of the dropped plans found their way into Rainbow 5, forced there by the march of events, so the effort expended in creating and updating them was by no means in vain.

It is true that the world war never reached the Western Hemisphere, except in the form of U-boat attacks, but there was no way to predict that at any time prior to or for much time after December 1941. The defeat of France in June 1940 quite naturally caused deep concerns over the role French possessions in the Western Hemisphere might play in advancing the European fascist war effort into the region. It took no great imagination to foresee the basing of long-range German patrol bombers or even U-boats at French bases in the Caribbean, or for that matter the introduction of German or German-controlled troops to defend those bases. There was also no telling at that moment, in which the United States was quite vulnerable to such events, the degree to which a collapse of the reeling British war effort might invite an even greater infiltration, for by then the United States had amply demonstrated, via the aggressive Neutrality Patrol, its barely fettered hostility toward the Nazi regime and its war aims.

On May 11, 1940, just one day after the German army assaulted the Netherlands, a combined Anglo-French force landed on Aruba and Curaçao in the Netherlands West Indies to prevent them from falling into Axis hands. (On the same day, the Japanese foreign minister demanded the maintenance of the political and economic status quo in the Netherlands East Indies.)

On May 21, the day the French army and British Expeditionary Force were encircled around Abbeville, France, General Marshall found on his desk an unsigned memo, possibly drafted by Brig. Gen. George Strong, chief of the army War Plans Division, that read in part, "In view of the present world conditions it is believed that this country should take immediate steps to acquire British and French possessions in the Atlantic." The next day, a group of army war plans officers submitted to Marshall a memorandum that cautioned against an attempt by the inadequate American military to try to cover all its bases—the Philippines, Guam, the Caribbean, the North Atlantic, and so forth—by dispersing its weak forces. This memo asked that Marshall and his peers determine priorities, or even one priority, at which a maximum concentration of forces might be rallied. The chief writer of this memorandum was Maj. Matthew Ridgway, whose considerable assets Marshall had noted during several encounters over the years and whose counsel Marshall was entirely disposed to factor into his own thinking. Ridgway concluded the memorandum with a suggestion that, in the near term, the United States' best interests would be served by concentrating forces in the Western Hemisphere and on out to the eastern side of the 180th meridian, which included Hawaii, Midway, and the Aleutian Islands but excluded Wake Island, Guam, and the Philippines. The day after Marshall received this memo, he showed it to President Roosevelt, Adm. Harold Stark (chief of naval operations since August 1939), and Under Secretary of State Sumner Welles. The four men agreed, in Marshall's words to war plans chief Strong, "that we must not become involved with Japan, that we must not concentrate ourselves beyond the 180th meridian, and that we must concentrate on the South America situation."

Next, on May 24, General Marshall and Admiral Stark instructed the Joint Planning Committee to provide a concrete plan to occupy the hemispheric possessions of all the western Allies—French, Dutch, Danish, and British—to keep them from German control.

The fear of a European fascist incursion into the Western Hemisphere came to something of a head, also on May 24, 1940, three days after Hitler's legions encircled the main bodies of the French army and British Expeditionary Force at Abbeville. A warning reached Washington from London that six thousand Nazi operatives had been loaded aboard merchant ships with the possible intention of landing in Brazil to seize the government with the help of merchant crews already in Brazilian waters. It is not known if the British were trying to be helpful or provocative, but in any case President Roosevelt directed Admiral Stark on May 25 to submit a plan to dispatch ten thousand troops to Brazil by air transport in order to create and hold a bridgehead for the arrival of one hundred thousand additional troops by sea. In only two days, Stark responded with Operation Pot of Gold, which, among other things, described a naval escort for the transport flotilla of four battleships, two aircraft carriers, nine cruisers, and three destroyer squadrons. Unfortunately, at the time Pot of Gold was promulgated, the United States had not the airlift capacity to fly a sensible fraction of ten thousand armed troops to Atlantic City, much less to far-off Brazil, which could be reached by air only by undertaking stopovers for refueling and maintenance at bases that had not nearly enough fuel or spare parts on hand. Nor did the navy possess a fraction of the required troop-lift capacity—not to mention cargo ships for equipment, supplies, ammunition, and large weapons such as artillery pieces and tanks. Fortunately, nothing came of the threat, and Operation Pot of Gold was shelved.

On May 30, the Joint Army and Navy Board set a triggering mechanism for the seizure of the Western Hemisphere possessions of defeated Allied nations: "The date of the loss of the British or French fleets automatically sets the date of our mobilization," which was taken to mean that the National Guard would be called up. A concrete plan for such a mobilization and an attendant national call to action was completed on June 7, 1940, and was approved by the secretaries of war and the navy on June 13.

The United States was not focusing on the German victory over the European Allies quite to the extent that it forgot to check in on events in the Japanese sphere of East Asia. It had been observed over a period of months that a large Imperial Army force had been conducting training on Hainan Island, off the coast of south China and opposite the coast of northern French Indochina. Speculation as to that force's ultimate mission naturally revolved around a move into the French colony, from which it would outflank neutral Thailand and British-controlled Burma. On June 17, 1940, the day the French sued for an armistice, the American embassy in Tokyo warned that "the Soviet and British attachés here are speculating with regard to possible Japanese invasion of [Indochina] in event of capitulation of France." The army War Plans Division further speculated that such a move by Japan might be preceded by an attack on the Panama Canal Zone or on the United States Fleet, which had just moved into Pearl Harbor. This news and speculation placed a deep conundrum before the U.S. military's top commanders. It had been assumed that the French and British fleets would dampen the Kriegsmarine's ambitions in the North Atlantic, leaving the United States free to base most of its growing fleet in the Pacific as a check on Japanese ambitions there. If the French Fleet was either neutralized by an armistice or, much worse, co-opted for use by the Axis, it would be necessary to shift more U.S. naval assets to Atlantic waters, and that could only embolden Japan in the Pacific and East Asia.

One immediate result of this conundrum being spelled out for General Marshall on this momentous June 17 was his instant decision to order army commands in Hawaii and Panama to go on immediate alert, "to deal with [a] possible trans-Pacific raid, to greatest extent possible without creating public hysteria or provoking undue curiosity." So hermetically hidden was the cause of the alert that many senior officers charged with maintaining it over many months had no clear understanding of its source.

Also on June 17, Marshall called in his War Plans chief, the chief of G-3 (planning and training), and the chief of G-4 (logistics and supply). According to notes taken at this conference, Marshall said, "We may suddenly find Japan and Russia appear as a team operating to hold our ships in the Pacific. If the French Navy goes to Germany and Italy, we will have a very serious situation in the South Atlantic. Germany may rush the South America situation to a head in a few weeks." The alignment of Japan and the Soviet Union arose from a concern that the two nations might undertake a mutual nonaggression pact, which is by no means the same as a military alliance, and a German rush to South America referred to ongoing concerns over a fascist coup, most likely in Brazil.

Marshall went on: "Are we not forced into a question of reframing our naval policy . . . [into] purely defensive action in the Pacific with a main effort on the Atlantic side? There is the possibility of raids. . . . The main effort may be south of Trinidad with action north thereof purely on the basis of a diversion to prevent our sending materiel to South America. This seems to indicate that we should mobilize the National Guard."

Then Marshall turned to possible consequences arising from President Roosevelt's month-old decision to base the United States Fleet in Pearl Harbor rather than several West Coast ports: "Should not Hawaii have some big bombers? . . . It is possible that our opponents in the Pacific would be four-fifths of the way to Hawaii before we knew they had moved." (If only that had been so!)

And on this important June 17, General Strong, the chief of the army War Plans Division, offered Marshall three policy revisions to consider putting forth to Admiral Stark and then taking to the president: assume a purely defensive position in the Pacific without recourse to interfering with Japanese adventures there; withhold further materiel transfers to the European Allies because they were all going to be defeated anyway; and immediately mobilize to undertake a credible hemispheric defense effort, to include calling up the National Guard and increasing the size of the Regular Army as well as simply seizing French, British, Dutch, and Danish possessions throughout the hemisphere. This package was considered too radical to take to Stark, but the army indeed went to the navy chief with three concrete derivative proposals: maintain a strong presence in the Pacific and resist pressure to undertake commitments elsewhere; go to any extreme, including "belligerent participation" to sustain France and Britain in Europe; and begin a sustained effort to stymie any sort of German or Italian "domination or lodgment" in the Western Hemisphere.

The three proposals were the subject of long discussions between army and navy seniors and planners until June 22, by which time helping France was out of the equation. On that date, Marshall and Stark placed the services' proposals before the president in the form of a draft document entitled "Basis for Immediate Decisions Concerning the National Defense." At the June 22 meeting, attended by only Roosevelt, Marshall, and Stark, only Marshall appears to have made notes, fairly rough in nature. A summary of the army chief of staff's account covers nine topic areas:

1. Marshall and Stark agreed that the loss of the French Fleet directly to German control would necessitate a transfer of a major portion of the United States Fleet from Hawaii to Atlantic ports. The president agreed but added that a decision with respect to returning those fleet units to the Pacific would be made as soon as possible.
2. The service chiefs expressed their concern about releasing additional war materiel to Great Britain because doing so from America's understocked warehouses might jeopardize America's war-making capacity. They even recommended against allowing war materiel being directly supplied to Great Britain by American manufacturers, who might otherwise produce goods for use by the American services. Roosevelt gave his qualified approval, the qualification being that any bullet fired by the British at the Germans and Italians benefited the United States by keeping it out of the war a bit longer.

3. The defense of the Western Hemisphere might involve occupation of British, French, Dutch, and Danish possessions in both the Atlantic and Pacific. Roosevelt exempted the British Falkland Islands because of an outstanding Argentinean claim for them (and Argentina was a nation closest to aiding the Axis). He suggested that the International Date Line serve as a western extremity of occupation.

4. All agreed that occupation of strategic positions in the Caribbean and Latin America then under control of hemispheric nations be undertaken only by prior agreement with those nations.

5. It was decided to support local governments in the hemisphere, particularly those under some sort of pressure to side with the Axis. The president stipulated that the support be reassessed on a "day-to-day basis."

6. Except for rifles and machine guns, no arms were to be provided to hemispheric nations. This reflected shortages for U.S. personnel and stipulated that ammunition for any arms that were supplied not be transferred until after March 1941, by which times U.S. arsenals might conceivably catch up with demand.

7. This was a legalistic stipulation regarding economic matters arising from national defense in Latin America.

8. The service chiefs recommended that arms production in the United States be speeded up by imposing on manufacturers a six- or seven-day work week of two or three shifts per day. They also recommended that the government provide unemployed workers with the necessary education to undertake factory work. Roosevelt balked here, noting that he preferred getting all of the nation's many unemployed workers trained and put to work before offering overtime to trained workers with jobs. He suggested that the arms producers themselves provide the necessary education to unskilled workers.

9. The service chiefs asked that a selective service act, long a planned solution to mobilizing a wartime army and navy, be enacted at once and then closely followed by full mobilization. Roosevelt, who was running for an unprecedented third term, was not ready to go to the mat with Congress on these matters, and he did not believe the services could absorb, train, or arm so many men so soon. He suggested a "progressive" mobilization that offered young men a choice of the army, the navy, work in the war industry, mechanical training, or a place in the Civilian Conservation Corps or similar national service. This response was already moot; a bill calling for a national draft had already begun wending its way through the Congress.

General Marshall and Admiral Stark rewrote Marshall's notes on the June 22 review of the national defense proposal and resubmitted them to the president on June 27. The revision made the following recommendations: a defensive posture by the United States; nonbelligerent support of Great Britain, the British Commonwealth, and China; hemispheric defense, including possible occupation of strategic positions and bases in possessions of defeated Allied nations; close cooperation with hemispheric governments; a speed-up of production and training of manpower for increased war production; passage of a draft act and "progressive" mobilization; and preparation of concrete plans for an "almost inevitable conflict" with Germany, Japan, and Italy, as well as cooperation with nations opposed to those powers.

On July 8, 1940, the Joint Army and Navy Board's Joint Planning Com-mittee issued a memorandum outlining a plan to seize French possessions in the Caribbean in the event the new Vichy French government allowed them to become a fascist springboard into the Western Hemisphere. And on July 30, a nervous gathering of twenty-one Western Hemisphere foreign ministers in Havana agreed to the Act of Havana, which called for a joint defense of the hemisphere in the event of incursions from the outside, meaning of course European fascist incursions. The Act of Havana bound the nations of the Western Hemisphere to a common purpose against incursion from outside the hemisphere.

A Policy of Forbearance

Throughout the critical first nine months of the war in Europe, the U.S. armed forces had been crippled in their planning by not having a clear objective by which the planning could be guided. President Roosevelt had an idea that he favored the Allies over the Axis, and so did most Americans, but this was not translatable into policy in the face of assured congressional opposition to war, per se, nor in the face of the economic and social realities of the day. The United States was able to mount the Neutrality Patrol and enforce hemispheric neutrality in large part because the Kriegsmarine had not yet even begun to build out its U-boat fleet to take on operations in the Western Hemisphere. And Japanese intentions and capabilities glued the larger and better equipped portion of U.S. naval fighting power to the Pacific.

As the extent to which the United States lacked a coherent, integrated war plan sank in, the best minds the services and the government could deploy worked over the possibilities against a backdrop of unfolding events that could barely be imagined, much less accounted for, in a proactive planning cycle. The war in Europe sucked the United States involuntarily forward in ways and to places it could not guess, nor wanted to go. But such alarming events forced decisions that forced and shaped policies that somehow, over time, added up to a coherent whole.

On June 27, 1940, only ten days after France capitulated, at a time Britain might very easily have been defeated, President Roosevelt heard his service chiefs make a series of six concrete and attainable recommendations that added up to a complete, reality-based strategy for racing to a better stance vis-à-vis the potential enemies: do not voluntarily get into a war with any of the presumptive enemy states, much less all of them; support Britain and her allies, the best friends and best future allies the United States could have in the inevitable war to come; speed up production of all the things the armed forces needed to win a war when the nation inevitably joined the war; build up the manpower of the armed forces through an urgent but orderly process of mobilization and conscription; protect the region nearest to home, even if that brought a full-blown entry into the war sooner than might otherwise occur; and put a positive outcome in Europe ahead of any outcome in Asia and the Pacific.

Unanticipated Benefits

For all that a great deal of planning effort (and eventually manpower and hardware) was expended on hemispheric defense, the military planning agencies were not so consumed as to fail to recognize that the source of nearly all the near-term dismay lay in Europe. It is important to note, then, that the planning for defense of potential Axis targets in the hemisphere was actually a program to counter the European Axis, per se. And that realization spawned the greater realization that the antidote to any incursions into the hemisphere, by any nation or coalition, was to generally raise the capabilities of the U.S. land, sea, and air forces. It was also noted that certain Latin American nations would side with the Axis if it came down to it, but that many others were prepared to side with the United States and the Allies against the Axis if it came down to that or, indeed, even if the war was fought outside the hemisphere.

As active planning for a hemispheric defense waxed and waned, and especially with respect to a watchful Congress, the Roosevelt Administration and the military planners concluded that touting and doing something about a vigorous defense of the Western Hemisphere would sugarcoat the idea of generally building up the air, ground, and naval forces many of the planners felt the services would need early on in a war in Europe, east Asia, the Atlantic, the Pacific, the Caribbean, or Latin America—or any combination of these potential war theaters. Looking ahead, for example, to the possible use of air ferry routes between the Americas and Europe (and even east Asia) via Africa, the planners realized that several Latin nations fronting the western South Atlantic might host bases exploiting the shortest over-water legs of a journey between the continental United States and transit points in western Africa, especially those in British and French colonies scattered throughout the westernmost portion of Africa. Consonant with securing these aircraft ferry routes, the American military planners drew up schemes for protecting the Latin American nations in which ferry bases would have to be built, of which Brazil was the chief contender.

At a rather elevated and mostly theoretical strategic level, such contemplation, discussion, and planning led the United States away from the *passive* defense plan (and mindset) mooted during an earlier period as a sop to the Congress's active and dominant isolationist and peace lobbies. By defining a concrete hemispheric defense force and then actually drawing up even as unworkable an emergency plan as Operation Pot of Gold for its use, which went so far as to specify the components of a naval escort flotilla, the planners slipped into a state known as a *dynamic* defense—you don't need to come to us; just dare to get close enough and we'll come to you. While still technically a defense that required a precipitating action by an enemy, it was a spring-loaded defense, complete with triggering mechanisms that could be set to react anywhere from very slowly to almost immediately. It was, then, an important waypoint in getting from no means for making war to a strategy of aggressive deterrence by way of a strategy of meaningful disincentive.

One other benefit derived from the planning exercises in behalf of a hemispheric defense was that it got the best planners the army and navy had into the same mental and intellectual working space. This courtship phase, in which each service learned *operational* details about the other that neither service had bothered to study for going on two decades, was vital to whatever the services might achieve together on yet unknown battlefields, beginning only eighteen months hence. In sum, during this worrisome but otherwise fruitless interval, the services took the first steps toward achieving a war-winning operational partnership, the means for working together in the field during a military expedition or a full-blown war, which is distinct from the lofty and somewhat theoretical realm of joint strategic planning. While the organs of discussion—chiefly the Joint Army and Navy Board—were bodies designed simply for consultation on a narrow range of issues of common concern, the service chiefs and their topmost subordinates and chief planners carried forth the impetus of the hemispheric defense assessment and planning exercises to the point of ongoing and deepening operational coordination. And they developed bonds of trust. In due course, senior army officers learned who the go-to guys further down the naval pecking order were, and vice versa. At a very high level, each service learned things about the other service that each needed to factor into any of its own plans requiring operational support from the other. And so forth. It is more than enough that the hemispheric defense exercises brought the services together in meaningful and useful ways, and that they did so at the earliest possible critical juncture, ultimately affecting an otherwise very bleak joint future.

Chapter 16

Army Expansion

Rivers of Wealth

IN THE EIGHT MONTHS between the German invasion of Poland on September 1, 1939, and the end of April 1940, U.S. Army budgeters and logistical planners were so wrapped up in their numbers and old ways to prioritize needs, as they had for decades, that they barely perceived that the Congress, the Roosevelt Administration, and indeed the army's own top leaders (especially Marshall and Arnold) were open to any and all notions regarding the influx of equipment, materiel, and manpower, up to and even beyond the minimums set in the 1920 Protective Mobilization Plan. Nevertheless, on May 7, 1940, three days before the German army and Luftwaffe launched their lightning war against Belgium, the Netherlands, and Luxembourg, the army supply division awoke sufficiently to submit a revised plan for reasonably near-term expansion. Basically, the new plan outlined the focus of yet more planning for funds to purchase items critical and essential to raising and equipping an army of 1,166,000 troops; to provide shelter, pay, rations, and everything else required for a full year; and to build the Air Corps up to 5,806 aircraft and the establishment required to maintain and fly them.

The army supply division's planning effort was further spurred by a presidential inquiry on May 9 as to the status of the Air Corps equipment program. The next day, of course, the entire military establishment and all the civilian agencies attending to it were spurred to urgent action as German ground and air forces burst into western Europe. On May 16, the president delivered to the Congress a message in which he outlined his support for all the funding the services said they needed to get to a war footing in the shortest time they could handle the growth. The near-term funding bill totaled $732 million, at which the Congress barely blinked.

An immediate result of the earliest new funding was an authorization for the army to grow from 227,000 troops to 255,000 and for provision of munitions to see a 750,000-man army into battle. For his part, Marshall, whose inner vision was complete, ticked off before the Senate Appropriations Committee on May 17 a list of immediate requirements, including additional plants to produce gunpowder, automatic weapons, and ammunition, and storage for these items. He said the Air Corps needed two hundred heavy bombers "of the most modern type," as well as contracts with more than the nine civilian flying schools at which many flying cadets were then undergoing preliminary training, an overall increase in pilot trainees from 2,700 per year to 7,000 per year, and an increase in enlisted personnel to support the training expansion. He also asked that the Regular Army's immediate overall manpower cap be set at four hundred thousand troops.

From the May 17 hearings alone flowed an immense river of wealth. What had been impossible in April became urgently fundable in mid-May. Almost without debate, the Congress sent a spending bill to the president amounting to a hair under $1.5 billion. This new spending bill was signed into law on June 13, but by then the estimates that supported it had been raised. On May 23, in the face of an enormous influx of news and data from western Europe, Marshall raised his manpower requirements to a fully equipped Regular Army of five hundred thousand men by July 1, 1941; one million men by January 1, 1942; and as many as two million men by July 1, 1942. Thus, on May 28, Marshall began to push for a supplemental spending bill of more than $506 million, of which $300 million was just for airplanes that could credibly challenge the Luftwaffe. The very next day, at the order of the Department of War, Marshall added $200 million to the supplemental for construction of new production facilities. (Much of the Department of War planning was actually undertaken or overseen, or at least urged by, Col. James Burns, executive assistant to the assistant secretary of war, the very same Burns whose 1923 memo had helped jump-start the Army Industrial College.) Thus, a supplemental bill for $500 million was laid before the Congress on May 31, two weeks *before* the underlying bill was signed into law. What the rattled Congress actually passed out, almost without opposition, was a spending bill for $821 million and a further contract authorization for more than $254 million. The chief aim of the supplemental was to massively build up military production facilities. A supplement to the supplement authorized an increase in the Regular Army to a total of 375,000 enlisted personnel. When passed on June 26, the overall supplemental brought the total War Department appropriation for 1941 to nearly $3 billion.

At this point, the entire budget and manpower process overran all prior planning models. As was the case for the 1941 Department of War appropriation, it became common for urgent supplementals to be submitted before underlying bills were codified in law, and it became common for the Congress, with little or no debate, to add substantially to the funds the army said it needed. Throughout the army, planning staffs came under intense pressure to grind out immensely complex requests in narrower and narrower time frames.

General Marshall on June 13, 1940, directed that the army control rates of production large enough to field a combat-ready force of one million men by October 1, 1941. Thus, the army planners prioritized the service's needs of everything from pay, rations, training, shelter, and transportation to new arsenals, new depots, new posts, expansion of the Air Corps, accelerated procurement, industrial mobilization, and additional civilian staff. Simply maintaining the massive and growing list of necessities, much less getting events in the right order, was a mind-boggling task that continued to suck in planners from throughout the army's corps of professional officers.

How Big an Army?

Beginning in February 1940, senior army planners realized that they were aiming at a moving target. No one knew how big an army the United States was ultimately going to be able to put in the field, or when. Even the best guesses proved serially inaccurate as appropriating began to lead planning. Perhaps the most qualified person to put his superiors' feet to the fire was Col. James Burns, who was really the person in charge of overseeing the strategy behind the build-up. Without knowing the army's real target end strength for a given interval, Burns could not aim the tools or power at his disposal. A February 1 memo from Burns to Marshall laid out Burns' needs and concerns regarding a timeline: How many troops do you need industry to equip, and in how much time will you need the men and their equipment? The memo went unanswered, largely because Marshall had no answer to give. Meanwhile, industry was making commitments to provide war production without knowing how much it needed to produce in how much time. This impasse threatened to put kinks in war production, production for friendly foreign nations, or civilian production, or all three. Moreover, industry could not hire and train workers before it received contracts and clear instructions.

At length, President Roosevelt became aware of the impasse. As he had in December 1939, to straighten out the competition between the American services and the French and British over aircraft production allotments, Roosevelt created a commission, the Advisory Commission to the Council of National Defense. He named but one person to the new council, himself; the commission reported just to him as well as keeping the departments of War and the Navy in the loop. The advisory commission's first meeting, with Marshall attending, was held at the White House on May 30, 1940. William Knudsen, who was in charge of production planning, asserted that he could not move forward efficiently without hard numbers on military growth and thus could not reliably allocate industrial output for three sectors—the U.S. military, foreign allies such as Britain and China, and the American domestic market.

On June 11, Knudsen followed up with the Department of War by demanding of Assistant Secretary Louis Johnson answers to just two questions: "How much munitions productive capacity does this country need, and how rapidly must it become available?" Johnson bucked the question back to its original source, Colonel Burns, who immediately wrote a memo with the data he had in hand. Burns then stated that only President Roosevelt and the Congress could hash out end-strength numbers and a timetable for manpower growth. And he then admitted that the Department of War had failed to advise Roosevelt in his capacity as commander-in-chief what its manpower requirements were, but he also asserted that answering Knudsen's two pressing questions were beyond the Department of War's statutory jurisdiction. Burns closed with a suggestion that the president be enlisted to set long-range manpower levels. Knudsen then had a memo prepared, incorporating all of Burns' points, over the signature of Assistant Secretary Johnson. The following is the progression of end strengths by date: production sufficient for a combat ground force of one million men by October 1, 1941; of two million men by January 1, 1942; and four million by April 1, 1942—about double the growth that Marshall had outlined for the Congress on May 23. As to the Air Corps, the memo to the commander in chief estimated that it was necessary to build up *capacity* to produce nine thousand airplanes per year by October 1, 1941; eighteen thousand airplanes per year by January 1, 1942; and thirty-six thousand airplanes per year by April 1, 1942.

Knudsen's memo was immediately hand-carried to the deputy chief of staff along with a note from Colonel Burns that bluntly required a comment within *thirty* minutes. The memo was immediately handed off to Marshall, who wrote in his own hand, "I concur in the above quantity objectives, but I consider it of imperative importance that means be found to advance the date for the needs of the first million men herein scheduled for October 1."

The program and schedule went to Roosevelt, who reduced the overall budget request from $11 billion to $7.3 billion. The plan was adopted on June 20 and sent back to Louis Johnson, who was by then the acting secretary of war. And so forth. On June 27 Marshall asked Johnson to go back to the president for more money to fund an expanded and accelerated program for the four-million-man army.

Chickens Come to Roost

The army's April 1940 maneuvers, which made the first use of corps headquarters in the field since 1918 and constituted the first field test of the triangular division, were unflatteringly instructive as to what the army lacked in the way of fighting power. The army's artillery backbone of 75mm field guns, still in service because of budget issues, was seen as wholly inadequate and in need of early across-the-board replacement by the new and really quite splendid home-grown 105mm howitzer. This implied, among other things, the parallel procurement of powerful, ruggedized trucks capable of moving the 105s, ammunition, and their crews under battlefield conditions. The maneuvers revealed a critical shortage of antitank weapons, and indeed of tanks themselves. These were not new revelations, but ideas driven home by attention to the war in Europe. Coordination between air and ground units pointed to neglect by both arms. Only two of thirty-four aerial missions requested by ground forces were actually performed, but only thirty-four missions were even requested.

Reports on and discussions about the maneuvers' shortcomings were blunt among general officers required to be in the loop, but the whole matter of shortcomings was squelched outside the highest circles lest the United States fall early prey to the exploitation by a vigilant enemy, or to the army's enemies lying low in the Congress.

✳

The Sticking Point

It was all well and good for the army to arrive at a commendably bold expansion program, including its most urgent requirements, but it took only until the last days of June for industry even to respond with the news that it had not the means to meet the army's timetable. If it takes great care, endless planning, and constant rejiggering of priorities for as hierarchical and disciplined an enterprise as the U.S. Army to develop itself at an efficient pace and all in the right order, why would anyone think that the anarchic, decentralized, and competing institutions of American commerce could do any better when its turn at bat arrived?

The main problem, brought to the attention of seasoned industrialists William Knudsen and Edward Stettinius, was that the domestic production of machine tools could not match the army's demands. Moreover, steel and iron production capacity was not sufficient to do their share to equip a four-million-man army in the time allotted, though the needs of a two-million-man force might possibly be met. The upshot of the news was that Marshall was given a stark choice: equip a two-million-man army soonest or wait an indefinite period to equip a four-million-man army. Following consultation with key subordinates, Marshall opted for the two-million-man bird-in-hand. He wrote to Acting Secretary Johnson on June 27 that the army could manage to defend the Western Hemisphere and eastern Pacific with such a force, probably for as long as it took to build out to four million troops, which the army had long considered its optimal offensive strength.

A conference was held on June 28, attended by Johnson, Marshall, Knudsen, and Burns. The four worked out a new six-step framework that took industry's sobering reality check into account:

1. Procure all necessary items and reserves to maintain a combat-ready field force of one million men.
2. Procure all necessary items and reserves for the acquisition and long-term maintenance of a two-million-man combat-ready field force.
3. Create production facilities to supply a balanced ground force of four million men.
4. Procure up to a total of eighteen thousand combat-ready airplanes, plus sufficient spares and spare parts to maintain a ready air force at the eighteen-thousand-plane level.
5. Create sufficient production capacity to build eighteen thousand complete airplanes per year plus spare parts to maintain them.
6. Assure necessary storage for all army equipment and other stocks.

The new outline was turned over to G-4 for budget figures, and on June 30—in only two days—a complete budget amounting to nearly $5.9 billion dollars was handed off to Acting Secretary Johnson, who immediately got it to the president. Roosevelt checked the budget with senior aides and, that very day, returned it to

Johnson for reconsideration of several issues. Along with concerns over the size and storage of reserve stocks, Roosevelt said he hoped to keep the army's entire 1941 budget beneath $4 billion—for political reasons. After explaining why the larger figure was the right figure, Marshall complied with Roosevelt's request, and Roosevelt approved the budget on July 3. Internal budget processing, with some give and take involving Roosevelt, ended on July 10, when the president sent the budget to the Congress as a request for "total defense." There were critics on all sides of "too much" or "too little" or even "too late."

The real hero in all this was Col. James Burns, who exceeded the perquisites of his rank and station—but not his deep knowledge of the issues—to force his superiors to make not only timely decisions, but decisions at all. Love it or hate it, the U.S. Army by mid-July 1940 had both a global military strategy in place and a concrete and orderly plan for building itself up to undertake that strategy.

Chapter 17

Under New Management

Stimson and Patterson

FROM THE PERSPECTIVE of the White House, it finally came time to relieve Secretary of War Harry Woodring, whose isolationist views and exasperating propensity to absent himself from all decisionmaking no longer suited President Roosevelt's worldview or needs, nor his politics, nor the nation's politics. Woodring was allowed to resign, effective June 20, 1940.

Assistant Secretary of War Louis Johnson—who had willingly borne the burden of nudging even the president toward a more realistic, more robust approach to rearmament than the president himself initially espoused—rightfully felt that he was next in line to move up to head the Department of War. Alas, the pressing need to cement a seamless national political unity on the issue of the looming war obliged Roosevelt's closest advisors to look across party lines for a successor to Woodring. When the profoundly disappointed but loyal Johnson heard of this decision, he gave notice that he would resign without a whimper when the new secretary and a new assistant secretary were appointed. In the interim, he served well and faithfully as acting secretary of war.

Following a talent search and a selling campaign by Supreme Court Justice Felix Frankfurter, a savvy politician and close Roosevelt confidante, the spotlight fell on Henry Stimson, a lion of the Republican Party who had distinguished himself in the Great War and had many times served in high government office.

Born on September 1, 1867, in New York City, Stimson graduated from Yale in 1888 and from the Harvard Law School in 1890 and then worked as a young lawyer under the tutelage of Elihu Root. By 1901 he was a full partner in Root's law firm. In 1895, President Theodore Roosevelt appointed Stimson U.S. attorney for the Southern District of New York. When Stimson ran for governor of New York in 1910, he was defeated, but in 1911 President William Howard Taft appointed him secretary of war, and he served until Taft left office in 1913.

Stimson had served in the New York National Guard between 1898 and 1907, so when the United States entered the Great War, he sought to renew his commission at the age of forty-nine. He was inducted as a lieutenant colonel and assigned to a National Guard artillery regiment. Later, he was promoted to full colonel and given command of another artillery regiment. He was so proud of his military service that he let it be known after his return to civilian life that he preferred to be addressed as "Colonel."

Following nearly a decade of practicing law, Stimson was appointed by President Calvin Coolidge in 1927 to arbitrate an election dispute in Nicaragua. He next served as governor general of the Philippines between 1927 and 1929, and then as President Herbert Hoover's secretary of state from 1929 to 1933. In the latter capacity, spurred on by America's humiliation in context of the Japanese invasion of Manchuria, he formulated the Stimson Doctrine: The United States would not recognize territories or diplomatic agreements acquired through aggression. He also terminated the Department of State's code-breaking program on grounds that "gentlemen do not read each other's mail," a policy that was itself terminated as he cleared the Department of State portals on the last day of the Hoover presidency.

For all that Stimson was a staunch Republican, he had publicly supported the Roosevelt Administration foreign policies, which is one reason he was Justice Frankfurter's first choice to head the Department of War. President Roosevelt was initially cool to the notion, but Stimson's candidacy was clinched when, immediately upon the fall of France, he, on his own, made a radio address urging the public to support American military preparedness.

Stimson was a cold, unloved man, but he was deeply admired and universally respected. Although he was seventy-two and in only so-so health when the call came, the call did come, and Stimson accepted. He was sworn in on July 10, 1940. For this, even though he brought Republican values and some patronage to the otherwise homogenous Democratic administration, he was read out of the Republican Party.

As a replacement for Assistant Secretary Johnson, Justice Frankfurter sought suggestions from a bipartisan group of New York State movers and shakers that had helped him come up with the Stimson candidacy. The perfect candidate turned out to be a New York State lawyer, a Republican known for being so selfless in service of his nation that Roosevelt had appointed him in 1939 to the United States Court of Appeals for the Second Circuit. Judge Robert Patterson, once a law student of Justice Frankfurter's, had served in the Punitive Expedition in Mexico in 1916, had commanded a company and then a battalion of New York National Guard infantry in France, and, indeed, had earned a Distinguished Service Cross and a Silver Star in hand-to-hand combat. When his name came up, he was on leave from the bench, having reenlisted in the New York National Guard as a forty-nine-year-old private so he could take a refresher military course at the newly reopened Plattsburg, New York, training camp—at which he had been commissioned a generation earlier—in order to realign his mind, body, and spirit for the new war.

Justice Frankfurter made the case for Patterson, and President Roosevelt made the nomination. The Senate Committee on Military Affairs voted out the nomination on July 26, 1940. Three days later, as soon as the full Senate voted its will, Patterson resigned from the bench, and from the National Guard as well. Many people who knew Patterson wondered why he had signed away his future to serve a Democratic administration that would surely be driven from office following the November 1940 elections.

Of all the civilian appointments President Roosevelt made in the years and days after the Aircraft Meeting, few were as crucial as Patterson's. In Robert Patterson, America had hired a tireless worker and a patriot in the highest and finest tradition. As much as anyone, and considerably more than most, Patterson was the man who built America's victorious World War II army.

Knox, Forrestal, and Stark

The driving force behind many of the navy's advances during Franklin Roosevelt's first two terms as president had been the administration's first secretary of the navy, Claude Swanson, a Virginia political lion who served from 1933 until his death in July 1939. Replacing Swanson on an acting basis was Charles Edison, the inventor's son and heir. Edison had served as a Navy Department aide during Roosevelt's own tenure as assistant navy secretary in the Woodrow Wilson Administration and had himself been appointed assistant secretary of the navy in January 1937. He served as acting secretary until Roosevelt formally elevated him to the top post on January 2, 1940, but he stayed only until June 24, 1940, when he resigned to run for governorship of New Jersey. During his tenure in the Navy Department, Edison had been a strong advocate for construction of the large, swift *Iowa*-class battleships.

Upon Edison's departure, President Roosevelt decided to make another goodwill gesture toward the Republican Party. He had been contacted some months earlier by Frank Knox, a former Rough Rider turned newspaper mogul who had served with distinction as a National Guard artillery colonel in France and later run unsuccessfully for vice president on the doomed Alf Landon Republican ticket in 1936. Though a rock-ribbed Republican, Knox had fully and effusively embraced Roosevelt's brand of internationalism, especially the president's support of Great Britain. He had bluntly asked to serve in a meaningful post in the administration. Knox took office on July 11, 1940, but his tenure was not particularly meaningful, in that Roosevelt did indeed incline toward being his own secretary of the navy. Moreover, Knox was simply not the right man to bridge a gap in trust that had grown between the Roosevelt Administration and some of the top admirals, most notably Rear Adm. James Richardson, who had been appointed United States Fleet commander in January 1940. It is said of Knox that he was so marginalized and had so little to do that he fell back on running the *Chicago Daily News* out of his navy department office.

Under a newly adopted plan and division of labor, the Department of the Navy stood up the new Office of the Under Secretary of the Navy, which was to oversee procurement and production in roughly the same manner as the Office of the Assistant Secretary of War oversaw and harmonized the army's procurement and production requirements. President Roosevelt's selection of James Forrestal to head the new secretariat was both routine and something of a reach. A bond salesman before the Great War, Forrestal had volunteered for pilot training and had earned his wings as a naval aviator before being assigned to the navy department for the duration of the war. He had then become a publicist for the Democratic Party in New York State, and it was in this capacity that he had met Franklin Roosevelt. Forrestal returned to bond sales in 1923 and rose to the presidency of a leading firm in 1937. He was known as a cold man, a compulsive workaholic who neglected his family in favor of work and career. In June 1940, President Roosevelt appointed Forrestal as an administrative assistant specializing in financial matters, then as the first under secretary of the navy on August 22. For all that he was cold toward humanity at large and neglectful of his family, Forrestal's compulsive work ethic made him ideal for his navy job, which required someone who could mobilize, organize, and oversee the production of a modern navy.

Rounding out the navy's triumvirate of command for the immediate prewar period was Adm. Harold Stark. Born in Wilkes-Barre, Pennsylvania, on November 12, 1880, Stark was appointed to the U.S. Naval Academy in 1899 and commissioned in 1903. From 1907 to 1909, he served in the battleship *Minnesota*, which took part in the Atlantic Fleet's epic Great White Fleet cruise around the world. Subsequently, Stark served extensively in torpedo boats and destroyers, and he rose in 1917 to command the Asiatic Fleet's torpedo flotilla, five obsolescent, coal-burning destroyers that he led through restive seas from the Philippines to the Mediterranean to take part in Great War operations. As a reward for his leadership, Commander Stark was transferred to London to serve on the staff of U.S. Naval Forces in European Waters from November 1917 to January 1919. Following the Great War, Commander Stark served as executive officer aboard the battleships *North Dakota* and *West Virginia*, attended the Naval War College, commanded the ammunition ship *Nitro,* and served in Washington at the Bureau of Ordnance. During the late 1920s through the mid-1930s, Captain Stark served as chief of staff to the Battle Fleet's destroyer commander, aide to the secretary of the navy, and commanding officer of the battleship *West Virginia*. Between 1934 and 1937, Rear Admiral Stark was chief of the Bureau of Ordnance, commander of a cruiser division, and commander of the Battle Force's cruisers.

He was posted chief of naval operations, with the rank of admiral, on August 1, 1939. Stark's distinguished career was justification enough for the appointment, but the factors that sealed the deal were that he was both especially diplomatic in pushing the navy's line to isolationist members of Congress *and* a soul mate of Franklin Roosevelt: he deeply believed in the president's vision of a navy second to none in the world. Stark was also a truth-teller; he had no qualms about speaking truth to power, a trait Roosevelt found especially appealing in key subordinates. Put simply, Stark was the right man for the time.

Of the navy's three key leaders during the run up to the United States' active participation in World War II, Knox competently ran his newspaper,

Forrestal competently built up the navy, and Stark competently ran the navy and promoted naval expansion to the Congress. Indeed, it was Stark's idea to quickly build up the surface navy to undertake the Neutrality Patrol by recommissioning and refurbishing mothballed destroyers.

Stark's first real opportunity to speak truth to power came about because of a presidential order issued on May 7, 1940, a month after Germany invaded Norway and three days before it invaded the Netherlands and Belgium. The United States Fleet had spent most of April and the first days of May conducting a fleet exercise in Hawaiian waters. At the conclusion of the exercise, the fleet made ready to return to West Coast home ports, but the president ordered it to berth in Pearl Harbor. Admiral James Richardson, the United States Fleet commander-in-chief, shot back a protest that the base was not up to berthing, servicing, or even victualing the entire fleet. Stark fully backed Richardson's objection and took it to Roosevelt, adding that many thousands of navy families living around West Coast ports would be effectively abandoned by the precipitous move. Roosevelt replied that he needed the fleet based in Pearl Harbor at that moment in order to make Japan think twice about her aggressive intentions toward the United States and the otherwise fully engaged European Allies, whose Pacific and East Asian possessions the Japanese openly coveted. Stark survived the wrangle because it was his *job* to tell the president the truth as he saw it, but Richardson, who had been appointed only in January 1940, became a marked man. (He was relieved and replaced in February 1941 and then allowed to serve in Washington until his retirement in late 1942.) And the United States Fleet, which was eventually renamed Pacific Fleet, remained forward deployed at Pearl Harbor while it and the base around it were built up nearly to a war footing.

Chapter 18

Mobilization

The Draft

THERE WAS A PLAN detailing how to use the vastly expanded army and its Air Corps. There was a plan to equip, arm, and maintain the vastly expanded army and its Air Corps. But how were the army and its Air Corps to be vastly expanded?

As the events in western Europe in the spring and early summer of 1940 consumed every bit of thought any of the national political leaders had to offer, there was no sentiment at army headquarters for a national conscription effort to be put into place to double, then quadruple, then octuple the size of the May 1940 Regular Army, at least not until the nation was officially at war.

The White House did not yet believe it could garner enough votes in the Congress to enact draft legislation, and the army feared it did not yet have enough experienced officers or trainers to absorb and make soldiers of the millions of recruits a draft would make available. Even with a plan—indeed a commitment—to build an army of two million men by January 1, 1942 (still eighteen months away) General Marshall and the army's overworked staff departments could not conceive of undertaking an orderly flow of men and materiel quite until much more groundwork had been completed at an institutional level. There was no point in launching as politically sensitive a measure as universal draft registration, much less a call-up, quite as soon as the summer of 1940. Moreover, young men were needed to work in those sectors of the economy that would build the planes and tanks and rifles and trucks, and indeed the airfields and training camps, the army would need in due course for use by many of those same young men. And it was an article of faith that the ground army and Air Corps could grow to the one-million-man level by the October 1, 1941, target date on voluntary enlistments alone.

And then fate and patriotic duty intervened in the form of a dinner attended on May 8, 1940, by Great War veterans, mainly former Army Reserve officers, who belonged to the Military Training Camps Association. The dinner was to commemorate the twenty-fifth anniversary of the opening of the first camp (at Plattsburgh, New York) dedicated to making officers of civilian volunteers.

The spark plug for a movement, first discussed at this old-comrades' dinner, to call upon the government to institute a national draft ahead of a declaration of war, was Grenville Clark, a prominent attorney. Clark's proposal fell favorably upon the ears of several hundred influential men, including those of William J. Donovan, a powerful Wall Street lawyer who had attended the Columbia School of Law with Franklin Roosevelt; Elihu Root Jr., son and namesake of a man who had served as both secretary of state and secretary of war; Henry Stimson, himself a former secretary of state and secretary of war; and Robert Patterson, a federal judge. (This was weeks before Stimson and Patterson were called upon to head the Department of War.) Just as in the years of and the decades after the Civil War, America's leading citizens and their sons had flocked to the colors during the Great War, and their heartfelt patriotic sentiment, not to mention their influence, in the affairs of the nation was at all times active throughout their lives. Many of those attending the silver anniversary dinner agreed to use their cumulatively vast influence to back Clark's proposal to call upon the Department of War and the White House to initiate the legislative process that, if successful, would lead to the first peacetime draft in U.S. history.

Deputized on the spot to carry the gathering's proposal to General Marshall was Brig. Gen. John McAuley Palmer, a Regular Army retiree who had had an important role in developing the Draft Act of 1917 and putting together the American Expeditionary Force for the Great War. He had been subsequently tapped by Gen. John J. Pershing to become operations officer of the American armies in France. After the war, Palmer had been in on the development of the National Defense Act of 1920, and his theoretical work greatly assisted Pershing in evolving the old army general staff into the modern, streamlined organization that still existed in 1940. Along the way, Palmer had worked closely with a younger George Marshall, who considered the older man both a mentor and a friend.

Palmer met with Marshall on May 25, 1940, but the chief of staff was not able to respond in any meaningful way, because he felt obligated to hew to President Roosevelt's lead on the issue of a draft, which amounted to no expressed view Marshall knew about. But neither could Marshall leave his old friend in the lurch. He offered to send a delegation of qualified officers to meet with the Military Training Camps Association executive committee in New York City. For this he tapped three army officers from the Joint Army and Navy Selective Service Committee, which kept up the plans for execution of an order to conscript soldiers and sailors via a draft law. (One of the army officers was Maj. Lewis Hershey, whose name would become synonymous with "draft" for going on two generations.) The three were ordered to take in the views of the committee and, as things developed, help its members draft a conscription law.

Six days after General Palmer met with Marshall, the chief of staff acceded to a request for a half-hour meeting with Grenville Clark and Julius Ochs Adler, a decorated Great War veteran who was at the time general manager of his family's newspaper, the *New York Times*. The two civilians bluntly asked Marshall to recommend to the president that a draft law be enacted forthwith.

Just as bluntly, Marshall refused, on among other grounds, that the army was in no way prepared to absorb the tidal wave of recruits that a draft would carry to it.

Far from calling for a draft, Marshall on June 4 wrote a memo to Acting Secretary of War Johnson in which he asked that the Regular Army use a standing program, the Civilian Volunteer Effort, to recruit the next required bloc of 120,000 new enlisted soldiers, which would bring its strength to 400,000. Johnson later wrote to President Roosevelt to recommend the use of the Civilian Volunteer Effort in cooperation with state authorities.

In the meantime, the influential men of the Military Training Camps Association made an end run on Marshall and the uncommitted Roosevelt Administration. Spokesmen for the group met with Senator Edward Burke, a Nebraska Democrat known to favor the draft, and on the House of Representatives side, a meeting was arranged with New York Republican James Wadsworth. From this alliance emerged the Burke-Wadsworth Bill, which was introduced in the House on June 20. It found greater support than anyone had dreamed.

To help bring President Roosevelt into line, the committee asked Henry Stimson to carry its water. Nominated to become the next secretary of war but not yet confirmed, Stimson personally and forcefully prevailed upon the commander in chief to reject the Civilian Volunteer Effort proposal and support Burke-Wadsworth. For the first time sensing that a draft bill might just pass both houses of Congress, the president gave a qualified commitment. On July 8, while still only the secretary-designate, Stimson met in his Washington home with Marshall, officers from G-1 and G-3, and Grenville Clark. Stimson asked Marshall to pledge the army's support of Burke-Wadsworth on the promise that Stimson would work with Marshall on finding solutions to the problems the chief of staff had heretofore voiced as objections to a draft act. Marshall immediately agreed to Stimson's proposal; perhaps he had just been waiting on his civilian bosses all along for official guidance and their sufficient attention to the inherent problems.

The White House would make no public effort to support Burke-Wadsworth until debate in both houses of Congress generated sufficient enthusiasm among legislators and the public at large to indicate that it might well pass. A little presidential nod could not hurt the bill's chances, but in the meantime more subtle devices were used to favor the bill. One of the strongest was the July 12 testimony by Chief of Staff Marshall before the Senate committee responsible for marking up Burke-Wadsworth prior to a final vote. Marshall directly stated that he supported a draft and, on top of that, favored legislation that would allow the president to call National Guard units to active duty for an entire year of rigorous training.

The success of the Burke-Wadsworth bill and the National Guard's call to federal service would bring immense numbers of untrained and semitrained men into the army fold, but that in no way mitigated Marshall's stated objections. How was the army to absorb so many men in so short a time? The Regular

Army had on its active roll nine nominal infantry divisions, of which just five were actual divisions, but not even one of them was functionally ready to enter combat. The National Guard's main strength was eighteen square infantry divisions, perhaps a little less nominal but nonetheless useless for purposes of fighting a war. There were also two absolutely nominal armored divisions, just activated.

The goal was to raise a functional two-million-man army in eighteen months. The two million men implied two million trained and conditioned men. It also implied two million men armed and equipped to do battle against at least one well-trained, well-equipped, and experienced Axis army on a battle-field far from home, with all that getting an army there and maintaining and supporting that army entailed. If *all* those things could not be done in eighteen months, then the two million men called to the colors in that period would be just that: two million men, and no more.

Here is why a draft flew in the face of everything George Marshall knew and felt and hoped as he read and rode the political winds of the early summer of 1940, and as he ultimately bowed to them. In the first place, the bulk of Marshall's experience in war was his role as chief trainer of the 1st Infantry Division in 1917 and 1918. The Draft Act of 1917 had come up with enough men to quickly fill out that twenty-five-thousand-man organization before it shipped over to France, but it had not allowed sufficient time to fully equip the division, nor to adequately train it. Thus the bulk of the division's—and Marshall's—time in France was devoted to training and equipping rather than to combat. It took long months to align American industrial output with wartime produc-tion requirements, and one reason for the long training cycle was that the minuscule pre–Great War army had fewer combat-experienced trainers than might be expected in light of the various expeditions in which it had partici-pated in the two decades prior to its entry into combat in France. The flow of materiel caught up with the needs of the troops in France, and then the war had quickly blooded a generation of American soldiers. But the two decades between 1919 and 1940 had once again left a shadow army bereft of modern weapons and equipment and with very few combat-experienced officers and noncommissioned officers who, over the years, had had few opportunities to train or be trained, so complete had been the functional destruction of the army's interwar combat arms. But even such training as had been administered was not administered to enough men to begin to match the needs of fielding a battle-ready combat force of up to 1.5 million men. Not even close.

Marshall knew the scope of the problem, and he had a solution. His idea was the same one he applied to building up weapons and materiel, to grow the army in orderly, achievable stages: First, build up three to five adequately trained, conditioned infantry divisions that were capable of being sent out into the Western Hemisphere to protect American interests there. Then draw intel-ligent, hardened officers and noncommissioned officers from these divisions—but not so many as to cripple them—to serve as cadres and trainers for three or more additional infantry divisions that could enter a war in progress, protect other locations in the hemisphere, stand as a reserve fire brigade, *and* serve as a manpower pool from which sufficient intelligent, hardened officers and noncommissioned officers could be drawn to train yet more divisions. And so forth. If there was no emergency requiring a deployment of any of the full-strength ready divisions, so much the better, because the process would go faster. With embellishments and following several bouts of hiccups, this was indeed the basic concept for what came to be known as the "division-making machine" that saw eighty-nine U.S. Army combat divisions into battle the world around in the period 1942–1945.

The availability of many millions of potential draftees, and the implied obligation to use them soonest, nearly destroyed the deliberate nature of the army's plan for growth during and beyond the eighteen-month period set aside to build a two-million-man army. And the helpful agreement to call up eighteen undertrained and undermanned National Guard divisions, with their often questionable local leaders in command of the troops, was at best a mixed blessing. On the negative side, doing so would add to the pressures on the army to house, victual, and train masses of troops, as well as lead them with an insufficient army-wide core of qualified officers and noncommissioned officers. On the positive side, the National Guard was in the business of training recruits and thus came complete with large numbers of experienced and effective trainers, of whom the most senior were often combat veterans. And the average National Guard division, though deficient in numbers, was often rich in equipment suitable for the training mission; many National Guard units, though not in any way equipped to undertake maneuver warfare in mid-1940 terms, were better equipped than almost any of the Regular Army divisions of mid-1940.

Besides, there was no choice. The nation wanted to be drafted, it wanted a protective mobilization, and it pretty much demanded both in the wake of the unbelievably rapid utter defeat of two European superpowers in May and June 1940. So, if there was no choice, what was an undermanned professional army to do to transform itself from a temporarily overmanned, under-led, and under-equipped mob into an adequately manned, adequately led, and adequately equipped, professionalized army capable of bearing any burden under any conditions on any given battlefield the world around?

First and foremost, if there was to be a draft, and if the Guard was to be called up, best get the dual projects going while it was warm enough throughout the nation to immediately and vigorously train and condition officers and men alike. Suddenly, every clement day counted. On top of that, each day congressional approval was delayed saw a speculative rise throughout the nation in the cost of the building materials that would be required to house and serve a vastly expanded army. Early congressional approval became increasingly critical as each day passed. But it was not to be.

❈

Delays

There was agreement. The chief of staff, the secretary of war-designate, the president, a large part of the public, and a large part of the Congress all wanted to proceed with the draft law. Yet the draft law lingered in a very long congressional gestation period.

Marshall, who had a wonderful relationship with the members of the congressional committees to which he reported, used emphatic terms in favor of a draft—and a separate National Guard call-up—when he testified before a Senate panel on July 12, and again somewhat later before the House Committee on Military Affairs. He emphasized at both hearings that the army felt an urgent need to get fully manned, fully equipped, and fully supported divisions ready to go to war in the hemisphere to counter any moves there by the fantastically war-ready German military. He also revealed that the actual issue regarding his desire to call up the National Guard had to do with the possible (some would say likely) dispatch of three to five Regular Army divisions to foreign shores. The plan at first was to call up four guard divisions to replace those Regular Army ready divisions as units to be made ready, but that had morphed into a plan to call up the entire Guard (which included many independent units and might yield eighteen unattached infantry regiments—enough for six new divisions—once its divisions were triangularized).

But the Congress dithered, not just on the draft and Guard issues, but on funding issues having to do with the expansion and creation of military camps and bases as well as road improvement around them, plus a large web of related issues. It took until August 27 for the Congress to pass a joint resolution authorizing the federalization of the National Guard and Army Reserve components. It was signed into law the same day, and the wheels immediately started turning. On Saturday, August 30, the first sixty thousand National Guardsmen were called to national service.

Nearly three weeks ensued before the Congress acted on the Selective Training and Service Act. The president signed it into law the day it was passed, September 16. Exactly a month later, October 16, records indicated that sixteen million men had so far registered for the draft, which made those who were physically and mentally fit available to the army and the navy, as needed. The first drawing for the draft, which was set up as a lottery, took place that day, October 16, but the actual swearing in of the first draftees would take place after they had been given thirty days to put their affairs in order, November 15, 1940.

In the case of the army, and taken together, the federalization of the National Guard and the draft would in a very short term provide the means to bolster the thin National Guard divisions and independent units from the national pool of draftees. This was another good reason to call up the entire Guard: to provide each unit with an equitable distribution of the entire draft pool that, after a sufficient interval for basic training and equipping, would yield eighteen more battle-ready infantry divisions. Trained draftees who would be assigned to Guard units (best say *former* Guard units) would benefit from long-standing structure and esprit, for some of these units traced lineage back to the Revolutionary War and many nineteenth-century wars. The dilution of a unit's hometown flavor would be difficult for many guardsmen to bear, but it would quickly become a given as reality and the new guys settled in.

As to ancillary requirements such as encampments and roads, the president partially bridged the gap left by the dawdling Congress when he provided $29.5 million out of his personal contingency fund while the weather was still reliably good enough to build them, but that only went so far. (Marshall spent nearly the entire amount on improving just one base, Fort Dix, New Jersey, which he later volunteered was an error). The delays in the Congress caused enormous dislocations in what was to have been an orderly call to arms. The tense world situation did not become less tense as the Congress dawdled. And the reasons for calling up the Guard and instituting the draft, as articulated in June, were no less dire in August and September, when the authorizations were finally enacted, or later still, when the troops began to arrive from home.

The Order of Things

As civilians were debating and rationalizing all the draft and National Guard issues, the army concentrated on working with the putative combat formations it had on hand. Such as it was, the 1st Division (renamed 1st Infantry Division in early 1942 along with all the other infantry divisions) resided at its permanent home, Fort Hamilton, New York. The 2d Division was based at Fort Sam Houston, Texas. The 3d Division was based at Fort Lewis, Washington. The 5th Division, activated at Fort McClellan, Alabama, in October 1939, was based at Fort Benning, Georgia, by April 1940. And the 6th Division, also activated in October 1939, was based at Fort Snelling, Minnesota, by June 1940. Two other old-line divisions were on the army roster long before the period of expansion: the Hawaiian Division was headquartered at Schofield Barracks, Oahu; and the Philippine Division, composed of Regular Army and Philippine Scout units (mainly the latter), was headquartered at Fort McKinley, Luzon. All of these Regular Army divisions were understrength by a wide margin, but all had been triangularized and were undergoing training as triangular commands based on the modern tactics developed at The Infantry School during Lt. Col. George Marshall's tenure.

While awaiting the Congress's pleasure regarding the draft and the National Guard, the army got ahead of the game by reactivating headquarters and templates for four additional Regular Army divisions: the 4th was activated at Fort Benning, Georgia, on June 1, 1940; and the 7th, 8th, and 9th divisions were all activated on July 1 at Fort Ord, California; Camp Jackson, South Carolina; and Fort Bragg, North Carolina, respectively. On August 1, the new 4th Division was redesignated 4th Division (Motorized) and became the focus of experimentation along those lines. (On July 15, 1940, the army also activated the 1st and 2d Armored divisions, of which more will be written later.)

The nine numbered infantry divisions were unequally manned and at no time during this period a great deal more than meager representations of their future selves, waiting to be filled up with officers, troops, weapons, and all manner of gear. But they were complete from a table-of-organization point of view, in that all the combat regiments and battalions were represented by real officers and troops in training mode, if not very many of them. The old-line 1st, 2d, and 3d divisions had had the longest to prepare, and were thus closest to being ready to go. They got the first cut as new everything became available, because they were the army's ready force, so to speak.

As planning for the Guard call-up proceeded, it was quickly and intuitively understood that there was no way the army infrastructure could handle the simultaneous call-up of eighteen divisions at one time. The call to federal service, when it came, was thus handled over a period from mid-September 1940 to the first few days of March 1941. The order of mobilization depended on the availability of basing and the readiness of the divisions to be called up. The first four National Guard divisions—30th, 41st, 44th, and 45th—were activated on September 16. (See Appendix A for details about origin, basing, and other data on all U.S. Army divisions activated by November 30, 1941.)

Training the 1940 Army

Army General Headquarters (GHQ) was established on July 26, 1940, as the nucleus of a command structure that would serve the chief of staff's needs in the event he directly commanded an expeditionary force in its overseas deployment. This was the holdover of an idea long espoused by General Pershing and arising from his experience in France in 1917 and 1918. The 1940 action reflected the notion that one American field army or army group would be dispatched to one foreign theater. It was a concept that, for a time, was consonant with the Europe-first grand strategy of the United States. The central idea was that the army chief of staff would command the fighting army.

Selected by Marshall to command GHQ with title of chief of staff, GHQ, was Brig. Gen. Lesley McNair, a brilliant artilleryman whose special forte was training. As a major, he had served with Marshall in the 1st Infantry Division in France and had followed Marshall to AEF headquarters, where he became principal staff officer for artillery with the temporary rank of brigadier general.

The ascension of a man widely regarded for his training skills was reflective of the idea that GHQ needed to first train the army it was to oversee in battle. This led to the assumption by GHQ, as soon as it was activated, of prime responsibility for the ground army's training program and of McNair as the ground army's trainer-in-chief.

GHQ immediately faced the daunting task of overseeing the definitive training for an immense conscript army and the entire National Guard, all at once. And for all that GHQ had immense responsibilities, its officer complement at the outset was merely seven. By June 1941, only twenty-three officers had been assigned. Yet, under McNair's able hand, GHQ performed exactly as Marshall desired.

The fundamental objective of American military training was, through successive training steps, to integrate the individual soldier into his squad, the squad into the platoon, the platoon into the company, and on up to the field army level by way of battalion, regiment, division, and corps. Every level of command was ultimately undertaken by an officer or noncommissioned officer who had demonstrated his aptitude for commanding or overseeing every level of the organization, from the squad on up to his current level of responsibility. In 1940, the army hewed strongly to this philosophy because both Marshall and McNair had had to work especially hard to overcome a long army tradition of hasty, incomplete training while they served in France in 1917.

Obstacles to Marshall's wishes and McNair's effort vis-à-vis training the army of 1940 were: the acute shortage of weapons, starting with rifles and ending in tanks and adequate 1940-era artillery; insufficient numbers of experienced trainers; and a fundamental uncertainty as to whether the best and brightest officers and noncommissioned officers in the standing divisions ought to be transferred to training duties or left in the divisions in the event they were called to combat in the near term.

When nearly overwhelmed by the influx of draftees and undertrained (or untrained) National Guardsmen, McNair fought every attempt to speed up the process, to introduce shortcuts, to do anything that might harm the individual soldier's ability to fully contribute to victory and, indeed, to inhibit his chances of survival. In essence, McNair insisted upon every new soldier's training in all the basics of soldiering ("basic training") ahead of his training in any specialty, from rifleman to antitank gunner to cook to railway gandy dancer. At the level of units and commands, none would advance to their own types of specialized training—amphibious or combined-arms exercises—until it had mastered the most basic sort of unit operations, beginning with marching in step and culminating in days-long field exercises, including night holding attacks, against other units and commands.

A very good reason for calling up the entire National Guard more or less at the front end of the army's expansion cycle was so the Regular Army could gain access to the Guard's many seasoned trainers as well as to a very large store of weapons that was also thus federalized and could be used in training up the Guard itself as well as training the early blocs of draftees.

The National Guard call-up alone overshot by several hundred thousand the army's plan to grow to four hundred thousand men during the first phase of the 1940–1942 expansion program. There was no way to reconcile the planning numbers with the actual numbers; there was only pressure to deal with the real numbers. Meanwhile, after much debate, the Congress passed out appropriations bills commensurate with an interim strength of five hundred thousand, which the army was thus obligated to adopt as its first-phase target. By December 31, 1940, however, the actual strength of the army was a shade under 621,000 men, of which 68.7 percent were Regular Army, 25 percent were National Guard, 3.6 percent (all officers) were Army Reserve, and only 2.7 percent (about 16,700) were draftees. (The all-officer Army Reserve bloc amounted to 46.5 percent of all army officers on active duty on December 31.) By June 30, 1941, the army would be awash in draftees, who by then amounted to 44.6 percent (or 607,000) of the 1,361,462 enlisted troops on active duty.

Nearly everyone in the army in 1940 had to be trained or retrained to 1940 standards on 1940 equipment for service in 1940 unit organizations preparing to take part in a 1940 war of mobility. This included generals, sergeants major, and raw recruits alike. And it included the trainers themselves. The complexity of the exercise cannot be overdescribed. But the army had long had a way to deal with complexity. Each complex problem was routinely broken down to its irreducible components, analyzed, discussed, reanalyzed, put to trial action, made as efficient and routine as possible, and reconstructed in the form of a standard operating procedure that was then reduced to a multistep manualized cycle of discrete actions. As time passed, actual experience triggered suggestions from any and all for changes that were serially analyzed, tested, and, if accepted, phased into the standard cycle of steps. The whole operation hinged on one central question: How will we train the stupidest, least coordinated recruit we can allow into the training cycle? If that recruit is able to pass through the system to become an effective soldier, then anyone smarter or better coordinated will, too—more or less. Anyone who can't make it through basic training can only be a danger to himself, his comrades, and by extension to the entire war effort. Does anyone need that spelled out?

More Roosting Chickens

If the army's April maneuvers had been eye-opening and alarming for the highest-ranking soldiers in the nation, the follow-on maneuvers conducted at the field army level in the summer gave the nation as a whole an alarming inkling as to how far its army had to go before even "defense" became a viable function.

On the positive side, the maneuvers incorporated the efforts of ninety thousand officers and men, the largest assembly of U.S. Army troops in two decades. Many of these troops were members of National Guard divisions not yet federalized but subject to federally overseen annual training. All of the units engaged in the maneuvers were understrength, and they were perceived as such by a public attuned to German battlefield successes in Poland and western Europe. This relatively unschooled but keenly interested public knew that the Guard divisions had a paper structure for twenty-two thousand troops, and it learned that the average Guard division engaged in the maneuvers numbered just over ten thousand troops. It also knew that devices designated "cannon" were iron pipes, and that aircraft designated "bomber" were often Air National Guard light observation planes of obsolete design. It learned that only about one-quarter of the participating riflemen were armed with actual rifles.

The practiced eyes of professional soldiers charged with evaluating the maneuvers saw once again the pronounced material deficiencies pointed up in the April maneuvers—there had been no time to fix them—but they also noted deficiencies in nearly all the *qualities* a modern army needed to mount even a successful defensive effort, much less a successful offense.

Called into question were levels of expertise and professionalism in areas such as reconnaissance, communication, sanitation, and, most chilling, leadership itself. The execution of small-unit tactics fell short of expectations, not to mention needs; as did the ability of the troops to maintain contact with enemy forces; as did the collection, dissemination, and use of front-line intelligence; and so forth.

This was stunning stuff. And this time, word of the U.S. Army's demonstrated deficiencies spread far and wide. So far and wide, in fact, that it was the subject of commentary in the leading Soviet military newspaper.

Rather than look upon the demonstrated deficiencies as proof the sky was falling, the clear-headed professionals at the army's helm agreed that the maneuvers presented a baseline from which they could extrapolate proof of real progress out of future maneuvers. They saw in the deficiencies in equipment proof positive that their many, many requests for modern weapons and equipment was fully justified, and they noted that new designs and updated specifications were being forwarded to federal arsenals and civilian factories.

They saw in deficiencies in lower-level leadership vindication for holding the line on training cycles that went slowly but produced thoroughly professional outcomes. They understood that new weapons and types of weapons would require that men who had undergone painstaking training on old systems be painstakingly retrained on the new systems. But they scored that to the age-old friction between needs for war now versus war in the future.

In the few months between the summer maneuvers and the first phase of the National Guard call to federal service, those in charge of training polished and implemented plans to assure that each Guard unit was greeted upon arrival at a training base by seasoned trainers possessing a definitive training plan and the best training courses and equipment the army could then provide. Each training cadre was instilled with esprit for the mission, which it was expected to instill on its trainees.

Lessons learned were constantly the source of new training goals and techniques. For example, as soon as the first four Guard divisions began their training, feedback from the camps caused General McNair to recommend that the remaining fourteen National Guard division staffs be called up ahead of their troops for remedial training—that deficiencies were as prevalent at the top as they were at the bottom. In due course, as growth of the ground army proceeded beyond the National Guard call-up, GHQ designed a training program for any newly assembled divisional staff of at least a month's duration before that staff got down to the business of even planning the functional activation of the new division. Moreover, the new division staffs were to be fully manned ahead of definitive advance training. (In due course, all the same procedures applied to the staffs of regiments and even battalions prior to functional activation. Eventually, even new corps headquarters underwent similar advance activation and training.)

Always in that early phase there was the constant backwash of too little equipment and not enough weapons for too many men. But shortfalls were made up as and when they could be. Troops could be and often were retrained or had their training upgraded. More and more experienced trainers emerged from the process, and the sense of the whole immense enterprise was always one of moving forward.

Chapter 19

Armor

The Origins of the Armor Force

THE TANK WAS INVENTED by the British in the middle of the Great War solely as a means for crossing from their trenchline to a German trenchline in the face of the sort of heavy defensive fires that had been amply proven as fatal to infantrymen in the same setting. There was no other use contemplated for tanks; they were simply armored battering rams designed to advance at walking speed—two or three miles per hour—while absorbing all manner of fire that infantry and even some artillery could put out. They could smash through barbed-wire barriers, so infantrymen advancing in their shadows could walk across that sort of barrier. The larger tanks were festooned with large cannon that could blow up barriers and defensive positions, and their several machine guns made them moving pillboxes that were more or less impervious to enemy machine guns.

Tanks, as conceived, designed, and built, supported advancing infantry. Nothing more. There were large tanks and small tanks, but it all came down to the same thing. When the Germans got into the game, there were even tanks to fight other tanks, but they were sent into battle within the context of trench warfare.

At the end of the Great War, the U.S. Army had manufactured under license 952 French-designed Renault M1917 (FT 17) six-ton light tanks and 100 British-designed Mark VIII 40-ton heavy tanks. Except for a small number of virtually hand-crafted experimental models, the United States manufactured no tanks, per se, from 1920 through the early 1930s. The experimental models more or less kept pace with tanks that were designed abroad, but, unlike military aircraft, there was no commercial market for tanks, so no cross-pollination took place. Indeed, the heavy, rugged engines required to impel a heavily armed and armored vehicle forward over rough terrain did not exist in industry, so it was difficult to even experiment with fully armored yet reasonably speedy designs that might remotely have a chance of going into full-scale production.

The Americans studied tanks, but inasmuch as the lumbering tanks had not been of much use during the final stage of the Great War, when a highly mobile infantry army was employed mainly to achieve breakthroughs followed by long, swift pursuits of fleeing German troops, American infantry officers became highly dismissive of tanks, which could not keep up with marching road-bound infantry. A cavalryman who had commanded the AEF's tank center, then a tank brigade, in France, George Patton Jr., was all for looking into further development of the fighting system. But Patton initially found very few fellow devotees in the cavalry branch, and he was given jobs far from the spheres in which he could further the creation of a tank force or even experiment with tank tactics. One professional officer who shared Patton's enthusiasm was a brilliant 1915 West Point graduate named Dwight Eisenhower, an infantryman who had been exposed to tanks when he was held back in the United States to train tank crews. The two hooked up early on and from time to time conspired to push for an armored corps. They were polar opposites temperamentally, but both had genius-level minds and shared a passion for tanks. They became fast friends despite a five-year difference in age, disparate ranks, and a world of breeding.

Under the National Defense Act of 1920, the wartime Tank Corps was disbanded, cavalrymen were returned to the cavalry, and the tanks were placed in the hands of the infantry. *All* of the army's tanks were formed into a "brigade" assigned to The Infantry School at Fort Benning, Georgia, and thus it became all but impossible for any specifically *armor* developments to take place.

Conversely, a few thinkers in the cavalry branch had interest in poking around the doctrinal edges of mechanized warfare, but the assignment of all the tanks to The Infantry School was the general staff's way of preventing that. So cavalrymen went ahead with experimental "combat cars," small, lightly armored vehicles on treads that looked and acted remarkably like light tanks armed with several machine guns.

One of the cavalrymen credited with knowing the most and thinking the best about tanks was Adna Chaffee Jr. A lieutenant colonel serving on the general staff in 1930, Chaffee succinctly summarized the roles of tanks as "first to assist the infantry of the combat divisions by directly preceding them and neutralizing the organized resistance in the main battle, [and] to use the light tank as the backbone itself of a force. . . . Along these lines may develop a great part of the highly mobile combat troops of the next war."

In 1931, the cavalry was authorized to stand up the Mechanized Force—one experimental mechanized cavalry "regiment," in reality a squadron of tracked combat cars and a squadron of wheeled armored cars and unarmored wheeled scout cars. The following year, the Mechanized Force was expanded to one mechanized "brigade," the 7th, consisting of the mechanized cavalry regiment supported by two light artillery batteries. Most cavalrymen of the day turned up their noses at any notion that steel would, could, or should replace horse flesh, but a small, growing, and fairly influential minority leaned toward the use of fully tracked combat cars in the same roles cavalry traditionally filled: reconnaissance; raids on supply lines and against headquarters; screening the movements of large, friendly formations; and pursuit of a broken enemy. Traditional horse cavalry had played almost no significant role in France during the

Great War, and the cavalry branches of most western armies clearly foresaw a day when they would be abolished from the battlefield, so playing with combat cars wasn't idle work. What this group of upstarts had in mind to begin with was the retention of traditional cavalry roles accompanied by a move from horses to full mechanization. They thus were at odds with the larger part of the cavalry community *and* the infantry's advocates for an infantry-controlled tank force that would move across future battlefields at the speed of infantry (as the gods of war intended).

Where the mechanization-minded cavalrymen saw resurgence of the cavalry in dashing armored sweeps deep into enemy territory, the infantry continued to see tanks as a plodding aid to infantry's getting from here to there under fire. There was in fact a place for both jobs on a modern battlefield, but, except for a sprinkling of visionary cavalrymen and infantrymen, neither branch was in the mood to give in to the other, and they certainly weren't about to put their heads together. So, while the combat-car enthusiasts in the cavalry toiled on in isolation, the infantry merely used its aging Great War tanks as props in the training of infantry officers, until these antiques ran out of spare parts and stopped running altogether. The only positive development for some years was the addition in 1936 of a second mechanized "regiment" to the 7th Cavalry Brigade.

The Cavalry's Search for Relevance

After September 1939, there was no longer any reason to believe that horse cavalry, no matter how adapted to a modern role it might become, had any place on a modern battlefield. (Only the Soviet Union was to make extensive use of cavalry in World War II.) Cavalry had played no relevant role as the Great War in western Europe matured into a static set piece, and most western European cavalry organizations were disbanded to provide fillers for the attritional infantry war that dominated. Tank warfare in Poland in 1939 and western Europe in 1940 left no doubt that playing at cavalry combat on the modern battlefield was a suicide pact between horse and rider. It only remained to be seen if western cavalrymen would find a useful role for themselves, without their beloved horses.

The cavalry officer who had the greatest influence on the U.S. Cavalry modernists remained Adna Chaffee Jr., son and namesake of a cavalry general who had retired with three stars and himself a 1906 West Point graduate who loved horses and was a world-class equestrian. Chaffee served as a staff officer in France during the Great War and rose to temporary rank of colonel before coming home to resume his captaincy. He was an instructor at the Command and General Staff School and was appointed G-3 of the 1st Cavalry Division in 1921 with rank of major, attended the Army War College, and commanded a cavalry squadron from 1925 to 1927. He then served on the War Department General Staff, where he had a hand in developing army doctrine for mechanized and armored warfare (the Mechanization Study of 1928), and as head of the troop-training section. Ranked lieutenant colonel and considered a mechanization visionary, Chaffee next served as executive officer of the newly transformed 1st Cavalry Regiment (Mechanized). He returned to the War Department in 1934 to serve as chief of the budget and legislative planning staff and then went back to Fort Knox in 1938 to command the 1st Cavalry (Mechanized). Promoted to brigadier general in November 1938, Chaffee moved up to command the 7th Cavalry Brigade, which he led in various maneuvers of the period.

Chaffee had been marked as future general quite early in his service, and he served notably in all the important assignments that marked his career. Along the way he became the cavalry's visionary in chief. Early on Chaffee saw that the cavalry needed to move from horses' hooves to tracks and wheels, and he made the case at every opportunity, marking himself as a bore in some circles and a prophet in others. Among his favorite rants: "Mobility is needed to carry the war home, to reach the decision, to conquer. Mobility means live men arriving and establishing themselves in possession of the military objectives. To live and move quickly against the gun requires protection. Armor gives protection in movement. The gasoline engine moves armor. And so we come to what is called mechanization." And: "The tank is not a new weapon; the Roman legionnaire with his shield, the armored elephants of Hannibal . . . were in reality tanks using the best motive power then available."

It can be argued that German combined-arms blitzkrieg doctrine, which married fast tanks and low-flying tactical aircraft at the forwardmost fighting front, arose from the 1931 exposure of an influential German army officer to lectures by Lieutenant Colonel Chaffee and like-minded American cavalrymen.

Chaffee's vision, first espoused as a complete doctrine in 1927, was holistic; it foresaw the organization of a cavalry mechanized division all the way up from tank platoon to division, the interplay of swift tanks and armored infantry, and the interplay of both with observation (but not attack) aircraft, all along the forwardmost line of battle. He foresaw the creation within each cavalry mechanized division of two operational task force headquarters (combat commands in the later armored divisions), to which squadrons (cavalry battalions) and troops (cavalry companies) could be added and removed as the situation warranted. He foresaw the use of fast and unfettered mechanized cavalry as both the breakthrough force (which horse cavalry had rarely ever been) and the pursuit force (which was a traditional horse cavalry role). He saw cavalry transformed by high-powered engines and armored skins—speeded up and impervious to many forms of gunfire—in other traditional horse cavalry roles: in reconnaissance ahead of the slower infantry army, and as slashing raiders against enemy lines of supply and rear installations. He saw mechanized cavalry so swift and maneuverable that it could avoid enemy tanks and, indeed, enemy troop concentrations it could not overwhelm.

The Armored Force

After the main body of American cavalrymen had spurned a horseless modern role long enough, mechanization and armor advocates turned their backs on that faction, closed it off, and fought their own battles. Coming up on army maneuvers in April 1940, the army G-3, Brig. Gen. Frank Andrews (the ousted and demoted GHQ Air Corps commander, who had been rescued from exile by an admiring George Marshall), ordered the chief of the cavalry branch to transfer troops from a horse regiment to the 7th Cavalry Brigade. The cavalry chief flat-out refused, and that led Andrews to order the creation of a provisional tank brigade to be formed out of the 7th Cavalry Brigade (Mechanized) and the 6th Infantry Regiment. During the second phase of the maneuvers, the provisional tank brigade was bolstered with The Infantry School's tank brigade. As such, this powerful, large formation so thoroughly defeated the 1st Cavalry Division as to humiliate it. An after-action conference was chaired on May 25, 1940, by Andrews and attended solely by infantry and cavalry officers who favored the adoption of horseless armor commands, including General Chaffee and Colonel Patton. The gathering was unanimous in recommending the creation of an armored force separate from the cavalry branch. Shortly, Andrews conferred with Chief of Staff Marshall, and the die was cast. Mechanized cavalry units were stripped from the cavalry branch, and infantry tank units were stripped from the infantry branch. Notwithstanding negative comments from the chiefs of infantry and cavalry, the plan moved forward with alacrity.

The Armored Force was created to activate two experimental armored divisions that happened to be organized pretty much along the lines Adna Chaffee had been advocating for years and had actually set down in 1939, but with the addition of an infantry regiment and a medium tank regiment per division. The Armored Force itself was stood up with Chaffee as branch chief on July 10, 1940. It was composed initially of the I Armored Corps headquarters at Fort Knox, Kentucky; the 1st and 2d Armored divisions; and a GHQ Reserve tank unit, the 70th Tank Battalion (Medium), at Fort Meade, Maryland. All these units shifted assets and personnel among themselves to make like units more or less alike.

On July 15, 1940, 1st Armored Division was activated at Fort Knox, Kentucky, and the 2d Armored Division was activated at Fort Benning, Georgia. Besides being the places at which mechanized and tank units had long been based, there is something symbolic, a setting of tone, a statement of larger intent, in the selection of the two stations, which were the home bases of the cavalry and the infantry branches, respectively. In October 1940, Chaffee was promoted major general, given command of I Armored Corps, and retained as chief of the Armored Force. He is still referred to as the "father of the armored force."

Chaffee turned out to be wrong about one vital detail. For most of his tenure as mechanization visionary in chief, emphasis in tank development had been on the tracked combat car, which was in fact another name for light tank (indeed, the M1 combat car was redesignated the M2 tank). Chaffee gave in to the infantry's vision of a tank force whose mission it was to slow down to the speed of infantry, as the first, inherently slow tanks had been forced to do in France.

He was willing to concede a need for tanks to maneuver alongside infantry, but he wanted none but speedy light tanks in his armored divisions. The line between the light, fast-maneuver tank and the heavier, slower, medium tank was the capability of internal combustion engines during most of the interwar years. There was no engine durable or powerful enough to move a heavy tank fast enough to keep up with the light tanks that formed the backbone of the 1940 armored division. To be a force capable of the "slashing," cavalry-like attack contemplated by the mechanization school of thought, the Armored Force had to embrace light tanks, which were capable of moving across open terrain at twenty-five miles per hour. The armor and total weight of a medium tank could not be impelled across any terrain, or even along roads, faster than about sixteen miles per hour, much more than the speed of marching men yet much slower than the speed of light tanks. But this was all moot in 1940. The army had not yet acquired a decent medium tank, and the obsolete and obsolescent models it did have were in short supply and thus assigned mainly to the armored divisions. In the near term, if the infantry needed tanks, it got light tanks. All this made it easy for Chaffee to concede the point to the infantry, just as long as doing so did not dent the schedule for bringing sufficient light tanks into the first two and succeeding armored divisions.

That an infantry regiment and a medium tank regiment were forced on the new armored division formation was the army's way of getting the armor enthusiasts to take notice of the reality of battle. As fast and as dashing and slashing as tanks alone could move across a battlefield, it was necessary to hold some former enemy ground for there to be a lasting point to the exercise. Following maneuvers in 1939, Chaffee conceded the issue of what he called the "holding power" of infantry units attached to armored commands. Also, face it, tanks alone, especially light tanks alone, must go around heavily defended terrain, woods, fortifications, fortified towns, or other tank-resistant obstacles, but infantry, especially infantry supported by powerful enough and highly mobile tank guns, is required to comb or reduce such impediments to tanks. That means infantry must be stitched into an armor formation. And infantry requires heavier tanks with heavier guns than light tanks could bring to bear on heavy fortifications. It also requires mobile infantry, which at the time was to say motorized infantry. So when the 1st Armored Division was activated, the 6th Infantry Regiment was retained as the 6th Infantry Regiment (Armored), and it became the test bed for the kind of motorization and organization that would best serve an armored division. Likewise, and with the same mission, the 41st Infantry Regiment (Armored) was activated at Fort Benning and assigned to the 2d Armored Division.

In sum, after the various points were demonstrated in maneuvers in 1939 and 1940, and in early reports concerning German medium tanks in action in France, Chaffee and his acolytes fully accepted that there was a place for medium tanks and fast-moving infantry units in the armored divisions. As a result, an infantry regiment was included in the 1st and 2d Armored divisions when they were activated up in July 1940, and specifications for one medium tank regiment per armored division were set forth in August.

Light versus Medium

Where Chaffee and his armor people went wrong was in the armament any light tank of the day was able to bring to bear on the modern battlefield. The lightly armored light tank was able to convey itself into high-speed, miles-eating battle only if it was very lightly armed with the army's standard antitank gun of the day, the puny 37mm. But this is understandable. As the American armored divisions were being created on paper in the wake of the German assault on Poland, a reality check would have revealed that the dominant German tank of September 1939 was the 7.2-ton, twenty-five-mile-per-hour Panzer II light tank, equipped with a 20mm main gun. Most of the U.S. Army's four-hundred-odd 11.6-ton, thirty-six-mile-per-hour M2 light tanks (a 1935 design) were equipped only with machine guns, but a small number of M2A1 variants were equipped with a 37mm main gun. All the M2 variants were better armored and speedier than the Panzer II, though the Panzer II featured thicker frontal armor.

As the 1st and 2d Armored divisions were being formed, the invasion of the Low Countries and the fall of France was spearheaded by large numbers of the thoroughly modern Panzer III, a medium tank that weighed in at twenty-two tons and got up to speeds between twelve miles per hour off the road and twenty-five miles per hour on the road. Most of the Panzer IIIs deployed in France were equipped with 37mm main guns. Thus, M2A1s and Panzer IIIs were equipped with equally powerful main guns, but the Panzer III was better armored (and its turret had been built to accommodate a 50mm main gun).

The American M2 light tank series was replaced before American armor went up against German armor, but M2A1s were deployed in the Philippines and by the Marine Corps at Guadalcanal. In 1940 and 1941, M2s adequately served I Armored Corps as a means to test tactics and tactical formations. Nevertheless, the upshot is that the American armor force foreseen by Chaffee and his fellows had fallen behind the German technological curve before it was fully activated. For all that, the follow-on M3 series of light tanks, which did see action against the Germans, was also armed with 37mm main guns.

With respect to medium tanks, the Germans for the first time fielded in France the Panzer IV, designed as a medium infantry-support tank and armed with a 75mm main gun. While the relatively few Panzer IVs deployed in France could not badly hurt the heaviest French and British tanks, they overwhelmed any light tank they encountered in relatively few tank-versus-tank confrontations. Faced with the reality of German tanks that clearly outclassed American tanks, General Chaffee had the good grace to step down from his light tank high horse and graciously accept the inevitable solution to the problem.

In mid-1940, the U.S. Army had only sixty outmoded medium tanks in hand. In development was the lightly armored M2 medium tank, which was to be armed with a 37mm gun. This was clearly a nonstarter. Retaining the basic chassis design and most of its parts, the M2 was transformed into a hybrid, a medium tank dubbed M3 that was equipped with a turret-mounted 37mm gun as well as a hull-mounted sponson equipped with a low-velocity 75mm gun. The stumbling block to building a "normal" medium tank was that neither the army nor industry could yet produce a 360-degree turret large enough and inherently strong enough to accommodate the forces generated when even a medium-velocity 75mm gun was fired. The 10.5-foot-tall M3 medium tank was the worst of all worlds—a high-profile target that had to swivel on its tracks while exposing its hull in order to bring its main gun to bear. But it was technologically achievable in the short interval before the United States might be drawn into the wars in Europe and Asia. Even as the M3 medium tank was tested, revised, and first produced, the follow-on design for its successor, the M4, went ahead at full speed. The M4, only nine feet tall, was to field a more powerful 75mm low-velocity main gun in a 360-degree turret. In any event, the first M3 medium tank pilot model was not even built until March 1941, and the first M4 pilot did not appear until September 1941.

If the 1st and 2d Armored divisions went to war against Germany in their mid-1940 configuration with their mid-1940 equipment, they were going to be defeated. But they provided hope for the future.

Chapter 20

The Cousins

A Shadow Alliance

ON SEPTEMBER 11, 1939, President Roosevelt opened what was to become a voluminous personal correspondence with Winston Churchill, who had just been appointed first lord of the Admiralty, a position Churchill had held during the Great War:

> Dear Churchill:
> It is because you and I occupied similar positions in the world war that I want you to know how glad I am that you are back in the Admiralty. Your problems are, I realize, complicated by new factors but the essential is not different. What I want you and the Prime Minister to know is that I shall at all times welcome it if you will keep me in touch personally with anything you want me to know about.

Churchill responded cordially, and a regular correspondence between the two grew out of Roosevelt's invitation.

In a May 15, 1940, letter, Churchill, who had been elected British prime minister by his party only five days earlier, laconically asked his shipmate, Roosevelt, for "the loan of 40 or 50 of your old destroyers." Roosevelt was at that time obliged by law and politics to refuse this request, but Churchill took the rebuff in stride and suggested in a follow-up letter that Roosevelt might reconsider within a year.

Hanging by a Thread

Utter calamity in Europe was averted, or at least delayed, as tens of thousands of British, French, and some Belgian troops were evacuated from Dunkirk by June 4, 1940. They would be absorbed into the rump of the British Army that had stayed at home and meagerly requipped from reserve stores to defend the British Isles against a German invasion then considered a sure thing. On June 9, also, the last organized Allied force was evacuated from Norway, thus adding some little strength to England's defenses.

On June 15, the British Admiralty set up a working group intent upon harmonizing and regularizing British and American naval interests and contacts, and on June 20 the British informed the U.S. naval attaché in London that they desired to open informal conversations between British and American staffs, either in Washington or London.

The British ambassador to the United States reminded President Roosevelt that, in 1917, during Roosevelt's tenure as assistant secretary of the navy, the United States had dispatched to London a "special naval observer" whose presence had done much to harmonize the operations of the U.S. Navy with those of the Royal Navy when the United States finally entered the war. Roosevelt discussed the idea with Secretary of the Navy Frank Knox and Adm. Harold Stark. Thus, on July 12, Knox and Stark proposed that Rear Adm. Robert Ghormley, the assistant chief of naval operations and one of the best-briefed men on naval matters in the nation, be dispatched to London. As Ghormley was being briefed as to protocol and American aims, Roosevelt decided to send an army representative as well. Brigadier General George Strong, chief of the War Plans Division, was added, as was Maj. Gen. Delos Emmons, the commanding general of GHQ Air Force. The three were briefed by their services, given oral instructions by the president, and sent off to England on August 6 on a secret mission that was widely reported in the media on August 8.

Meeting as the Anglo-American Standardization of Arms Committee because the ensuing discussions in the United Kingdom were fraught with legal strictures and perils, the talks, which included the U.S. naval and military attachés, were wide-ranging and freewheeling. The only limitation, again because of legal issues, was that the Americans could discuss issues and make recommendations but not make any binding agreements. It is highly instructive of the sheer importance the British placed on the meeting that their represen- tatives included Admiral of the Fleet Sir Dudley Pound, first sea lord; Gen. Sir John Dill, chief of the Imperial General Staff; and Air Chief Marshal Sir Cyril Newell, chief of the Air Staff—Britain's top military executives. It was Newell who came clear about British hopes and intentions in the official minutes: "In our plans for the future we were certainly relying on the continued economic and industrial cooperation of the United States in ever-increasing volume. . . . [They] were fundamental to our whole strategy."

General Strong had been the officer who had written a blunt June 17, 1940, memo to Marshall that allowed as how supplying the British might be a waste of materiel the United States urgently required for itself. Strong reversed himself when asked how the two nations might share information. The minutes note that "it had been agreed in principle . . . that a periodical exchange of informa- tion would be desirable. [Strong] thought that the time had come when this exchange of information should be placed upon a regular basis."

A rather startling admission the British made was that they were not at that moment prepared to go to the mat to defend Malaya or Singapore against Japan if doing so cost them the security of holding their position in the Atlantic. This was an important insight, especially in light of the recent American decision to abstain from mounting a relief expedition to save Guam or the Philippines.

Generals Strong and Emmons returned to Washington at the conclusion of these ground-breaking talks, while Admiral Ghormley remained to indeed serve as the president's special naval observer. Strong came away with information and ideas that went straight into a plan produced by the War Plans Division he oversaw. The resulting ten-page memo, issued on September 25, incorporated the first fruits of the London discussions, but it did so with added context provided by Col. James Burns, executive assistant to the assistant secretary of war, as well as input provided by the assistant chief of the Air Corps and the naval officers serving on the Joint Army and Navy Board's Joint Planning Committee. The caption over one section of the memo provided insight into General Strong's new views relative to sharing: "Necessary additions to the national policy covering release of munitions and production to Great Britain and other nations." Here, then, military planners overseeing the monumental task of rebuilding and rearming the U.S. military signed off on the imperative that, from this point onward, the United States was a British ally in fact if not in name, and that the fates of both nations in the current war were intertwined. America was thus pledged to share her wealth and burgeoning industrial capacity with her Anglophone cousins the world around, for better or worse.

On August 5, 1940, as a symbolically well-timed down payment on America's growing generosity toward the British war effort, a British mission headed by Sir Henry Tizard, chairman of the Aeronautical Research Committee and one of the fathers of radar, arrived in the United States to pretty much exchange everything the British knew for pretty much everything the Americans knew about adapting science, especially radio science and electronic science, to weapons and systems that would help the Allies win the war. Admiral Stark established some general ground rules to govern the exchange of information, but it was pretty much a sure thing that the cousins were not going to hold very much too close to the vest and perhaps risk the outcome of the war.

For all that, the new alliance of sharing was fraught with problems. On August 27, the Congress had authorized the president to call up the Army Reserve and National Guard, the first contingent of sixty thousand guardsmen had been called up on August 31, and the president on September 16 had signed the newly enacted Selective Training and Service Act into law. Presumably hundreds of thousands—perhaps millions—of American soldiers would have to be transported, housed, fed, equipped, and trained in very short order, and the British and Commonwealth armies and navies would be supplied from U.S. arsenals and factories as well.

In September, President Roosevelt acceded to the very first request Prime Minister Churchill ever made of him, "the loan of 40 or 50 of your old destroyers." Only it wasn't a loan, it was a swap made under an executive agreement. In return for Roosevelt's transfer of fifty Great War–vintage destroyers to the Royal Navy, Churchill agreed to lease, for ninety-nine years, bases in or bordering the Caribbean: Antigua, Bermuda, the Bahamas, British

Guiana, Jamaica, St. Lucia, and Trinidad. The trade represented enormously important accommodations by both nations to a shared destiny. The United States transferred the first eight destroyers to the Royal Navy on September 6.

Adding considerably to the mountain of concerns American planners and logisticians had to face up to as a result of the virtual alliance with Britain and the rapid expansion of the army was news on September 27 that Japan had formally signed on with the European Axis powers, thus creating a true worldwide alignment of enemies who might at any time declare war on the United States or, in the case of Japan, attack British, Dutch, and American bases and possessions in the Far East and the Pacific. The world became a hundred percent more dangerous before the United States could actually ship a button or bullet off to the British.

Too Many Options

The United States had reached a point at which there was literally too much going on and too many worries to consider in anything like an orderly manner. There was absolutely no assurance that Japan might not pounce at any moment upon the possessions of European powers that had been swept away in Europe— the Netherlands, Denmark, and France—or upon the possessions of a weakened United Kingdom, or indeed upon the possessions of an unready and overextended United States. Perhaps the Japanese had somehow learned of the recent Atlantic-first decision or of the Americans having written off their own possessions west of the 180th meridian. Perhaps Spain and Portugal would enter the war on the side of their fascist cousins, or perhaps the rump of France under the German-yoked Vichy regime would be terminated, all of which would provide the Kriegsmarine with a host of new Atlantic ports, well south into northwest and west Africa and as far out into the Atlantic as the Azores, Canary, and Cape Verde islands, at which U-boats, commerce raiders, surface warships, and long-range bombers could be based. What if Gibraltar fell? What if the putatively neutral Vichy French outpost at Dakar, Senegal, fell? What if *all* of French West Africa fell? What if the Germans actually did move into French, Dutch, and Danish possessions in the Caribbean and nearby? What if Germany and Italy were actually able to establish puppet regimes in Latin America?

Could the United States, even with British assistance, eject fascist forces from the places it was determined to eject them from? If not now, how soon?

Army and navy planners were consumed with these and scores of other possibilities. Consumed, yes, but not dazzled or overwhelmed. The pace was frenetic, but the planning was cool-headed and linear. The one answer that addressed most of the questions was obvious: Build up the army, build up the navy, build up the Air Corps. Also, show restraint in dealings with Germany and Japan even though it was an open secret that war would eventually come between the United States and both those nations and their partners.

It is axiomatic: Never underestimate the opposition's propensity to find itself in untenable positions. By the late summer of 1940, the German army had pretty much admitted to itself that it had no way to cross the English Channel, and thus it had no expectation of invading England in 1940. The first encounters of the Battle of Britain had been fought in July (by British accounts, but not until September by German reckoning), when there was still some hope of invading Britain, and it had rapidly spun up to history's first exclusive clash of air forces, taking on a logic of its own as the RAF defiantly opposed a Luftwaffe effort to bomb England into submission. Though the continuous air campaign tied up and consumed immense British resources, it also tied up and consumed immense German resources, and a bombing campaign against cities did not especially hamper the raising and training of an army to replace the army that had been lost in France. As to the Japanese, the Imperial Army dominated the nation's political machinery, and it was content for the time being to enslave vast regions of China; as an institution, it as yet had no reason to pick a fight with the United States.

So, for all the crises and worries and possibilities facing the United States and the United Kingdom in mid-1940, both were actually in a safe zone, free to build up their legions, fleets, and air armadas in a bubble of relative security. It was just that they had to do so with alacrity. And they had to do it together, melding American industrial might and distance from the battlefields with the lessons the British and their allies were gaining at a high price in blood and so close to home.

Admiral Stark said it best. At the October 5 meeting of the Standing Liaison Committee (State, War, and Navy departments) in which a British request to send an American naval squadron to Singapore was rejected as too provocative with respect to Japan, the chief of naval operations went on record to the effect that "every day that we are able to maintain peace and still support the British is valuable time gained."

At about this time, President Roosevelt went silent with respect to *the* vital decision the United States had to make regarding its growing alliance with Great Britain. Roosevelt was fully embroiled in a heated run for an unprecedented third term in the White House. The things the Roosevelt Administration were willing to do to aid the British war effort were not the things the American public was yet prepared to do. So, at a time the president had to publicly promise that no American boys would be sent to fight abroad, he had to distance himself from even the most critical decisions that he alone could make.

After winning the 1940 election, Roosevelt got back into the game. And well he did.

Plan Dog

On November 12 a draft proposal by Admiral Stark that had languished for a month was formalized and presented to Secretary of the Navy Knox. It had been vetted and agreed to with adjustments by General Marshall, Admiral Ghormley in London, and Adm. James Richardson at Pearl Harbor. The memorandum offered four possible plans for immediate action: (A) placing a limit on American naval activity with respect to defense of the Western Hemisphere; (B) making Japan the primary object of naval planning and the Atlantic region secondary; (C) making Japan and the Atlantic equal; or (D) conducting a strong naval offensive in the Atlantic while mounting a defensive campaign in the Pacific.

All of these options had been on the table for more than a year, at least since Germany had invaded Poland. All had been discussed endlessly. Yet, in the mind of the chief of naval operations, no concrete decision had yet been forthcoming; he and the navy had no firm, definitive, official guidance by which they could build and deploy their ships, planes, and men.

The immediate need for working space and time to build up the fleet as well as build up the British war effort militated toward the first option, as presented: Don't make waves. But the *real* option the U.S. Navy had to adopt, given a balanced worldview, was the fourth, Plan D, or in naval parlance, Plan Dog. This is the option Stark argued for. To get there, he strongly recommended that the U.S. Army and U.S. Navy immediately enter into continuous secret technical discussions with the British in London and the Canadians in Washington. (The basis for talks with Canada had already been ratified on August 18, 1940, as the Ogdensburg Agreement, and the Permanent Joint Board for the Defense of Canada and the United States had been created on that date.) Similar talks would take place in Singapore with the British and in Batavia, Netherlands East Indies, with Dutch officials acting beyond the reach of the German occupiers of their homeland.

At roughly the same time, the British first sea lord, Admiral Pound, had prevailed upon the British ambassador to the United States to renew a plea to establish a regular exchange of information with the U.S. Army and U.S. Navy, as brought up by General Strong at the August London meetings. (Due to the U.S. election cycle, this thread had, to the consternation of the British service chiefs, been left dangling despite frequent inquiries.) As it turned out, Admiral Stark fully concurred with Admiral Pound, and the two joined forces to get something set up. Stark took the proposal to Marshall, who agreed with it, and then Stark set up the first meeting that winter of what came to be known as American-British Conversations (ABC).

In the meantime, Stark's recommendation for his November 4 Plan Dog, which mainly involved a naval perspective on a national strategy, ran onto some shoals when it reached the army War Plans Division, to which it was referred by General Marshall. The devil was in the details. Underlying Plan Dog's basic strategy of offense in the Atlantic and defense in the Pacific was a network of policies the army planners felt were as yet beyond the capabilities of the United States to undertake simultaneously and in the immediate term. This led in turn to discussions that involved the president and the Joint Planning Committee. National policy would be made, but in the meantime Stark still had no firm policy on which to build or deploy the expanding navy. Somewhat frustrated, he wrote on November 22 to Marshall: "Over here we are much concerned with the possibility of having a war on our hands due to precipitate Japanese action."

More discussions ensued, bringing in Under Secretary of State Sumner Welles. But by November 27, Marshall could only tell Stark that the Department of War was not ready to back the detailed plans undergirding the strategic concept embodied in Plan Dog. And so it went; memoranda were exchanged between all the relevant parties and entities, and high-level meeting followed high-level meeting.

The army was worried about Japan. The navy was worried about Japan. The State Department was worried about Japan. But everyone was equally worried about Britain and the Atlantic, and there was no way in late 1940 that the United States could undertake equal presence in the face of both threats. Yet Japan was merely a threat, while Britain and the Atlantic were under siege.

When Secretary of State Cordell Hull was read into the discussion on January 3, 1941, he punted. The thrust of the discussion as he saw it was a technical military matter best left to the services to hash out.

Decision Time

And then news of the impasse reached the president. On January 16, 1941, Roosevelt called to his office Secretary of State Hull, Secretary of War Stimson, Secretary of the Navy Knox, General Marshall, and Admiral Stark. In notes taken by Marshall and redrafted after the meeting, the president is depicted as raising the possibility, which he rated one in five, of the United States being attacked simultaneously by Japan and Germany. He further stipulated that such an attack might take place *any* day.

The president asked the others what they thought the United States should do if so attacked, and when and in what order. He asked them how the nation might publicize its priorities ahead of an attack with respect to the Philippines, use of the navy, or support of the British. He asked for the assemblage's views regarding a range of responses to Japanese aggression and the possible curtailment of shipments to the United Kingdom, an eventuality he felt the United States must overcome, at the very least in order to preserve Britain as a base from which American and British forces could liberate occupied Europe. The president thought that even in the event a surprise attack cut off the sea lanes between the United States and the British Isles, an eight-month maritime campaign would suffice to reopen them before Britain collapsed for lack of North American goods and war materiel.

Marshall's notes finally summarize the basis of thought and agreement on which the landmark January 16 meeting ended:

> That we would stand on the defensive in the Pacific . . . that there would be no naval reinforcement of the Philippines. . . .
>
> That the navy should be prepared to convoy shipping in the Atlantic to England . . .

That the army should not be committed to any aggressive action until it is fully prepared to undertake it; that our military course must be very conservative until our strength [has] developed; that it was assumed we could provide forces sufficiently trained to assist to a moderate degree in backing up friendly Latin American governments against Nazi inspired fifth column movements.

That we should make every effort to go on the basis of continuing the supply of materiel to Great Britain, primarily in order to disappoint what [the president] thought would be Hitler's principal objective in involving us in a war at this time, and also to buck up England.

With that, Marshall and Stark, their principal assistants, and their staffs went to work on the army's and navy's concrete, policy-based war plans built on an articulate and coherent national grand strategy.

On January 29, 1941, British representatives took part in the first American-British Conversation, ABC-1, which was followed closely by ABC-2. This round of combined planning (one nation with another), which lasted until March 27, cast a yet-somewhat-plastic strategic plan known as Joint War Plan Rainbow No. 5, which was the detailed embodiment of Stark's Plan Dog. It also emplaced a firm understanding upon the British that their American cousins were in it for the long haul, and it provided an equitable division of labor for the immediate term, in which one cousin would manufacture as much as it could of what the other cousin needed to stay in the fight. The meetings themselves, not to mention the agreements, were of enormous relief to the British, who never doubted America's good intentions but had run out of patience with the time it took for Americans to sort out the options, overcome the politics, and simply get on with things.

Chapter 21

Naval Operations, Expansion, and Aid

The Pointy End of the Spear

The U.S. Navy's expansion and modernization between the German invasion of western Europe and the end of 1940 proceeded apace that of the army, but the army had a whole lot more quiet time to do what it needed to do as large parts of the navy engaged in a shadow war the whole time the service was expanding and modernizing. While good for rigorous, on-the-job training as well as for inuring thousands of officers and sailor to the rigors of wartime routine, the operational tempo forced the navy to deal with wear-and-tear issues to a degree it was not prepared to handle. This was a good thing, overall, because it got systems and materiel and trained men and better designs and better ideas in place before the navy found itself in a real war. As in real war, sailors and their officers found numerous procedures that could be streamlined, and streamline they did. Likewise, the exigencies of the Neutrality Patrol forced parts of the navy, especially air patrol units, to learn to set up and operate from ad hoc bases far from the comforts of established home ports and stations. This expeditionary flavor, not to mention the experience of coping with and even overcoming spartan conditions, made parts of the navy stronger, more prepared for the coming naval war than anyone then imagined.

As the seagoing navy learned what it could about prolonged wartime duty and conditioned its men and ships to cope with an unrelenting operational tempo, the sphere of the Neutrality Patrol got much larger, and the conditions became more dangerous.

The navy also got larger. In addition to expanding its enlisted and officer ranks via new enlistments, the service encouraged reservists to volunteer for active duty, at least to catch up with technical advances and take on responsibilities at typically higher ranks than those at which they had previously served. Indeed, the reserve officer component became so important to running the hard-working and expanding active navy that Rear Adm. Chester Nimitz, the chief of the Bureau of Navigation (which oversaw personnel and training), decided that reserve officers would not wear any markings that distinguished them from regular officers, a break with a rather odious British decision that signaled that reserve officers were inferior to regulars. When the need for the skills reservists brought to the game became particularly acute and could no longer be bridged only by volunteers, Secretary of the Navy Knox, on October 25, 1940, placed all reserve units and aviation squadrons on short notice for call to active duty, en bloc, and he gave the Bureau of Navigation the authority to call up individual fleet reservists as necessary, voluntarily or not.

Rising Stakes

The Kriegsmarine suffered serious losses at the outset of the invasion of Norway. On April 9, the day the invasion began, one of its two 8-inch heavy cruisers was mortally damaged by Norwegian shore batteries near Oslo, one of six German 6-inch light cruisers was sent under by a British submarine, and another light cruiser was sunk by Royal Navy dive-bombers, a first in history. The very next day, two of the ten German destroyers covering the occupation of Narvik and several German supply ships were sunk in the first phase of the Battle of Narvik by Royal Navy warships just arrived from ports in the United Kingdom. Two British destroyers were also sunk on April 10, but in the second phase of the battle, on April 13, a British battleship and an accompanying destroyer flotilla sank the remaining eight German destroyers and a U-boat, leaving the Kriegsmarine with only twelve destroyers in commission. This series of battles seriously crippled the German surface fleet and had enormous long-range consequences to the battle for the Atlantic that was then still only shaping up. During the course of the Norway campaign, Britain and her allies suffered some pretty terrible losses of their own: one British cruiser sunk, three British cruisers damaged, two British destroyers lost, one French destroyer sunk, and one Polish destroyer lost—nearly all to German shore-based aircraft. Also in April 1940, four Allied and neutral merchant ships aggregating twenty-five thousand tons were sunk by U-boats, and one U-boat was sunk by a British destroyer.

While the United States remained avowedly neutral, fallout from the widening European war inevitably touched its maritime trade. On April 10, President Roosevelt extended the maritime danger zone set forth in the Neutrality Act of 1939 to cover all of Scandinavia, including neutral Sweden.

On May 3, the local government in Greenland, a Danish crown colony, requested protection of its sovereignty by the United States as it came under pressure from the German conquerors of the home country. It was an honor indeed, but for the moment no one in the United States had the vaguest idea about how to respond.

The German occupation of Denmark on April 9, 1940, also severed communications with Iceland, whose parliament, on April 10, elected to take control of its own foreign affairs, which included a declaration of neutrality. Notwithstanding this declaration, the British had a very good idea about the usefulness of Iceland as an advance aerial search base—for themselves or the Luftwaffe. Thus, on May 10, a British invasion force arrived in Reykjavík harbor. The government of Iceland issued a protest against this "flagrant violation" of Icelandic neutrality but that very day asked Icelanders to treat the British troops as guests. In due course, the basing opportunities the United States and Britain gained in the former Danish possessions in the North Atlantic were to profoundly affect the course and outcome of the war in the North Atlantic and Europe.

On May 11, three days before the Royal Netherlands Army capitulated to the Germans, British and French forces launched preemptive invasions of the Netherlands Antilles, chiefly Aruba and Curaçao, in order to protect oil-production facilities there. Royal Netherlands armed forces in the Caribbean willingly threw in with the Allies.

The U-boat war remained stagnant in May, because the as-yet quite small U-boat force was tied up supporting operations in western Europe. U-boats sank ten Allied and neutral merchant ships aggregating fifty-five thousand tons. On the other hand, while Allied forces were evacuated from Dunkirk between May 17 and June 4, German land-based aircraft sank three British and two French destroyers. On June 8, as the last twenty-five thousand Allied evacuees fled Norway, a pair of German battlecruisers beset the Royal Navy aircraft carrier *Glorious* off Narvik and sank her with gunfire.

The United States Reacts

On May 17, partly as advance planning ran its course but largely influenced by the disastrous events on western Europe, President Roosevelt authorized the navy to refurbish another thirty-five Great War–vintage destroyers for duty at sea. Less than a month later, on June 12, the navy awarded contracts for twenty-two new warships, and on June 14 (the day the German army occupied Paris) the president signed the 11 Percent Naval Expansion Act, which authorized new warship construction totaling 167,000 tons and auxiliary ship construction totaling 75,000 tons. A day later, Roosevelt approved a naval aviation expansion up to ten thousand airplanes, and on June 17, Chief of Naval Operations Harold Stark requested of the Congress new appropriations of $4 billion to cover construction of a "two-ocean navy," meaning in effect the simultaneous deployment of world-class naval forces in both the Atlantic and the Pacific.

The official American reaction to the Franco-German armistice of June 22—that of a neutral nation—came first in the form of a presidential edict and a new law. On June 27, President Roosevelt (who on June 11 had declared the Mediterranean Sea a war zone under the Neutrality Act) went all out by declaring a national emergency and invoking the Espionage Act of 1917 as a means to control access of world shipping to U.S. territorial waters and waters near the Panama Canal. On July 2, the Congress passed the Export Control Act, which authorized the president to prohibit or curtail the exportation of military hardware, munitions, or supplies whenever he believed doing so was "necessary in the interest of national defense."

On July 19, the Naval Expansion Act of 1940 was signed into law. It contemplated the two-ocean navy cited by Admiral Stark in his June 17 testimony before the Congress. The new bill authorized a 70 percent increase in the size of the navy. In it were provisions adding to previous authorizations sufficient to build combatant ships to an aggregate of 1,325,000 tons, auxiliary ships to an aggregate of 100,000 tons, and 15,000 new airplanes. This translated to eleven new battleships of several classes, eleven new *Essex*-class aircraft carriers, six "large" cruisers (in effect battlecruisers), fifty light and heavy cruisers, and one hundred destroyers. (Many of these ships were never built, including 58,000-ton *Montana*-class battleships, but many other ships were built in their place, including nine light aircraft carriers built on light cruiser hulls.) The first contracts for 210 of these ships, including 12 aircraft carriers and 7 battleships, were awarded on September 9.

The immense naval expansion required that the shipbuilding industry expand its operations to two shifts, or three shifts in places. It also required that new shipbuilding facilities be built and, of course, that many thousands of workers be hired, first to be trained and then to be turned loose in the biggest game of catch-up in human history.

Best estimates showed that all the frenetic naval construction activity would cut a six-year task to two years. This was admirable, but it meant the American fleet would not be up to fighting an end-of-1940-type war until the end of 1942. This reality thus bolstered all the rationale that had gone into providing munitions, arms, and equipment to keep Britain and its Commonwealth and allies in the war, which of course placed greater pressure on the American economy to transform itself into a hell-bent, full-out war economy.

The French Possessions

Cheered on by local Dutch authorities, the British and French had taken part in the occupation of the Dutch colonies of Aruba and Curaçao in May 1940, but it remained to be seen who would hold sway over French colonies spread from offshore Canada in the north to French Guiana in the south after France capitulated in June. All of the French possessions in the Western Hemisphere were strategically located and would make terrific bases for whichever side held them, but all of them had legal ties to the neutral French rump state whose capital was Vichy.

When the United States offered to "protect" French possessions in the Caribbean, the Vichy government tartly declined, with a reminder that it and its possessions were declared neutrals. Of special interest, however, was Fort de France, Martinique, where a Vichy French aircraft carrier, a cruiser, a gunboat, and six tankers lay at anchor, and 112 American-built warplanes were gathered to await transport to France aboard the aircraft carrier. Fort de France was also the best harbor in the Lesser Antilles.

Rather than go to war with Vichy France and perhaps the entire Axis over control of Martinique—which a U.S. navy-marine expeditionary force was prepared to do from a military standpoint—the Roosevelt Administration worked behind the scenes at the June 1940 Havana Conference of American Republics. The result of an adroit diplomatic effort led by Under Secretary of

State Sumner Welles was a June 30 declaration that the transfer of territory in the Americas from one nonhemispheric nation to another nonhemispheric nation would not be tolerated. The agreement established the Inter-American Commission for Territorial Administration to oversee any territory that changed hands in an unapproved manner. The conferees also rather pointedly renewed their backing of the U.S. Navy Neutrality Patrol.

An American admiral was dispatched to ask the French admiral commanding at Fort de France to switch his allegiance to the new Free French movement and place his facilities in its hands. This the French admiral felt honorbound to refuse, but he agreed to a set of terms that effectively neutralized the base, its armaments, and all its ships and planes. In return, the United States agreed to provide regular food shipments, medical supplies, and gasoline purchased with French funds in blocked accounts in U.S. banks. (On June 20, the American heavy cruiser *Vincennes* had arrived at the New York Navy Yard with two hundred tons of the Bank of France gold reserve aboard for deposit in U.S. banks, so French credit with the U.S. government was nothing short of spectacular.) Thereafter, Martinique, neighboring Guadeloupe, and the penal colony in administratively linked French Guiana were monitored by American ships and patrol bombers based in Puerto Rico and, in due course, at the leased British base at St. Lucia. The French kept to their agreement.

The governor general of Miquelon and St.-Pierre, French island possessions near Newfoundland, declared for Vichy France, but to keep the economy afloat, he was forced to ask the United States for loans guaranteed by the French treasury, which pretty much neutralized the place. Because of the islands' proximity to vital convoy routes, Canada considered mounting an invasion, but the British governor general of Canada never authorized the plan.

A Scare in South America

On May 30, 1940, the U.S. minister in Uruguay reported in a telegram to Secretary of State Cordell Hull that the political situation in Montevideo was "deteriorating," that the Uruguayan government was "well meaning but weak, undecided and confused," that events were "drifting," and that "people [are] climbing on the Nazi band wagon." The minister further warned that "armed movement is a possibility."

The next day, May 31, the U.S. ambassador to Argentina met with the minister in Montevideo, and the two jointly suggested to Secretary Hull that "if the situation in the Far East permits," a "large U.S. naval force, 40 or 50 vessels [sent] . . . to the east coast of South America" would "strengthen the position of those who desire to combat Nazism, as well as restore the confidence of those who are now wavering." The two went on to suggest that a U.S. naval squadron "more or less permanently [stationed] in these waters would be an added assurance that we are prepared to give effective and immediate assistance if required." This recommendation was bolstered by the views of the State Department's resident South America expert and seconded by Under Secretary of State Welles.

Hull replied to his men in Montevideo that President Roosevelt had just ordered the heavy cruiser *Quincy* to proceed immediately to Rio de Janeiro, Brazil, and then to Montevideo for "friendly visits of courtesy." On June 1, Under Secretary Welles informed the U.S. ambassador to Brazil that *Quincy* was en route to Rio de Janeiro and Montevideo "to furnish a reminder of the strength and the range of action of the armed forces of the United States."

Admiral Stark, on June 2, dispatched a memorandum to President Roosevelt in which he laid out the navy's options with respect to the overall political situation in South America. The president thus decided to send one additional heavy cruiser to South America, continue ongoing and routine destroyer shakedown cruises to South American waters, and utilize only those ships already assigned to the Atlantic Squadron, so as to avoid weakening the fleet in the Pacific. This was not quite the show of force the U.S. diplomats in South America wanted, but it was extra attention.

Quincy arrived in Rio de Janeiro on June 12 and reached Montevideo on June 17. On June 20, the new destroyer *O'Brien* called at Buenos Aires during her shakedown cruise, and on June 27 she stopped off at a Brazilian port. On June 20, light cruiser *Phoenix* sailed from Hawaii to begin a goodwill cruise to ports on South America's Pacific coast. Thereafter, such port calls by a succession of U.S. Navy warships became routine. In aggregate, this activity added up to quite a spectacle and undoubtedly had the desired effect. As early as June 18, in fact, the U.S. minister in Montevideo reported that the Uruguayan government had arrested eight leading Nazi sympathizers and that the Uruguayan chamber of deputies had met in secret session to study a report on Nazi activities in their country. As a backup, with an eye on quite different options, the submarine tender *Bushnell*, between April 9 and June 15, undertook a hydrographic survey off the coast of Venezuela that charted 2,200 nautical square miles of ocean depths.

The Battle of the Atlantic

The German occupation of numerous Atlantic-facing ports from the Arctic Circle to the Bay of Biscay during the spring of 1940 bore out Great Britain's worst nightmare with respect to the spread of U-boat attacks to a much broader reach of the Atlantic than the German submariners had been able to access via their traditional Baltic ports. (The Vichy French did not turn over their bases in northwestern and western Africa to the Germans, but neither were the bases of use to the reeling British.) Immediately upon the fall of France, the German U-boat force forward command post was established in Brest (but soon moved to Lorient), and work began on turning the French navy's submarine pens at St.-Nazaire into an immense bomb-proof home port for the bulk of the German U-boat fleet. But such facilities would be months in the making, and there were as yet few U-boats to use them.

The short-term results of German access to and domination of broad swathes of Europe's Atlantic seaboard were simply staggering, once even the small German U-boat fleet of the day sallied from its Baltic ports after the fall of France. In June alone, following two very quiet months, Allied and neutral shipping losses mounted to fifty-three merchant ships aggregating 297,000 tons, plus three British armed merchant cruisers sunk—against two U-boats lost to unknown causes (which is to say *not* through British action). The bulk of the merchant ships lost were caught sailing alone or in unescorted ad hoc convoys. While convoys bound for England from the main gathering point at Halifax, Nova Scotia, were large, slow targets, they were aggressively escorted by corvettes, destroyers, and armed merchantmen quite unafraid of German undersea raiders, so for the moment the U-boats steered clear.

No more than fifteen U-boats were ever at sea at one time through the end of 1940. Except for Bergen, Norway, which was made operational in a matter of days, satisfactory U-boat bases had to be built and supplies laid in. Rather, a host of coastal air bases had fallen into German hands, and these were exploited almost immediately by long-range search aircraft tied into the submarine radio network. So, while the number of U-boats on patrol barely rose in June 1940, their patrols were optimized by eyes in the sky. On the other hand, relations between the Luftwaffe and Kriegsmarine were not very good. The airmen manning the long-range patrol bombers were frankly jealous of publicity accorded the U-boats, so they often alerted the crews of straggling ships that they had been spotted by mounting bombing attacks rather than simply standing off to report the whereabouts and progress to the Kriegsmarine.

The British did what they could to stem the renewed U-boat assault, but their strategic defenses had been outflanked by the German seizure of Atlantic-facing air and naval bases, and their defensive plan had been destroyed. The area in which they needed to search for U-boats became too large to handle with the resources at hand; it soon extended southward to waters off north-western Africa. When the Germans figured out the secrets of sonar (which the British called asdic) salvaged from a French destroyer, the U-boats changed tactics. Sonar could find submerged targets, so the Germans attacked on the surface, at night. Radar might have countered this tactic, but it had not yet been shrunk down to a size suitable for small surface escorts.

The British and their remaining allies became very serious about creating convoys and guarding them with suitable escorts, but it took time for many independent-minded ship captains to fall in line, and the same for freeing up escorts (of which the best armed were held in British home ports as long as invasion worries were realistic). It took much more time, also, to arrive at a suitable escort doctrine. Data over time revealed that even strongly escorted convoys suffered greater losses while traversing some areas than they suffered traversing others, so some areas were blocked off and the safer routes were patrolled more aggressively against incursions by U-boats and long-range search aircraft. It took the Germans very little time to tumble to these adjustments and reposition their U-boats.

July was a bit milder than June: U-boats sank thirty-four Allied and neutral merchant ships aggregating 173,000 tons, plus one Royal Navy destroyer, and a U-boat was sunk by a British escort and aircraft in the Irish Sea. August 1940 yielded about the same attrition to U-boats as July: thirty-nine merchant ships aggregating 190,000 tons were lost, as were one British escort and two armed merchant cruisers serving as convoy escorts. The uptick in combatant losses was a factor of more escorts being more aggressive when U-boats were located.

One U-boat was sunk in August by British aircraft. On the downside, heavily armed, long-range German maritime bombers capable of sinking merchant ships with bombs began to operate from Bordeaux, France.

In late September, to seal the southern extremity of the Atlantic battle area, British troops, accompanied by the first Free French ground force to be identified as such, were dispatched to negotiate with Vichy French forces holding Dakar, Senegal. The Vichy troops refused to yield, and they prevailed following two days of fighting.

September 1940 was also the month in which German U-boats were first organized into wolfpacks. Employing data from a decrypted British naval code, the wolfpacks wreaked havoc on the convoys. In one night, one U-boat sank seven of the eleven ships sunk from just one convoy bound from Halifax to the United Kingdom. In September, fifty-three merchantman aggregating 272,000 tons and two British escorts were sunk, and *no* U-boats were lost. In October, the Germans sank fifty-six merchant ships aggregating 287,000 tons. One of these, a 42,000-ton liner, was sunk by bombs planted by a Luftwaffe maritime patrol bomber. One Royal Canadian Navy destroyer was sunk, and one U-boat fell prey to a team of British destroyers. In addition, a German commerce raider arrived in France to report that she had sunk or seized ten small ships aggregating 59,000 tons during a six-month foray in the central Atlantic. And the pocket battleship *Admiral Scheer* sailed from Germany to begin a commerce-raiding expedition in the South Atlantic and Indian Ocean.

As the seas became heavier with the onset of colder weather, many light escorts had to be withdrawn from convoy duty, not to return until the spring. This necessity naturally left the convoys more exposed to the wolfpacks, which typically deployed as many as nine U-boats at a time to undertake ruthless, minutely controlled, set-piece operations that significantly magnified their effectiveness. In December, the wolfpacks, reinforced by newly commissioned U-boats, began to operate routinely in the mid-Atlantic, where Canadian air patrols from the west and British air patrols from the east did not mesh, owing to distance.

Destroyers for Bases

The American Neutrality Patrol played a very minor role as the Battle of the Atlantic shaped up between April and the end of October 1940. The United States was not ready to go to war, and the Roosevelt Administration did not want to goad the Axis beyond a certain level of productive assertiveness. But the reality of the situation was that British naval and maritime assets were being very roughly handled as the tempo of the Battle of the Atlantic increased. The Royal and Royal Canadian navies were fighting gallantly but falling further and further behind the curve of U-boat production and upgraded tactics. As the fate of Britain became increasingly perilous, questions over an efficacious American defense of the Western Hemisphere became increasingly disturbing. In the end, both issues—increased convoy security and hemispheric defense— were handled at one stroke.

Following discussions across a range of options, President Roosevelt, Prime Minister Churchill, and Secretary of the Navy Knox arrived at a very simple agreement on July 24, 1940. In exchange for the transfer of fifty Great War– vintage destroyers to the Royal Navy in seaworthy condition, the British would grant the United States ninety-nine-year leases on naval and air bases in British possessions in the Western Hemisphere.

Though the deal had been struck, and Roosevelt's word was certainly good enough for the British, it was urgent that the transfer of ships begin immediately. This point was made rather strongly in a July 31 telegram sent by U.S. Ambassador Joseph Kennedy to Secretary of State Hull. In it, Churchill asked that as many destroyers as the U.S. Navy could spare be transferred to the Royal Navy as soon as possible. In the previous ten days, Churchill noted via Ambassador Kennedy, the Royal Navy had lost four destroyers, and seven others had been damaged. "If we cannot get reinforcement," Churchill bluntly stated, "the whole fate of the war may be decided by this minor and easily remediable factor."

The U.S. Navy began to select and even prepare some destroyers, but notwithstanding Churchill's plea, there were a few legal niceties the Roosevelt Administration had to cope with. On August 2, Roosevelt and his cabinet met for a "long discussion" concerning "ways and means to sell directly or indirectly" fifty or sixty destroyers to Great Britain. All agreed that "the survival of the British Isles under German attack might very possibly depend on [the British] getting these destroyers." But all those present agreed that it was necessary to accomplish the goal via legislation, which could be very time-consuming and might actually fail.

On August 5, the British ambassador provided President Roosevelt with a list of the facilities the British government might be prepared to lease to the United States. The matter was then discussed at length on August 13 by Roosevelt, Secretary of the Navy Knox, Secretary of War Stimson, Secretary of the Treasury Morgenthau, and Under Secretary of State Welles. As a result of this conference, Roosevelt, in a telegram from Welles to Ambassador Kennedy, informed Churchill that "it may be possible to furnish to the British Government . . . at least 50 destroyers," but only if "the American People and the Congress frankly recognized in return . . . the national defense and security of the United States would be enhanced." Roosevelt therefore insisted that, in the event the British Fleet were run out of home waters, it be dispatched to other parts of the empire rather than turned over to the Germans or sunk, and that the British government lease to the United States, for ninety-nine years, air and naval base sites in Bermuda, the Bahamas, British Guiana, Jamaica, Newfoundland, St. Lucia, and Trinidad.

A relieved and grateful Churchill responded in two days that "the worth of every destroyer that you can spare to us is measured in rubies" and that the "moral value of this fresh aid from your Government and your people at this critical time will be very great and widely felt." The very next day, August 16, Roosevelt called a press conference to announce that the United States was in discussions with the British about acquisition of naval and air bases to defend the Western Hemisphere and the Panama Canal. No other details were given. The effect of the president's news was greatly heightened just a day later, when the German government rather maladroitly announced that it was about to establish a "total blockade" of the British Isles and warned that all ships transiting British waters would be sunk without warning.

On August 18, President Roosevelt and Canadian Prime Minister MacKenzie King signed the Ogdensburg Agreement, which established the Permanent Joint Board for the Defense of Canada and the United States. The first meeting of the board took place in Ottawa on August 26.

August 27 was a key date. The president met with secretaries Knox, Stimson, and Hull concerning a legal impasse that had arisen over the destroyers-for-bases agreement. Roosevelt then conferred with Admiral Stark, Secretary Knox, Secretary Hull, and the British ambassador. During the meeting, Stark certified that the destroyers selected for transfer to the Royal Navy were no longer essential to the defense of the United States. This certification cleared a major legal hurdle to their transfer. Later, Attorney General Robert Jackson delivered to the president a ruling in which the legal framework for the transfer was set forth. According to Jackson's ruling, the transfer and signing of leases could be accomplished under presidential authority without need for congressional approval.

On September 2 the British ambassador and Secretary of State Hull signed the final agreement. It granted the United States rights to bases in Antigua, Bermuda, the Bahamas, British Guiana, Jamaica, Newfoundland, St. Lucia, and Trinidad. The first eight destroyers, already refurbished for prospective duty with the Neutrality Patrol, were handed off to British crews at Halifax, Nova Scotia, on September 9. American naval officers embarked immediately on a tour of the prospective bases to assay their potential use and the resources the new facilities would require, but the first fruits of the deal did not ripen until November 17, when a squadron of tender-supported PBY seaplane patrol bombers mounted its first search missions from Bermuda.

Also, on September 9—the day the first shipbuilding contracts were awarded under the Naval Expansion Act of 1940—Germany finally fired a shot across America's bow with its formal announcement that *all* ships transiting Axis-defined war zones were subject to attack "regardless of nationality." The Germans, who had briefly contemplated severing diplomatic ties with the

United States, were not yet ready to take on the United States in a face-to-face declared war, so they let all their understandable grievances go at that. Americans, who were even further from ready to go to war with Germany, nevertheless saw the German announcement as a pointed threat.

Yet even as a quite angry Hitler stood down from any overt attack against the United States, he ordered that plans be drawn up to seize several potential air-base sites on islands across the central North Atlantic. Among the proposed base sites were the Azores, a possession of the Axis-leaning Portuguese fascist government at which U-boats sometimes refueled. The westernmost island, Flores, lies only 1,200 miles from St. John's, Newfoundland. Hitler hoped, perhaps via a lease deal, that a base in the group might eventually support long-range bombers then in development for operations against the northeastern United States.

Here, Hitler ran into the consequences of neglecting his Kriegsmarine during the late 1930s. While the Luftwaffe came up with a plan to transport paratroops to various islands, the chief of the badly weakened Kriegsmarine averred that his service had not the strength to guarantee the lines of supply and communication between mainland Europe and new island bases. Any notion of using U-boats to guard the lines of supply and communication would bring some of them within the Pan-American Safety Zone, and that might well lead to an as-yet unwanted shooting war with the United States. Hitler backed down, and the plan was scrapped for all time, a profound if bloodless American military victory. As a seeming sop to the Axis (but really to pull American ships back from an exposed position), the U.S. Navy on October 22 disbanded a small battle force in the western Mediterranean that had been monitoring the Iberian Peninsula since 1936. The end of the Spanish Civil War had obviated the excuse, if not the need, for that little flotilla.

By November 26, 1940, the Royal Navy had received all of the fifty promised destroyers from the U.S. Navy (and by April 1941, a bonus of ten 250-foot U.S. Coast Guard cutters would also be transferred). These surface warships could not in themselves turn the tide in the war with the U-boats, but they could—and did—hold the line and buy time.

A footnote to the destroyers-for-bases deal was laid down in early October when the Uruguayan government asked the United States to provide two or three old destroyers to its virtually nonexistent navy. The request was dismissed out of hand as impracticable, and Secretary of State Hull followed up with a note to the U.S. minister in Montevideo that such a gift would encourage like requests from all the Latin states. Maybe so, but the coldness of the refusal, if not the refusal itself, seriously angered the Uruguayans, who noted that it was the Americans who had asked the Latin nations to cooperate in the defense of the hemisphere.

Methods Short of War

After many quiet months, there occurred several confrontations that once again placed the Neutrality Patrol in the bull's eye. On October 24, the German freighter *Helgoland* departed Puerto Colombia, Colombia, in a bid to get back to Germany. Three American destroyers pursued her for several days, but the ship was able to evade near the Lesser Antilles, and she arrived at St.-Nazaire on November 30.

On October 31, the German freighter *Rio Grande* sailed from Rio de Janeiro. After eluding Neutrality Patrol ships and planes, she made her way to Bordeaux in mid-December.

Destroyer *Plunkett*, patrolling off Tampico, Mexico, on November 15, observed a German freighter and a German tanker as they prepared to make a break from the port. The next day, destroyer *McCormick* thwarted the breakout attempt by the German freighter, which returned to her berth. *Plunkett* blocked the tanker, *Phrygia*, whose crew scuttled her.

Once again off Tampico, on November 29, a pair of destroyers shadowed the German freighters *Idarwald* and *Rhein* as they bolted for freedom. A slow sea chase by relays of Neutrality Patrol destroyers ensued until, on December 8, a British light cruiser intercepted *Idarwald* near the Yucatan Channel. Rather than face capture, the freighter's crew scuttled her within sight of the American destroyer *Sturtevant*. American ships shadowed the *Rhein* until December 11, when a Royal Netherlands Navy destroyer approached her near the Florida Straits. As the American destroyers *MacLeish* and *McCormick* looked on, the crew of *Rhein* also scuttled her to avoid capture.

First Blood

The first American-flag vessel lost in World War II, the SS *City of Rayville*, sank off Australia on November 8 after she struck a mine laid by a German commerce raider. Thirty-seven crewman reached safety, but one was killed, the first American to die in action beneath his nation's flag in World War II.

Chapter 22

Arnold's Air Corps: Part 2

A Race Against Time

THE ARMY AIR CORPS had been consumed in frenetic planning and acquisition activity since the November 1938 Aircraft Meeting, but it had surprisingly little to put in the air by the time France fell in June 1940. It was larger than it had been in late 1938, and it had better airplanes on order or just reaching its operational units, but it was by no means a match for the Luftwaffe in offense or nearly the size of the Royal Air Force in defense.

The first real plan to expand the Air Corps to a viable wartime establishment had been formulated in the spring of 1939, when a balanced roster of twenty-four bombardment and pursuit groups had been set forth. Once agreement was reached on the twenty-four groups, the Air Corps planners looked to acquiring airplanes, support vehicles, tools, spare parts, men to operate the planes and equipment, and so forth. It was a daunting task. An air group's airplanes, pilots, and aircrew were only the tip of the spear. On the ground, airplanes require an immense amount of servicing, and that requires a very large maintenance staff. Also, spare pilots and aircrew must be assigned to each group, as must administrative and support staff.

The original plan was to build out the twenty-four fully manned and combat-ready groups by June 30, 1941, but world events overran the plan long before it reached fruition. In May 1940, the goal was reset to forty-one combat-ready air groups, and then in July it was raised to fifty-four under the rubric First Aviation Objective. By the standard of the day, putting fifty-four combat-ready groups in the air required a basis of 4,000 airplanes, 187,000 enlisted personnel, 15,000 pilots and pilot trainees, and nearly 17,000 officers to man nonflying billets.

Though not without stresses and strains, there were ways to enlist and direct the requisite number of warm bodies—even trained warm bodies—to the plethora of billets that would open up in a fifty-four-group Air Corps. (The Air Corps was a popular branch selection for voluntary enlistees who did not want to take their chances being conscripted and sent to the infantry. Between July 1, 1939, and July 1, 1941, the number of Air Corps personnel was to jump from 20,503 to 152,569.) But there was not yet enough airplane construction capacity in the United States to build out a fifty-four-group equipment roster as well as provide combat and other aircraft to America's allies, chiefly the British. Money was not an issue, especially after the fall of France; there was more than enough money to expand military aircraft production. Time was the chief cause of anxiety. There were irreducible minimums on the production side, for building aircraft factories, for mining and converting raw materials, for training skilled workers, and so forth. Likewise, there were irreducible minimums for training pilots, aircrew, and groundcrew; insufficiencies in the training regime inevitably led to deaths and total equipment loss. Training programs could be compressed, but not by much. They certainly needed to be expanded to accommodate tens of thousands more trainees than the Air Corps had seen in two decades, and that of course begged the same question the ground army faced in its precipitous expansion: from whence the trainers? Pulling experienced men out of operational units to train recruits weakened those units, but the Air Corps as a whole would eventually benefit via superior training of its recruits. This was a classic war-now-versus-war-later dilemma.

Industry did its share, albeit with government subsidies in the form of outright grants or increased orders. In very little time, as 1939 gave way to 1940, single-shift factory schedules were doubled and then trebled. This required the doubling and then trebling of the corps of skilled and trained factory workers, which took the time it took and was always the subject of an important caveat: Would the newly trained military-age workers be subject to conscription?

The aircraft-building program involved the entire economy, because each airplane required thousands of separate components—compasses and gyroscopes, for example—that had to be fabricated or built outside the aircraft plants and shipped to them for installation. Facing a shortage of an item because of limited utility or limited demand in the civilian world, the Air Corps materiel planners and industrial liaisons had to join with the aircraft manufacturers to induce increased parts production sufficient to match or exceed increased aircraft production. Sometimes it was sufficient for a component manufacturer to go to second or third shifts, but sometimes they had to expand their facilities. This resulted in attendant costs and pressures on the commercial real estate markets and, always, pressure on a job market that was inevitably going to end up competing with military recruitment for its manpower. One enduring solution that the Army Industrial College provided was to offer "educational orders" to manufacturers who made sort of the same thing as the aircraft factories needed in quantities that exceeded the output and even the potential output of the traditional component suppliers. Thus, a manufacturer of wristwatches that was just chugging along in the economy might be given an educational order for a military item that required pretty much the same skill sets as the manufacturer deployed for civilian production. The wristwatch manufacturer might be asked to take a stab at producing the timing devices for precision fuses for bombs and then, if that worked out, given a long-term contract that made it worthwhile to switch over completely to meet the military's needs, or expand somehow to stay in business as a watch manufacturer (because the military requires watches) *and* produce precision timing devices. Until tens of thousands of issues like this example were worked out and those new suppliers got up to speed, producing thousands of ready-to-fly warplanes per year was a bit of a pipe dream.

To a large degree, laws pertaining to competitive bidding went by the board. Building warplanes to an impossibly truncated schedule was not the right venue for slavish adherence to such niceties. If a plant could produce, it got the contract. Besides, the Air Corps officers who oversaw production were reliably tightfisted. At one point, early on, some very senior Air Corps officers used to getting their way—among them Hap Arnold—nearly negotiated Boeing right out of B-17 production by sticking to a price for finished airplanes that was well below Boeing's cost of production, even with economies of scale factored in. The Air Corps learned the limits then, but its production czars remained functionally tightfisted.

As noted earlier, the army and navy settled on standardizing common parts, from wing nuts to pressure pumps to only two machine gun types, which influenced economies of scale and saved time. In due course, the British were induced to adopt some of the American standards in the equipment they ordered from U.S. plants, and that relieved pressure on the entire system. But there were real, unbridgeable differences between some the navy's and Air Corps' needs, not to mention between British and American needs, and thus incompatibilities lingered on for years. On top of that, the Air Corps and navy expended huge efforts and huge sums on research and development on every aspect of their aviation needs, from more rugged wing nuts to longer-ranged, faster, more reliable, more survivable airplanes. The services even stopped production runs in order to incorporate, on the spot, improvements suggested by combat experience over western Europe and North Africa. This tendency, good for achieving battle superiority, played havoc with the production process, at times down to the very foundations of the production process, but it was not so much tolerated as encouraged.

On May 16, 1940, President Roosevelt asked the Congress to raise the ceiling on aircraft building capacity to an output of 50,000 airplanes per year. This was to be divided, 36,500 and 13,500, respectively, between the Air Corps and the navy. It was double the capacity the aircraft industry controlled when the request was made, but throughout 1940 the real production rate soared to 250 percent of the 1939 capacity. Most of the growth was achieved after the fall of France, which suggests a much higher percentage in real growth.

During the first nine months of 1940, the aircraft industry as a whole delivered 3,770 military aircraft of all types. At that juncture, there remained unfilled orders for 16,649 Air Corps airplanes, of which 9,122 (nearly 55 percent) were combat types, and most of the remainder were training aircraft. Projections of increasing needs coupled with increasing production capacity suggested that the Air Corps could take delivery of up to forty thousand airplanes of all types, counted from January 1, 1939, to December 31, 1941. Moreover, a much higher proportion of this avalanche of airplanes represented larger, heavier, increasingly complex multi-engine types, especially heavy bombers. This makes the numbers far more impressive, given simply the time and material consumed on larger aircraft.

Pilot induction and training were massively expanded as the war in western Europe ran its course. Generals Marshall and Arnold were summoned to the White House on May 14, 1940, and told directly by President Roosevelt that the not-fully-developed old plan to train 4,500 pilots was to be expanded to accommodate 7,000 new pilots in a year's time. Then, on August 8, Roosevelt directed that 12,000 new pilots be produced within one year, a number he raised on December 17, 1940, to 30,000. Goals for production of aircraft and everything the Air Corps needed to maintain and support them were proportionally raised as well, as were recruiting and training goals for aircrew and non-flying personnel.

While the early phases of flight training for many would-be pilots was left in part to civilian contract flight schools under the supervision of GHQ Air Force and certification of the Civil Aeronautics Authority, the Air Corps had to render special and in-type training—fighters, bombers, observation, and transport—at its own facilities. The Air Corps Training Center at Randolph Field, Texas, was massively expanded from July 1940 onward, and a growing inventory of new training bases for pilots and aircrew was being built in areas that enjoyed good weather most of the year around. Tried-and-true curricula were compressed to the degree they could be without wasting lives or tampering with the finished product, and lessons derived from the war in Europe were introduced on a continuing basis. The chronic shortage of instructors was incrementally alleviated when it dawned on the planners that some of the top graduates in any given training class could be dragooned, usually against their will, into instruction billets, usually with guarantees for posting to combat units following some fixed period of servitude.

As the training bases, many of them new, churned out pilots and aircrew for assignment to newly activated units, those new units required space for unit training, and thus it was necessary to develop more airfields from scratch. In many cases, as at new ground-army camps, the bias was toward cheaper, temporary facilities, including tarpaper barracks that could be built swiftly and, some day, torn down without a trace. This was not pleasant for the airmen stationed at such outposts, but it unwittingly inured them to life at even worse forward bases in the Pacific and, much later, in continental Europe. Most bases were built in areas of predominant good weather, often in remote desert regions far from decent towns. If there was not much solace with respect to living conditions, it did mean a lot of flying days, and that was a good thing all around.

By the end of 1940, the Army Air Corps still had an immensely long way to go to reach competitive war footing. But the nation was behind it, and there was the basis of a plan, even if its outcome kept moving out of reach. Ultimately, as the war in Europe took unexpected turns, the Air Corps finally arrived at a firm mission to which it could peg its immediate planning for growth and improvement, something to focus all the frenetic energy. The German invasion of western Europe had made real hitherto vaguely felt threats against strategic points in the Western Hemisphere.

The Air Corps and Hemisphere Defense

By mid-June 1940 it became all too easy for American military planners to envision a world in which the whole of Europe had fallen under Nazi domination and the German and Italian navies had been massively bolstered by the capture of large portions of the French and British fleets. In a traditional sense, all that could possibly stand between these Nazi-controlled fleets and their utter domination of the eastern littoral of the entire Western Hemisphere was the weaker portion of the frantically expanding U.S. Navy.

Thoughts along these lines were daunting enough to Americans planning a hemispheric defense against amphibious assaults on weakly fortified (or unfortified) bases in the region, but their woes ratcheted up precipitously when they factored in the new air bases the Germans had acquired or might acquire in areas directly facing the Atlantic Ocean, from Norway to Senegal. Factoring in the ranges of only German twin-engine tactical bombers, it became easy to see how, with a hop, a skip, and a jump, German aircraft might eventually become active over eastern Canada and the northeastern United States. For example, a hop by German army units to seize bases in Iceland would place German bombers within range of Newfoundland, a skip to southern Greenland or the western Azores would expose the Canadian Maritime provinces to German bombs, and a jump from French West Africa to islands far out in the eastern Atlantic would help interdict shipping lanes as far west as Brazil. And if the Kriegsmarine was bolstered with former French and British surface squadrons, amphibious assaults to gain air bases in the West Indies were not improbable.

It wasn't only the military planners who put two and two and two together. Large portions of the American public could read maps, and they clamored for action by their government and the military. Utterly buried in the upheaval of concern was any discussion of defensive action as another way of saying "preparation of war," the rubric beneath which even prudent preparations had been killed off for twenty years. Far from it: the public wanted action, and it wanted action it could see, touch, and count on.

The best means the United States had for fending off the threat of German aerial forays into the eastern Atlantic littoral were: a strong U.S. naval presence associated with a strong and free British naval presence, the extension of search and bombardment fans far beyond those possible to maintain from the U.S. mainland alone, and the competent physical defense of as many vulnerable Atlantic islands and island groups as possible in whatever time there was left.

This was the basis for bolstering the British war effort at such great expense to America's own military buildup, it was why the United States was throwing so much money at the notion of a two-ocean navy, and it was why the ground army was tripping all over itself to prepare an expeditionary force of at least three combat-ready and fully supported infantry divisions in the shortest time possible.

The American planners also fully recognized the means by which the Germans had achieved some of their stunning successes before war actually broke out in Europe. These included such ruses as using ethnic solidarity groups to undermine target regimes, as in Czechoslovakia; using the German national airline, Lufthansa, to map aerial routes to be used later by bombers; using German commercial firms to smuggle arms and money to German sympathizers; and establishing so-called fifth-column cells that looked and acted like student or trade organizations while conducting or preparing to conduct espionage missions. Most of Latin America was vulnerable to these ruses. If the United States and Canada were suddenly called upon to take in tens of thousands of British refugees, how many would be in the pay of German intelligence organizations or outright saboteurs?

There was a lot the United States could do to dampen the effect of such ruses in the Western Hemisphere, but there remained much still that the country could not anticipate or counteract. What the United States *could* do was foresee the threat to gain footholds in the Western Hemisphere that would place bases at the disposal of German forces. The United States could interdict such bases if it had sufficient forces and long-range ships and airplanes at its disposal.

Accompanying President Roosevelt's request for additional military expenditures that reached the Congress on May 14, 1940, was a message that pointed all this out, made a plea that "the American people must recast their thinking about national protection," and the watchwords, "Defense cannot be static. . . . Defense must be dynamic and flexible." The message especially pointed out the most modern antidote to Axis projection of power into the hemisphere: *offensive* air power.

President Roosevelt's May 14 love note to the Air Corps put to an end a decade's worth of stupid frat-house polemic over which service had pride of place with respect to meeting an enemy invasion force as far out from American shores as possible, as if participation in defending the United States was a zero-sum game. *Of course* the navy was to do so, if and when and where it could. And *of course* so was the Air Corps, if ever and whenever and wherever. And both services were prepared to do so, the navy by means of long tradition and more than a century of preparation, and the Air Corps by means of a June 1938 doctrinal study entitled "Air Corps Mission under the Monroe Doctrine." By March 1939, the Air Corps had honed its planning for hemispheric defense to the point at which the primary defensive mission was to be the "destruction of enemy aviation at its bases." That is, in 1940 terms, if German long-range aircraft could reach targets in the Western Hemisphere, then American long-range aircraft could reach the German bases from bases of their own at or near those targets.

Thanks to the president's newly announced position, the Air Corps in June 1940 set out its hemispheric defense mission in six steps:

1. Deny hostile air forces the ability to establish air bases in the Western Hemisphere.
2. Defeat hostile air forces that have become lodged in the region through attacks on their bases.
3. Defeat hostile air forces by bringing them to battle in the air.
4. Prevent the approach of enemy invasion flotillas and defeat landing operations in progress through interdiction from the air.
5. Support friendly ground operations.
6. Operate against enemy battle fleets alone or in support of friendly naval flotillas.

The new June 1940 defense doctrine leapfrogged, by a wide margin, the reasoning for maintaining an army Air Corps. While the Air Corps still espoused a doctrine embodying its battlefield role with respect to direct support of army ground forces, it clearly established operations *at a distance* as its major obligation to the national defense. This doctrinalized the long-range bomber as the U.S. Army Air Corps' primary weapon of choice. Indeed, as early as mid-1939, the Air Corps had specified a four-engine bomber with a combat radius of up to three thousand miles, and in June 1940, it specified a follow-on design leading to a four-thousand-mile combat radius, which is four thousand miles out and four thousand miles back plus hover time. This specification eventually led to development of the Boeing B-29. Meanwhile, the B-17 was considered sufficient for dynamic defense of the Western Hemisphere.

For the time being, the American bases closest to all the potential hotspots in the Caribbean and Latin America were Puerto Rico and the Panama Canal Zone. On August 18, 1940, close on the release of the new Air Corps hemispheric doctrine, the United States and Canada established the Permanent Joint Board for the Defense of Canada and the United States under the Ogdensburg Agreement of the same date. Unlike an outright military alliance that might have goaded the Axis to action against the United States, the new, much closer arrangement with Canada was placed under the rubric of adherence to the Monroe Doctrine, which had been placed in force in 1823.

For the near term, Canadian forces were given the task of defending British bases from Newfoundland in the north to British Guiana in the south. Meanwhile, the Americans were read into the scheme via the Permanent Joint Board on Defense.

The Air Corps began to build up its strength in Puerto Rico and Panama as soon as it had new units to deploy. A composite wing headquarters was transferred to Borinquen Field, Puerto Rico, on November 1, 1940, as was one heavy bombardment group. As well, the Panama Canal Air Force and a new bombardment wing headquarters were activated on November 20, 1940, at Albrook Field, Panama Canal Zone, where an old-line bombardment wing headquarters had been based for years to oversee one medium bombardment group and two pursuit groups. (Army ground forces in the area included one Regular Army infantry regiment on Puerto Rico, plus two Puerto Rico National Guard infantry regiments not yet called up, and three Regular Army infantry regiments permanently based in the Panama Canal Zone. There were also several naval facilities in Puerto Rico and the Canal Zone.)

Important and urgent as the strategic defense of the Western Hemisphere was to the nation and its allies, the ground army and Air Corps simply had no more than these commands and units in 1940 to allocate to locations outside the eastern continental United States. Nevertheless, there were, in principle, air, ground, and naval commands and units allocated to an expeditionary force concept in the event any Axis incursions were made in the region from Newfoundland to Brazil.

Army Aircraft of 1940
Heavy Bombers

The Army Air Corps bomber enthusiasts continued to pin their hopes on the long-range, self-defending strategic bomber throughout the first full year of the war in Europe, even though the breathtaking German blitzkrieg strategy was built upon the partnership of tanks and armored infantry on the ground and light, swift tactical bombers and fighters operating at various levels above the ground, from quite low to quite high. While the RAF was the only other air force in the world that subscribed to the strategic bomber concept, its first four-engine heavy bomber, the Short Stirling, was not ready for in-service testing until May 1940 and would not make its combat debut until February 1941. As well, the four-engine Handley Page Halifax would not make its combat debut until June 1941. The RAF filled the strategic bomber position for the first sixteen months of war with twin-engine bombers such as the long-range Vickers Wellington, which mounted its first combat mission on September 2, 1939. Therefore, the Air Corps had no real experience by any other air force in the world on which to base its high hopes. Nevertheless, the sale had been made; the United States produced small numbers of B-17s through 1940 and expected to continue doing so in much larger numbers.

For all that the B-17 was literally the biggest thing in Air Corps circles after 1937, the Air Corps in 1939 invited Consolidated Aircraft to design a bigger, faster, longer-ranged, higher-payload, higher-flying heavy bomber than the B-17. As it happened, Consolidated was well along in designing a long-range flying boat it hoped to sell to the U.S. Navy as a patrol bomber. The key feature of the flying boat design was the low-drag Davis wing, an innovation designed specifically to move heavy airplanes over great distances through lower fuel consumption. Built around the Davis wing, the new heavy bomber design, dubbed Model 32, was accepted by the Air Corps in March 1939, almost as soon as Consolidated offered it. Designated XB-24, the new design, which was actually a bit smaller than the B-17, made more space for bombs than the

B-17 by incorporating much deeper bomb bays in which bombs were mounted vertically, nose down. To boost range and speed, the low-drag wings were mounted on the shoulders of the fuselage, which also enhanced low-speed handling. The bomb-bay doors were innovative in that they rolled into the fuselage, which produced less drag than bomb-bay doors lowered into the slipstream. The XB-24's tail assembly was composed of a pair of distinctive endplate fins and rudders.

The XB-24 prototype flew for the first time on December 29, 1939, and the first order for seven in-service test models was written almost immediately, and followed almost as quickly by an order for 36 B-24As for the Air Corps and a whopping 120 for the French air force. The first B-24s, which incorporated upgrades arising from in-service testing, were ready for delivery only after the fall of France. The French B-24s were picked up by the British, who were queued up by then to receive 164 of their own. The British dubbed their B-24s Liberator, and Consolidated dubbed the RAF model LB-30 (for "Liberator bomber"). The Liberator nickname eventually stuck to the American B-24s. The first RAF test model flew on January 17, 1941, and the first batch sent to theUnited Kingdom was unarmed examples to bring over rotations of ferry crews for the rest of the combined British and French order. Many of the RAF airplanes were considerably modified in Britain to serve as radar-equipped, rocket-firing maritime patrol bombers over the North Atlantic. Because of the urgency of the British war effort, the RAF was given precedence over the Air Corps, which did not receive its first airplanes— actually configured as unarmed LB-30s—until June 1941. In the meantime, England ordered forty-two examples of the new B-17D model, incorporating upgrades such as self-sealing fuel tanks and better crew armor, after the fall of France.

The Medium Tactical Bomber

Once the four-engine Boeing B-17 was on the Air Corps rolls, it was designated a heavy bomber. In the late 1930s, lighter, swifter, shorter-range twin-engine bombers (chiefly the Douglas B-18, a design variant of the Douglas DC-2 airliner that was first ordered in January 1936) were reconceived and reclassified as medium tactical bombers and nominally assigned the task of intermediate and distant support of ground forces. Billy Mitchell had even conceived a tactical antishipping role for speedy, multi-engine tactical bombers. Beginning with the initial Air Corps tests in March 1934 of the all-metal, twin-engine Martin B-10, which could cruise at 193 miles per hour at a service ceiling of 24,200 feet to a combat range of about five hundred miles with a bomb load of 2,260 pounds, the medium bomber was medium in all things—size, payload, operational altitude, range, mission, and expectations.

During his tenure as chief of GHQ Air Force, as the B-18 was entering service, Maj. Gen. Frank Andrews had argued long and hard against the entire notion of an intermediate class of bombers, in part because their limited range but relatively large size made it difficult to move them to far-off places if they could not simply fly there, even in stages. Andrews was willing to countenance light bombers employed in an attack role, mainly as a sop to the needs of the ground army. But he considered the B-17 and its class of large and long-range, four-engine strategic bombers as being so versatile that it could be adapted as needed to a lower-level, closer-in tactical role. In an impassioned January 1938 memo to the secretary of war regarding the fate of the B-17 program, which the civilian leaders wanted to abort, Andrews bolstered his overall argument in favor of the B-17—and against medium bombers that would divert scarce funds needed for strategic bombers—by noting that, on the one hand, the long-range B-17 could be fitted with bomb-bay fuel tanks to render it even longer ranged, and, on the other hand, that it was so adaptable that its payload, with or without long-range tanks, could be tailored to specific missions, including medium-range or even short-range sorties in support of ground forces, at low level, with small bombs—whatever. This sort of relentless argument cost Andrews his job and his stars in March 1939.

The supporters of medium bombers noted rather more diplomatically that the type could be designed and exploited to fill all the many niches between on-the-deck direct support of ground troops and precision bombing missions hundreds of miles behind enemy lines. This line of thinking, and a good deal of British and German experience with twin-engine tactical bombers throughout 1940, led to a doctrinally sound medium-bomber program in the United States.

The first effort to build on the experience of operating a total of 350 Douglas B-18s was a Douglas model designed in 1938 from the ground up and designated B-23 by the Air Corps. The B-23, which was the first American bomber to incorporate a tail-mounted "stinger" machine gun, seemed like a good idea when an order for thirty-eight was placed just before the outbreak of the war in Europe, but enthusiasm waned precipitously as attention was drawn to German models that obviously outclassed the B-23. The small and only production run was relegated first to coastal patrolling and later to towing gliders.

More work on a replacement for the inadequate B-18 began with a new 1938 specification that led in January 1939 to the first flight of a North American Aviation twin-engine airplane capable of carrying a 1,200-pound bomb load. The Air Corps was encouraged, but it sent North American back to the drawing board with a list of desired modifications, including a larger payload. The result, in September 1939, was a suitable airplane the Air Corps ordered under the designation B-25 and nicknamed Mitchell, after Billy Mitchell (the only American military airplane ever named after a person). At first, 184 B-25s were ordered, but the cure for a design flaw and the addition of crew-space armor and self-sealing fuel tanks led to a redesignation of B-25A. Only twenty-five B-25s and forty B-25As were built before further changes were ordered, and the United States would be drawn into World War II before any B-25Bs were delivered.

In 1939, the Air Corps requested designs for a very fast light bomber with enough payload to double as a medium-altitude precision bomber. The Glenn L. Martin Company responded with a design it guaranteed would meet or exceed the specification, to which the Air Corps replied with an unprecedented 201-plane production order before a test model was built. Indeed, no test example was ever built; the first production airplane, designated B-26, flew on November 25, 1940. The new medium bomber had a maximum speed of more than 250 miles per hour and an internal bomb capacity of 5,800 pounds for short-range missions—nearly as fast as a pursuit with nearly the payload of a B-17. The big problem the B-26 presented was that it tended to stall at speeds of just under one hundred miles per hour, which made it tricky for novice pilots to land. The answer to this was a set of modifications and better pilot training.

Pursuits

The Air Corps attempted to field good pursuit aircraft prior to the outbreak of war in Europe, but the impetus of war there quickly outran the best American designs of the day. The Seversky P-35, of which seventy-six were delivered by August 1938, was clearly a nonstarter, and eighty more commandeered from a Swedish order in October 1940 were of little use, even though forty-eight of them were ultimately dispatched as a stopgap to front-line units in the Philippines. Seversky, renamed Republic Aviation in 1939, upgraded the P-35's engine and supercharger under the XP-41 designation, and other changes led to a further redesignation of P-43. Thirteen in-service P-43 test examples were ordered in March 1939, and deliveries began in September 1940. Testing went well, but the P-43 in no way reached the level of pursuits already in action over Europe. The Air Corps eventually ordered 907 units of an improved version, designated P-44, but in the end production was cut off at 53 P-43s and 80 P-44s, plus 125 P-43As that eventually were shipped to the Chinese air force. All of the P-43s and P-44s accepted by the Air Corps were ultimately converted for use as photo-reconnaissance aircraft and shipped to Britain.

Back at the drawing board, Republic's chief designer married the biggest, most powerful rotary engine then available with what turned out to be one of the largest single-engine piston fighters ever built, a highly evolved P-35 the Air Corps designated P-47. An order for one test example was placed in September 1940. It would fly for the first time in May 1941, but the first production P-47 would not be delivered until March 1942.

In the end, the Air Corps entered 1941—the *second* full year of war in Europe—with a thoroughly inadequate operational pursuit roster: small numbers of outmoded and inferior P-35s and P-36s, and small numbers of reasonably modern P-39s and P-40s.

Part IV

THE FORGE

February 1, 1941
–
November 30, 1941

Chapter 23

Lend-Lease

You Fight, We Build

BY THE BEGINNING OF 1941, the United States had crafted an exceptionally good deal for itself with Britain. The United States got to be one of the good guys while, for as long as possible, only the world's other English-speaking peoples and a corps of refugees from mainland Europe did the dying.

There was a greater good in play within this deal. The longer the United States stayed out of the actual war in Europe and the looming war in Asia and the Pacific, the faster it could build its own world-class war machine. The less material wastage the United States itself suffered in battle, the more goods would be available for Britain, its imperial and Commonwealth forces, and its allies. It would clearly take direct and massive American involvement in combat to wrest Europe back from Nazi domination, but first the Americans had to build a competent military force equipped to fight on at least an equal footing with the demonstrably superb and immensely strong Wehrmacht. And that would take time. Thus, the Allied forces in the fight remained steadfastly in the fight while giving the United States a moral pass to sort itself out, build itself up, and create and export priceless war goods in the meantime. For as long as no nation attacked the United States or declared war on it, for as long as the American military establishment grew stronger by the day without suffering war's inevitable expenditures in lives and treasure, for as long as American industry could keep the Allies in the fight, which was the better option: war now, or war later?

The Road to Lend-Lease

When the European war broke out in September 1939, President Roosevelt had been obligated to invoke the Neutrality Acts, which barred American firms or even the U.S. government from selling or otherwise transferring arms and other war commodities to any belligerent nation, which is to say Germany and Poland, and any of their allies who declared war on one or the other of the initial belligerents. Very quickly, as Americans began to feel hemmed in and increasingly alarmed by the pattern of German and Japanese military and political triumphs following close on the heels of the invasion of Poland, there was increasing domestic pressure to help one side at least stand up to the other.

While there was much altruism associated with the impulse to somehow aid Britain and France as they prepared to stand up to the Nazi war machine, so too was there much hope that their doing so would spare the United States and its citizens an experience of war.

President Roosevelt had for some time been urging the lifting of the total arms embargo with respect to the European war. America's allies needed the goods, American industry needed the impetus and income to expand, and American workers needed the jobs. The president had been lobbying for a change since before the war actually began.

In an urgent policy speech before the Congress on September 21, 1939, two weeks after he had declared a limited national emergency, Roosevelt called for repeal of the all-encompassing arms embargo with respect to Poland, Great Britain, France, Australia, and New Zealand. There was great division in the Congress between interventionists and non-interventionists (as the old isolationists were suddenly labeled), but the matter was settled very quickly, as these things went, under the can't-miss rubric "aid to democracies." The bill that the president requested passed both houses on November 4, 1939, and was put into effect as the Cash-and-Carry policy, which was fashioned to evade some prickly financial problems arising out of arms sales to belligerents—especially Britain—during the Great War. If England, France, and their allies wanted to buy American munitions, war machines, or other war commodities, they only needed to pay in full when they placed the order. Many of the other neutrality measures remained in force, including a ban on U.S.-flag vessels transiting defined war zones, which effectively meant that U.S. vessels could not carry American-made war materiel to England, France, or any other destination in a war zone. Aircraft sales were limited to oldish models without the latest accouterments, a restriction that was modified on March 25, 1940, to include some better types with better equipment, but not the best. After France fell to the Wehrmacht, the British assumed responsibility for all undelivered French orders.

The Army Air Corps' fifty-four-group program, not to mention orders from the U.S. Navy, severely impinged on British aircraft purchases, but the Air Corps, on July 23, 1940, graciously allowed British orders for aircraft urgently needed to fight the Battle of Britain and deter Japanese ambitions in Asia to be placed at the head of the queue. On September 13, 1940—the same day the Italian army invaded Egypt from Libya—the Joint Aircraft Committee, headed by the chief of the Air Corps, was established to oversee all aircraft output for the industry's three largest clients, the U.S. Army Air Corps, U.S. Navy Bureau of Aeronautics, and the British Purchasing Commission. In January 1941, the Joint Aircraft Committee took under its control all contracts, foreign and domestic, for all aircraft material. The committee also established a master production schedule for the entire industry.

Centralizing and bureaucratizing all the processes of aircraft production and allocation erased uncertainty and confusion, and it gave all parties equal footing in claims on (rising) capacity. But the system did not get to Britain's emerging concern, which was that its dollar reserves were shrinking out of sight as the aggregate of goods purchased in the United States steadily mounted. By the end of January 1941, the British government would have gone entirely through the $4.5 billion in gold and financial instruments it had tied up in investments in the United States on September 1, 1939. This money, plus other British resources, and French money while it lasted, had an immense impact; together with America's own spending, it so thoroughly primed the pump of American industry as to keep it running for fifty years. But, in the short term, Britain was rapidly running out of financial options, American law was still American law, and that law was Cash-and-Carry.

Lend-Lease

Much concerned about Britain's approaching penury with respect to the Cash-and-Carry law, President Roosevelt, during a November 1940 post-election cruise aboard a U.S. Navy cruiser, worked with his principal personal advisor, Harry Hopkins, to devise a solution that would be palatable for the American people and their elected representatives. The basic concept was that the United States would establish new government armories, plants, and shipyards to bolster American industry's rush to build out the U.S. military as authorized under several statutory expansion plans. Also, the private-public effort would create sufficient excess capacity to allow for lending or leasing many categories of items, including food, to anti-fascist nations at war with Germany, principally Great Britain and its imperial and Commonwealth partners. To a lesser and less overt degree, similar aid would be provided to China. How Britain and other nations might pay the United States for such goods was left vague, something to be skirted in the public relations groundwork the plan would require to get support in the Congress and across the nation.

Upon his return to work, Roosevelt began to lay the political and public relations foundation for the resulting plan. The first foray was a presidential press conference on December 17, 1940, in which the lend-lease formula was first revealed. On that same day, Secretary of the Treasury Henry Monganthau Jr. appeared before a congressional committee to say that Great Britain was "scraping the bottom of the barrel" and could no longer pay the cash it took to carry off American war goods. On December 29, the president delivered a fireside chat via commercial radio, a device he had long used to speak directly to the American people:

> My Friends:
>   This is not a fireside chat on war. It is a talk on national security, because the nub of the whole purpose of your president is to keep you now, and your children later, and your grandchildren much later, out of a last-ditch war for the preservation of American independence and all of the things that American independence means to you and to me and to ours. . . .

At this moment, the forces of the states that are leagued against all peoples who live in freedom are being held away from our shores. The Germans and the Italians are being blocked on the other side of the Atlantic by the British, and by the Greeks, and by thousands of soldiers and sailors who were able to escape from subjugated countries. In Asia the Japanese are being engaged by the Chinese nation in another great defense. . . .

Some of our people like to believe that wars in Europe and in Asia are of no concern to us. But it is a matter of most vital concern to us that European and Asiatic war-makers should not gain control of the oceans which lead to this hemisphere. . . .

Does anyone seriously believe that we need to fear attack anywhere in the Americas while a free Britain remains our most powerful naval neighbor in the Atlantic? And does anyone seriously believe, on the other hand, that we could rest easy if the Axis powers were our neighbors there?

If Great Britain goes down, the Axis powers will control the continents of Europe, Asia, Africa, Australia, and the high seas—and they will be in a position to bring enormous military and naval resources against this hemisphere. It is no exaggeration to say that all of us, in all the Americas, would be living at the point of a gun—a gun loaded with explosive bullets, economic as well as military. . . .

The British people and their allies today are conducting an active war against [the Axis]. Our own future security is greatly dependent on the outcome of that fight. Our ability to "keep out of war" is going to be affected by that outcome. Thinking in terms of today and tomorrow, I make the direct statement to the American people that there is far less chance of the United States getting into war if we do all we can now to support the nations defending themselves against attack by the Axis than if we acquiesce in their defeat, submit tamely to an Axis victory, and wait our turn to be the object of attack in another war later on. . . .

The people of Europe who are defending themselves do not ask us to do their fighting. They ask us for the implements of war, the planes, the tanks, the guns, the freighters which will enable them to fight for their liberty and for our security. Emphatically we must get these weapons to them, get them to them in sufficient volume and quickly enough, so that we and our children will be saved the agony and suffering of war which others have had to endure. . . .

Democracy's fight against world conquest is being greatly aided, and must be more greatly aided, by the rearmament of the United States and by sending every ounce and every ton of munitions and supplies that we can possibly spare to help the defenders who are in the front lines. And it is no more unneutral for us to do that than it is for Sweden, Russia, and other nations near Germany to send steel and ore and oil and other war materials into Germany every day in the week. . . .

American industrial genius, unmatched throughout all the world . . . has been called upon to bring its resources and its talents into action. Manufacturers of watches, of farm implements, of linotypes, and cash registers, and automobiles, and sewing machines, and lawn mowers, and locomotives are now making fuses, bomb packing crates, telescope mounts, shells, and pistols and tanks. . . .

I want to make it clear that it is the purpose of the nation to build now with all possible speed every machine, every arsenal, every factory that we need to manufacture our defense material. . . .

As planes and ships and guns and shells are produced, your government, with its defense experts, can then determine how best to use them to defend this hemisphere. The decision as to how much shall be sent abroad and how much shall remain at home must be made on the basis of our overall military necessities.

We must be the great arsenal of democracy. For us this is an emergency as serious as war itself. We must apply ourselves to our task with the same resolution, the same sense of urgency, the same spirit of patriotism and sacrifice as we would show were we at war.

We have furnished the British great material support and we will furnish far more in the future. . . .

Known as the Arsenal of Democracy Speech, this masterful message set the stage for passage of Lend-Lease by the Congress. The themes the president struck home on December 29 were struck home again during his January 6, 1941, State of the Union Address to the Congress.

The administration jumped the gun a bit when it signed a letter of agreement with the British on February 23, 1941, ahead of a bill passed in both houses of the Congress. Following hot national and congressional debate, the first Lend-Lease Act was passed on March 11. During the March 15 signing ceremony, President Roosevelt struck an important political note: "This decision is the end of any attempt at appeasement in our land; the end of urging us to get along with dictators; the end of compromise with tyranny and the forces of oppression." That very evening, Roosevelt attended the annual White House Correspondents' Association dinner for the first time since his election in 1932. There, to a crowd whose members reached into most American homes on most days of every week, the president hammered home anti-fascist concerns and drew further attention to his premise that supplying Britain and her anti-fascist allies in the near term would help prevent the loss of American blood. A few choice sentences: "We believe firmly that when our production output is in full swing the democracies of the world will be able to prove that dictatorships cannot win."

"But now the time element is of supreme importance. Every plane, every other instrument of war, old and new, which we can spare now we will send overseas. That is common-sense strategy."

"The great task of this day, the deep duty which rests upon us, is to move products from the assembly lines of our factories to the battle lines of democracy now."

At a March 17 meeting of army supply chiefs, Secretary of War Henry Stimson expressed his view of the far-reaching consequences of Lend-Lease; Stimson stated in unequivocal terms that the new program was going to take the United States to war. On March 20, General Marshall wrote in a memo to Stimson on the effects of Lend-Lease on aircraft production, "Such a program cannot be sustained as a military requirement unless we are willing to state that we are preparing for an *offensive* campaign in the air against a foreign power."

Hitler's Reaction

There was undoubtedly relieved cheering from London to the most remote outpost of the Allied battlefront when news of Lend-Lease reached them. There was only the gnashing of teeth and rattling of sabers in Nazi Germany's highest councils, for Lend-Lease was the latest and most objectionable show of American support for Germany's otherwise reeling principal enemy. Many of Hitler's closest advisors urged that he immediately declare war on the United States, if for no other reason than to stop the flow of goods from American shores to Britain and its war fronts. But Hitler demurred.

These same advisors had had to reel in the German despot when he reacted to the destroyers-for-bases deal in September 1940. Now, however, Hitler and his army and air force chiefs and their staffs were plotting a massive spring assault on the Soviet Union. Except for the U-boat fleet, there were no assets to provide teeth to a declaration of war against the United States, and the U-boat fleet, while growing quite fast, was not yet so large as to be able to initially overcome a sudden active offensive by American antisubmarine vessels and bombers. Hitler was angry enough to declare war, but he was yet lucid enough to stay the impulse. There would be time and force sufficient to the task following the projected collapse of the Soviet Union in, the generals promised, September. With a margin to allow for the transfer of fully reequipped veteran ground forces to western Europe and North Africa, that suggested that the declaration of war would be made in October or November.

In this, there was a meeting of minds: Roosevelt's military brain trust *hoped* the United States would not be drawn into any war until the end of 1942, but the president, who hoped for the same, pretty much concurred with Hitler; he *expected* the United States to be at war with Germany, like it or not, by the end of 1941.

Implementation

Key among the early implementers of Lend-Lease was the ever-handy James Burns, who had been promoted to major general in October 1940 and still served as executive officer to Under Secretary of War Robert Patterson. Many believed that the hard-working Burns, the brains and driving force behind so many other matters, from ordnance and industrial mobilization to national strategy, was the key to the early successes the Lend-Lease program required to stay in favor with its numerous stakeholders. Burns, born in Pawling, New York, on September 13, 1885, graduated West Point as an artillery officer in 1908. He served in the Vera Cruz expedition of 1914 and, with rank of colonel at age thirty-three, served under the American Expeditionary Force's chief of ordnance. After helping to dream up the Army Industrial College and set it up, Burns had graduated from the new institution in 1926. He attended the Army War College in 1927, served in the Philippines from 1932 to 1935, and in the office of the chief of staff in 1935 and 1936, from which he went to the office of the assistant secretary of war. (He would be named the army's chief of ordnance in April 1942.)

At its working end, the Lend-Lease Act was nothing without the cash to buy things. The British had no more ready cash, but the solution to that problem arrived on March 27, with a congressional authorization for $7 billion in credits.

As well on March 27, the U.S. and British military staffs meeting under the rubric American-British Conversations (ABC) presented ABC-1, which set forth an outline for a grand strategy to be implemented in an Anglo-American war against Germany. They followed two days later with ABC-2, a template for the implementation of a combined air offensive over Germany and occupied Europe and a guide for aircraft production in the United States that would satisfy the burgeoning needs of the RAF and Commonwealth air forces, the Army Air Corps, and U.S. naval aviation. The Joint Aircraft Committee's role was expanded to include allotment of aviation materials provided under Lend-Lease. As such, the committee doubled as the Defense Aid Supply Committee, which worked up a basic policy statement.

The sum of all the parts was that the allocation of all war goods produced in the United States gave precedence to Britain's needs, because it was fighting the war. Setting back the American rearmament timetable, given how far the American armed services yet had to go to effective war-making power, was deemed the least of all evils.

On July 9, the president asked Secretary of War Stimson and Secretary of the Navy Knox to provide a joint estimate of "overall production . . . required to defeat our potential enemies." This was in aid of the Office of Production Management, which had to reconcile needs with production capacity. Among the staggering requirements laid out in the September 11 response was an outline of Air Corps needs for more than forty-three thousand new airplanes (including trainers) by 1944, a minimum for conducting an aerial offensive over Europe sufficient to have a strategic effect. Taken with the needs of Allied and naval aviation, the September 11 report suggested a grand total in airplanes alone of more than seventy-two thousand by 1944.

Combined and taken in total, the projection of British and American war-production needs was staggering. Yet, as a collation was being presented in late September, a rather buoyant President Roosevelt made the first moves to incorporate them into a plan that would be dubbed the Victory Program, the grand economic strategy for pooling resources and output to defeat the Axis.

Soviet Needs

The president's request regarding overall production requirements vis-à-vis American and British needs, not to mention the response, was made *after* Wehrmacht spearheads crossed into Soviet-occupied Poland on June 22, 1941, and pushed the Red Army and Soviet air force far back into their motherland. This was good news to Britain, because it bled off the bulk of the Luftwaffe from British and western European skies. Nevertheless, it very quickly impinged on growing but not fully grown American production capacity, because the Soviets quickly and urgently asked the United States for warplanes and other war goods, and the United States could not say no, for powerful reasons the president had outlined in his Arsenal of Democracy speech (even though Comrade Josef Stalin's workers' paradise could not, by any construction, be deemed a democracy by the American president).

In early August, the United States pledged an initial token delivery to the Soviet Union of forty P-40 pursuits and five B-25 medium bombers. (The delivery of these and follow-on aircraft allocations to the Soviets required the establishment of air ferry routes via Alaska, and that required an aggressive airfield construction program in that remote U.S. territory.) An Anglo-American mission was dispatched to Moscow with full powers to map out long-term Soviet munitions requirements under Lend-Lease.

The Anglo-American mission to Moscow met with Premier Stalin when it arrived, and by October 1, the British and American ambassadors, along with the Soviet foreign minister, signed the first agreement, which essentially placed a preliminary order with the United States for 1,800 airplanes, mostly combat models. The Soviet Union officially became part of the Lend-Lease program on November 1.

The modest initial Soviet requirement was added to the nascent Victory Program, as were follow-on orders that would affect production into 1942. But even sanguine observers had the sense that the sands were running out of the American peace bubble, both with respect to a deteriorating political climate between the United States and Japan, and with respect to German forbearance of American support for Britain and, now, the Soviet Union.

Upside, Downside

For a U.S. Army struggling to absorb hundreds of thousands of troops rated untrained to semi-trained, and to equip them with modern weapons and transportation at a time the nation's industrial base was not yet fully changed over to war production, Lend-Lease was enervating, to say the least. Every truck sent to another nation was a truck some American troops missed riding in during a long road march. Every airplane sent abroad was one less the Air Corps or naval aviation had in hand to train a pilot and crew or use as a platform for training aerial gunners. Or for fighting a war. Every Lend-Lease 75mm artillery piece lost on a battlefield in France or North Africa was, even though obsolete, one less to be used to train an American gun crew and one more shaved from the war-now-versus-war-later equation that guided so much of the effort to build out the American ground army.

Still and all, there was an upside. As General Marshall had said to a senior Air Corps general in the autumn of 1940 regarding a transfer, then in discussion, of twenty still-rare B-17s to the RAF, "battle tests are better than peace tests." Moreover, American generals and admirals soothed themselves by noting that clearing out early models of modern weapons by sending them to the British meant that American forces had access to the newest upgrades, which were themselves often prompted by British "war tests."

In the end, it was what it was because the president wanted to keep the British and Chinese, and ultimately the Soviets, from going under. To do that, Roosevelt was willing to push back by a considerable interval the fielding of the perfect American army, navy, and air forces.

There was a range of problems arising from incompatibilities between American specifications and British specifications. For example, the British service rifle of the day was the bolt-action .303-caliber Lee-Enfield, while both the old American Springfield '03 and the new Garand M1 fired a .30-06-caliber round. If the United States was to simply give the British the smaller American round, the bullets would have to be accompanied by tens of thousands of .30-06 rifles meant for American troops at a time when the U.S. Army had not enough rifles of any type merely to train its recruits. *Or* a number of American munitions lines would have to be retooled to produce hundreds of millions of .303-caliber rounds for a British army at war.

The first impulse was to send bullets then in hand, of which one hundred million were declared surplus for that purpose on May 22, 1940. General Marshall shortly promised another fifty-eight million by December. But the bullets were .30-06s, and the May 22 promise, even if practicable, would have left the U.S. Army with thirty million fewer rounds in hand than would be required merely by training demands arising from implementation of the Protective Mobilization Plan. Moreover, the ability of U.S. arsenals to make up the difference was as yet inadequate. As the army looked more deeply into its own reserve versus its own growing needs, it was reported in early August 1940, as the National Guard call-up and draft were being pushed, that bullets needed for the much larger army translated to a total shortfall of nearly 1.1 *billion* rounds. By September 20, G-3 reported to the general staff that the army had just 520 million rounds in hand, of which 135 million were stored at numerous overseas sites, such as the Philippines and the Panama Canal Zone. That left 385 million rounds at a time when one year's training cycle alone would consume a projected 468 million rounds.

On February 19, 1941, by which time nearly the entire National Guard and several newly activated divisions were undergoing training, the British requested nine hundred million .303 rifle rounds. If filled, the new order would further impinge on the production of .30-06 rounds and thus leave the U.S. Army short by about 60 percent the number of training rounds it needed, even though bullet production had by then been substantially increased. This to say nothing of the shortfall the United States faced if the nation was dragged into the war.

And on and on and on it went. Each request the British made was received with genuine sympathy, and every effort was made to fill every order. But delicate balances within just the army were constantly disrupted, and the time and energy it took to constantly rebalance the equation was time and energy lost to a hundred or a thousand other urgent planning demands. Moreover, it was quickly apparent that gearing up whole factories to produce just British-designed weapons was relatively inefficient, because many British designs were inherently less efficient than American designs filling the same niches. The British Lee-Enfield service rifle, for example was a ten-round bolt-action weapon, a 1907 design similar to the five-round bolt-action American Springfield '03, a 1903 weapon; it wasn't ever going to be in the same class as the eight-round gas-operated semiautomtic M1 Garand of 1930s design, even if it was made in American factories. Another example of an American perspective on an "inefficient" weapon involves the standard British artillery piece, the 25-pounder field gun/howitzer, a 1930s design that fired an 87.6mm round out to a maximum range of 13,400 yards (about 7.6 miles). This compared to the American 105mm field howitzer, a 1919 design updated and first built in the 1930s that could fire its larger round out as far as 12,325 yards (7 miles). Though longer ranged, the 25-pounder round had less burst radius than the 105, which is to say it was less lethal when it got where it was going. American arsenals declined to produce 25-pounders for the British.

As the U.S Army grew in size through the first half of 1941, well beyond the dreams of men who had fashioned the Protective Mobilization Plan of 1920, the ordnance planners had to lay down the law. It wasn't enough to merely recruit men; those men had to be adequately trained with real weapons, equipped with real weapons, and eventually sent off to war with real weapons. To make sure there were enough real weapons to go around in the burgeoning ground army alone, the weapons and ammunition that would be sent to Britain and other Lend-Lease nations had to give way at least to a rational degree to needs at home. Thus, the United States curtailed production of some foreign weapons and munitions for reasons of efficiency and in order to expand capacity for its own needs. For example, the United States continued to produce the .303 round used with British Lee-Enfield rifles, along with Lee-Enfield rifles themselves, mounting to more than a million by 1945, but the somewhat different .303 machine gun round was left to the British to produce on their own.

As matters developed, even as fixes to some problems were worked out, the situation became increasingly complex. The effort to keep apace demand led to strains and some fractures between the United States and foreign combatants as well as between and among American representatives of numerous constituencies that were obligated to compete vigorously for finite resources and then defend vigorously their minor triumphs, each for excellent reasons. There was no point in 1941, not even a fleeting moment, at which the whole thing balanced out: not even close. Committee after committee held meeting after meeting to discuss study after study and reach solution after solution, but the entire enterprise was never at rest long enough for any solution for any subsystem to completely take hold, so interdependent were the parts upon one another. The whole enterprise seemed to move forward and even gain momentum, but the U.S. forces never could say exactly when any of them, much less all of them together, would reach some tipping point at which even the most sanguine player could declare the U.S. military as being ready for war. That was an existential state that would have been difficult enough—perhaps impossible—for the American military-industrial-political partnership to achieve in 1941, even without the urgent need for and vast expenditure of time, effort, raw materials, and finished goods devoted to supplying other warring nations.

War Delayed

Early in 1941 Hitler had hoped to bring the Soviet Union to its knees in September and declare war on the United States from a position of strength in October or November. From June 22 onward, the Germans had done *very* well in rolling up the Red Army and laying waste to the Soviet air force across an immense front and well into the Soviet rear, but the invasion had been delayed at the outset. This delay was triggered when a bumbling Italian army had invaded Greece on October 28, 1940. After months of humiliation at the hands of the Greeks, the Italians asked the Germans for help. To do so from their marshalling positions to the north, a vital core of German combat divisions had to invade both Yugoslavia and Greece. This began on April 6, 1941. The Royal Yugoslav Army surrendered on April 17, and Greece surrendered on April 19, but British and Commonwealth troops who had fought beside the Greek army retreated and set up shop with Greek troops on Crete. The Germans needed a month to prepare; they invaded Crete on May 20, and the last defenders surrendered on June 1. Fast, efficient, and brutal, the on-the-spot German actions in Yugoslavia, Greece, and Crete showed the German army at its very best. Nevertheless, the commitment of crack German divisions to Yugoslavia, Greece, and Crete over two crucial spring months had delayed and somewhat weakened the larger, more visionary offensive.

Even though German battlefield successes in the Soviet Union were running at or ahead of schedule, the whole invasion was out of kilter, and reliably rainy autumn weather was slowing it down. A revised estimate placed a prospective

Soviet collapse and capitulation in November or December, immediately upon the fall of Moscow.

So maybe Hitler could transfer powerful forces to western Europe and all across North Africa by January or February and then declare war on that supremely maddening Roosevelt and his supremely maddening navy in March or April 1942.

Chapter 24

Industrial and Scientific Mobilization in 1941

The Victory Program

THERE WAS A STRATEGY, Joint War Plan Rainbow 5. There was a policy for sharing with allies, Lend-Lease. There was a vague sense of a far-off goal of victory. The armed services knew what they needed to do to prepare for war, and the navy even had a decent idea about how to prosecute a war in its milieu. But in early 1941 there remained no systematic plan to turn from rearming America to fighting *and winning* a multi-front war on land and sea, and in the air. There was no central planning authority, no central clearing house that could systematically match the needs of the individual services to the overall plan. There was no clear sense of what victory would, or even should, look like.

The Lend-Lease Act was passed on March 11, 1941. It took approximately no time at all for its requirements to bump up against the requirements of the American armed services, but there was no referee. There was a statute that made the Office of the Assistant Secretary of War the nation's military logistician-in-chief, but there was no sure mechanism that would allow Assistant Secretary Robert Patterson to actually oversee all of the nation's war production; the path to harmonious planning petered out somewhere just beyond the portal to Patterson's Department of War office suite. The navy wanted to go its own way; the Maritime Commission wanted to go its own way; even the Air Corps wanted to go its own way.

Less than a year earlier, in June 1940, Col. James Burns, had stubbornly forced the national command authority to provide a clear strategic vision that would guide his and the assistant secretary's effort to purpose-build an army for the onrushing war. Burns' influence had been golden; men of far higher rank and station had bowed to his iron will, and the nation had advanced. (Since then Burns had been promoted two ranks but yet remained as Patterson's executive officer.)

The new man of the hour was Col. Henry Aurand, a senior G-4 staffer. It was he, on April 7, who pointed out that there was no one in the Department of War hierarchy who had the actual authority to reconcile Lend-Lease acquisition requests with military acquisition requests. Assistant Secretary Patterson concurred in an April 18 memo to Secretary of War Stimson in which he noted that future requirements had to be charted as soon as possible so that everyone's needs could be met, and that it was time to force needs to intersect with industrial capacity by means of a long-range but nonetheless detailed plan. Patterson said that to establish and prioritize needs, he required from the people over his head a clear statement of the nation's settled war policy. Patterson wrote that "a decision should be made as promptly as possible, on the production effort necessary to achieve victory on the basis of appropriate assumptions as to probable enemies and friends and theaters of operation. . . . It is suggested that a joint committee be created to make appropriate recommendations, and to consist of representatives of the Army, Navy, Maritime Commission, and of the [newly created] Office of Production Management." Patterson, who in this statement made the first official effort by a high government official to project needs all the way out to final victory, then made a pithy demand that could not be ducked: "In any event this office needs a decision as to the ultimate production required by the War Department so that appropriate plans can be started."

The urgency of Patterson's April 18 request was not matched by presidential action until July 9. The interim was full of urgent competing demands on the president's time and thought processes, and this one slipped through the cracks. Nevertheless, the memo was circulated within the Department of War. General Burns sent Secretary Stimson a copy on April 29, along with Burns' recommendation that the issue be placed before the Joint Army and Navy Board. The War Plans Division shortly chimed in that it required an early solution because it needed to make commitments right away to Britain and China while also arming American troops. A War Plans officer told his chief, "The situation is extremely confused. Confusion will reign until an agency for formulating a policy based on all strategic plans is designated."

The Office of Production Management (OPM), which worked for the president in overseeing just these matters, revealed to a May 17 conference of army leaders that it was "getting very definite pressure from the White House to get an intensified effort from industry." (American industry, even at this late date, had not definitively switched a large proportion of its capacity over to war production, and it could not be ordered to do so without a declaration of war.) The OPM representative listened well and eventually asked the vital question, "Is it true that if your supply or procurement service knew your whole objective, you could place that load easier than if it was placed in successive bites?" The army officials and officers in the room who had been grappling with this very conundrum realized that they had not succeeded in fully communicating their needs to the civilian hierarchy. The short answer was "yes," but General Marshall, who was hosting the meeting in his office, spoke at greater length: "If procurement of these essential items, which amount to several billion dollars, would help you, we might possibly get them and store them against future use. However, another complicating factor is the priorities question. What will the bomber program [a request for five hundred bombers that the president supported] do? The president has said to step up the cruiser program."

All well and good, but OPM was merely the latest executive agency whose weakness became evident to all the players as its swiftly growing staff struggled to build momentum while being held hostage to action by the president. Established by executive order on January 7, 1941, OPM turned out to be a mere reshuffling of the older and quite toothless advisory commission to the Council of National Defense. The council's only member had been the president, and the chief of both was William Knudsen, the chairman of General Motors. So, even though OPM finally got the message about a long-term plan, the only way for it to get from confusion to a solution was via President Roosevelt, and he had no time just then to grapple with the problem.

Frustrated and dead in the water, army War Plans sent a memo to navy War Plans outlining the dilemma in the hope the navy would realize that, like the army, its plans and needs were tied to those of the other service and Lend-Lease. Navy War Plans (whose brilliant but mercurial chief, Rear Adm. Richmond Kelly Turner, was famously prone to getting into unexplained snits) failed even to respond, so on June 7, Brig. Gen. Leonard Gerow, the army War Plans chief, formally laid the matter before the Joint Army and Navy Board. At roughly the same time, General Marshall required Gerow to prepare for the general staff a *brief* and clear-cut rough estimate of strategic needs for ground, air, and even naval forces. Marshall wanted answers to all the unresolved questions that had been dogging the services for months. The G-4 branch also pointed out that the absence of a firm, long-term, reality-based plan was depriving industry of a clear road map.

It turned out that the logjam was less a function of presidential fiat than of the army bureaucracy's inability to assign the required task to a specific agency. Everyone everywhere in the chain of responsibility had pretty much signed on to the need for a clear road map showing the path, not so much to preparing for war, as to *winning* a two-ocean war fought nearly the world around. Marshall's order to Gerow for such a plan jogged the system sufficiently to break the logjam. The job was given to Maj. Albert Wedemeyer, a formidably brilliant 1919 West Point graduate.

The task was far more complex than anyone had imagined, but led by Major Wedemeyer, a small staff with an immense reach provided by the army chief of staff built its case and found its solutions. It took all of Colonel Aurand's time to provide the planners with basic data compiled by the G-4 branch. The early intercession of Secretary Stimson produced a start at cooperation from agencies beyond Stimson's purview, but a July 9 letter from President Roosevelt finally and completely turned the tide. In very short order, Aurand became trustee of immense piles of data compiled and sent to him under the auspices of OPM, the Office of the Secretary of the Navy, the chief of the Maritime Commission, and the British Supply Council.

Of these agencies, the navy itself was least cooperative. It had ranked highest in terms of the largesse offered by the Congress throughout the interwar years, particularly since the mid-1930s, and especially since September 1939. This was simply because the navy was in the best position to defend the U.S. mainland against foreign aggression before it touched America's shore. But, as the army's mid-1941 information-gathering process went forward, even the navy grudgingly admitted that "only land armies can finally win wars." This statement appeared on September 5 in the navy's War Plans Division's long-delayed response to President Roosevelt's July 9 call for cooperation with the Wedemeyer project. It appeared in a sixteen-page document dubiously and self-servingly entitled "Proposal for the National Defense Policy of the United States." The document, a product of the irascible Admiral Turner's War Plans Division, was delivered less than a week before the scheduled release of the Wedemeyer report. It was a good thing it was so short and lean in data, for it triggered no extensive recalculations. Perforce, the Wedemeyer plan was able to shed very little light on the navy's needs within the matrix of cause and effect it set forth.

All the data that was going to be turned over to Wedemeyer's team was studied and compiled in an orderly and logical process, and it was allowed to speak for itself; there appeared to be no forced conclusions drawn. On September 10, Major Wedemeyer launched his team's detailed plan, dubbed the Victory Program, up the chain of command.

As a look into the future, from the perspective of the future, the Victory Program had mixed results—unknown, of course, when it was issued. It forecast an army end strength in 1945 of 8.7 million, and the true number was a close-enough 8.2 million. But it also forecast an army of 215 combat divisions, where only 89 were in service in 1945. The sixty-one armored divisions forecast became sixteen, ten airborne divisions became five, and only one mountain division was activated of ten estimated. It was also wrong about the number of army antiaircraft units and troops, because it did not foresee developments in air superiority that unfolded in all active theaters; instead of the nearly 465,000 antiaircraft troops cited in the forecast, fewer than 250,000 troops manned antiaircraft units in 1945.

But the Victory Program was logical in all its parts; it arose from the real and observable world of mid-1941, and above all it turned into exactly the forecast the planners required to break through the confusion that tied up the system before the plan was circulated. Navy War Plans, which had been passive-aggressive throughout the process, quibbled and quibbled over details, but President Roosevelt embraced the program and remained quite engaged in asking follow-up questions.

Ultimately, the Victory Program did what was required of it. Though it did not survive the first shot fired by the enemy—no military plan ever does—it was promulgated at a critical moment in American history. It did the job. It fixed the focus of the men who made the decisions. It got the ball rolling.

The Victory Program was a closely guarded secret until the third week of October. At that time, in order to quell rumors arising from leaks (and perhaps to sow some misdirection), President Roosevelt spoke its name in public and laid some of the details he calculated the American public needed to know. The October 27, 1941, issue of *Time* magazine reported, "The Victory Program means civilian curtailments beyond anything yet dreamed of by U.S. citizens, increased burdens (and a demand for increased efficiency) upon the defense agencies for production, subcontracting and priorities. By 1943 the United States should be not only an arsenal but an armed camp."

Scientific Mobilization

Over and above the concerns expressed and actions taken by the Roosevelt Administration, the Congress, the military services, and other public institutions was the patriotic fervor acted out by civilians who were in positions materially to aid the mobilization and rearmament efforts. In but one example, a prominent scientist, Dr. Vannevar Bush, on his own initiative, convened a voluntary *action* group calling itself the National Defense Research Committee (NDRC).

Vannevar Bush was born in Everett, Massachusetts, on March 11, 1890. He graduated from Tufts College in 1913, worked briefly at General Electric, and taught college courses until being accepted to the Massachusetts Institute of Technology (MIT) electrical engineering program. Bush received his doctorate in engineering in 1917 and during World War I worked with the National Research Council on development of submarine detection techniques. In 1919 he returned to MIT to teach electrical engineering and was tenured in 1923. Dr. Bush constructed an electro-mechanical "differential analyzer," a working computer that was capable of solving differential equations with up to eighteen independent variables. This work was crucial to later development of digital circuit design theory. From 1932 to 1938, Bush served as MIT's vice president and dean of engineering, and he rose to prominence as a leading scientist of the day.

Dr. Bush in 1939 became president of the Carnegie Institution of Washington, which was in the business of awarding large stipends for scientific research. Bush was thus able to direct a sizeable portion of research grants toward military objectives and was therefore in a position to advise the government on scientific issues. Also in 1939, Dr. Bush was appointed chairman of the National Advisory Committee for Aeronautics (NACA), a political appointment he held through 1941.

Stemming from what Bush had seen during the Great War as a lack of cooperation between civilian scientists and the U.S. government, and concerned about the lack of militarily relevant coordination within the scientific research community, he proposed a new federal agency to direct such research. The matter was often discussed among NACA colleagues, including Frank Jewett, president of the National Academy of Sciences; Karl Compton, president of MIT; and James Conant, president of Harvard University. Early in 1940, the secretary of NACA began work on a draft proposal for a National Defense Research Committee (NDRC), which Bush intended to have introduced to the Congress. Before the draft was completed, however, Germany overran most of western Europe. Riding the new sense of urgency sweeping the nation, Dr. Bush directly approached President Roosevelt and managed to get a meeting on June 12, 1940. Roosevelt approved Bush's plan in a matter of minutes.

The NDRC was officially established by the Council of National Defense on June 27, 1940, with Dr. Vannevar Bush as its chief. Bush appointed four leading scientists to the committee: his NACA colleagues Drs. Jewett, Compton, and Conant, and Dr. Richard Tolman, dean of the graduate school at California Polytechnic University. Compton was put in charge of radar, Conant was put in charge of chemistry and explosives, Jewett was put in charge of armor and ordnance, and Tolman was put in charge of patents and inventions. Military liaisons included Brig. Gen. George Strong, chief of the army general staff's War Plans Division; Rear Adm. Harold Bowen Sr., director of the Naval Research Laboratory; and Rear Adm. Julius Furer, the navy's coordinator of research and development. Another, and vital, member was Commissioner of Patents Conway Coe.

In June 1941, Bush was named head of the new Office of Scientific Research and Development (OSRD), a larger operation that superseded NDRC. Indeed OSRD controlled the forerunner of the Manhattan Project, the super-secret S-1 Section, until 1943, when it was taken over by the army. As head of OSRD, Dr. Bush reported to just one man, and that was Franklin Roosevelt, who gave the agency access to virtually unlimited funds and resources.

In all during World War II, OSRD under Dr. Bush's able leadership ultimately employed thirty thousand workers to oversee development of approximately two hundred weapons and other devices of war, including radar, sonar, loran, the proximity fuse, rocket-propelled weapons, the Norden bombsight, jet propulsion, improved and versatile aerial bombs, improved detonators, improved infantry weapons, and an array of amphibious vehicles. It also contributed to the mass production of sulfa drugs and penicillin, and the development of many other life-saving medical products and techniques used on and behind American and Allied World War II battlefields.

It can be said with a high degree of certainty that the early intervention of the NDRC and OSRD probably knocked a full year off the length of World War II, and by no means entirely as a result of its pioneering work on the atomic bomb. For example, work done by NDRC led to the appearance in 1941 and 1942 of effective air-search, surface-search, and gunnery radar sets scaled down for use aboard ships as small as destroyers and submarines. Some models were even packed aboard airplanes. Altogether, such radars were a decisive factor in the outcomes of both the Pacific War and the Battle of the Atlantic.

Chapter 25

The Army in 1941

A New American Army

THEY WERE AMERICA. They came from every American city and large town, no doubt from every county and borough. Some were sons of American families going back to the first Siberian settlers of a vast and empty continent, while others had arrived only very recently from Europe, South America, and even Asia. Among them, they spoke or understood every major language on Earth and more minor tongues than probably thrive to this day. Their forebears had fought in every American war and most of the wars of historical Europe. They practiced religions that went back thousands of years, or a matter of months. Some who were forbidden by their religious beliefs from going to war had overcome those scruples in what, to them, was as obviously a looming war against the Devil incarnate as any war had ever been. Some, who would not bear arms, became medics with the intent of succoring the wounded on far-flung battlefields.

Some of the older, senior soldiers had fathers who had fought on either side in the Civil War, had themselves been blooded at Château-Thierry and the Argonne Forest, and had led soldiers throughout their adult lives. Some had first fought as recently as 1939 or 1940, when their homelands had been overrun by Nazi legions.

Some were unrepentant thieves and liars, some had never worn hard-soled shoes, and some had never eaten in a restaurant. Some were cowards who would always be cowards, but most were unformed teenagers who would do heroic things because heroism was the common standard to which they would unthinkingly and unblinkingly adapt. Some had never spoken to, or even met, a Jew (much less taken orders from one), and some had never seen a black man, nor broken bread with a Catholic. Some had never seen an ocean or a ship, had never eaten fish, or had never lived in a building made of milled wood. For some, a tarpaper barracks on a military base was an immense step up in life, but for many it was humbling. For others, access to fresh produce of any description was a new and wonderful experience. For many, the discipline of regular exercise was a bitter shock and then a source of immense pride. For most, living out of a duffel bag—to say nothing of a light field pack—was a deprivation of immense magnitude, as was cooking, sewing, lying in the mud, voiding behind a bush or in the open, or even just following orders. For the most part, the army would be an unforgettable waypoint in life, but a waypoint nonetheless. For some, the army would become home for thirty and more years followed by decades of pining for that home.

Some were men of letters, eloquent and talented writers and speakers of all types, while others could not read or write—or even speak English—when they enlisted. Some were wealthy beyond description: men who had never wanted for a thing money could buy. Others enlisted solely to eat or to sleep off the ground regularly. In the democracy of battle, the latter would teach the former how to survive in a self-dug hole in the wet ground or sand. And because the crucible of war does strange things to men, some of the lowest would rise to become the mightiest, and vice versa.

Friendships—indeed, a brotherhood of love—would bind men across all classes and talents for the rest of their days, and a grateful nation would offer the survivors, one and all, an opportunity to better themselves for the glorious decades that would follow their war. But that was in an unknown and unknowable future. The task these men and boys—some as young as twelve—faced lay ahead in 1940 and 1941, when the army caught the first whiff of a war it might have to fight. No promises were made, except to some potential pilots, whose future tuition would be paid to the tune of $500 a year if they enlisted for pilot training at the end of their second year of college. The rest—the immense majority—were entitled to three hots and a flop on the best of days, a little pocket money (if there was anyplace to spend it), a hope of glory, a fear of personal humiliation in front of buddies, and an opportunity to look Death in the face. To get any of those choice items, they had to undergo a rigorous training program that sometimes seemed pointless and was always cutting-edge insulting to a young man of merely average intelligence. If war came—*when* war came—they might spend years beyond the reach of loved ones, cut off from even the worst their society had to offer, to say nothing of the best. They arrived for training in the tens and hundreds of thousands, few quite realizing that death and maiming might lay ahead, that their lot in life might include bad and even infrequent food, crowded and stinking troop holds, drowning at sea, maiming on land, or perhaps only unreasonable discipline at the hands of sadists.

Many men came to the army in 1941 by enlisting in it, but the army picked a very large percentage of its troops by lottery. As long as a fatalistic draftee or enthusiastic enlistee met the minimum physical and mental requirements, he was taken in and given a democratic opportunity to raise or lower himself in life, as the case may be. The new army was filled to brimming with amiable bumpkins, guileless rubes, and hard-bitten ignoramuses not quite dumb or innocent enough to reject, but also with college dropouts, college graduates, and even savants also named "Private." The army mixmaster mished and mashed a random cross section of America by dressing it to look the same and conditioning it to salute anything that moved, ignore stupidity, react in a split second to the sound of gunfire, and, above all, obey, obey, obey.

Slow Going

Notwithstanding the passage in mid-1941 of an unprecedented $9,825,000,000 no-strings spending bill for the army alone, the task of building a balanced war-ready ground army for the coming war was the hardest thing Americans have ever had to do as a nation. The organization, while run by authentically brilliant men, was so broken following two decades of willful neglect that the task appeared well nigh impossible when taken against any rational expectation of when the United States might be plunged into the deepening crises overseas. Heavy betting supported the idea that the United States would be a combatant in the war by April 1, 1942, but there was nothing to suggest that it would be ready for effective combat operations by then.

The worst problem the struggling ground army faced was uncertainty: What was the timeline? What was the upper limit of combat-ready divisions and essential combat-support and service-support units that could be ready to ship out to who-knew-where in three months, six months, or a year? And, hardest of all, would the National Guard and hundreds of thousands of trained and semi-trained conscripts even still be in the army when the axe finally fell?

The draft and the Guard call-up were both statutorily timed for one year, beginning on the date of issue in the case of the Guard and on the date of induction for individual draftees. In the case of the Guard, whose call-up had to be staggered over many months, some units were expected to be sent home long before other units had been sufficiently trained. Moreover, most Guard units were short many men; each Guard division had spaces for more than twenty-two thousand officers and men but averaged only a little more than ten thousand when called to federal service. The holes had to be filled by men drawn from other sources who would be left high and dry if or when their units were sent home.

There were a lot of other things wrong with the Guard divisions of late 1940–early 1941. As did the regular divisions, they lacked many of their authorized weapons and most of the equipment fully competitive combat units needed on the new war's battlefields. Many Guard units were not necessarily trained as well as the army's lowest expectations foresaw. It was discovered early on that many community-based units, especially those from rural areas, and down to platoon level, had been used as ad hoc local welfare organizations that had recruited men because they were down and out and not because they could possibly make good soldiers. Trainers working with such units found privates as old as forty-five who could not read or write and might have any number of low-grade but nonetheless debilitating illnesses along the lines of heart disease, lung disease, arthritis, and even missing digits. Sending these men home without the Guard paychecks their families depended on to eat was just plain heartbreaking, and filling the resulting vacant billets set back the entire army, not to mention the national effort.

It did not help one bit that American industry was not yet up to producing all the goods the army needed, or that so much industrial capacity at this critical juncture was given over to keeping Britain in the war. There was no way seen that might mitigate the resulting shortfalls, save for giving the industrial sector the time it needed to get up to speed.

More Than a Year?

The army leadership did not deal directly with the looming release of the National Guard and draftees for a long time. It had no solutions to offer on its own, and the draft had passed the Congress by a narrow margin, so there was no stomach for a legislative fight as long as the nation was not directly molested, in which case the Congress would surely grant a healthy extension. The leadership thought about the issue and even discussed it, but no one actually grappled with it for many months.

The first time the National Guard extension matter came up in an official public venue was when a congressman asked General Marshall about it during a hearing of the House Appropriations Committee on March 5, 1941. "We do not know yet," Marshall averred. "It depends entirely on the situation. If the good Lord is good to us, they will be returned to their homes." The congressman pressed Marshall over a rumor that, if the Guard was demobilized, the army would retain its equipment for use by the Regular Army. Marshall assured the man that no such thing was contemplated.

On March 7, two days after this exchange, newspapers reported on a Department of War plan to retain the National Guard for twelve to eighteen months beyond the mandated year of federal duty. The department denied the report.

Next, in April, Marshall was once again pressed on the topic while testifying before the House Appropriations Committee. He responded definitively: There were no plans to hold any Guard unit for more than one year; enlistees, draftees, and reserve officers assigned to Guard divisions would be reassigned to regular units as their Guard units stood down; and the eighteen Guard divisions would remain at home as a general army reserve, to be federalized again only in event of a dire national emergency. When a questioner asked, Marshall noted that, short of a presidential order following a formal declaration of war, it fell to the Congress to legislate a longer term of federal duty for the Guard, and that "the decision does not have to be made until three months before the first units of the National Guard have completed twelve months of service." Ever helpful, the army chief of staff did the math: "That would be in June."

Rumor was rife inside the Guard units on active duty. The National Guard Bureau received so many queries from individual guardsmen that its beleaguered chief had to tell Marshall that it appeared that the Guard as a whole expected the army to extend its tour but that the ranks would remain restive until definitive news came down.

The army had a plan for either eventuality, for proceeding with its build-out with or without the Guard. Of course, the loss of eighteen fairly well organized divisions, plus the eighteen infantry regiments that would be shorn from them if they were triangularized, would be a major loss. So would be the enormous and wasted expense of having fed and trained them for a year, but the army was past crying over spilled milk. There was too much to do for time to be expended on might-have-beens.

At a press conference held at the White House on June 17, President Roosevelt stated that the issue of a one-year extension of National Guard service was under consideration. The president was waiting on a report from Secretary of War Stimson. On June 20, Marshall forwarded to Stimson his best arguments for an early decision: guardsmen, their families, and their civilian employers needed to plan a future with or without the guardsmen; the army needed to plan a future with or without the guardsmen; and state governments and communities throughout the nation needed to know if they must organize some sort of home guard to undertake domestic missions normally undertaken by the National Guard in time of civil emergency.

The Department of War made its recommendation to the White House on June 24, 1941, coming down unequivocally on the side of extending the Guard's tour by a full year. It did the same with respect to reserve officers who had been summoned to active duty, and with respect to draftees, who were all one-year men.

A leading congressman assured the executive branch that the extension would be voted into law quite soon, but it was not to be. The hubbub of the Guard extension had been thrown off the front pages by several riveting events in the progress of the war. First and foremost, the bulk of the Wehrmacht invaded the Soviet Union on June 22, a front-page story if ever there was one. And the Department of State ordered all Italian consulates throughout the United States to be closed down, a response to a German and Italian order of the same nature with respect to U.S. consulates. And in belated response to the May sinking of an American merchant ship by a U-boat, the Department of State publicly branded Germany guilty of piracy. Once bumped from the front pages, few issues regained that stature. The army's woes were no longer topical.

Facing up to the fizzled extension of the Guard, reserve, and draftee duty cycle, General Marshall used the occasion of his first biennial report as chief of staff, issued on July 3, 1941, to revive the matter. "When and where these forces [the reserve and National Guard] are to serve are questions to be determined by their Commander-in-Chief and the Congress, and should not be confused with the problem of their readiness for service. . . . The materiel phase of our task is generally understood. The personnel phase is not, and it is here that the legal limitations, acceptable at the time of their passage, not hamstring the development of the Army into a force immediately available for whatever defensive measures may be necessary." Marshall amply bolstered his position by pointing out, for example, that each regular infantry division on the current army roster was officered by reserve officers to the tune of 75 to 90 percent, an average of six hundred officers per division who, unless they volunteered on an individual basis to stay, would be going home when their one-year term of service expired. Further, only two Regular Army divisions were manned entirely by regulars and three-year enlistees; the others were composed, up to 50 percent, of one-year draftees. Simply stated, the army could not possibly respond to a declaration of war with a competent field force—not to mention field forces—without retaining its hundreds of thousands of trained and often vital one-year men, officers and enlisted.

The Selective Training and Service Act of 1940 contained specific language with respect to retaining draftees for an extra year, by presidential decree in response to a national emergency. But the president and his key players did not want to rile the Congress over the draft when that might jeopardize the extension of the Guard and the reserve, which was the Congress's responsibility. Unless directly confronted during testimony, the Department of War and the army went silent on the matter, even with respect to ordinary internal planning documents that might become public.

While the army and the nation waited on tenterhooks, the isolationists (now styled non-interventionists) in the Congress had their last hurrah. And a jolly good party it was. It took more than half the summer of 1941 to get the required measure to a vote. The long interim was consumed within a bitter fighting withdrawal by the isolationists, who gave and received no quarter in committee-room battlefields or on the House and Senate floors. The Senate, as a body, was more kindly disposed to the army's dignified and direct reasoning processes, and it passed its version of the draft extension a week ahead of the House. The more rabid last-ditch efforts of House isolationists held up passage in that body until August 12, and the vote that day came out 203 to 202 in favor. Such was the retained animus that the Senate was warned to adopt the House version as-is rather than risk reopening the debate and possibly losing a new vote in the House. It was the height of the congressional summer recess, but early passage was essential; too much time had been frittered away rekindling dead causes, and the hundreds of thousands of officers and men waiting on a firm outcome had grown restive. Senate leaders sent airplanes to bring senators back for a vote that was taken as soon as possible and forwarded immediately to the White House for President Roosevelt's signature, which he affixed on August 18.

The army leadership breathed a sigh of relief; as far as the generals were concerned, the manpower part of the equation was fixed and settled.

But it *wasn't* settled.

Manpower versus Materiel

The consequences accruing from the slow pace of the army's materiel acquisition reached critical mass in September 1941, when several army agencies and bureaus finally realized that the successful expansion of manpower and training of troops had far outpaced the army's ability to definitively equip those troops either for specialized training or especially for an onset of combat. American industry was ramping up on schedule, but so much of its burgeoning output was going to the aid of Britain that the army's balanced plan for modulating the pace of training to the availability of equipment, and vice versa, had come completely undone. The choice thus facing the army was to either inadequately equip about thirty combat divisions by the end of 1941 or definitively equip far fewer.

After much discussion, the choice finally came down to stopping the influx of draftees and enlistees—that is, cap the size of the army until the acquisition process caught up—or send home all or part of the National Guard while still taking in new recruits and activating new regular divisions. Both solutions were fraught with peril in an increasingly unfriendly world.

A long-time Marshall friend, Lt. Gen. Lesley McNair, General Headquarters (GHQ) chief of staff and thus the army's trainer-in-chief, put forth one idea. His plan was to send home the "best" Guard divisions and replace them with new divisions composed mainly of newly recruited soldiers and reserve officers, stiffened by a large cadre of trained men. General Marshall did not want to open a can of worms by characterizing any Guard divisions as "best," because that begged the question of which were worst, but he found merit in McNair's suggestion. Marshall and McNair assumed that the Guard divisions that were to be sent home—perhaps all of them, in the order in which they had been activated—would be recalled for war at a time before the gains they had made in a year or more of active-duty training had dissipated. Meanwhile, the Regular Army would use ex-Guard bases to activate and train new divisions, employing the non-guardsmen and non-Guard equipment from the inactivated Guard divisions as cadres.

President Roosevelt, who normally could be counted on to make the difficult choices, was of two minds on these competing issues. He had a long, long list of things he wanted the expanding army to do in a growing number of faraway places. But he was firm in his commitment to the British. At the moment many army venues realized that the one was incompatible with the other, Roosevelt came down somewhat more on the British side than on the army's. This was instructive, of course, and it had the effect of erasing doubt. The decision was thus made on October 31, 1941, to send the entire Guard home in the order of activation, and to begin doing so in February 1942. Plans were drawn up to use fourteen of the bases housing Guard divisions as bases for replacement divisions and the other four bases for training replacement troops for the combat arms.

Recruit Training

The bedrock of American military strength in the 1940s was embedded in American industrial tradition. The cotton gin—a machine that could perform uniform repetitive tasks formerly done by many hands—was only one of Eli Whitney's inventions. Whitney's greatest contribution was his innovative efforts to assemble interchangeable parts (a concept put forth in France) into finished, identical rifles and pistols; he was the first to apply the idea in what could be called an industrial setting. The fact that every part, made up in batches (production runs), was *exactly* the same for every weapon of the same specifications vastly speeded up serial production of completed weapons and allowed any part from one weapon to be replaced by a like part from another weapon or from a stockpile of spare parts: a means for putting broken weapons swiftly back into service. Before Whitney, spare parts had to be fabricated as needed and finished by hand, as one-off replacements. Now think of a newly trained rifleman as a spare part for an existing infantry squad, or a double handful of newly trained riflemen as the parts from which, with a few experienced noncommissioned officers, a brand-new infantry squad could be fabricated—and another, and another, as long as the need was there and the supply of new recruits held out.

Even as late as 1939, the American aviation industry had much to learn from an inventor more than a century in his grave. What Eli Whitney did that was unique in the early nineteenth century was to marry the idea of interchangeable parts to a combination of power machinery and a division of labor. This innovation revolutionized serial fabrication of almost any type of product and set the United States on a course for industrial domination. Adding luster to Whitney's accomplishment was Henry Ford's invention, a century later, of the assembly line, on which automobiles built from prefabricated, interchangeable parts were assembled serially with breathtaking speed by a stream of specially trained workers. They divided up the labor by specific and repetitive task, this one to weld bodies, that one to mount doors, and so forth, from the beginning of the line to its end, a length measured temporally rather than linearly.

Now think of a highly charged, minutely scheduled training environment as analogous to a factory. In that context, why shouldn't Americans charged with rapidly bringing into being a vast, new army from a feedstock of unformed civilians not look on new recruits as unfinished but ultimately interchangeable parts in the mechanism of an entire wartime army? And why not serially assemble these interchangeable recruits as uniform basic soldiers on something akin to an assembly line composed of waystations overseen by specialists such a drill instructors and marksmanship instructors? Thus, an assembly line was placed in constant operation to turn raw recruits into trained infantrymen (or medics or artillerymen or tank crewmen, etc.). Then, another assembly line built tactical units (rifle platoons, for example) from parts (individuals) and subassemblies (three off-the-shelf infantry squads plus a serially trained platoon leader and a few noncommissioned officers). Somehow, it was comforting for Americans to know that their army, built to defend American values, was a product of bedrock American innovation.

To a man of George Marshall's long experience, including duties as a divisional and field army trainer of raw recruits in France in the Great War, the notion held much appeal. A basic uniform recruit emerging from a fixed program devoted only to training such men would unburden an existing unit (such as an infantry battalion heavily enough burdened by battle) from taking on the traditional role of training its own replacements in all of the many fundamentals of soldiering, from general obedience to accurately firing a rifle to reliably undertaking intricate battlefield maneuvers under hostile fire. It would further unburden the tactical unit from having to send its best men back, away from the battlefield, to train new men to replace the dead and wounded. It would place the raw recruits in the hands of specially selected and well-trained trainers who had no cares in the world beyond training, and no way up the ranks except by performing well as trainers. And it would give the well-trained trainers time to wash out the meek and the stupid from assignment to tasks beyond their abilities as well as allow them to identify, early on, the brave and the brilliant for consideration for entry into elite units or for training as officers.

Basic training, as it was called, was a purely American innovation, unique among the world's armies, a reflection of American technological genius merged with American organizational genius. (U.S. Marines had opened their first attempt at standardized basic recruit training in 1818, and Marine Corps boot camp had become a permanent fixture in 1911. The U.S. Navy also opened its first boot camp in 1911.)

The army organization ultimately charged with developing and overseeing the standard program of recruit training for the various branches was General Headquarters (GHQ), which had been revived in July 1940 under then-Brig. Gen. Lesley McNair, an artilleryman, with title of chief of staff, GHQ. McNair was directly subordinate to Marshall and stood between him and the four regional field army commanders. GHQ was established to oversee a new American expeditionary force abroad, and it was this eventually aborted mission that got it into the business of recruit training, as had been undertaken by Pershing's American Expeditionary Force in France. Until the primary mission was changed to training in mid-1941, however, there was no pressing need to man a large GHQ, because the United States was not at war and the army had no expeditionary force to oversee. It took a push from Marshall to get GHQ manned by enough officers to definitively take on the immense and growing training challenge, and it took all the energy of the enormously energetic McNair to deal with a thousand emerging issues and friction points, not to mention push-back from holders of more traditional views.

Unit Training

While General Marshall was a major force behind standardized recruit training, his real passion was for unit training, a discipline in which he had immersed himself during his tour at The Infantry School. To Marshall, soldiers became real soldiers as they systematically practiced the art of war "in the field," honing individual and group skills on successively larger and more difficult field problems, starting with tiny, set-piece maneuvers by infantry squads and advancing by stages to larger field exercises, culminating (in 1940 and 1941) in immense war games involving the movement and maneuver of entire field armies across the breadth of one or two states. Marshall himself had always excelled at maneuvering large forces against other large forces, and he felt that mastery of such exercises marked the real combat general. As a rule of thumb, the men Marshall would hand-select to be the first to go to war as the commanders of divisions, corps, and armies were the ones who excelled, as had he in his day, in large field exercises, usually through a demonstration of well-honed instincts or a knack for command, an ineffable "something" that was new and fresh and bold enough without being reckless. The fortunes of many an officer of any rank rose or fell based on their performances on the mock battlefields on which Marshall's new army sparred and parried and drove for the jugular.

To one-third of new troops freshly doled out to tactical units from the shock conditioning under the new basic training curriculum, army life seemed to consist of pointless make-work interspersed with endless rounds of dumbplay. Tens of thousands of the troops went to "the field" armed with broomsticks masquerading as rifles, trucks masquerading as tanks, or stovepipe masquerading as artillery. Indeed, throughout their training at regimental level and above, the enlisted troops were thought of and treated as mere props in an officers' game of command and control. The troops, who in the field were typically maneuvered around mapboards like so many inanimate chess pieces, learned little and suffered greatly in the real outdoors; they had no idea what was afoot and benefited only to the extent the rough living inured them to further rough living. Their attention became entirely devoted to griping.

Conducted mainly by new soldiers and witnessed by many thousands of civilians living on or near the mock battlefields, the large war games showcased the army's many, many deficiencies, many quite appalling given what was going on in the world beyond America's shimmering shores. It was plain enough for the new soldiers and appalled civilians to see that the army was in desperate straits, unable to fight a war, much less win one. Where were the rifles? Where were the machine guns? Where were the tanks and field radios and mortars and artillery pieces? Where on earth was the expensive Air Corps? And where on earth were sufficient live rounds for definitive training of riflemen, machine gunners, and mortar and artillery crews?

For all its trials as an unintended social experiment, this new national army was filled with intelligent, inquisitive young men who required nurturing and a sense of worth to motivate them toward glory. Marshall, who heard rumblings by way of a senior officer whose son was a draftee, could only try to explain the materiel shortcomings as temporary snags in the industrial processes then ramping up, but he responded forcefully to shortfalls in educating the troops by insisting that officers throughout the chain of command explain the object of each part of a field exercise, to share the plan and explain the means. Giving the troops military education beyond mere fieldcraft would benefit the army as a whole, and morale on that front was soon raised. But it took modern weapons and gear to raise morale further and keep it raised, and there was not enough of that in 1941.

Of this the leaders of the new American army were certain: The goal of every unit leader worth his salt, from corporal to general, was to integrate disparate America into a fluid, competent whole capable of undertaking intricate dances with Death in order to survive combat and emerge as kings of the battlefield. But in 1941 it all had to be done and set before a single one of the modern formations, revised tactics, latest and ingenious weapons and tools, and tens of thousands of newly minted officers were worth taking to hell in a handbasket. If all these new men and new ideas and new stuff didn't jell at first contact with the enemy—today, tomorrow, or a year away—the United States of America might be compelled by History to live on the wrong side of twilight. But knowing that was good, understanding that was vital, taking that to heart was key. It made would-be historical figures, from the commander in chief on down, very, very serious about the soundness of their thought processes, the consequences of their decisions, and the purity of their ideals.

Readiness

On November 30, 1941, the size of the army stood at 1,644,212, up only 183,214 over its June 30 end strength. This aspect of slow growth was a reflection of the materiel problem facing the army; Marshall judged there was little point in expanding the manpower base without the tools to equip a much larger army, and he personally stood in the way of immediate growth.

Of the total on November 30, 121,094 were officers, of which 16.9 percent were Regular Army, 66.8 percent were reserve officers, and 16.3 percent were National Guard officers. Of the 1,523,118 enlisted men, 34.8 percent were Regular Army, 14.1 percent were National Guard, and a whopping 51.1 percent were draftees.

By the time the War Plans Division issued a report on readiness as of October 1, 1941, the old army had been spread so thin throughout the new army that it provided hardly any stiffener at all—and just *one* infantry division (of twenty-nine) was *almost* ready to fight. Actually ready to fight were five antiaircraft regiments, two bombardment squadrons, and three pursuit groups, which is reflective only of the public's fear of air attack on American cities. But there was ample reason for hope. In the same report, War Plans speculated that by January 1, 1942, two divisions would be combat capable along with one mechanized cavalry regiment, seven antiaircraft regiments, three bombardment groups, one bombardment squadron, and four pursuit groups. Then, by April 1, 1942, the effective units might well have mushroomed to three infantry divisions, the I Armored Corps (two armor divisions and one motorized division), one mechanized cavalry regiment, nine antiaircraft regiments, seven bombardment groups, and seven pursuit groups plus two pursuit squadrons.

Going beyond these numbers, which were depressing enough, Secretary Stimson convened in Washington, D.C., on December 3, 1941, a conclave of leaders to discuss the army's *quality* based on an after-action assessment of major maneuvers that had been concluded in the Carolinas on November 30. All the civilian big guns from the Department of War were there, as were Marshall, his three assistant chiefs of staff, and the army's chief trainers—McNair and Brig. Gen. Mark Clark, the GHQ deputy for operations and training.

In a nutshell, the field army commands, corps commands, and divisional commands had done well, and so had the regimental commands. But smaller units—rifle platoons, infantry companies and artillery batteries, and combat-arms battalions—had performed below McNair's exacting standards.

But that made sense. Most of the generals and many of the colonels commanding regiments, divisions, corps, and the field armies had served in France and then gone on to soldier hard and train hard over the two intervening decades. But lower-ranking officers—especially lieutenants and captains, but many majors and lieutenant colonels as well—had not been to the army schools, had not been in battle, had not had the opportunity to sufficiently polish the skills required to move forty or two hundred or nine hundred men forward on fire-swept ground, nor even on ground swept by make-believe fire. They had not developed the insights or gained the experience a leader or commander needs to marshal when planning, executing, and fine-tuning an attack. They were not yet as well trained or seasoned as war requires of men at their various levels of leadership and command.

The solution was obvious to the professional soldiers in the room: more training to even more pressing standards. Rifle platoons, artillery batteries, and infantry battalions were the vital components in the attack. If rifle platoons could not competently press forward, if artillery batteries could not provide spot-on fire support, if 850-man infantry battalions could not function independently, day or night, then the U.S. Army's—and George Marshall's—favorite tactic, the holding attack, could not be successfully brought off. And if battalions in the offense could not reliably seize ground from an enemy, the entire American strategy for war—a war of movement undertaken primarily by infantrymen on foot—could easily bog down as the German strategy in 1914 France had bogged down, with a result similar to the static four-year stalemate that nearly bled European manhood to death. (It is not true that generals tend to refight the last war; modern generals typically and emphatically do all in their power to *avoid* refighting the last war. Marshall, McNair, and their fellow American generals of 1941 knew very well what refighting the Great War would do to America and the world.)

One of the major outcomes of the post-maneuver conference was a decision, whose roots went back many months, to slow down the army, to allow the reality of sluggish materiel acquisition to reverse itself in its own time, while the ground army significantly slowed its head-long expansion program and put its money on qualitative goals, to stop the army from making so many new units and bias itself toward improving the performance of the units it already had in hand, particularly the tactical units down the chain of command upon whose battlefield prowess the entire national war effort would necessarily hinge. For the near term, then, the army's leadership opted for war now ahead of war later, to complete work on several dozen war-capable divisions ahead of having on its hands several score half-baked divisions.

McNair presented an excellent, detailed plan that might very well have done the job he envisioned. But it was December 3, 1941. There were only a few grains of sand yet remaining in the hourglass.

Chapter 26

The Navy in 1941

New Ships, New Men

FROM THE MID-1930s the navy did everything it could short of taking up a collection from its sailors to assure that the onset of a new war anywhere in the world would not find it deficient in numbers and modern types of both warships and auxiliaries—not to mention the trained, confident crews—a true maritime power needed to see its merchant fleets safely across the world's oceans and seas. Thus, on the eve of America's entry into the new world war, the navy had seven fleet aircraft carriers in hand and twelve on order, seventeen battleships in hand and eight on order, and thirty-seven cruisers in hand and dozens more on order. The navy had 171 destroyers, old and new, on its active role, and many, many more on order, along with a whole new type of small escort destroyer. A class of swift motor torpedo boat was being built. More than one hundred patrol craft, gunboats, and Coast Guard cutters of all sizes and varying capabilities were felt (by all except their hard-pressed crews) to be abundant, and there were orders in for many more. One escort carrier was in hand and others would soon join the fleet. There were 112 submarines in commission, including new fleet boats that were larger, longer-ranged, and armed with more torpedoes than earlier classes still in service. Transports and cargo ships were being converted from civilian liners and merchantmen, which were in turn being supplemented by several classes of purpose-built transports and cargo ships. In all, on the eve of war, there were thirty-one transports, six new attack transports, two hospital ships, twenty-two cargo ships, four munitions ships, one aircraft transport (the old *Langley*), nine provisions ships, and three store ships. A total of twenty-nine old and new fleet oilers were in service, and more were coming into service. Thirty-two tenders for seaplanes, seventeen destroyers and other surface ships, and fourteen submarines were also being rushed into service. There were sixty-six minelayers and minesweepers, plus fleet tugs and yard boats of every description.

As fast as the new ships were laid down, commissioning crews were formed and trained, and all the new ships were launched, commissioned, shaken down, and pushed into service as quickly as the shipyards, recruiters, and trainers could manage. Even as new ships and new types of ships were coming into service, ship after ship after ship was called into the yards for upgrades of every type: better guns, better sonar, early types of radar that were supplanted by more and better types—search, gunnery, and antiaircraft. As a result, it was necessary to find more berthing space for the new types of specialists who knew the ships' secrets. And with it all came promotions unheard of in the moribund peacetime navy. Men who had long languished at ranks far short of the loyalty and professional mastery they had long demonstrated rode a moving escalator to exalted ranks and vastly increased power, leavened by obligations as trainers and mentors. Further, they were the keepers of the navy's soul in a close-in world filled with landlubbers who dressed as navy men but acted like farmers or haberdashers or truck drivers, or whatever unnavy-like trades had spawned them and left them without the good sense to throw up topside and outboard, but, Jaysuss, *not* into the wind!

In 1941, as the operational tempo grew and the distance to war perceptibly contracted, the navy was tired but never at loose ends. It had a mission and a purpose. It was content.

New Airplanes

The doctrine naval aviation would employ in a 1940s war had been pretty much set by the mid-1930s, and the types and main characteristics of the airplanes that would be set loose to carry the doctrine to America's enemies had also been pretty much set. Carrier air boasted three types of warplanes: torpedo/level bombers, scout/dive-bombers, and fighters. Land- and sea-based air-search units composed of seaborne or amphibian multi-engine, long-range patrol bombers were meant to supplement carrier air by their reliance on either fixed bases near or far from home, or by basing from tenders that could be distributed almost anywhere a ship could anchor. The final classes of naval aircraft foreseen in the 1930s were small, light scout and gunnery-observation floatplanes built for launch and recovery from battleships and large cruisers. Largely as a result of the Air Corps' claims regarding coastal defense, the navy expended little thought on land-based maritime bombers, even after British and French aircraft buyers went out of their way to place large orders for them in 1939 and 1940. Several of these types, meant for the RAF, fell into U.S. Navy hands after the United States entered the war, but it took a long time before the navy concentrated on how to best exploit long-range land-based bombers.

SBD

The U.S. Navy's standard scout/dive-bomber of late 1941 was the Douglas SBD-3 Dauntless (S for scout, B for bomber, D for Douglas). The SBD-2 had entered active service with the Marine Corps in mid-1940 and become operational aboard U.S. Navy carriers in March 1941. The SBD-3 had a top speed of 250 miles per hour (quite speedy for a dive-bomber of the day). Its combat radius, fully loaded, was only 250 to 300 miles, but it boasted a substantial search range—up to 1,750 miles under ideal conditions. Its payload was usually a 500-pound bomb on a search mission, a 500-pound depth charge on antisubmarine patrol, and a 1,000-pound bomb on a strike mission. The extremely robust yet highly maneuverable SBD-3 was well adapted to defending itself with two cowl-mounted .50-caliber machine guns fired by the pilot, and two linked .30-caliber machine guns mounted on a free-moving ("flexible") frame fired by the rear-facing radioman-gunner. As a dive-bomber, the SBD could fall upon an enemy vessel at a seventy-degree dive angle, the steepest performer in the world, thanks to perforated dive flaps that split out from the trailing edge of each wing. The SBD was highly maneuverable even in a seventy-degree dive; its pilot could easily correct his aim on a ship attempting to maneuver out of his way at high speed.

Designed as an offensive dive-bomber and a long-range scout, the SBD was also typically employed close to a friendly carrier deck for antisubmarine defense or, in extreme cases, as a last line of defense against low-flying torpedo bombers. The SBD was a fine airplane.

F4F

As the onset of war in the Pacific loomed, most carrier fighter squadrons were equipped with the Grumman F4F-3 fighter variant, an unarmored, midwing monoplane with four .50-caliber wing-mounted machine guns, a fairly modern gunsight, and decent performance characteristics, thanks in part to a two-stage supercharger that enhanced it for high-altitude performance. (The F4F-3A subvariant lacked the two-stage supercharger but was otherwise identical.) The early addition of heavy makeshift armor plate on a field-expedient basis negatively affected the F4F-3's performance but made for a more robust combatant. Ditto two factory-installed self-sealing fuel tanks to prevent fatal combustions as a result of bullet strikes. In December 1941, six of seven carrier-based fighter squadrons were equipped with F4F-3s and F4F-3As.

A fully loaded F4F-3 with armor and self-sealing tanks weighed 7,450 pounds. It had a top speed of 329 miles per hour at 21,000 feet and could climb 2,460 feet per minute to 10,000 feet and 2,174 feet per minute thereafter to 20,000 feet. While an F4F-3 with all the additions was nominally rated to a range of 816 miles at 150 miles per hour in ideal conditions, its real combat radius was something on the order of 200 to 250 miles. Strangely, the navy would completely neglect to equip any of its carrier aircraft with supplementary fuel tanks—much less droppable tanks—until nearly the end of 1942.

Because of limited range, Wildcat fighters were not ipso facto expected to undertake escort duties for air strikes; if enemy targets were well within the Wildcat's 250-mile outer combat radius, these fighters might be sent along all or part of the way. Or none might be sent with the bombers. The Wildcat was primarily a point-defense interceptor: Beginning months before the United States got into the war as a named combatant, at all times during the day in a combat zone, a patrol of Wildcats was aloft over the friendly carrier, and others were ready to take off at short notice. U.S. Navy surface warships accompanying the carriers as antiaircraft escorts could certainly put up formidable antiaircraft defenses, as could the carriers themselves, but the burden of defense fell upon a barrier of interceptors whose primary mission was to fend off incoming enemy air attacks. Wildcats might supplement the bombers on antisubmarine patrols around the friendly carrier, but that practice would be in decline by mid-1942. A distinctly tertiary role—after bomber escort—was the provision of strafing during hit-and-run raids against shore targets, or even against ships, and in a still-nascent role of support for friendly forces ashore.

The Wildcat fighter was a mixed blessing, but the full extent of the mixture was not completely known, even after the type had weathered a fair number of fighter-versus-fighter engagements. On the other hand, every Wildcat in the U.S. Navy inventory had a reasonably modern two-way radio. This was a terrific boon, for individual fighters could be precisely controlled from afar, and fighter pilots could warn one another about impending danger as well as coordinate their tactics, or simply yell for help. Also, the Wildcat could absorb a terrific beating. Some performance was sacrificed to the likes of radios, self-sealing fuel tanks, and heavy armor plate behind the pilot's seat, but all these features added appreciably to the overall effectiveness of the fighter and the longevity of the pilot, so the sacrifices in performance were seen as trade-offs that by far favored the Wildcat's overall ability to fight and survive.

TBD

By early 1939, an assay of Japanese carrier aircraft indicated that the TBD, which had entered service in 1937 as the best torpedo bomber in the world, had fallen sharply behind the development curve. This led to an open competition aimed at replacing the Devastator as quickly as possible. The Grumman TBF Avenger design was selected, and its development was well along by the start of the war, but no TBFs would be available to the fleet before June 1942.

PBY Upgrade

In 1939, a test example of the then-current Consolidated PBY-4 long-range patrol bomber was fitted with landing gear, thus creating a true amphibian that could operate from runways as well as from the surface of the sea. By the end of 1939, Consolidated was producing the sea-based PBY-5 and amphibian PBY-5A variants, which in typical flying conditions and at standard operational settings had an overall range of 2,545 miles. The larger, longer-ranged, and better armed Martin PBM patrol bomber/transport began service in early 1941, but it did not come close to the PBY in numbers built (at least three thousand) and ubiquity in a range of missions, from long-range patrolling to air-sea rescue, through the entirety of World War II.

The Pacific Fleet

The United States Fleet had been based at Pearl Harbor since June 1940, and the commander in chief of the fleet, Adm. James Richardson, had been in hot water with the Roosevelt Administration for exactly as long. Blunt and cerebral, a doer, Richardson had neither gotten over being blindsided by the basing change nor stopped fuming about the fact that his advice was routinely ignored. At length, Richardson had been marked down as a complainer, and this limited his incumbency.

Richardson had made several telling points at the outset of the venture: Pearl Harbor was not so developed in mid-1940 that it could efficiently host as large a fleet as was based there. The harbor entrance was narrow and might prove a death trap if ships under attack had to sally through it one at a time. And the families of ships' crews lived at former home ports on the mainland. Nothing changed with respect to the second and third points, but base facilities of every type were upgraded in the interim, the base itself was expanded via a number of land purchases, and the land-based aircraft and ground units guarding the base were steadily built up.

By early 1941, the navy was ready for a two-fold change. On February 1, the navy reactivated the Pacific Fleet at Pearl Harbor, subordinated it to the United States Fleet, and placed both under the command of Adm. Husband Kimmel, with headquarters at Pearl. Richardson was given a desk job until his earliest optimal retirement date rolled around in 1942.

Pacific Defenses

The road map for development of naval bases in the Pacific under Plan Orange (and later under Joint War Plan Rainbow No. 5) was the finding of a commission of naval officers chaired by Adm. Arthur Hepburn, who had commanded the United States Fleet between June 1936 and January 1938. Mandated by the Congress in May 1938, the Hepburn study's entire purview was a look into the navy's need for new Pacific bases dedicated to basing and/or servicing patrol planes, submarines, and the smaller, short-range types of warships, either by building shore facilities such as airfields, fuel depots, and repair shops or merely providing anchorages for tenders and refueling tankers.

The Hepburn Report, delivered in December 1938, recommended the development, in Alaska, of a patrol plane and submarine base in the Aleutian Islands at Dutch Harbor (in addition to the small Coast Guard station and navy radio station already at Dutch Harbor), a patrol plane and submarine base at Kodiak, and a patrol plane base at Sitka. The report recommended the construction at Guam, which was practically defenseless, of a robust defense establishment capable of holding off Japanese air, naval, and amphibious attack until a relief expedition could be mounted; and at Midway, the development of a patrol plane base and a submarine base, plus dredging of the lagoon to accommodate tenders and tankers. On Oahu, the report called for the enlargement of Pearl Harbor's Ford Island Naval Air Base and construction of a new patrol plane base at Kaneohe. Recommendations for Wake included the development of a patrol plane base and a submarine base plus dredging the lagoon to accommodate tenders and tankers. The report also recommended that some limited development work be done in a number of far-flung American possessions around Hawaii that might serve as early-warning posts or aircraft ferry stops. Money was allocated to dredge the lagoons at Canton, Johnston, Palmyra, and Rose (in American Samoa) atolls for use by patrol planes and tenders.

The Congress passed the development measures for Alaska, Oahu, Midway, and Wake, and the smaller places, but a hot debate failed to produce any improvement funds for Guam. Those opposed to defending Guam said they did not want to provoke the Japanese, who occupied the rest of the Mariana Islands group.

While the Hepburn Report resulted in reasonably large efforts in Alaska, Oahu, Midway, and Wake, most of the smaller Pacific islands and atolls that came under U.S. oversight or administration were not fully developed until very late in the game and, indeed, several were not developed at all until just before or after war engulfed the Pacific. In addition to their roles as military bases, Midway and Wake were well-established and reasonably developed refueling stops on Pan-American Airways' China Clipper commercial seaplane route; military airfields were first built there in 1940 and 1941, respectively. Johnston Atoll, a bird sanctuary, was another refueling stop at which a seaplane base and airstrip had been built in 1936. Palmyra Atoll was privately owned until taken over by the navy in 1938; a man-made lagoon was completed in early 1941 to serve as a ready anchorage for a seaplane tender and a clutch of patrol bombers, and there was just enough room to accommodate a narrow airstrip, which was established on August 15, 1941. Canton Island, an isolated, jointly owned British-American territory, was a link in the Pan American Clipper route to New Zealand last used on December 4, 1941; it was not developed as an air base until after the start of the Pacific War. Even less developed was Christmas Atoll, a lonely, uninhabited U.S. possession far to the south of Hawaii that was prized for its guano deposits; it was developed with a weather station and airfield after the outbreak of war. Baker Island, another isolated guano source, was not occupied until after the start of the war. Howland Island was the uninhabited site of several earthen airstrips graded in 1937 for the arrival of Amelia Earhart, who never got that far; the island was not occupied until after the start of the war.

By the eve of war, detachments from several U.S. Marine Corps defense battalions (armed with anti-ship and antiaircraft weapons) occupied Wake, Midway, Johnston, and Palmyra. The latter two locations had functioning airstrips by mid-August 1941 but no aircraft were permanently based at either location. Midway and Wake could service navy patrol bombers, but Midway had no land-based aircraft when the war began, and an advance detachment of twelve marine fighters arrived at Wake on December 4, 1941. A full marine defense battalion was shipped to American Samoa between December 1940 and March 1941; it supervised the recruitment of a local provisional infantry battalion, but a planned airfield at Tuituila was not completed until after the start of the war.

✳

The Far East

In addition to its own priorities in the Pacific, the U.S. Navy took time in 1941 to discuss with the British their plans for a response to an eventual declaration of war by Japan. The Royal Navy did not feel its naval operations in the Atlantic and Mediterranean would leave it with enough warships to meaningfully defend or relieve the pivotal base at Singapore, which the British considered vital to holding open trade routes from Australia and New Zealand to India and the Suez Canal. The British asked the U.S. Navy to split the Pacific Fleet in half in order to provide cover for Singapore and possibly help Royal Netherlands Navy units hold the so-called Malay Barrier between Singapore and the Netherlands East Indies.

The American contact, Rear Adm. Richmond Kelly Turner, director of the navy War Plans Division, thought the request was ridiculous. The British knew that Rainbow 5 did not contemplate a naval relief of even the precious Philippines, so what were they on about with regard to Singapore and the Malay Barrier? In the end, the only accord this round of navy-to-navy meetings reached in minutes recorded on February 10, 1941, was "that for Great Britain it was fundamental that Singapore be held; for the United States it was fundamental that the Pacific Fleet be held intact"—an agreement, then, to disagree. Even the Australian government chose to announce that its small navy (though not its army) would be kept close to home rather than contribute it to the defense of Singapore, and New Zealand so subscribed in due course. Much later in 1941, the Royal Navy said it would send at least six capital ships to Singapore if the U.S. Navy agreed to support Royal Navy units in the Mediterranean, a pact made too late to bear fruit.

The ABC-1 report of March 27, 1941, cemented the Pacific and East Asia strategy for both nations: "If Japan does enter the war, the military strategy in the Far East will be defensive. The United States does not intend to add to its present military strength in the Far East but will employ the United States Pacific Fleet offensively in the manner best calculated to weaken Japanese economic power, and to support the defense of the Malay Barrier by diverting Japanese strength away from Malaya." The important point that lay in these words was that the United States committed its navy to a *dynamic* defense of whole regions of the Pacific and East Asia, and not a merely passive defense of existing bases. Moreover, ABC-1 turned the entire Pacific region over to the sole defense of the United States, an arrangement that required no consultation with the British with respect to setting goals and schedules. For the navy, it meant dominance over planning in a vast region in which it should be dominant.

With respect to the Far East, again, meetings between American, British, and Dutch officers were held in Singapore during the week April 21–27, 1941. There were so many variables, so many possible actions the Japanese might take, that the planners simply could not get down to cases, much less agree to specific responses. There was agreement only that events and eventualities would be tied entirely to what the Japanese did, how far and in what direction they went in who-knew-how-soon. The so-called ABD (American-British-Dutch) Agreement that came out of this meeting was so vague, except for excessive British-engineered attention to Singapore, that Admiral Stark and General Marshall rejected it on July 3, 1941. The American service chiefs were so concerned about the British motivation to hold Singapore at all costs that they revoked an earlier agreement to subordinate the small American Asiatic Fleet to British command for fear it would be sent straight to the relief of that one base. On November 5, however, Stark and Marshall recommended to President Roosevelt that the United States ratify three of the ABD Agreement's many contingencies by establishing a policy of automatically declaring war on Japan for: a "direct act of war" by Japanese forces against any of the ABD signatories; a move by Japanese forces in Thailand west of a line from Bangkok to the Isthmus of Kra; or Japanese occupation of Portuguese (East) Timor or the (Free) French Loyalty Islands off New Caledonia in the South Pacific.

Chapter 27

The Air Corps in 1941

The Army Air Forces

THE RAPID ONSET of the Air Corps' expansion following the German invasion of Poland eventually shed a good deal of light on the command structure's many inadequacies. At that time, the chief of the Air Corps oversaw administration, recruitment, and materiel acquisition, while the chief of GHQ Air Force was charged with overseeing combat operations and pilot and aircrew training. This bifurcated arrangement had not worked especially well at the outset, and the early fix had been to unite the command structures under one individual, Hap Arnold, beginning shortly after he took over as chief of the Air Corps in October 1938. The fix worked for awhile, but the expansion proceeded at such a brutal pace that it eventually overwhelmed the attention span of one of the military's most practiced workaholics. There was simply too much going on in each sphere for one man to follow on a day-to-day, hands-on basis.

As part of a general Department of War reorganization that took effect on November 1, 1940, GHQ Air Force was accorded separate status under the army's commander of field forces, and its chief no longer reported up the Air Corps chain of command. That is, it was more closely bound to the fighting army, per se, than ever contemplated by Air Corps officers. In anticipation of this cleavage, however, Arnold had been appointed acting chief of staff of the army for air, a new provisional position created to raise the impact of air planning on the army as a whole. And he retained his place as chief of the Air Corps. So, in the end, while losing direct control of GHQ Air Force, Arnold, as acting deputy chief of staff, was in a position to oversee it by other means, albeit at one remove from his previous direct control.

There remained much that was awkward and inefficient in the new arrangement, especially insofar as how much Arnold still had on his plate. Thus, in March 1941, Secretary of War Stimson saw to it that the defunct office of assistant secretary of war for air was reinstated. Selected for the post was Robert Lovett, a Texas-born New York banker and Great War naval aviator who, since December 1940, had been Stimson's special assistant for air. Lovett was known for his organizational abilities, and, indeed, it was his primary task to streamline the Air Corps organization as well as oversee the production of aircraft, which is to say he was to organize the aircraft industry for wartime needs.

Lovett's concentration on Air Corps reorganization bore first fruits on June 20, 1941, when his office created the Army Air Forces (AAF), a new command level placed atop the co-equal Air Corps and the new Air Force Combat Command (AFCC), a more robust successor to GHQ Air Force. Arnold, who was named chief of the Army Air Forces, reported directly to Marshall and oversaw all policies and plans affecting army aviation. The primary features of the new arrangement were that Arnold benefited by being served directly by a new air staff (including the new Air War Plans Division, AWPD) and that the chiefs of the AAF and AFCC reported directly to him. Major General George Brett was named chief of the AAF, and Maj. Gen. Delos Emmons was named commanding general of AFCC. Arnold, who remained dual-hatted as deputy chief of staff of the army, was granted four-star rank. And, although Arnold was nominally Marshall's subordinate, he was to be accorded effectively equal status to Marshall and Admiral Stark in the highest military councils of the age.

For all that the new arrangement seemed to have raised the status of the Air Corps, proponents of an independent air force carped that it blocked the realization of their dreams and was perhaps merely a sop to their sensibilities. Moreover, as a solution to any extant problems, it was as flawed as any before it by vague lines of authority between combat functions and service functions, and it remained to be seen what the AAF's actual relationship with its Department of War bosses really was. These matters had not been settled by the time war overtook the nation.

Scrambling for Airplanes

Lend-Lease was choking the Air Corps. There was no way the proposed organization of combat and service groups could hit any of its target dates as long the warplanes just off the assembly lines were allocated to Britain, in particular in the numbers—roughly 50 percent—prescribed by President Roosevelt. Yes, Britain put the aircraft to excellent use against the Luftwaffe over western Europe and the North Atlantic as well as against the combined German-Italian air forces over eastern North Africa. And, yes, that helped keep the wolves from America's front door. But there was persistent and growing alarm, for good reason, that the United States was running out of time and would thus need its own robust, well-trained, well-equipped air groups to defend its long coastlines, its possessions in the Caribbean and the Pacific, and the leased British bases facing the western Atlantic. There was, indeed, no point holding those bases if they could not be defended.

Though growing impressively, the nation's aircraft-building capacity was not remotely there yet. Just 3,770 new American-built military airplanes, many of them highly complex multi-engine bombers, were accepted by their various users, including the navy and Air Corps. So, while the Air Corps took in sufficient personnel to meet its 1941 targets, it took in too few airplanes and thus did not activate the number of groups it intended to activate—not even the old fifty-four-group plan requiring 21,470 training and combat aircraft by April 1, 1942.

There was, however, encouragement on the fiscal front: between January 1 and August 31, 1941, the Congress appropriated $6.5 billion for construction of fifteen thousand new airplanes and to fund the expansion and construction of aircraft factories. This was nearly four and a half times the money Congress had authorized for aircraft construction in 1938, 1939, and 1940 combined.

Training

In 1941, the Air Corps was all about training. Even measures-short-of-war operations to bolster the naval Neutrality Patrol with coastal observation were more like training than like combat flying.

Pilot training in 1939 sought to add 1,200 new aviators to the Air Corps roster, but in 1940 the goal was first raised to 7,000 new pilots, and then to 12,000. By February 1941 the goal for the year was set at 30,000 new pilots, then raised to 50,000 to accommodate a proposed and still somewhat theoretical long-term expansion to *eighty-four* active air groups.

It was by no means difficult to recruit pilot trainees. If anything, too many young men applied for the available slots. Selection criteria, which had been traditionally held to ridiculously high standards as a means to exclude the bulk of eager pre-1940 volunteers, were relaxed to reasonable levels, certainly levels low enough to allow sufficient overage for the large number of men who were weeded out or killed during the intense training cycle.

In order to hit its personnel goals, the Air Corps had to build numerous new training facilities, engage more civilian flying schools for primary training, generally streamline the training program, and spend less time on military niceties and a larger proportion of time on flying and gunnery. In essence, the Air Corps had to industrialize its pilot training (and aircrew and groundcrew training) in much the same way the aircraft industry had to industrialize its formerly slow plane-building process. The metaphor of the day was "assembly line."

The precipitous expansion of groundcrew training, begun in late 1938, was largely accomplished in civilian-run, military-supervised contract schools located all around the nation. The Air Corps made no concerted effort to train its own earth-bound technicians until November 1941, when it had to do something to help the contract schools achieve a goal of one hundred thousand graduated ground-service technicians per year.

Aircrew training took place at or under the supervision of the Air Corps Training Center at Randolph Field, Texas, and three bases set up in areas of the country where good flying weather was the norm. GHQ Air Force was in charge of crew training until it was superceded by the Air Force Combat Command, but the Technical Training Command was inserted into the command structure in March 1941.

The wonder of it all was that, through most of 1941, the vast Air Corps expansion was accomplished solely from a base of volunteers. This was because the initial draft act was prescribed under law as a one-year solution, and the Air Corps needed a year or most of a year just to train its aircrew and ground technicians, leaving roughly zero time to put draftees, once trained, to good use. There was no shortage of enthusiastic young volunteers, though the enthusiasm of many stemmed from the fact that the Air Corps wasn't the infantry.

It is well worth noting that the base of enthusiastic volunteers for pilot training included many black youngsters—and a number of seasoned black aviators—who were qualified in every way but for the color of their skin. Nevertheless, on January 16, 1941, on orders from President Roosevelt and at the insistence of Congressional statute—but to the great chagrin of the Department of War—the Air Corps formed its first training squadron composed entirely of black aviation cadets at Tuskegee Institute in Alabama. In March 1941, the 99th Pursuit Squadron was activated at Chanute Field, Illinois, with an initial complement of several white ground officers and 250 black enlisted ground-crewmen. The 99th was transferred to Tuskeegee's Moton Field in June 1941, but it would be a year before a logjam of racially motivated delays was overcome sufficiently to allow the first five black pilots to join the squadron, and nearly another year to get it overseas.

War Games

The Air Corps took part in every war game held in 1940 and 1941. Each and every one of the assessments that took place at the highest levels following each war game showed the branch lacking in exactly the tactical-support missions it had been neglecting since it became fixated on heavy bombers and strategic bombing in the 1930s. The ground army learned throughout the cycle of war games that it could not depend on support from the sky, that the Air Corps had failed in every aspect of its ground-support mission, from pilot training to development of control of aircraft by ground-based observers, to the development of radios with which pilots and ground observers could communicate.

For some reason, despite almost universally harsh criticism from ground commanders, the Air Corps was not placed on sufficient notice to clean up its act. With few exceptions, all that was lacking in December 1941 would be just as lacking when battle was joined between U.S. Army and Axis forces in late 1942 and on into 1943.

Hemispheric Defense

From the Air Corps' doctrinal perspective, defense of American shores—or any base—was centered on meeting an approaching enemy fleet or air attack as far out from shore as possible. There is nothing in this to explain why the Air Corps did absolutely nothing for decades to press for long-range pursuit aircraft, but the perspective does bolster the rationale for the B-17 heavy bomber, and indeed for less long-legged bombers like the B-18 or even the earlier B-10. Notwithstanding any agreement with the navy to stand down its mission to defend shorelines by flying far out to sea, the Air Corps had long stuck to its views, had long prepared to defend land bases by flying its bombers far out to sea to engage the oncoming enemy.

The Air Corps' persistent view of its role, long a worry for the navy, was seen as a very good thing in 1940 and 1941. The navy, while growing and gaining experience far out at sea in the Atlantic and Caribbean, was by then willing to accept help from any quarter. Its carrier fleet—the means by which it expected to engage an enemy fleet far out at sea—was still small and almost hopelessly dispersed. Its fleet of long-range patrol bombers was made up of PBYs and PBMs, which flew far but carried insignificant payloads and could not defend themselves at any one time against more than a few enemy fighters, if that many.

By March 1939, the Air Corps had been allowed to openly state one of its cherished war missions, that of defending against air attacks on friendly bases by attacking, with long-range bombers, the bases from which enemy attacks would be mounted. Indeed, this openly stated mission became the Air Corps' primary mission, even ahead of utilizing its pursuit aircraft to protect friendly bases directly overhead.

By June 1940, after the United States had experienced increased sensitivity with respect to defense of the entire Western Hemisphere, the Air Corps had taken upon itself a total of six linked strategic missions. These were codified in a study entitled "Air Corps Mission under the Monroe Doctrine," and they were a statement of current Air Corps doctrine in themselves. In order of importance, they were: prevent enemies from establishing bases in the Western Hemisphere; attack the bases of any hostile air forces that became established in the hemisphere; challenge enemy air units in the air and defeat them; attack transports and cargo ships attempting to unload enemy forces and their supplies; support the efforts by friendly ground forces to defend their bases or seize enemy bases in the hemisphere; and support or take the place of friendly naval forces against enemy naval forces.

These six self-assigned missions shaped the World War II Army Air Corps in that they required a particular balance of forces centering on particular types of aircraft built to particular specifications. There was room in the planning and implementation for everyone, especially bombers, but the pursuit, transport, and observation arms could also find work.

Topping the Air Corps' wish list for achieving full implementation of its integrated doctrine—which was obviously defensive in all its parts—was a longer-range bomber than the B-17 and even the newer B-24. The Air Corps claimed, with complete justification, that the farther out at sea an approaching enemy fleet was first met, the more attacks could be conducted against it over a longer period across a dwindling range. Also, longer-ranged bombers could reach enemy lodgments farther from their fixed bases than could shorter-ranged bombers. This obvious argument was highly sensible when one glanced at a map to see where bombers of the day, operating from a line of fixed bases, could reach at extreme range. It wasn't all that far: Natal, Brazil, which was

1,600 miles from the nearest point in western Africa, was 2,600 miles from the nearest American base, in Puerto Rico.

The United States did not undertake the destroyers-for-bases deal in September 1940 because it wanted to diffuse its limited fighting forces over a wider area, nor did it do so solely to help the British cope, nor was its sole aim the distant defense of the Panama Canal, without which it had no hope of waging a two-ocean naval war. Bases in British Guiana were half as far from Natal as bases in Puerto Rico and that much better able to reach air ferry routes between, say, Dakar and Natal. In November 1941, the United States was also granted rights by the local authorities to base airplanes in Dutch Guiana, which was closer to Natal than British Guiana. Also, several friendly Central American nations liberalized air routing across their territory and even approved the building by Americans of several auxiliary airfields. Further, airfields, interlocked for mutual defense, were built or improved in some of the bases granted by the British.

At the other end of the hemispheric defense line, in the north, the Ogdensburg Agreement with Canada led to an October 1940 U.S. survey of possible military use of Newfoundland Airport, in Gander Lake. German bombers of the day could reach Boston and New York from Norway if they could make a refueling stop in Newfoundland, so a strong air-defense contingent based at Gander could challenge a German effort to seize a base site elsewhere in Newfoundland or even in Greenland, some eight hundred miles east of Gander.

The best way to defend Greenland turned out to be by sitting on Greenland. When German bombers began flying too close to settled areas in the Danish possession for the comfort of the local authorities, and with several German attempts to establish meteorological stations there, the Danish minister to the United States once again asked the Americans to defend the immense island. What had only been a quandary a year earlier, after Denmark went down before the blitzkrieg, was a real boon in the world of early 1941. Formal trade agreements between the United States and local Greenland authorities had been in effect since July 1940, and American survey teams were already visiting likely airfield sites. Spurred by a German air attack on Iceland—only four hundred miles east of Greenland shores—in February 1941, it was no stretch by early 1941 for the United States to agree to build several bases in Iceland from which air and sea routes could be patrolled and interdicted and, indeed, through which aircraft could be more easily and safely ferried to theUnited Kingdom from the United States via Newfoundland Airport. Thus, on April 9, 1941, the Danish government in exile formally extended basing rights in Greenland, in return for which the United States undertook to keep the Danish territory safe from German occupation.

It was a safe argument that Greenland lay within the Western Hemisphere defense zone defined and justified by the Roosevelt Administration's invocation of the Monroe Doctrine. But the four hundred miles separating Greenland from Iceland was another matter. It took a great deal of stretching to apply the Monroe Doctrine to this other, more distant Danish North Atlantic possession.

Fortunately, the local Icelandic government (under coercion from the British government, which needed its twenty-five-thousand-man garrison back) asked the United States to base troops there. On July 7, 1941, President Roosevelt transmitted the request to the Congress along with a message that a U.S. naval force and a U.S. Marine brigade had just arrived in Reykjavík to supplement the British force that had been there since May 1940. Under terms of the agreement, plans leading to the replacement of all British forces in Iceland were first promulgated in June, the first Air Corps aircraft reached Reykjavík on August 6, and the first U.S. Army ground troops arrived in September. It is well things turned out as they did, because American military planners had for some time written into their strategic plans a definite operation to seize bases in Iceland as soon as the United States and Germany were at war.

Often forgotten in discussions of hemispheric defense concerns and solutions in the 1940–1941 period is the matter of defending the Panama Canal against Japanese attack. While at the outset the Panama Canal Zone defenses were weak, all of the services appreciably built up the defenses, but there were few options available to distant defense out into the Pacific. The only land in air range to the west and south of Panama are the Cocos Islands, a possession of Costa Rica; Malpelo Island, an uninhabited rock under Colombian governance; and the Galapagos Islands, a distant province of Ecuador. Ticklish political ties with each of these nations prevented any discussion of basing rights from even being raised in the 1940–1941 period. Thus, in the near term at least, American forces in the Panama Canal Zone would have to undertake a close-in defense if attacked from the Pacific side, another great reason for basing B-17s there while pressing for the development of even longer-ranged bombers.

As with the western approaches to the Panama Canal, Alaska and the Aleutian Islands were of considerable concern to those who took in a complete view of the meaning of hemispheric defense. It took until 1935 for Air Corps concerns over the defense of Alaska to result in congressional authorization for construction of just one adequate military base within America's far northwest territory. It took until 1939, however, before work began on the base, which was located outside Anchorage. Also, the Civil Aeronautics Authority began work on a string of emergency landing fields in Alaska that could be adapted to military usage. As the base at Anchorage was being built up, arrangements were made with Canadian aviation authorities under the Ogdensburg accord to develop air routes over and use of emergency airfields in Canadian territory. The Air Corps was also made responsible for air defense over the naval base at Dutch Harbor, on Unalaska Island, in the Aleutian Islands, a project that eventually required development of an advance airfield on Umnak Island, farther to the west.

Pacific Defenses

The main American bases in the Pacific were in Hawaii and the Philippines. A number of tiny, isolated atolls and islands had been marginally developed with airfields or as temporary bases for tender-supported seaplanes, or they provided or might provide waystations to and from the larger possessions as well as along several commercial air routes. These were Midway, Wake, Canton, Christmas, Johnston, Baker, Howland, and Palmyra. Guam, in the otherwise Japanese-occupied Mariana Islands, was an old coaling station taken in the Spanish-American War and permanently garrisoned by small navy and marine detachments; it had no airfield because the island was indefensible and thus bound to fall into Japanese hands at the outset of war. The Air Corps' stake in these far-flung places under control of the navy was wrapped entirely in their potential as waypoints on various potential B-17 ferry routes between the U.S. west coast and the Philippines.

Hawaii and the Philippines had both fallen into American hands in 1898 and both had been home to American garrisons from the start. Each was defended by a large U.S. Army ground force concentrated near their capitals, Honolulu on Oahu and Manila on Luzon. Hawaii was mainly home to a naval base protected by an army garrison and several Air Corps bases. Luzon was mainly home to an army garrison augmented by a major naval base and filled out with several Air Corps bases. The Philippines was a colony consciously and wholeheartedly on its way to independence while Hawaii was a territory possibly on its way to statehood. The military centers on Oahu and Luzon were elaborate and large, and both were at the center of broad webs of ancillary garrisons and bases, some quite far away and isolated. The main difference between the two in 1940 and 1941 was that the Philippines were going to be defended to the last but not relieved or even reinforced or resupplied once the expected war began. Hawaii, however, was going to be defended by whatever means the United States needed to expend. The Philippines were too far away to keep, and Hawaii was too close to lose.

For a very long time, the Army Air Corps had had a plan to defend the Philippines, but in this case, more than every other, the exigencies of Lend-Lease traded the defensibility of an American possession for long-term British security. The Air Corps could not long hold back a Japanese landing, staged from Formosa against Luzon, but it might very badly bloody the Japanese, perhaps give them a reason to reassess their options. But that might only take place if there were enough modern pursuits to overwhelm Japanese escort fighters and keep Japanese bombers from hitting Luzon's array of air bases, as well as enough heavy bombers to fully implement the Air Corps' stand-off doctrine as embodied in the report "Air Corps Mission under the Monroe Doctrine." Done right, with alacrity, there might even be time to build up an air establishment on Luzon and distant Mindanao large enough to deter the Japanese entirely, or for a long time, from any attempt to reach into the Pacific from what in 1941 stood as the empire's eastern boundaries.

Grand Strategy

The role of the Air Corps in a coalition war beside Great Britain was defined in the March 27, 1941, final report of the first American-British Conversation

(ABC-1). At its root, ABC-1 established the Germany-first strategy set forth in America's 1940 Joint War Plan Rainbow No. 5 as its long-term primary goal. As did Rainbow 5, ABC-1 included goals for the early elimination of Italy from the Axis coalition, and the eventual defeat of Japan once full attention could be diverted to the Pacific and Asia.

The Air Corps' mission in the grand plan was to join with the other services and various allies to hermetically defend the Western Hemisphere against Axis incursion and, "in collaboration with the Royal Air Force," to mount "a sustained air offensive against German Military Power, supplemented by air offensives against other regions under enemy control which contribute to that power," and to attain "superiority of air strength over that of the enemy, particularly in long-range striking forces." This bomber offensive against Germany, for that is what it all added up to, was the only offensive operation set forth in the ABC-1 strategy discussion.

This directive in ABC-1 must have made the bomber boys swoon. The mask could be removed; the Air Corps was to be a fully sanctioned offensive organization after all. Nevertheless, the Air Corps and RAF were also directed to allocate resources—considerable resources—to support the ground armies and naval forces of the Allied coalition.

The best estimate on an initial Air Corps contribution to the ongoing British bombardment offensive against Germany and occupied Europe was thirty-two bombardment and pursuit squadrons—fewer than ten combat air groups—if the United States was drawn into the war as early as late 1941. This was a puny down payment on an immense venture, but it was reflective of the pressure Lend-Lease put on equipping the Air Corps for a host of missions, from the British Isles (or perhaps Egypt) in the east all the way out to the Philippines in the west. This comprised a battlefront encompassing more than half the globe, half of which was over stretches of open water that came very close to defying the ability of unshippable large airplanes to get from the center—the United States—to either end of the line.

Recognizing that the United States was still not at war with any nation, ABC-1 suggested that the British and American military communities exchange permanent military missions acting in behalf of the various service chiefs. The missions would initially concentrate on exchange of intelligence but also begin work on joint war planning and joint transportation services. This was a very fine proposal, because it got more and more British and American officers working together, getting into one another's thought processes, sharing the fruits of practical experience, and learning how to make concessions that benefited the enterprise rather than the parochial interests of one nation or the other.

The adoption and early implementation of ABC-1 caused the army and navy War Plans divisions to recalibrate Rainbow 5. Indeed, on May 14, 1941, Joint Army and Navy War Plan Rainbow No. 5 was formally adopted for the first time by the Joint Army and Navy Board as *the* leading strategic vision that would direct the American war effort whenever war came to America. The only update to the plan, a response to the deteriorating relations between Japan and the United States, was a November 1941 Joint Board–approved rush to get combat aircraft out to the Philippines.

The German invasion of the Soviet Union on June 22, 1941, caused the British staffs overseeing implementation of ABC-1 to take a fresh look in light of the new situation. The British-authored review was presented to the British chiefs of staff on August 11. Insofar as it fine-tuned the role of a contemplated combined Anglo-American bomber offensive against Germany, the new study called for a far greater, far more sustained effort than ABC-1 originally contemplated. As a goal, in fact, the paper suggested that the only limiting factor on such an air offensive be the maximum number of warplanes that could be accommodated on however many airfields could be built in the United Kingdom. The paper then went on to define the goal of the bomber offensive as a *cumulative* victory—a level of defeat far beyond a military defeat, for it envisaged taking down the entire German economic and industrial bases through a massive war of attrition that would bring the entire nation to its knees. This was a vital distinction. Germany had sued for peace in November 1918 as a result of a military defeat. The German economy, especially food-production sectors, had been strained beyond its ability to cope with more war, but the German industrial base had been untouched by war. This led to a theory embraced by a majority of humiliated Germans that their beloved fatherland had been "stabbed in the back" by traitors—Jews and Communists came immediately to German minds and tongues. That viral conclusion, dead wrong, led to the ascension of the Nazi regime, total dictatorship, and a new war in less than a generation. The enduring bootprint of cumulative victory on the Nazi posterior would leave no doubt as to who brought Germany down in the 1940s, and that lack of ambiguity in the final outcome, the British authors of the revision hoped, might lead to a lasting European peace insofar as Germany was concerned. And it has. Somewhat naively, the planners also hoped that a bombed-out Germany might sue for peace before the Allies had to mount a land invasion of occupied Europe.

The American response to the new British modifications was muted. It was noted rather dryly throughout a virtual interlinear American commentary that this major revision of ABC-1 contemplated the deployment of terror bombing against civilians—which the British called "morale bombardment"—as the effective means for bringing Germany to its knees (or its senses, whichever came first). The Americans, who were not yet at war and whose urban centers faced little risk of bombardment, reported that this was an odious plan. Further, the Americans stated their belief that the British planners were staking too much on the air offensive, per se, when the British contemplated a victory over Germany as deriving from the attritional effects of bombing alone, an outcome the British went so far as to label as "probable." The American Joint Army and Navy Board rather soberly recommended that the British return to the plan set forth in ABC-1, a deliberate defeat of German arms, industry, and economy by all the means necessary, of which a sustained bombing campaign was but one.

The British were no doubt taken aback by the American response. A November 21, 1941, follow-up from the British Joint Planning Board hemmed and hawed and backed and filled, but it did not exactly back down. Withal, the discussion was overrun by events, and additions and changes to ABC-1 were made by partners fighting a world war side by side and hand in hand.

AWPD-1

The June 1, 1941, reorganization of the Air Corps had placed the new Air War Plans Division under the control of the Office of Deputy Chief of Staff for Air, but it did not create AWPD as an autonomous entity. Rather, AWPD was composed of air officers whose primary assignment was to the army War Plans Division. AWPD was a subset of the army War Plans Division, and subordinate to it. Nevertheless, in late July 1941 a senior Air Corps officer with responsibility to War Plans, Lt. Col. Clayton Bissell, met with Arnold to discuss air strategy for the coming war. Even this late in the game, there was no overarching air strategy and thus no definitive benchmark for the Air Corps expansion program. Between them, Arnold and Bissell decided to assign to AWPD the task of completing a first draft of a comprehensive air plan, including strategies and tables of organization and orders of battle. No one at the full War Plans organization blinked when AWPD pretty much convened on its own authority to do so.

Four Air Corps officers did most of the heavy lifting: Col. Harold L. George, the AWPD chief; Lt. Col. Kenneth Walker; Maj. Laurence Kuter; and Maj. Haywood Hansell Jr., of whom all would attain flag rank. The work began on August 4, and the plan, dubbed AWPD-1, was submitted on August 11, accepted by Army G-3 on August 12, and then approved in quick succession by the full War Plans Division, generals Marshall and Arnold, Assistant Secretary of War Lovett, and Secretary of War Stimson.

The planning bases for AWPD-1 were ABC-1 and Rainbow 5, and the Air Corps' mission in an upcoming war was divided into three headings: defense of the Western Hemisphere, defense of Pacific bases, and offensive operations against Germany. Such strategic operations would begin on what the army called M-day, the start of hostilities. Until M-day, the Air Corps was to concentrate on a rapid but orderly expansion along lines already set down in the fifty-four- and eighty-four-group programs. From M-day forward, the Air Corps was to work with the services generally to conduct dynamic defensive operations in the Pacific as well as begin and steadily ramp up an unremitting aerial offensive against Germany. At some future point, the operations against Germany would reach a level of violence at which it could be called an all-out attack, and that all-out attack was to be waged until Germany was on its knees. At that point, the strategic emphasis was to be shifted to an offensive against Japan that culminated in an all-out phase.

AWPD-1 was prescient in some areas and overly ambitious in others. For example, it cautioned that, while the offensive aviation operations would commence as early as April 1942, the Air Corps build-out would not be up to mounting the all-out phase against Germany until April 1944. The latter estimate was nearly dead-on; the first bombing missions against Berlin would take place in April 1944. But the starting date, April 1942, was half a year ahead of reality. An Air Corps light bombardment squadron would undertake a few symbolic missions in June and July 1942, and some fighter sweeps would be run out of England in August, but the first real American-run bombardment mission based out of England was one in which just twelve B-17s from one group would target a German airfield in France on August 17, 1942. The build-up from there would be painfully slow, and no American bombers would reach Germany itself until late January 1943, when fifty-five of ninety-one B-17s dispatched would strike the naval base at Wilhelmshaven.

AWPD-1 made a stab at placing combat groups in the various theaters—a total twenty-three bombardment groups and thirty-one pursuit groups were designated by type to cover the entire U.S. coastline, the Western Hemisphere outside the United States, the Philippines and Hawaii, Alaska, and whatever else might brew up in a time of war. These fifty-four groups were indeed on the Air Corps roster on M-day (see Appendix B), but many of them were paper organizations with few airmen or airplanes, not to mention little training and roughly zero experience at war. Arnold later quipped, "We had plans but not planes."

All five principal authors of AWPD-1 were bomber boys. (Colonel Harold L. George, the AWPD chief, was known throughout the Air Corps as "Bomber" George, the best way to distinguish him from Col. Harold H. George, who was known as "Fighter" George.) There is not much wonder, then, in AWPD-1's heavy reliance upon bombers to bring the war to Germany and Japan themselves. No effort was made to suggest that pursuits be upgraded for deep-penetration missions—which might include bomber escort—because the bomber boys, who dominated the Air Corps' upper echelons, believed wholeheartedly in the self-defending, do-everything bomber. Indeed, Lt. Col. Kenneth Walker, an AWPD-1 co-author, was to earn a Medal of Honor when he perished aboard an unescorted heavy bomber in January 1943.

AWPD-1 was as comprehensive and prescient a document as the far-looking officers who compiled it could imagine it was necessary to be. It was as good a place to start as any in the summer of 1941, but like every other plan written by men ahead of the events in question, it was doomed from the start to be overrun by reality. No one could have dreamed that summer how the Army Air Corps would actually evolve in the crucible of war. Armed with AWPD-1, a plan of its own by its own, the U.S. Army Air Corps labored long and hard that summer and fall of 1941 as the hours and minutes ticked inexorably toward peace's fire-drenched sunset.

New Airplanes
B-17 Upgrade

The first production example of an upgunned B-17 upgrade, designated B-17E, first flew in September 1941. The initial B-17E order was for 512 airplanes—

or nearly three and a half times the number of B-17s built between 1935 and mid-1941. All 512 B-17Es were scheduled for delivery within a year.

P-38

A result of a 1937 design competition was an ultra-modern and quite breathtaking design departure from standard aircraft design, the twin-engine, twin-boom Lockheed P-38. The Lightning, as it was dubbed, was a superb airplane that crammed more modern technological goodies and insight into its airframe than any pursuit airplane in the world at that time. Constant modification slowed the acquisition process (in-service test examples did not reach a tactical squadron until March 1941), but the P-38 pretty much redefined the pursuit concept by the time the first production models were built. The P-38 featured two boom-mounted supercharged inline engines pushing counter-rotating propellers; twin tail assemblies; fully retractable tricycle landing gear; and a powerful weapons package consisting of four .50-caliber machine guns and a 20mm cannon, all mounted in the nose.

Other Pursuits

But for the North American P-51, which started life as a British design concept to be executed in the United States, the American design push of the late 1930s pretty much equipped the Army Air Corps pursuit branch with the modern fighter types that would take it through World War II. Unfortunately, the best of this crop of home-grown pursuits, the Lockheed P-38 and Republic P-47, would not be available for combat use until well into 1942, and the early models of the others that were drawn into combat in 1942, chiefly the Curtiss P-40 and Bell P-39, were markedly inferior to the German and Japanese first-line fighters of the day.

Transports

The closest any prewar civilian airliner came to satisfying global needs in aerial supply and transportation—which the Air Corps did not yet clearly foresee—was the Douglas DC-3 airliner, a larger DC-2 upgrade that first flew civilian passengers in 1936. Military tinkerers noticed the larger, faster DC-3's potential right off the bat, but working through complex upgrade specifications and tight manufacturing schedules for Douglas exports urgently needed in overseas war zones contributed to delays that prevented the first contract from being written until as late in the game as 1940 and the first deliveries from being made until 1941. The DC-3's Air Corps variant was the C-47, a designation that became synonymous with "World War II transport plane." It was flown by every American service—and many foreign air forces—in every part of the world from 1941 onward. Many thousands were built, and there were still C-47s in service at the dawn of the twenty-first century.

The only other civilian airliner of the late 1930s that was large enough and long-ranged enough to have strategic potential was the 1937 design for the twin-engine Curtiss CW-20, a pressurized twenty-four- to thirty-four-seat airliner with a wide, 2,300-cubic-foot cabin (twice that of a DC-3) and 455 cubic feet of storage beneath the cabin floor. First flown in March 1940, the CW-20 was thereafter further modified for civilian use and adapted to Air Corps specifications as the C-46, which in transport configuration could haul fifty-four soldiers or more than fifty thousand pounds of cargo up to 1,200 miles under normal cruising conditions. The first Air Corps test examples were produced in late 1940, but the first, heavily modified, C-46 production airplanes would not reach operational units until mid-1942, because the Curtiss production facilities were clogged throughout the interim with urgent orders for combat aircraft from the American and many foreign services. Not nearly as numerous as the C-47, the C-46 was nonetheless used the world around under the most arduous conditions imaginable. By November 1941, the Air Corps had activated seven transport groups, which varied as to completeness and equipment when the United States was drawn into the war but was nonetheless a good start on a new concept.

Chapter 28

The Marine Corps

A Beachhead at Guantánamo

FOR THE FIRST 123 YEARS of its existence, the U.S. Marine Corps was, like its British parent, the Royal Marines, a branch of the navy composed of small, shipboard detachments that usually served as seagoing police or base guards but were sometimes employed as the core of detachments that boarded enemy ships or took part in brief forays to attack enemy ports and fortresses. This changed in 1898, when at Key West, at the start of the Spanish-American War, the Marine Corps organized and trained an expeditionary battalion of infantry and artillery to seize a beachhead at Guantánamo Bay, Cuba. On May 10, 1898, ten days ahead of a landing by the main U.S. Army invasion force, the marine expeditionary battalion secured the objective, which it then successfully defended against a superior Spanish force.

The use of amphibiously delivered marines to seize an advance base *and to defend it* was revolutionary. No such force was employed in the Philippines phase of the Spanish-American War and, indeed, Adm. George Dewey later lamented the oversight.

Following the Spanish-American War, and in light of its singular accomplishment at Guantánamo Bay, the Marine Corps argued that it was perfectly positioned to serve as a naval land component to assume the lead in a requirement that was emerging for the projection of American power into new areas of the globe, particularly in the Pacific.

In 1878, in the first such move of the century-old nation, the U.S. Navy established a permanent coaling station in Samoa. And in 1887 a treaty with Hawaii led to the establishment of a second coaling station, at Pearl Harbor. In 1898, a landing force from one of the warships convoying U.S. Army troops to the Philippines seized Guam from Spain, and thus a third link was added to the American chain across the Pacific. The Philippines themselves became the western anchor of the chain, also at Spain's expense in 1898.

For most of its history before 1898, the U.S. Navy saw itself as the guarantor of the Monroe Doctrine in the Caribbean and South Atlantic. But in 1880 some naval officers began to think about how their service might project force via the seizure and establishment of "advanced bases" there and elsewhere if the need arose. The U.S. Army, which was small and quite scattered at the time, would not be drawn into this line of inquiry, and no one thought of the Marine Corps in such a role, so distant was its traditional role and so small was its aggregate strength. Even with marines at their core, expeditionary landings of all types were traditionally composed in the main by bluejackets drawn from ships' companies. No one really debated the transformation of marines into self-supporting landing or advance-base forces until the opportunity of the war with Spain provided, first, sufficient manpower and, second, an actual mission. Only after an all-marine force had seized and defended Guantánamo Bay did it become obvious that the solution to a theoretical problem existed in a real setting. Indeed, as soon as marine expeditionary units could be organized and transported, marines established several advance bases in the Philippines, and thus began four decades of campaigning and base work there. So, too, began the century-long focus of the U.S. Marine Corps on innovation and practice in the arts of expeditionary and amphibious warfare—a relationship so powerful as to make those arts synonymous with "U.S. Marines."

Theory Becomes Practice

The line of thinking that followed the establishment of advance bases by marines in Cuba and the Philippines, and then in Panama, focused on the defense of such bases, and not on seizure of enemy bases by direct amphibious assault. The first classroom application of many theories and only a few practical examples was established in Newport, Rhode Island, in 1901, and a marine battalion undertook an initial field exercise as part of a much larger fleet exercise in the winter of 1902–1903 at Culebra, an island off the east coast of Puerto Rico. No formal course was established until 1910, and it was 1913 before enough theory had been laid down to warrant the establishment of a permanent advance-base force of about 1,750 officers and men. This force was divided into two regiments: a fixed-defense regiment composed of coast artillerymen, mine troops, engineers, communicators, searchlight units, and the like; and a mobile-defense regiment composed of infantry and artillery. Note the use of "defense" in characterizing both regiments. A small aviation contingent was added in early 1914.

In 1914, marines and bluejackets seized Vera Cruz in Mexico, in 1915 marines took part in landings in Haiti, and in 1916 they helped to establish order in Santo Domingo. American forces quickly withdrew from Mexico, but the burden of expanding and maintaining garrisons in the Caribbean—and Nicaragua in due course—hung heavily over the Marine Corps for two decades and, while it produced veterans, it drew resources away from planning and innovation in the advance-base role.

When the Marine Corps burgeoned to seventy-three thousand officers and men to take part in the Great War, it sent a brigade of two reinforced infantry regiments to France but maintained the bulk of its fighting establishment in base-defense and expeditionary roles in the Western Hemisphere. Indeed, it is probable that no more than half of the marine officers who would serve conspicuously and rise to high rank in the Pacific in World War II even set foot in France in 1917–1918.

The Pacific War Foreseen

As often happens in advancing theories, one man appears to have had more to do with pushing thinking toward a critical breakthrough than all the rest combined. The individual who drove the concept of amphibious *assault* toward its well-known conclusion was marine Capt. Earl "Pete" Ellis.

Ellis became obsessed with the notion that the U.S. advance into the Pacific beginning in 1878 at Samoa would lead to a war with Japan. By 1913, he had written a brilliant and widely discussed paper that highlighted the problems of waging the land component of a naval war across such vast ocean reaches. He reasoned that the United States and Japan would defend their respective advance bases (of which Japan had *none* in 1913), seize neutral ground to strengthen their strategic positions, and ultimately assault one another's bases against a backdrop of intense fleet activity. As part of his study and ongoing work, Ellis provided chillingly accurate detail as to how such a war would actually be conducted.

At the end of the Great War, Japan—an American ally—was indeed granted permanent mandates in former German possessions in the Pacific that enabled it to establish its own string of naval bases, west to east across the central Pacific, paralleling the American string of bases. In fact, the mandates outflanked the line of American bases, giving Japan an instant strategic advantage. Even though Japan agreed not to fortify these bases as part of the 1922 naval disarmament treaty, this sudden advantage of position gave Pete Ellis's prognostications immense support and helped lead in 1924 to the first formal revision of War Plan Orange, which had been written in 1911 as a strategic prescription for waging a war with Japan in the Pacific that would be supported by fixed bases such as those in Hawaii, Samoa, Guam, and the Philippines. Ellis's—and others'—chief focus on seizing neutral bases and assaulting Japanese bases was ultimately and quite naturally incorporated into the revised War Plan Orange, and it gave a free hand to Marine Corps officers to develop specific plans and an organization for assaulting and defending island bases.

The Advanced Base Force at Quantico, Virginia, was redesignated the Expeditionary Force in 1921 and was composed of infantry, artillery, engineer, signal, chemical, and aviation units. Its orientation was toward the Caribbean. A similar force, scheduled for basing in San Diego, for deployment in the Pacific, was hampered by postwar troop shortages and would not be effective for some years, even in the face of the suspected installation of Japanese bases in the Marshall, Caroline, and Palau island groups.

Also in 1921, Pete Ellis, now a major, modified his original treatise on amphibious assault, and it was adopted as Operations Plan 712: Advanced Base Operations in Micronesia. In a speech at the Naval War College in 1923, Ellis elaborated on his treatise in a reference to War Plan Orange: "On both flanks of a fleet crossing the Pacific are numerous islands suitable for submarine and air bases. All should be mopped up as progress is made." Ellis's genius is that he linked the role of the Marine Expeditionary Force to the U.S. battle fleet's progress across the Pacific. As technological progress was made, submarines and land-based aircraft increasingly became strategic weapons that would fill out the interstices not covered by a surface fleet. In fact, the progress of the actual Pacific War became inextricably linked to the ranges of land-based aircraft, and U.S. submarines played a vital role in holding advance lines of defense and undertaking maritime offensive operations.

Withal, the intellectual progress was not matched by physical progress. Cutbacks in military budgets and the ongoing "banana wars" in the Caribbean prevented the Marine Corps from doing much in the way of testing, evaluating, or practicing the emerging art of amphibious warfare. A reinforced regiment took part in Atlantic Fleet maneuvers in the winter of 1922, including a landing at Guantánamo Bay that incorporated a base-defense problem. In 1923, marines conducted landings in Panama and Cape Cod.

The 1922 and 1923 exercises were instructive in that they demonstrated shortfalls in types and numbers of landing craft, naval bombardment techniques, command and control, logistics handling, and stowage of equipment aboard ship. Each of these areas would prove to be vital to success in the Pacific, but there was little opportunity to improve. The last amphibious exercise of the era was held in Hawaii in 1925, when an amphibious command unit oversaw the landing of a simulated force of forty-two thousand marines. The commanders fared well, but all the other shortfalls that had showed up in 1922 and 1923 persisted.

The Interwar Slump

After 1925, the Marine Corps was unable to any launch meaningful exercises. Its strength was cut and its mission load was increased to include a regiment in the Far East, commitment to constabulary work in Nicaragua, and even to guarding the U.S. mails for a time. So few marines could be based at Quantico and San Diego that both bases were for a time in danger of closure.

For all that it was hobbled by budget and manpower cuts in practical experimentation and the acquisition of equipment, the Marine Corps' leadership was overjoyed in 1927 when the Joint Army and Navy Board officially directed the marines to undertake "land operations in support of the fleet for the initial seizure and defense of advanced bases and for such limited auxiliary operations as are essential to the prosecution of the naval campaign." This directive codified nearly three decades of intellectual and physical expenditure in the development of amphibious warfare since the 1898 landings at Guantánamo Bay and provided the Marine Corps with a strategically vital role in the projection of U.S. power and influence to the far reaches of the world.

✳

Resurgence

Marines were withdrawn from Nicaragua in 1933, and plans were afoot to withdraw from Haiti as well. This made sufficient troops available to man the stunted expeditionary forces, undertake exercises required to test theories and equipment, and hammer out doctrine.

In August 1933, Brig. Gen. John Russell, the assistant commandant of the Marine Corps, assembled a staff at Quantico to resume organizational planning for a marine force to be attached to the U.S. Fleet under the 1927 Joint Board directive. Russell proposed that the Expeditionary Force be renamed Fleet Marine Force or Fleet Base Defense Force. The former name was selected, and all the necessary proposals were approved so that the new Fleet Marine Force (FMF) could be stood up as an integral part of the United States Fleet under the operational control of the fleet commander. The decision, codified on December 8, 1933, gave new life and focus to the 158-year-old Marine Corps.

The commandant of the Marine Corps was given responsibility for manning, maintaining, and training the FMF, and for commanding it while it was based on land. Once embarked, however, senior FMF officers and the FMF itself would come under the command of the fleet commander—a naval officer—and serve at his operational direction. The arrangement made sense in that the Marine Corps was traditionally an integral part of the navy and thus subordinate within the navy command structure.

Despite the creation of a staff and infrastructure, the FMF could not be adequately manned at the outset. In August 1934, a year after General Russell's recommendation, no combat units were available to serve in the FMF.

Troops or no troops, planning and development continued. It was recognized, first of all, that a handful of papers and exercises did not in themselves constitute a doctrine for amphibious warfare. Thus, in November 1933, all classes at the Marine Corps Schools were terminated and all faculty and students were put to work to develop an amphibious warfare manual covering training and operations. This was issued in January 1934 as *Tentative Manual for Landing Operations*. It was renamed *Manual for Naval Overseas Operations* in August 1934, and *Tentative Landing Operations Manual* by the end of the year. As such, it was approved by the chief of naval operations and handed back to the Marine Corps for dissemination, evaluation, and testing. The modified but essentially intact manual was recompiled and reissued in 1938 as *Fleet Training Publication 167*. It was considered so authoritative that the U.S. Army accepted it in toto in 1941 under the title *Field Manual 31-5*.

Training and exercises were resumed in 1935 and conducted annually through 1941 in the Caribbean or at San Clemente, California. Each new exercise found kinks to be ironed out, but solutions to most of the problems waited on the development and acquisition of equipment, everything from troopships to landing craft to ruggedized field radios. The total dependence of the Fleet Marine Force on the navy to get it ashore in a modicum of order under a suitable umbrella of air and naval gunfire was driven home time and again, and it became essential that the junior service push the senior service toward better cooperation and integration.

Even as the final series of prewar exercises was underway, the Marine Corps and navy were made to face up to various critical shortcomings in mid-1940 when they were called on to prepare an expeditionary force to perhaps seize Martinique from its Vichy French masters. Formal amphibious exercises of the period usually involved some sort of fakery in which, perhaps, half-formed units stood in for full-size units, or equipment shortfalls were made up by substitution of, for example, a few land-based aircraft made to represent a full-fledged carrier air group that existed only on paper. The crisis over Martinique required actual ground units at whatever strength they really wielded, and actual ships, aircraft, and landing boats. The actual shortfalls, then, led to a lot of dashing to and fro to fill in and provide lift and cover for the designated units with full complements of troops, weapons, and supplies. It was not a pleasant experience, but it did sharply focus many minds.

As late as October 1941, Adm. Ernest King, commander-in-chief of the Atlantic Fleet, stated that "the Atlantic Amphibious Force is not in condition to be relied upon for the successful conduct of active operations." This was significant in that the bulk of the effort to build an amphibious ready force was taking place along the East Coast in support of the Neutrality Patrol and in preparation for a war with Germany as mandated in Joint War Plan Rainbow No. 5. King recommended the following as a way to "remedy the shortcomings" exposed by his study of the topic: creation of a corps-size amphibious force; provision of adequate equipment for the troops; acquisition of sufficient specialized troop transports and cargo ships to move the amphibious corps to far-off places and sufficient landing craft to carry the troops and their weapons, gear, and supplies ashore under fire; and planning of follow-on exercises to further test doctrine *and* further train the troops and their officers.

Getting There

As the doctrine for getting ashore was developed, the U.S. Navy and Marine Corps went to work to find the best means for transporting troops and equipment to the objective and then getting them ashore. Initially, it was thought that battleships and cruisers would double as transports and naval gunfire vessels, but berthing capacity was limited, gear and weapons were bulky, and too many other problems arose. More than thirty four-stack destroyers were ultimately converted to transport troops, but these could accommodate only an infantry company apiece and very limited supplies. Ultimately, in 1940 and 1941 the navy purchased commercial ships that were converted to transports and cargo vessels, and then went on to design attack transports and attack cargo ships from the keel up.

The design of landing craft of various sizes and types depended on the carrying capacity of the transports. All sorts of experimental craft were developed from the early 1920s onward, and much was learned, but serious design work did not take place until the large transports joined the fleet and carrying capacity was standardized. At minimum, a landing craft had to be portable via troop transport. It had to be large enough to carry a tactical unit—an infantry platoon, for example. It had to have a powerful enough engine to get through surf and had to be stable in the water. It had to be able to run up on a beach but also designed to be retractable from the beach under its own power, and it had to be low enough in the water to allow fully equipped combat troops to exit over the sides. This is a very complex set of demands. To make a very long and complicated story short and uncomplicated, the navy finally accepted a troop-carrying landing craft designed by the Higgins Boat Company of New Orleans. After the final Higgins design was selected but before it was put in production, the firm's president, Andrew Jackson Higgins, was shown a photo of a Japanese troop barge that featured a bow ramp. This idea was too good to pass up, so Higgins rushed through a redesign, built a sample that worked, and would go on to build thousands of ramped landing craft in several sizes. It is no small irony that the signature Higgins landing craft to which many credit victory in the Pacific was inspired at the end by a Japanese innovation. Beyond troop-carrying craft, the navy specified a range of tank lighters and other transportable landing craft.

As all this was taking place, years of development toward an amphibious tank led the Marine Corps down many false paths. But in 1937 the navy became aware of a swamp vehicle built in Clearwater, Florida. The fully tracked, fully amphibious Roebling Alligator was all but perfectly designed to transport supplies from a ship directly to inland supply dumps. Budget constraints kept the services from acting on the innovation until 1939, when the Marine Corps finally freed up enough money to request that Roebling build a military prototype. This was done, the design was accepted as the Landing Vehicle, Tracked, 1 (LVT-1), and a contract was let for two hundred machines. The first production LVT-1s came off the line in July 1941, and the Marine Corps stood up an amphibious tractor battalion in each division. For the time being, the unarmed and unarmored "amtrac" was relegated to a service-support role as an amphibious cargo truck, but it would have a distinguished future as a combat vehicle.

Growth

At the start of the war in Europe in September 1939, the strength of the Marine Corps stood at less than twenty thousand officers and men, of which the Fleet Marine Force—ground and air—counted fewer than five thousand. The FMF ground component consisted of two units grandiloquently designated 1st and 2d Marine brigades, each bolstered by a nascent marine aircraft group, plus one scouting detachment equipped with small floatplanes based in the Virgin Islands. The 1st Marine Brigade and the 1st Marine Aircraft Group were stationed at Quantico, Virginia, and the 2d Marine Brigade and the 2d Marine Aircraft Group were based near San Diego.

Things could only get better. Even in the face of possible war following the fall of France, the Marine Corps received less attention and money than the senior services. Nevertheless, on February 1, 1941, the two brigades were redesignated as divisions modeled on the U.S. Army triangular infantry division, and in July 1941 the two air groups were redesignated as Marine Aircraft wings. The total FMF strength on November 30, 1941, was nearly thirty thousand, of which nearly three thousand were aviators or aviation ground personnel.

Harkening back to the advance-base concept that had led to the formation of the FMF, the Marine Corps stood up four defense battalions in 1940. These were artillery units built for coastal and antiaircraft defense of U.S. possessions and bases. Marines also shouldered their traditional role in the form of detachments aboard a growing number of capital ships—battleships, cruisers, and aircraft carriers—as well as guard and military police units and detachments at a growing number of marine and naval bases and facilities.

The total involvement of the FMF in the Pacific was *not* foreseen before the United States was drawn into the war: hence, the basing of a full division and aircraft wing on the East Coast—ultimately at Camp Lejeune and Cherry Point in North Carolina, respectively. Marine security detachments ended up in strategic U.S. and British possessions in the Caribbean as well as Bermuda and Newfoundland. There was even a plan afoot in 1940 and 1941 to send a brigade of marines to the Azores to keep the islands out of German hands, or perhaps to seize the Vichy French naval base at Martinique. The biggest single prewar job marines tackled in the direction of Europe was the dispatch of the reinforced 1st Marine Provisional Brigade, built around the 6th Marine Regiment (6th Marines) and the new 5th Defense Battalion, to Iceland in July 1941.

On November 30, 1941, the total strength of the Marine Corps stood at just under sixty-six thousand officers and men. Of these, just over twenty-six thousand manned non-FMF billets in the United States, at five major bases, forty-three posts and stations, the Marine Corps headquarters, and four recruiting districts. Nearly thirteen thousand marines manned sixty-eight shipboard detachments, twenty-four overseas posts and stations, and three non-FMF tactical units (the 4th Marines—moving from China to Luzon—801 officers and men; the 1st Separate Marine Battalion in the Philippines, 725; and the 1st Provisional Marine Brigade in Iceland, 3,972). Fleet Marine Force units and detachments in the continental United States stood as follows: 1st Marine Division, 8,918 (less than half the authorized strength); 2d Marine Division (less the 1st Provisional Marine Brigade), 7,540; 1st Marine Aircraft Wing, 1,301; 2d Marine Aircraft Wing (less detachments in the Pacific), 682; 2d Defense Battalion, 865; and miscellaneous units and detachments, 633. Overseas, the Marine Corps fielded 5,621 troops, as follows: five defense battalions in the Pacific, 4,399; elements of the 2d Marine Aircraft Wing in the Pacific, 733; and elements of the 2d Marine Division in Hawaii, 489. These numbers hardly constitute a war footing, but the foundation had certainly been built, the framework was in, and buildup was progressing with all due speed.

The Pacific

Stated in rudimentary terms, it was the strategy of both the United States and Japan to advance their respective battle fleets across the Pacific, meet somewhere near the middle, and conduct a decisive *surface* battle that would, pretty much at one fell swoop, determine the war's outcome. To bolster their plans, both sides sought bases from which the fleet advances could be supported. And, as Pete Ellis had prophesied in 1913, each side laid down plans to deny the other the advantages of these bases, and indeed to seize whatever they could.

In the year or two before the onset of the war, as tensions rose, both future combatants sought new bases and built up older ones. The United States built up the tiny atolls at Wake, Midway, Johnston, and Palmyra, improved their anchorages, and built or improved airfields. It beefed up larger holdings—the Philippines and American Samoa, but not Guam, which would have to be conceded in the short term. Civilian contracting firms bolstered naval and marine forces in the various smaller holdings by undertaking most of the construction work. The bases were small and generally offered crowded, abysmal living conditions. Thus, through 1940 and 1941, military units rotated in and out to maintain the sanity and esprit of the troops.

As Ready as Possible

Things were falling into place for the Marine Corps. A bumpy forty-three-year ride from Guantánamo Bay was leading the junior naval service down a road tailor-made for the Pacific War as it actually unfolded. It is difficult to conceive that so many vital pieces fortuitously came together so late in a game whose rules only a very few visionaries could see at the outset. But there it is—an organization rounded off on the eve of a war that began earlier than expected; last-minute acquisition of the finest assault landing-boat design that has yet to emerge (the basic Higgins design would still be going strong after the millennium); the last-minute acceptance of transport and cargo vessels good enough for a long, far-ranging war in the Pacific; and great strides in doctrine taken in the immediate prewar years.

Part V

COUNTDOWN
TO WAR

Chapter 29

At Short-of-War with Germany

THROUGH NEARLY ALL OF 1941, the American strategic consensus set forth in Joint War Plan Rainbow No. 5 remained a concentration of offensive force against Germany and a stand-off defensive campaign against Japan, followed by a full-thrust offensive against Japan as soon as Germany had been brought to its knees. There was no guarantee that both Axis nations, along with Italy, would engage the United States and Britain at the same time, but the United States resolved, in the event it was initially faced down only by Japan, to hold the bulk of its forces ready to fight Germany when Hitler inevitably declared war, for it was plain to see that the seething Nazi dictator could not long stay his own hand against the United States.

Its strategy now set, the United States could turn all its attention to shaping its economy and armed forces to match the goals so clearly enumerated in Rainbow 5.

On November 1, 1940, in a purely housekeeping move made to better delineate lines of command and authority germane to the time, the relatively small U.S. Atlantic Squadron was renamed Patrol Force, United States Fleet. On December 17, command of Patrol Force, United States Fleet, passed to Rear Adm. Ernest King, a distinguished sixty-two-year-old late-blooming naval aviator known for the clarity of his thought and the abrasive directness of his manner.

Following is an extended chronology of mostly naval and maritime events and incidents that unfolded mostly in Atlantic waters between mid-January 1941 and early December 1941. The glue that binds these at-times wildly disparate events together is the growing animus the U.S. government and swelling numbers of American citizens felt toward Germany as the days and weeks rolled by. Matters became nastier and more deadly as the press of events rolled on.

January 16, 1941: President Roosevelt made an urgent appeal to the Congress for $350 million to build two hundred merchant ships.
January 17: The chief of the naval War Plans Division assured Adm. Harold Stark, chief of naval operations, that the navy was on course to begin convoy escort duty between U.S. ports and Scotland by April 1.

January 20: The 3d Battalion, 3d Infantry Regiment, departed New York to defend St. John's, Newfoundland.

January 30: Germany announced that *any* ship carrying goods to Great Britain would be sunk without warning.

February 1: The navy reorganized its fleets. The Patrol Force, United States Fleet, was redesignated Atlantic Fleet, and Ernest King was named commander in chief with rank of full admiral.

February 13: A company of U.S. Marines arrived at Argentia Bay, Newfoundland, to take possession of what would become the site of the principal American naval operating base and naval air station supporting convoy and antisubmarine operations in the western North Atlantic.

February 19: An act of Congress established the Coast Guard Reserve.

March 1: The navy stood up Support Force, Atlantic Fleet, under command of Rear Adm. Arthur Bristol, a distinguished naval aviator. The new command, headquartered at Newport, Rhode Island, was to oversee destroyer squadrons and a patrol plane wing assigned to protect convoys in the North Atlantic.

March 11: The Lend-Lease Act took effect.

March 30: The Coast Guard seized all of the two German, twenty-eight Italian, and thirty-five Danish merchant vessels tied up in American ports.

March 31: The South Greenland Expedition arrived in Godthaab, Greenland, aboard the Coast Guard cutter *Cayuga* to collect hydrographic data and survey sites thought to be suitable for seaplane bases, radio stations, meteorological stations, aids to navigation, military bases, and especially air bases suitable for support of ferry operations involving American-built airplanes bound for Britain. The expedition was composed of experts from the War, Navy, State, and Treasury departments and aided by a light searchplane based aboard *Cayuga* (and later the cutter *Northland,* which relieved *Cayuga* during the two-month data-gathering phase). The expedition would survey large swathes of Greenland shoreline that had never been surveyed before.

April 7: The navy established Naval Operating Base Bermuda and Naval Air Station Bermuda at Hamilton. Shortly thereafter, the Central Atlantic Neutrality Patrol (carriers *Ranger, Wasp,* and *Yorktown;* two heavy cruisers, and a destroyer squadron) was established at the new base. Operations in the area were generally uneventful.

April 9: Under terms of the Act of Havana, and based on new information regarding a German effort to establish an air base in eastern Greenland, Secretary of State Hull and the Danish minister in Washington signed the Agreement Relating to the Defense of Greenland, by which the United States pledged to defend and supply the Danish possession until such time as Denmark was freed. This agreement gave the United States complete control of military affairs on and around the huge, ice-bound island.

April 9: The battleship *North Carolina* was commissioned at New York.

April 10: As an adjunct to the destroyers-for-bases deal, President Roosevelt made a gift to the Royal Navy of ten fairly new Coast Guard cutters highly suitable for convoy escort work.

April 10: During the night, the new *Benson*-class destroyer *Niblack*, as she finished rescuing survivors from a Dutch freighter torpedoed off Iceland, got a sonar ping off a German submarine and attacked with depth charges. No damage seemed to have been done, and it was considered highly doubtful that the German crew even knew the attacker was a U.S. Navy warship. The U.S. Navy considered this to be its first action of World War II against a German military target, but German records revealed no such contact at the place and time.

April 16: The first food transfer was made to Britain under the terms of the Lend-Lease Act.

April 17: A German commerce raider sank the Egyptian passenger liner *ZamZam* with gunfire in the South Atlantic. An estimated 150 American citizens, foolishly traveling aboard a belligerent ship in a war zone, were killed.

April 18: The United States declared Greenland and Iceland to be in its sphere of interest, a diplomatic nicety that said the United States would defend the Danish possessions as if they were American soil. This declaration effectively placed Greenland off limits to German efforts to build an airfield and establish weather stations, unless the Germans were willing to go to war to obtain the privilege. Indeed, the Atlantic Fleet's Adm. Ernest King defined the Western Hemisphere as extending "from approximately 26 [degrees west longitude], westward to the International Date Line and, in the Atlantic, includes all of Greenland, all of the islands of the Azores, the whole of the Gulf of St. Lawrence, the Bahama Islands, the Caribbean Sea, and the Gulf of Mexico."

April 22: The Regular Navy's authorized strength was statutorily raised to 232,000.

April 24: The Neutrality Patrol area of responsibility was officially extended eastward to 26 degrees west longitude, just to the west of Iceland. Two days later, the southward extremity was extended to 20 degrees south latitude, nearly to Rio de Janeiro.

May 9: Royal Navy escorts captured *U-110* after she was forced to the surface and abandoned by her crew. A boarding party retrieved the boat's Enigma coding machine and current codebooks, which led to almost perfect eavesdropping on German naval communications.

May 15: The battleship *Washington* was commissioned at Philadelphia.

May 21: The U.S.-flag freighter *Robin Moor* was stopped by the German submarine *U-69*, then sunk by gunfire and a torpedo while transiting the South Atlantic on her way to South Africa and Mozambique. The crew, which was allowed to take to its lifeboats before the sinking, was given food and directions by the Germans. The sinking was especially galling because the Germans could not—and did not—excuse it as an unwitting act against a ship of unknown nationality. Indeed, President Roosevelt would angrily describe the act as "piracy."

May 24: The navy was authorized to construct or acquire 550,000 tons of auxiliary shipping.

May 24: The sinking of the British battlecruiser *Hood* by the German battleship *Bismarck* in the Denmark Straits precipitated an epic naval chase that drew in American naval assets covertly on the side of the British. For the duration of the chase, navy PBYs based in far-northern areas mounted search missions meant to box the German battleship in from the west. Bad weather precluded any sighting and forced the patrol planes to land anywhere they were able, fortunately without casualties. (Hitler's unleashing of *Bismarck* and her consort, the heavy cruiser *Prinz Eugen*, in North Atlantic waters was a furious reaction to the Lend-Lease food shipments to Britain, which had begun on April 16.)

May 24: President Roosevelt authorized the occupation of the Azores Islands by a brigade of marines. The marines began to train, but following consultation with Prime Minister Churchill in early June, the president would cancel the mission in favor of sending a marine brigade to Iceland so the British occupation force there could be dispatched to an active battle front. Under mild pressure from the British, the Icelandic authorities would actually invite the Americans to their island.

May 26: American naval observers riding in a pair of Royal Navy patrol bombers were the first to pinpoint *Bismarck* from the air.

May 27: British naval forces sank the *Bismarck*. The British defeated *Bismarck* without overt American assistance, but during the final engagement, the Coast Guard cutter *Modoc*, on a search for survivors of a torpedoed merchant ship, blundered out of an evening mist, right into the middle of the battle. She was fired on, and missed, by *Bismarck*'s antiaircraft guns and nearly run down by a British battleship.

May 27: As prospects for open war with Germany rose, President Roosevelt declared an unlimited national emergency, extended the service of the Neutrality Patrol, and—in keeping with promises made to the British—ordered about 20 percent of the Pacific Fleet to join the Atlantic Fleet. Selected for the transfer were the battleships *Idaho, Mississippi,* and *New Mexico;* the carrier *Yorktown;* and the light cruisers *Brooklyn, Nashville, Philadelphia,* and *Savannah*. The last of these ships would reach the Atlantic Fleet in June. As contingency planning still advanced for the possible operation to seize the Azores, three fleet oilers, three transports, and a number of auxiliary vessels were also transferred from the Pacific.

May 29: The navy extended the range of its Neutrality Patrol operations almost throughout the Atlantic Ocean.

June 1: Four U.S. Coast Guard vessels inaugurated the South Greenland Patrol. The task of the patrol was to stop German incursions, such as the establishment of meteorological stations, in the northern areas. The Coast Guard, which for many years had performed weather-watching and rescue duties in northern sea lanes under the designation of Ice Patrol, had many officers and crewmen knowledgeable of the maritime environment as well as cutters and other vessels specially built and equipped to handle a range of tasks the year around.

June 2: The navy commissioned its first escort carrier, *Long Island,* at Newport News. The new type of carrier, originally designated as an "aircraft escort vessel," was not initially considered for a combat role, merely as a means to move fully assembled carrier-type aircraft from place to place. The early escort carriers were converted merchant ships or tankers, but by October 1941 the navy would begin to commission purpose-built escort carriers and use them as platforms for active air interdiction of U-boat operations.

June 6: Unprecedented in peacetime was passage of an act of Congress requested by President Roosevelt that authorized the Maritime Commission to "requisition" any foreign-flag vessel "lying idle" in an American port. Many ships so seized would be turned over to the navy for conversion to cargo ships and transports.

June 12: The entire United States Naval Reserve was called to active duty.

June 20: In an incident unknown to Americans until after World War II, the German submarine *U-203* crossed tracks with the battleship *Texas* shortly after midnight between Newfoundland and Greenland. The U-boat skipper attempted to maneuver into a firing position, but the old, slow battleship drew beyond torpedo range. When news of the encounter was related to Hitler, he forbade his navy chief from plunging Germany into a war with the United States until the imminent invasion of the Soviet Union had reached a successful conclusion.

June 22: Germany and its allies invaded the Soviet Union.

June 28: Following a sixteen-month covert operation undertaken with the help of a double agent, American intelligence operatives and law enforcement rolled up several German espionage rings in U.S. cities.

June 30: The navy reported having on its rolls 1,899 vessels of all types and 284,427 active-duty personnel. The Coast Guard's end strength had climbed to 19,235, and the Marine Corps' to 54,359.

July 1: The navy established the Caribbean, Hawaiian, North Atlantic, Pacific Northern, Pacific Southern, Panama, Philippine, and Southern Coastal Naval Frontiers. These essentially shore-based organizations were to facilitate the defense of the assigned coastal region, the protection and routing of shipping, support of fleet operations, and support of the army and associated forces within the frontier region.

July 1: The Coast Guard inaugurated the Northeast Greenland Patrol. (The South Greenland Patrol and Northeast Greenland Patrol would be consolidated in October 1941 as the Greenland Patrol.)

July 1: The navy stood up a new patrol plane wing headquarters at Argentia, Newfoundland.

July 7: The president informed the Congress that his representatives had concluded a basing and protective occupation agreement with the government of Iceland. On that very day, a troop convoy reached Reykjavík and sent ashore the 1st Provisional Marine Brigade, composed of an infantry regiment, an artillery battalion, service and support troops, and an independent marine defense battalion. (The first U.S. Army ground and Air Corps tactical units were scheduled to reach Iceland in early August.) Taking most seriously the possibility that the occupation might trigger an immediate war with Germany, the navy organized a convoy escort of two battleships, two light cruisers, and thirteen destroyers.

July 15: The navy formally activated its new, uncompleted naval operating base and naval air station at Argentia, Newfoundland.

July 18: Following months of discussion, Secretary of the Navy Frank Knox ordered the construction of one hundred newly designed 1,500-ton destroyer escorts to be turned over to the Royal Navy at the rate of ten per month. The United States also agreed to build twenty minesweepers and fourteen rescue tugs for the Royal Navy, all to be used with the destroyer escorts on the North Atlantic convoy routes. In return, the Royal Navy agreed to turn over designs for tank landing ships (dubbed LSTs by the Americans) and to help build them.

July 19: Under orders from Adm. Ernest King, the navy's new Task Force 1 was formed for the express purpose of defending Iceland and escorting convoys to and from the United States and the island nation. Nineteen Canadian and three Free French corvettes were assigned to bolster Task Force 1, which immediately began active escort of ships from *all* friendly nations between Iceland and the North American continent, or merely through Icelandic waters. Further, the Royal Navy agreed to take care to prevent German surface warships and commerce raiders from reaching Atlantic waters via the passage between Iceland and the Faroe Islands. As well, Admiral King and his British counterpart agreed to take joint action in the event German combatants were located in waters patrolled by the Atlantic Fleet.

August 1: Naval Operating Base Trinidad was established.

August 1: Task Force 3, which had been stood up in mid-June at Guantánamo Bay, Cuba, and San Juan, Puerto Rico, was ordered to actively patrol the area between Trinidad and the "hump" of Brazil. Admiral King, who felt that an aggressive patrol regime off Brazil might trigger a war with Germany, ordered Task Force 3 to douse its lights at night, maintain itself on a war footing, and take care it not fall victim to sudden attack.

August 6: Two navy patrol plane squadrons were deployed to Reykjavík from Argentia, Newfoundland.

August 9: The Atlantic Conference on joint strategy was inaugurated at Placentia Bay, Newfoundland. The high-level American and British teams were led by the two national leaders, President Franklin Roosevelt and Prime Minister Winston Churchill. The purpose of the conference was to clear up many technical matters concerning combined operations and to make concrete high-level plans that would guide American naval and air forces set to join the convoy escort business in a very short time. Indeed, the conference was devoted mainly to maritime and naval matters and policies.

August 15: The Atlantic Conference ended with publication of the Atlantic Charter. Among other statements, the largely maritime-oriented agreement mentioned a peace in the future that "should enable all men to traverse the high seas and oceans without hindrance." It also foreshadowed a newer, stronger try at a league of world nations when it spoke of "a wider and permanent system of general security."

August 18: President Roosevelt announced that U.S. pilots were directly engaged in ferrying combat aircraft to British forces in the Near East via a route from Brazil to Africa. He did not mention that Brazil had been allowing American naval and air units to use Brazilian ports (Bahia and Recife) and other facilities since June.

August 26: The president invoked the Ship Warrants Act, which empowered him to order the Maritime Commission to establish cargo handling, ship repair, and maintenance priorities for U.S.-flag merchant vessels.

August 28: The Maritime Commission established the Supply, Priorities, and Allocation Board. The upshot of this and the invocation of the Ship Warrants Act was that the U.S. maritime industry had been effectively placed on a war footing under strict government control.

September 1: In a move that took the U.S. Atlantic Fleet from a short-of-war footing to a might-as-well-be-at-war footing—to the brink of actual combat as a partner of one belligerent coalition against the other—the navy announced that it would henceforth bear sole responsibility for escort of certain North Atlantic convoys between a rendezvous point off Argentia, Newfoundland, and the meridian of Iceland. While open to interpretation as an act of war, this direct participation in escort of convoys made up in large part of ships from belligerent nations—"shipping of any nationality"—was rationalized as merely seeing to the safety of ships taking part in delivering supplies to American forces between Argentia and Iceland. As a practical matter, U.S. Navy escorts under Support Force, Atlantic Fleet, assumed responsibility for certain convoys shepherded to a certain point off Newfoundland by Royal Canadian Navy escorts and then turned over the escort duty for all but Iceland-bound ships to Royal Navy escorts joining at a "mid-ocean meeting point" (MOMP). The same plan worked in reverse between Iceland and Argentia.

September 1: All U.S. Navy warships operating in Atlantic waters were placed on a war footing, ready to defend themselves aggressively in the event—or even at the threat—of hostile action.

September 1: Admiral King established a permanent task force as the Denmark Strait Patrol with responsibility for the area between Greenland and Iceland.

The Denmark Strait Patrol, based at Hvalfjordur, Iceland, was initially composed of three battleships, two heavy cruisers, and a destroyer division overseen by a destroyer squadron headquarters.

September 4: While on a mail run to Iceland, the American destroyer *Greer* was contacted by a British plane regarding a U-boat the British airmen were tracking nearby, about 175 miles southwest of Iceland. *Greer's* sonar located *U-652* as the airplane left the area owing to a low fuel state. During the three-and-a-half-hour contact, the U-boat fired two torpedoes that missed the destroyer, and *Greer* laid several patterns of depth charges that failed to touch her target. The first actual shooting affair of World War II between the American and German armed forces resulted in no damage or casualties to either side.

September 7: The American merchant ship *Steel Seafarer* was sunk by Luftwaffe aircraft in the Gulf of Suez. At the time of the sinking, she was on her way to deliver war goods to British forces.

September 9: The navy established the new Naval Coast Frontier Forces.

September 11: President Roosevelt broadcast news that he had formally authorized naval warships and aircraft to shoot on sight any vessel that so much as threatened any U.S.-flag ship or any ship under U.S. escort.

September 12: Following sleuthing work by the Coast Guard-supervised Northeast Greenland Sledge Patrol, the cutter *Northland* took a Norwegian trawler into "protective custody" in MacKenzie Bay, Greenland, as the trawler's German passengers engaged in setting up and servicing weather stations. The next day, *Northland's* crew rolled up a weather station 150 miles to the north. Inasmuch as the United States was not at war with either Germany or Norway, it was necessary for the crew of the cutter to arrest the trawler's crew and the men found at the remote weather station as "illegal immigrants" in order to shut down their activities.

September 17: Five U.S. Navy destroyers undertook the first American escort operation of the period, with Convoy HX-150, a fifty-ship groupment originating at Halifax, Nova Scotia. The American ships took over the escort duty at a point about 150 miles south of Argentia.

September 19: The Support Force, Atlantic Fleet, headquarters was transferred from Newport, Rhode Island, to the uncompleted naval operating base at Argentia, Newfoundland.

September 24: Five U.S. Navy destroyers out of Iceland picked up the first westbound convoy, ON-18, charged to American protection.

September 25: Convoy HX-150, the first eastbound convoy with American escort, was handed over to Royal Navy escorts at a MOMP south of Iceland. No contacts were made during this first American convoy escort, but an American destroyer rescued the entire crew of a merchant ship that caught fire. In this first test, the American escort commander noted under "lessons learned" that four-stack destroyers were too short-legged and slow to make effective escorts.

September 26: The navy was ordered to protect all commercial sea traffic in U.S. waters. Authorizations in behalf of this new policy included reporting, engaging, and destroying German and Italian combatants.

September 27: The SS *Patrick Henry,* America's first Liberty Ship, was launched at Baltimore. The construction of the ship in record time was largely a publicity stunt involving an unusually speeded up schedule, but the point was well made that America was in the race to build more ships more quickly than U-boats might sink them.

October 17: Five American and one British destroyers, along with a Free French corvette, joined forces near Iceland on October 15 in response to distress calls from a slow convoy under attack by U-boats. At 0200 hours, October 17, the new U.S. Navy destroyer *Kearney* was damaged by a torpedo fired by *U-568* as she gave way to a passing corvette in firelight from a burning merchant ship. Though eleven of her crew were killed and many more were injured, *Kearney* was able to reach Iceland under her own power. The entire incident pointed up the urgent requirement that escort vessels be equipped with surface-search radars, especially for night operations.

October 19: The U.S. merchant ship *Lehigh* was sunk off Sierra Leone by a torpedo fired by *U-126.*

October 20: The fleet carrier *Hornet* was commissioned at Norfolk, Virginia.

October 28: While escorting a navy task group that included the carrier *Yorktown* and the battleship *New Mexico,* about seven hundred miles east of St. John's, Newfoundland, the U.S. Navy destroyer *Anderson* made a depth-charge attack on a sonar contact. The result was a "considerable oil slick," but a lack of other evidence failed to produce confirmation of a kill.

October 30: The U.S. Navy fleet oiler *Salinas* was seven hundred miles east of Newfoundland, on her way back to Argentia from convoy-escort duty to Iceland, when she was struck by two torpedoes fired by *U-106.* As three other torpedoes missed her fore and aft, *Salinas's* own stern deck gun might have struck the surfaced U-boat, which submerged and evaded escort destroyers. The oiler's crew sustained no casualties, and *Salinas* was able to reach St. John's Bay, Newfoundland, on November 3 under her own power.

October 31: Five U.S. Navy destroyers were escorting east-bound Convoy HX-156 when a German wolfpack attacked it in the dark nearly six hundred miles west of Iceland. As the attack developed, the four-stack destroyer *Reuben James* interposed herself between the known position of the U-boats and the port side of the convoy. At about 0525 hours, as *Reuben James* turned toward a possible target, a torpedo fired by *U-552* blew off her bows and ignited a magazine. Forty-four of her crew survived and 115 perished. In a separate attack, a U-boat fired torpedoes at the four-stack destroyer *DuPont,* but none struck the American warship.

November 1: The U.S. Coast Guard was transferred from the jurisdiction of the Department of the Treasury to the jurisdiction of the U.S. Navy for the duration of the national emergency.

November 1: As his war against the Soviet Union appeared to be nearing a favorable conclusion, Hitler ordered his U-boat chief to make a point of directly challenging American-escorted convoys. This effort fizzled because the naval staff dispersed the submarines at sea to undertake weather reconnaissance or attack convoys in and near the Mediterranean.

November 6: The German blockade runner *Odenwald* was captured near the Equator in the Atlantic by Task Force 3's light cruiser *Omaha* and the destroyer *Summers*. At the time she was taken, *Odenwald* was masquerading as a U.S.-flag merchant ship. She was carrying a cargo of rubber from Japan to Germany.

November 8: Naval Operating Base Iceland was established.

November 10: In a radical departure from previous escort policy, which involved escort of goods ships only, a U.S. Navy convoy escort sailed in the company U.S. Navy transports and support vessels carrying the twenty-thousand-man British 18th Infantry Division bound from Halifax, Nova Scotia, to Basra, Iraq, by way of Cape Horn. Ships assigned to this effort include the carrier *Ranger*, two heavy cruisers, eight destroyers, a fleet oiler, and six transports. They were still at sea when the United States was drawn into the world war.

November 11: The U.S. Navy was formally authorized to attack any vessel that so much as threatened any U.S.-flag ship.

November 11: Lend-Lease was extended to Free French forces.

November 17: The Congress amended the Neutrality Act of 1939 to allow U.S.-flag merchant ships to be armed and to sail through areas previously excluded as war zones.

November 17: The U.S. Navy transferred the aircraft escort vessel *Archer* to the Royal Navy. *Archer* was the first of thirty-eight escort carriers the United States would turn over to Britain. Antisubmarine warplanes operating from these and numerous U.S. Navy escort carriers would have an immense impact on beating down the German U-boat force.

November 19: In what was probably the first success of its kind by an American warship, the destroyer *Leary*, while escorting Convoy HX-160, pinged a U-boat with her newly installed surface-search radar. The quick adoption and installation of these early radar sets, small enough for installation aboard destroyers, corvettes, and many cutters, opened up the night for American surface combatants (and, not much later, American submarines). Even smaller search radars would follow for service aboard patrol aircraft.

November 21: Lend-Lease was extended to Iceland.

November 23: U.S. forces occupied Surinam, Dutch Guiana, as part of an agreement with the Royal Netherlands government-in-exile to protect strategically vital bauxite mines.

December 2: The merchant ship *Astral* vanished without a trace in the North Atlantic. It was presumed at the time she was sunk by a U-boat, which was confirmed after the war.

December 3: The unarmed merchant ship *Sagadahoc* was sunk by torpedoes fired by *U-124* in the South Atlantic.

Chapter 30

Ready or Not

The Bang for the Buck

IN THE THREE YEARS between the November 14, 1938, Aircraft Meeting and the evening of December 6, 1941, billions of dollars had been lavished on the Army Air Corps for development and construction of a modern air fleet: facilities and training for many thousands of pilots, aircrew, groundcrew, and administrators; new airfields; new equipment of every conceivable type—a whole new, completely reinvented Air Corps when you get right down to it.

Seventy-three of a proposed eighty-four Air Corps air groups were in service on December 6, 1941, though many were fairly recent additions and few were ready for a fight. Of thousands of combat airplanes of all types and ages that had been received or ordered, 913 were posted outside the continental United States, east, west, north, and south. By the standard of fighting air forces of the day, and despite a hand from naval and Marine Corps aviation, this was pathetic for a nation that had had three self-aware years to prepare and had goaded its two prospective world-class enemies so openly and persistently as to have demanded a war, perhaps two wars, by the end of 1941—even though America's most sanguine air plan required at least one additional year to reach fruition.

The same was true of the army, navy, and Marine Corps. None was ready to go to war on its own terms in late 1941. The army was well short of its manpower and equipment goals for late 1941, and the 1941 goal was well short of its minimum wartime needs. The army was grimly prepared to act as a breakwater in every area in which it was deployed, but it had little to no hope of holding the line for very long in the face of a concerted blow at any point (not to mention multiple points) by any suitable expeditionary force composed of seasoned Japanese or German troops. Ditto the Marine Corps, which had a reinforced regiment and a defense battalion in Iceland and a clutch of defense battalions and parts of defense battalions deployed in Hawaii and across a sprinkling of isolated bases surrounding Hawaii. The navy was spread thin, but it could move quite easily to the sound of gunfire. It had six air groups based aboard fully war-ready carriers (of which the *Ranger* was not up to most of the exigencies of the day). A seventh carrier, *Hornet*, was in commission but not nearly ready for war. Moreover, the soonest even one of twelve newly started fleet carriers could join the war fleet was late 1943. Stopgaps were afoot in the form of smaller carriers of limited utility, but even these could not make their presence felt before mid-1942. Navy patrol squadrons equipped with long-range but slow patrol bombers and suckled by a fairly ample force of tenders were nearly as mobile as the carriers, and they fielded airmen who had effectively been at war for more than two years. Indeed, navy patrol squadrons were manned by the most experienced and war-savvy airmen and service contingents the United States had in the field in early December 1941. As well, tens of thousands of American sailors and Coast Guardsmen, and their officers all the way up to flag rank, had been operating on near-war and even full-war footing for more than two years; their ships and tactics were proven; and the command organizations, afloat and ashore, that had been at the forefront of the Neutrality Patrol effort were shipshape and squared away.

Destroyers for Bases

As soon as the destroyers-for-bases deal with the British was even contemplated, American planners began work to determine how many troops, ships, and large defensive weapons would be directed to the defense of new posts from Newfoundland in the north to British Guiana in the south. Beginning on August 20, 1940, the day Prime Minister Churchill first broached the issue in the House of Commons, Admiral Stark ordered the Joint Planning Committee of the Joint Army and Navy Board to prepare a survey of base sites and defensive zones in Newfoundland, Bermuda, British Guiana, Jamaica, St. Lucia, and Trinidad. Only a week later, the planners responded with a scheme to base navy patrol bombers at each of these sites and to build up facilities and provisions to support fleet combat elements at Newfoundland, Bermuda, and Trinidad. The army, in its part of the joint plan, set forth troop commitments that included large air elements and a reinforced infantry division to garrison Bermuda; two reinforced infantry battalions at Newfoundland; and a two-division expeditionary corps, plus transport aircraft, at Trinidad, to be ready to move into any Latin American nation that might fall prey to an Axis-inspired coup. One infantry regiment apiece was contemplated for Antigua, British Guiana, Jamaica, and St. Lucia, and later, an infantry battalion was slated for the Bahamas, which could easily be reinforced from the U.S. mainland. On September 6, 1940, General Marshall approved a proposal for army engineers to build airfields and support facilities. Long before it was implemented to the smallest degree, this comprehensive plan fell before the realities of the slower-than-anticipated effort to equip and train the ground army, and it was severely cut back.

Defense of the Continental United States

By the end of November 1941, all of the armed services had been drawn into the defense of the American eastern flank. There was a strong belief in circles high and low that Germany had been goaded as much as it could stand, and notwithstanding a deepening winter stalemate before Moscow, at least the Luftwaffe and Kriegsmarine were preparing to strike a blow in the Atlantic. The most likely target was Iceland, where the air defense was severely restricted owing to a lack of decent airfields and consistently terrible weather (which would also hamper Luftwaffe flight operations).

Air Defense

The topmost command responsible for aerial defense of the continental United States (the Zone of the Interior in military parlance) was GHQ Air Force. Doctrinally, this level of defense was to oversee strikes against distant enemy bases by means of long-range bombers and the close-in defense of point targets throughout the nation (but chiefly those within reach of enemy air bases or enemy carrier-based aircraft). Bolstering Air Force Combat Command in continental defense was the Air Defense Command, which was activated at Mitchel Field, Long Island, in late 1940. Air Defense Command, however, had no operational role; it was strictly a planning agency that aimed to integrate the hugely disparate air-defense system lines of command and coordination over major cities and industrial zones. Observers were sent to England beginning in 1940 to learn how the British defended their homeland, and they brought many valuable lessons home. Among these were a wider use of radio communications and an integrated and upgraded use of radar coupled with filtering and information centers. To place the home-defense operation in a more serious frame of mind, four regional administrative air districts that had been set up in October 1940 were redesignated air forces (which is to say *fighting* commands) in November 1940. These new air forces, numbered First through Fourth, were deployed thusly: First in the northeast, Second in the northwest, Third in the southeast, and Fourth in the southwest. (See Appendix B.) It should be noted that the air force regions differed somewhat from the ground army's deployment of its First, Second, Third, and Fourth armies. (See Appendix A.) Between late May and mid-October 1941, the continental air-defense structure was further refined by establishment of a variety of air commands (e.g., I Bomber Command) roughly analogous to corps commands in the ground army (which were also designated by roman numerals). Emphasizing the fighting character of the forces it oversaw, GHQ Air Force itself was redesignated Air Force Combat Command (AFCC) in June 1941.

Ground Defense

Technically speaking, the four ground field armies headquartered in the United States were prepared to defend directly their respective regions or come to one another's aid in the event of direct attack. And they would have, had such an attack taken place. Nearly the entire ground army and Marine Corps were based on the continent on December 6, 1941. Even though nearly all of both were not yet prepared to conduct offensive operations, a decent rump of them was in reasonably competent, armed, and equipped shape to defend the nation from within the nation. And certainly, in such an emergency, warehouses filled with goods bound for Lend-Lease partners would be stripped to arm and equip local forces.

Naval Defense

The navy in the continental United States in late 1941 operated via regional coastal commands, the naval frontiers. Mainly, these frontiers were responsible for routing ships within continental waters and providing air-search over these waters. The main focus was on U-boats. The navy maintained a number of fighting commands, such as the Atlantic Fleet and various numbered task forces and task groups, as mobile forces equally adept at conducting offensive and defensive operations. While all the Pacific Fleet battleships were based at Pearl Harbor, all the Atlantic Fleet battleships, though older and slower, were within reach of the East Coast, as were squadrons and divisions of cruisers and destroyers that were home-ported at various continental bases and from which ad hoc task forces could be fashioned on very short notice. The navy's traditional role was mobile defense of the littorals, and all of its many 1941 tasks were, at root, functionally defensive in nature, even as far out as the Philippines, East Asia, or South America.

Through December 6, 1941, at least, few American military leaders believed the continental United States was vulnerable to direct attack by any other nation. Submarines were definitely a threat, even quite close to the surf line, but ground assault, or even air attack, seemed a remote possibility. Nevertheless, it did no harm to train the air, ground, and naval forces based along the ocean littorals as if their areas of responsibility might be attacked. If nothing else, the mere act of training was beneficial, and the American public was reassured by seeing its fighting forces acting in its direct behalf.

The North Atlantic

If there was an area of authentic concern for attack in December 1941, it was the North Atlantic area, where Germany had been goaded to within a millimeter of tolerance and where it had real interests upon which its war with Britain might hinge. While goods that kept Britain in the war originated in safe, far-off Canada and the United States, they had to be lifted across the vulnerable northern ocean to add weight to Britain's stubborn propensity for staying in the war. Germany had a real ability to throttle the ocean trade routes on, under, and over the waves, but it had an increasingly difficult time maintaining the pressure because the United States insisted on adding its weight—significant in late 1941 and potentially more significant as time went by—to the heroic but otherwise (in German minds) doomed resistance. If it had not been for exigencies arising out of being Italy's military partner and the resulting late offensive against the Soviet Union, Hitler could easily have taken on the nascent but essentially ill-prepared United States at any time in the last quarter of 1941, or perhaps as early as August.

One thing the army and Air Corps could and did do to mirror and match German aspirations for the northern region was construct an integrated line of weather and communications stations straight across from Labrador to Baffin Island to Newfoundland to Greenland to southwestern Iceland. Ten stations in all had been emplaced by December 6, and many fill-ins were planned for warmer weather. But even the first handful of weather stations had an impact on the increasingly successful war against Hitler's U-boats.

Eastern Canada

The defense of eastern Canada naturally fell primarily to Canadian forces, but the chief American commands taking an interest in the region were First Army on the ground and First Air Force in the air. The promise of relief of some Canadian units by Americans was a hopeful but at first fairly toothless rhetorical gesture.

American survey teams dispatched to locate and lay out base sites began work in Newfoundland in October 1940, and then a garrison force of not quite a thousand men arrived in January 1941. The first American combat unit deployed in Canada was a 155mm gun battery that was set in to guard the harbor approaches at St. John's, Newfoundland. It was joined by an antiaircraft machine gun unit and engineers to build housing.

More than three thousand Air Corps troops, mostly base support personnel, found themselves at Newfoundland Airport alongside one reconnaissance squadron of six old B-18s that arrived in May. The B-18s were bolstered by eighteen transport planes in June, and replaced in August by another reconnaissance squadron of eight outmoded B-17Bs. The B-18s were used initially to map Labrador and other remote regions and to locate potential base and airfield sites. The Royal Canadian Air Force also based a clutch of B-18s at Newfoundland Airport, and it was hoped that an Air Corps pursuit squadron could be deployed there in November. A November uptick in U-boat sightings led to orders in early December for another B-17B squadron to base at Newfoundland Airport, but the squadron was held up waiting for a supply of depth bombs.

Detachments from army airways communications system squadrons were deployed at the St. John's, Newfoundland, airport, and Harmon Field in western Newfoundland. There was also a profound hope that an Air Corps pursuit squadron could be deployed that winter aboard Naval Air Station Placentia Bay, near the buzzing American naval hub at Argentia. The only navy aircraft assigned to bases in the region were patrol bombers serving under Support Force, Atlantic Fleet, but the naval surface forces, sometimes including an aircraft carrier, made a robust presence in the region as they came and went on convoy escort and patrol missions.

Greenland

Rough, remote Greenland, even its southernmost extremities, was hardly conducive to settlement by hearty Vikings much less the establishment of bases by technically advanced Americans manning fragile instruments. Surveys conducted in 1940 and the spring and summer of 1941 had revealed no suitable airfield sites on the huge island's eastern—weather—shore, but there were promising locations to the west and southwest. Of these, a major base was to be built from scratch at Narsarssuak, Greenland's southern tip, but there was not enough time left in 1941 to begin work before reliably bad weather set in. The only American troops to reach Greenland in 1941 were members of two aviation engineer companies and detachments of meteorological, communications, and airways communications system squadrons.

Iceland

The Germans had the ability to build an advance line of airfields in Iceland, and they might well have done so had the Luftwaffe not been all but completely tied down in the Soviet Union. British troops available to defend Iceland were few: so much so that Britain had implored the United States to defend the island in place of 27,500 British soldiers, sailors, and airmen already there but urgently needed elsewhere. The Americans had responded with the 1st Provisional Marine Brigade in July 1941, and the promise of a large army ground force in April or May 1942, which was thus the soonest British troops could be withdrawn. (The reinforced 5th Infantry Division was readied, but the commitment was ultimately reduced to less than a regiment.) On the other hand, the Air Corps devoted a reasonably healthy force of engineers and airfield service units to establishing a string of primary and secondary airfields on the island, over which German long-range maritime bombers flew with near impunity. The onset of bad weather made futile the lavish construction program until the spring thaw, but some progress was made.

One squadron of thirty P-40 pursuits and three observation planes shipped out for duty at Reykjavík Airport aboard the carrier *Wasp* in late July 1941, but they could hardly do much against a concerted German effort to seize or neutralize the base. The weather turned so bad in October that a robust patrol effort made by navy long-range patrol bombers had to be terminated as the PBYs and PBMs were withdrawn to warmer climes. The same bad weather precluded until spring the approved deployment of a squadron each of eight B-17 heavy bombers and eighteen B-25 medium bombers. The only bright spot here that winter, if it was indeed bright, was that American forces based in Iceland were ordered to fire the first shot if they found German forces within fifty miles of the island. On December 1, 1941, around four thousand Marines and just fewer than six thousand army troops were based in Iceland.

The Caribbean

In all the Caribbean, indeed in all the Western Hemisphere outside of the continental United States, the U.S. military valued no parcel of land more than it valued the Panama Canal Zone. No piece of real estate better defined U.S. maritime hegemony than the narrow, hand-wrought strip of blue that joined

Atlantic and Pacific 4,500 miles north of Nature's own passage. It was in Panama that the U.S. Army, in a June 1940 letter from its Panama Department commanding general to General Marshall, fully subordinated itself to the needs of the U.S. Navy in its Panama Canal mission, which was "to guard the Canal that it may at all times be available to the navy." Nevertheless, for all that the canal was so important to the navy, that service guarded its near approaches from *both* oceans on the cheap with four old destroyers, a gunboat, a handful of small patrol craft, and a force of twenty-four PBY patrol bombers.

By mid-1941 the strategic value of all the Caribbean islands to the defense of the United States was prospective, tied to the defense against U-boat incursions into American waters upon the outbreak of hostilities with Germany. As important, but more difficult to factor in, was the value of Caribbean bases to the distant eastern defense of the Panama Canal Zone. And also important, once again prospectively, was the impact air and naval interdiction might have on guarding the air ferry routes spanning the South Atlantic narrows between the hump of eastern Brazil to the hump of western Africa, routes by which flights originating in North America could by stages reach North Africa, the Middle East, and even south and east Asia. Land forces were needed to hold the Caribbean bases and perhaps quell Axis-led coups in Latin America, air forces were needed to defend the bases and transport combat troops, and naval forces were needed to screen the bases and escort troop ships.

By August 1941 the top soldier in the Caribbean region was the indispensable Maj. Gen. Frank Andrews, who, following his tour as army general staff G-3, had been named in late 1940 to command the Panama Air Force, which was activated in October 1940 and redesignated Caribbean Air Force in August 1941. Thanks to Andrews' singular organizational skills, the far-flung Caribbean air detachments, groups, and commands acted as a well-honed whole, capable of rallying from far afield to make a focused response at a point of contact with an enemy force. In August 1941, Andrews was promoted to lieutenant general and named to head the brand-new Caribbean Defense Command, which from headquarters at Albrook Field, Panama Canal Zone, oversaw all U.S. Army ground and air forces in the region and served as a joint all-services headquarters for the entire region.

The Panama Canal Zone

The moment the full impact of the German invasion of Poland came clear in September 1939, the Panama Department chief shot off a request for more troops to see him through a possible assault on the canal by one or more of America's enemies. Within a few months, the army and Air Corps garrison rose from nearly 13,500 to more than 37,500, including three Regular Army infantry regiments. Many of these troops were later withdrawn as an understanding of German war aims became sharper. But even as the ground force subsided, renewed appreciation of how easily a single carrier-based bombing attack might cripple the canal locks caused the department commander to ask for more warplanes—long-range bombers to locate and delay carriers, and pursuits to mount an overhead barrier against carrier bombers. New anti-aircraft units were dispatched, and a mechanized reconnaissance unit was added to the ground force in June 1940, but the request for heavy bombers was rejected.

The Panama Canal Zone was the focal point of the entire Caribbean air defense, because of what it was and where it was. Air Corps units operated from three major airfields: Albrook on the Pacific side, France on the Atlantic side, and Howard, a new base three miles from Albrook. Two auxiliary fields were also in use, five others were under construction, and several emergency fields could be used without further improvement. By December 1, 1941, 396 airplanes of all types had been allotted to the Canal Zone for permanent basing, but only 183 were actually on hand. Of these, three pursuit groups counted only seventy-one modern P-40s among them, plus a number of embarrassingly outdated Boeing P-26s. A light bombardment group was equipped with just twelve A-20s and a large contingent of obsolete A-17s. Of only eight B-17s actually assigned to two heavy bombardment groups headquartered at Albrook Field, four were based on Trinidad. Fortunately, all the Caribbean Air Force air units had been trained to rally in whole or in part to any base or bases in the region. Training also extended to support of expeditionary forces that might be sent to Latin American hotspots.

Puerto Rico

Despite its position athwart sea routes from the South Atlantic to southeastern U.S. ports *and* its status as a full territory of the United States whose people were U.S. citizens, the defense and exploitation of Puerto Rico received remark-ably little attention in the run-up to war. The only ground combat unit based in Puerto Rico during the interwar years was the 65th Infantry Regiment, a Regular Army unit recruited and trained in the territory. The 295th and 296th Infantry regiments of the Puerto Rico National Guard were called to federal service on October 15, 1940. Both were attached to regional commands but retained on the island.

Aerial defenses took surprisingly long to organize. The first air unit to reach the territory was a pursuit squadron that arrived from the mainland in December 1939. A full year later, the Air Corps approved the establishment of a composite wing deploying a pursuit group, a heavy bombardment group, a medium bombardment group, two base groups, two reconnaissance squadrons, and an observation squadron. A cadre of airmen reached Borinquen Field in early 1941, and all the units assigned to the composite wing were nominally activated by splintering the wing headquarters. In April 1941, by which time a small effort had been made to install antiaircraft defenses, the island's entire air complement stood at three obsolete A-17s and one B-18.

The navy took the most interest in Puerto Rico. The Caribbean Sea Frontier was headquartered at San Juan. Patrol bomber squadrons rotated through various locations around the island. Warships came and went, and a huge naval base was contemplated for the eastern part of the island at Roosevelt Roads.

The Virgin Islands

The largest military unit in this U.S. territory was a Marine Corps air base service detachment equipped with seven biplane utility floatplanes and a single light transport plane.

Bermuda

To American planners, development of a large base at Bermuda was considered essential to anchoring defenses off the U.S. East Coast. Thus, on August 28, 1940, General Marshall and Admiral Stark approved a plan to build up a force there of six navy patrol squadrons, a carrier battle group (one carrier and up to a dozen surface escorts), an Air Corps composite wing, and a reinforced infantry division.

The navy established Naval Operating Base Bermuda and Naval Air Station Bermuda at Hamilton on April 7, but no aircraft except patrol seaplanes could operate from the unfinished air station. Shortly thereafter, the Central Atlantic Neutrality Patrol, which was established to control the carriers *Ranger, Wasp,* and *Yorktown;* two heavy cruisers; and a destroyer squadron, was established at the naval operating base.

The army was very slow dispatching even a virtual handful of the thirty thousand combat and service troops it had committed to defending Bermuda, and very slow at building facilities for them. Only 1,280 Air Corps personnel and no ground troops at all were on hand there by December 1, 1941.

Trinidad

In an August 1940 joint plan, Trinidad was to have been the southern anchor of the Caribbean defense shield, a base large enough to accommodate a two-division reaction force supported by at least one group of Air Corps transports, and a large force of tactical aircraft, all on hand to either warn Axis forces away from Latin America or ready to mount the liberation of any Latin nation that fell to an Axis-inspired coup. In September 1940, the reaction force was cut from two divisions to one, and in October only 16,202 troops were still on the table. When the first army troops reached Trinidad in April 1941, there were only 1,303 of them, and on December 1, 1941, the total army garrison was 2,866. Of these, 400 comprised an Air Corps unit that managed air base operations at Picaro Airport, home to six B-18s.

Jamaica

Jamaica was also to have been a major defense locus; the initial army and navy budgets to develop bases and facilities there totaled $48.5 million. As events unfolded, Admiral Stark decided that Jamaica was located too far to the west and too near Puerto Rico to serve the navy's emerging needs, so he pretty much pulled out of the plan. With no naval base to defend, the army cut its troop allotment and building program. By January 1941 only 1,390 troops were even contemplated, and only 701 of them had been dispatched by December.

Other Caribbean Bases

The Joint Planning Commission report of August 28, 1940, allotted one infantry battalion and a composite air group to each of four remaining British possessions, Antigua, the Bahamas, British Guiana, and St. Lucia, but early enthusiasm quickly waned. There were few troops and airplanes to spare and too little return seen for committing so many.

Antigua was of some importance to American planners as the destroyers-for-bases deal unfolded in 1940, but only because of its proximity to Vichy French Guadeloupe. The Bahamas were so close to Florida as to make any bases there redundant to defensive measures and patrol efforts already underway in Florida, and they could be swiftly occupied in the event of a German move to seize them. British Guiana was rich in bauxite ore for aluminum and could serve as a waystation on the air route from the United States to Brazil (and on to Africa and beyond) as well as a spot from which Free French forces in French Guiana could be bolstered. St. Lucia was of interest because it was close to Vichy-controlled Martinique.

It took until May 1941 for President Roosevelt to overcome his own qualms regarding any commitment to these prospective bases, and he authorized only a reinforced infantry company for each. In time, engineering surveys in the Bahamas turned up no air base sites that could be quickly and cheaply exploited, and no such work was authorized. On November 30, 1941, there were 282 American troops on Antigua, none in the Bahamas, 288 in British Guiana, and 275 on St. Lucia.

The Americans expended time and effort in 1941 in planning to put troops ashore on the Dutch islands of Aruba and Curaçao, but the proposal hinged on a request by the United States that Royal Netherlands troops be committed to a possible expeditionary force to liberate Venezuela if it came under Axis control. This the Dutch politely declined to do, and the occupation plan fell through. Nevertheless, the Dutch were ever-mindful that all the petroleum produced in the Netherlands Antilles rode out on vulnerable tankers. Thus, the Royal Netherlands government-in-exile agreed to extend existing island runways to accommodate large American bombers in the event its island airfields were needed as stopover points or even just to extend the range of antisubmarine searches. The Caribbean Air Force sent technical detachments of thirty-seven men to each of the islands. (On February 16, 1942, a surfaced U-boat boldly shelled Aruba's refinery and several other U-boats sank five tankers with torpedoes.)

Ready or Not?

So, after three years of hard work readying itself for a war with Germany, was the U.S. military ready for that war?

One answer is "Yes." As History would very shortly show, there was no immediate threat to American security or interests from the European Axis that the U.S. military had not taken into account or could not overcome in relatively short order. There was a shortcoming—a simple lack of political will to turn out the lights of American coastal cities—that Hitler's U-boats would exploit within weeks to light up American coastal waters with burning ships and extract an unnerving tax in lives and goods. But there was no means, really, by which a German Wehrmacht fighting for its life in Russia's winter wastes could immediately disturb the orderly process of the American military build-out for execution of Rainbow 5, at least as that plan stood against Axis interests in Europe and even North Africa.

But the answer is also "No." After three years of hard work readying itself for a war with Germany, the U.S. military was not ready for the offensive war it had long (and illegally) contemplated.

The vast bulk of the air groups and combat divisions the U.S. Army had hoped to have, ready to go, by late 1941 would not be combat-ready for a full year. The first American bombing raid over occupied Europe would come on July 4, 1942. It would involve eighteen American airmen flying in six Lend-Lease A-20s borrowed back for the symbolic occasion from the Royal Air Force. And the first American fighter squadrons to get into action over Europe, in August 1942, would fly, of all things, British-built Spitfire fighters. The North Africa invasion of November 1942 would be spectacular in its interconti-nental breadth and boldness, but the land and air campaign that followed was muddled and amateurish. It would be mid-1943 before German troops faced a confident, professionalized U.S. Army on the ground, in Sicily. Part of the extra time it took to get it right was bound up in delays arising from the exigencies of Lend-Lease, but the other part of it was good old Yankee hubris. The fact that American industry did so much to save the British war effort gave Americans no grounds for ignoring, as they did, the lessons the British had learned at the cost of so much of their blood and treasure. But this gets light years ahead of this story.

So, yes, the U.S. military was in a good position to cope with the defensive dangers it encountered between late 1942 and mid-1943 as they related to a war with Germany. But, no, the U.S. military was yet and by far in no position to carry the war offensively to the German military save in one crucial arena. In due course, following a traumatic opening, the U-boat war was going to be won decisively by a steady, confident U.S. Navy that had been itching for two years to take the gloves off.

Chapter 31

Japan's Road to War

Ample Warning

THROUGHOUT THE LATE NINETEENTH CENTURY, Japan broke out of her feudal past with a ruthlessness and singlemindedness that would have scared Western nations had they been paying attention. Its modern navy was modeled on Britain's Royal Navy, its army was patterned on the Prussian army, and it imported its new modern industrial base from the best examples the world around. By 1894, Japan was ready to join in the game of empire that had so enriched Europe over the previous four hundred years.

Japan's first target for acquisition was Korea. In July 1894, it attacked the Chinese forces that outposted the peninsula and then declared war four days later. The Chinese were routed, and a peace treaty was signed in March 1895 that gave Japan access to Korea and Formosa. Shortly, France, Germany, and Russia informed Japan that they would oppose the outright absorption of Korea into a Japanese empire. Japanese leaders took this so-called Triple Intervention to mean that even the most modern Asian state was not to be granted an equal status to European nations. This only fueled Japan's newfound lust for empire.

Japan needed resources to realize its industrial ambitions. It possessed precious few of its own, but nearby Korea and adjacent Manchuria had them in abundance. This outlook cast Russia as a leading contender. As proof against the alliance that had denied it a complete domination of Korea, Japan signed a naval treaty with the United Kingdom in 1902. Under the treaty's terms, the Royal Navy was obligated to support Japan against Russia if Russia acquired just one active ally in a war against Japan. While this treaty raised Japanese prestige in the industrial world, Russia refused to yield in its hostility over the extent of Japanese exploitation of Korea.

Japan went to war with Russia on February 9, 1904. It opened with an attack on the Russian Far Eastern Fleet in Port Arthur and then declared war a day later. The Russian fleet was soundly defeated, and a Japanese field army in Korea invaded Manchuria. The Russians dispatched a field army of their own from Europe—which was six thousand miles away—and a land war ensued. Japan won the land war in a year, and the Russian field army retreated overland. At sea, the Russian Baltic Sea Fleet completed an eighteen-thousand-mile sortie that saw it utterly routed at Tsushima on May 27, 1905. This singular victory, more than anything, raised Japanese prestige among the leading European nations. The United States stood in as an interlocutor. By the terms of a peace treaty signed in September 1905 in Portsmouth, New Hampshire, Japan was allowed to fully incorporate Korea into its empire; it received a lease to exploit Manchuria's Liaotung Peninsula, adjacent to northwestern Korea; and it was given the southern half of Sakhalin Island, to its immediate north.

An outgrowth of the American role in the peace with Russia was a strengthened mistrust by the Japanese of the United States. The trouble actually started in 1898, with the American acquisition of Hawaii, Guam, and the Philippines. To the Japanese, these additions to an American empire appeared to be direct competition, a limiting factor in the event the new Japanese empire desired to expand eastward at some future date. Moreover, in 1900, the United States issued its "Open Door" proclamation, which was aimed in part to forestall direct Japanese aggression in China. There were also racist rumblings against Japanese—the "yellow peril"—in the San Francisco area, where many of the relatively few Japanese immigrants to the United States settled. Indeed, if California-based jingoists had had their way, the United States would have gone to war against Japan by 1908, the year a so-called gentleman's agreement caused Japan to restrict the emigration of blue-collar workers to the United States. President Theodore Roosevelt formed the Great White Fleet and sent it off on a world cruise—with a stop in Tokyo—as a sop to anti-Japanese elements in California. The whole purpose of the exercise was to intimidate Japan, but it only deepened its growing animosity toward the United States. By 1913, anti-Japanese sentiment had risen to the point in California and Hawaii at which Japanese were singled out among all immigrants to be denied purchase or even lease of land in many neighborhoods.

A war might have broken out between Japan and the United States by 1914 or 1915, but events in Europe forestalled it by giving Japan an opportunity to match the American Pacific empire at one swoop. Honoring its mutual defense treaty with the United Kingdom, Japan declared war on Germany on August 23, 1914. Immediately, a Japanese army besieged the German naval base at Tsingtao, China, which surrendered in November 1914. Shortly, Japanese troops mounted their nation's first amphibious assaults, against lightly defended German colonies in the Mariana, Marshall, Palau, and Caroline island groups. In 1915, Japan exploited the weakness of a civilian Chinese regime that had overthrown the imperial system in 1911. It issued a long list of demands for commercial concessions, and the Chinese, who lacked any European backers because of the Great War, acceded to most of them.

The 1919 peace conference in Versailles granted Japan a mandate over all the former German Pacific possessions north of the equator, and most of the concessions in China remained intact. What Japan was unable to get at Versailles was an explicit expression of racial equality. This it blamed directly on President Woodrow Wilson.

As the Russian Revolution moved eastward across the huge land mass of Siberia, the Imperial Japanese Army intervened in its own behalf. To counter Japan's obvious imperial interests, the United States landed its own troops in Siberia as a somewhat more than tacit statement that it would not countenance a direct seizure of land or wealth north of the prewar Japanese spheres.

When it was revealed in 1919 that a Japanese expeditionary force sent to maintain order in Siberia might not leave when a similar American force was prepared to pull out, Washington noted its displeasure by pointing out that the United States had not signed the Versailles Treaty and was thus under no obligation to recognize the mandates granted under the treaty with respect to former German colonies in the Pacific. A transfer of American fleet components to the Pacific added teeth to the U.S. position. The event rankled the Japanese.

Japan's feelings were further hurt when, at the Washington Naval Conference of 1921–1922, it was placed on a footing by which its allotted tonnage in warships was only 60 percent that of the United Stated and the United Kingdom. This rankled beyond the explicit advantage offered the United States; it gave explicit voice to the deeply rooted belief that the United States saw Japan and the Japanese as inferior. Nevertheless, as a practical matter, the 1922 round of treaties boosted the Imperial Navy to the number-three position in the ranking of the world's navies.

The United States mended a lot of fences in Japan with an outpouring of aid and charity in the wake of the 1923 Tokyo earthquake. But in 1924, trumping all of the previous insensitivity and stupidity in its apparent program to rile Japan on racial grounds, the United States imposed the new Immigration Act to override the merely insulting gentleman's agreement of 1908 by specifically forbidding *any* Japanese immigration.

War in East Asia

The Showa Emperor, Hirohito, ascended to the throne upon the death of his mentally ill and alcoholic father, Taisho, on Christmas Day 1926. Taisho, perhaps as a reflection of his mental instability, was all for military adventures in East Asia and an eventual showdown with the United States, but Hirohito took an opposite view. He favored a more peaceable approach to Japanese industrial and trade expansion. This placed him at odds with the generals who had exploited and dominated the mad Taisho. But Hirohito was the emperor, a living god, so they could not act against his person, nor even in a way that appeared to contradict his absolute authority. Fortunately for the generals and their ambitions for conquest, the ascetic Hirohito, a talented and dedicated marine biologist, was not given to hands-on management of Japan's affairs. He reigned while others ruled in his place.

By the late 1920s, talk concerning expansion of the Japanese imperial base on the mainland was done under the rubric of "bringing order" to lawless China and its outlying provinces. After the Chinese revolution of 1911, the nation had Balkanized into a network of fiefdoms that became the private plantations of warlords. There was no powerful central authority that ruled China in more than name. Quite aside from the opportunities of empire, there were prominent Japanese who felt that Japan's true destiny was to bring order to lawless, Balkanized China.

With the emperor's attention drawn far from the affairs of state, Imperial Army officers began to plan in earnest a campaign that was to eventually bring all of China under Japanese domination—either for purposes of bringing order or outright expropriation of China's assets, its work force, and its untapped natural resources. The first step was directed against Manchuria, for two reasons: it was only just across the narrow Sea of Japan, and its wild rivers could be harnessed to create immense reserves of hydroelectric power that would in turn foster an aggressive industrial reformation. Also, Japanese troops already had a foothold in Manchuria's southern province, including around the Manchurian capital, Mukden.

The Imperial Army's Manchuria plan opened on the night of September 18, 1931, with the detonation of an explosive device beneath a railroad track near Mukden. The device had been planted by Japanese under orders from the commander of the Japanese Kwangtung Army (based in Korea and southern Manchuria), who acted in defiance of orders from Tokyo to stand down an invasion plan. Within hours, ostensibly to "bring order," Japanese troops stormed the city of Mukden, seized the Chinese army arsenal, and moved out to conquer all of Manchuria. When a League of Nations investigation pinpointed Japanese culpability in the railroad bombing, Japan withdrew from the league, which placed it outside the strictures of international law, such as it was in 1931.

The success of the adventure—which started off with a mutiny against the national authority!—added gloss to the Imperial Army's resume and brought forth a rise in the already overt influence the army had over politics. Moreover, a rather bizarre tradition had sprung up in Japan with respect to the assassination of uncooperative civilian politicians whose policies clashed with the army's fine sense of what was and what was not in the interests of the emperor's greater glory. When army officers felt they needed to guide events in behalf of the emperor, they laid on a culturally acceptable coup d'etat by either tacitly wielding their prerogative of assassination as a tool of intimidation, or by actually cutting off heads. In the wake of the Mukden incident, a military plot against the cabinet was indeed planned, but it was uncovered. No one died, but the government was reliably intimidated, and the conspirators received slaps on their wrists. Everyone paid lip service to an admonition that the Kwangtung Army stand down, but it did no such thing.

Go North, Go South

The Japanese venture into Manchuria was a mixed blessing. The wild areas could not be tamed by force of arms, and it cost as much to defend industrialized areas as the exploitation earned. The military factions that held the most sway in Japanese government had for more than a decade been divided over the issue of where to turn next. One faction embraced the "go north" strategy, meaning both Manchuria and the Soviet Far East; the other advocated a "go south" strategy, meaning resource-rich Southeast Asia, the Netherlands East Indies, and perhaps the Philippines. Either way meant war, either with the Soviet Union, or with the Dutch and British, and perhaps the United States.

At first, it was just a debate, but by the end of 1935, the go-north clique felt it had lost the argument. Thus, on February 26, 1936, go-south army officers of middle rank seized a portion of the capital and assassinated several imperial ministers. For once, Hirohito took firm personal control. He ordered his imperial guard to liberate the capital and restore order, which was accomplished fully by February 29. The emperor ordered the mutineers to be court-martialed, but senior army commanders ignored the order and merely reported it had been carried out. This false report, when it was revealed via news outlets, caused foreign ambassadors in Tokyo to advise their governments that when Japan went to war, it would move south rather than against the Soviet Union.

Also in 1936, the Japanese announced their withdrawal from the odious and unequal terms of the Washington naval treaties of 1922 and London naval treaty of 1930. The Imperial Navy had long been finessing the self-policing aspects of the treaty, lying outright about the tonnages and numbers of their warships, but the withdrawal from the treaty made outside inspection impossible even if the other signatories had asked.

To counter the alarming influence of the military over the affairs of state, Hirohito in early 1937 named Prince Fumimaro Konoye as his premier. Konoye's brief was to bring the military in line with the emperor's views. Prince Konoye tried for a time to impose the emperor's will, but he lacked will of his own, and the military slipped further from imperial control than ever it had been. (It must be said that Konoye was one of the emperor's few close friends, someone whom Hirohito apparently could not find fault with, much less rebuke, and even less dismiss.)

Konoye had been premier for only six months when the army manufactured or exploited an incident at the Marco Polo Bridge, in a demilitarized zone near Peking. A Japanese soldier went missing on the night of July 7, 1937, and the Japanese demanded Chinese help in finding him. The broad implication that the missing man had been kidnapped by Chinese troops led to a number of brawls and shootings that in turn led to pressure on Prince Konoye to sanction the outright invasion of several Chinese provinces. Konoye, who had turned passive in the face of army demands, acceded.

The Japanese seized all of their objectives well within a six-week time frame offered to Konoye, but throughout the period Hirohito refused to declare war or otherwise personally sanction the conquest. World opinion easily saw through the stated cause of what Japanese diplomats, who had to obey the emperor, painfully referred to as the China Incident.

In November 1937, the utterly compliant Konoye proclaimed the Greater East Asia Co-Prosperity Sphere, a name that seemed to stand in opposition to the domination of so much of China's trade by European nations and the United States. Suddenly, Japan recast itself as the guarantor of Asian rule in Asia. Chiang Kai-shek, the Chinese supreme warlord whose ideas ran more along the lines of Chinese rule in China, immediately declared war on Japan and ordered a nationwide mobilization.

In Chiang's declaration of war, Japan's militarists found a license to run amok in China. It got crazier and crazier from there.

The Republic Strikes Back

Japanese excesses in the China War are too numerous to describe. The first to strike home to Americans came on December 12, 1937, when Japanese naval aircraft guided by an army colonel out to foment immediate war with the United States attacked the clearly marked and neutral U.S. Navy gunboat *Panay* in the Yangtze River near Nanking. Three oil barges under escort by the *Panay* were attacked at the same time. The gunboat and two of the barges were sunk, and three lives were lost. President Franklin Roosevelt was so outraged that he considered withholding oil from Japan, and he gave a speech in which he suggested that Japan be quarantined. But the United States took no formal action, on advice of its ambassador to Japan, Joseph Grew, who warned that the empire might simply move to capture oil fields in the Netherlands East Indies if oil was embargoed. Roosevelt thus followed up his speech with letters in which he asked leading American industrialists to voluntarily curtail trade with Japan. Far from working against the Roosevelt Administration's marathon program to reverse the Great Depression, the letter simply pointed out that business might be more profitably and efficiently carried out with European trading partners. The industrialists responded positively to the call, and the Japanese were duly alarmed when Roosevelt was revealed as the promoter of falling bilateral trade.

No real political consequence arose from the trade curtailment, and the Imperial Army certainly didn't hold back in its treatment of Chinese civilians, of whom hundreds of thousands were murdered. Indeed, with full realization that its oil had to be purchased from American and Dutch sources that might be shut off at any time, the Japanese went into overdrive to purchase and store huge reserves while they still could. Also, the Konoye government was replaced in January 1939 by a crew of extreme militants that considered peace no option.

In May 1939, culminating an amphibious campaign to secure most of the China's South China Sea coast, the Japanese Army invaded Hainan Island and thus took firm military control of Chinese maritime trade routes. The move also placed Japanese forces on the flank of northern French Indochina. As it turned out, the capture of Hainan was the last major Japanese gain of the period. The war in China had reached an impasse; China was too big to digest and the Imperial Army was too strong to push back. The chief consequence of this stalemate was that the Imperial Navy, by far the junior military arm, found an opening to give voice to the go-south strategy long sought by it and a considerable wing of the Imperial Army. Real planning thus began in secret.

At this stage, President Roosevelt felt it was necessaruy to fire a shot across Japan's bow, just so it might simply begin to pay some attention to the many American protests regarding its behavior in China. Thus, out of the blue on July 26, 1939, the United States gave the required six months' notice that it intended to abrogate its 1911 Treaty of Commerce and Navigation with Japan. After January 26, 1940, Japanese trade with the United States would be subject to terms, some perhaps arbitrary, set forth at the discretion of the president or the Congress. As it turned out, American public opinion was for once behind the use of such power.

Relations between Japan and the United States ebbed and flowed over the next year; following the formation of a somewhat more moderate Japanese cabinet on January 16, 1940, there was briefly real hope for reconciliation, but the general drift remained downward. The key driver was Japanese treatment of Chinese civilians and an ongoing string of outrages against American citizens living in conquered areas. The successive Japanese governments spoke of reconciliation, but none gave in on absolute Japanese rule and control of all trade in occupied China.

The United States countered the mounting problems with increased and increasingly obvious fleet movements in Hawaiian waters. By the time Adm. James Richardson took over as commander in chief of the United States Fleet on January 6, 1940, a large detachment of his cruisers and destroyers, home ported on the West Coast, appeared to be more or less permanently tethered to anchorages in Hawaii. On March 31, the Roosevelt Administration called attention to its naval presence in the Pacific via a public announcement that annual fleet maneuvers would take place in Hawaiian waters. On April 4, a concerned and outraged Japanese Navy Ministry spokesman told *his* nation's newspapers that if the maneuvers lapped across the International Date Line, Japan would regard the action as tantamount to "brandishing a big sword," which is to say a provocation toward war.

On April 15, the Japanese foreign minister reinvoked the Greater East Asia Co-Prosperity Sphere, a rather broad hint that Japan had set its eye on nations and colonial possessions beyond China's borders. This seemed a logical enough transition, given the obvious military stalemate in China. Chillingly, the announcement referred to "relations of economic interdependence and of co-existence and co-prosperity between Japan and . . . the Netherlands East Indies." Secretary of State Cordell Hull issued an immediate press release in which he warned that a Japanese incursion into the far-flung Dutch colony "would be prejudicial to the cause of stability, peace, and security."

The main body of the United States Fleet sallied from West Coast ports on April 2. Fleet Problem XXXI was to be conducted until May 9 well to the west of the International Date Line, but on May 7 the entire fleet was ordered by a chain of command beginning with President Roosevelt to conduct an extra two weeks of war games and then to base itself at Pearl Harbor. Admiral Richardson, who was completely surprised by the change of plans, cabled Chief of Naval Operations Stark that very day to ask, "Why are we here?" To which Stark replied, "You are there because of the deterrent effect which it is thought your presence may have on the Japs going into the East Indies."

On May 10, the Wehrmacht kicked off its murderously efficient campaign in western Europe, and the Netherlands capitulated in only five days. The Royal Netherlands forces in the East Indies pledged their fealty to Queen Wilhelmina when she went into exile, and they supported her continuing stance on the side of the Allies.

Prince Konoye returned to power on June 22, 1940. This time around, the emperor's friend appointed Gen. Hideki Tojo, an ardent anti-Russian and anti-American militarist, as minister of war. Tojo had been an early supporter of the invasion of China, and he was all for going to war in Southeast Asia and, by extension, the Pacific. The fierce strength of his convictions, vehemently stated, brought to mind the deadly 1936 coup, and this swiftly cowed the other ministers into submission.

Equally portentous, Konoye also named Yosuke Matsuoka foreign minister. Matsuoka had lived in poverty in Oregon as a youngster but had earned a degree at the University of Oregon despite his many hardships. He hated Americans for their racism, whose sting he had certainly felt. Though Matsuoka took office at a time of extreme delicacy in U.S.-Japanese relations, he went out of his way to advocate alliances with Germany and Italy.

The sagacious Ambassador Grew, on sizing up the new Konoye cabinet, warned that French Indochina might be an early target of Japanese aggression. Certainly it would be a prime target if the Japanese wanted to choke off supplies to the Nationalist Chinese via Hanoi, one of only two routes with access to the Nationalist capital in Chungking.

On July 2, 1940, the United States Congress passed the Export Control Act, which authorized the president to prohibit or curtail the export of munitions, military equipment, tools, or materiel whenever he deemed it "necessary in the interest of national defense." Three days later, Roosevelt invoked the new act with respect to Japan, thus prohibiting the exportation without license of strategic chemicals and minerals, aircraft engines, spare parts, and other equipment.

On July 18, three days after the French army capitulated to Germany, the Japanese insisted that Britain close the Burma Road, which besides Hanoi was one of only two lines of supply from the outside world to Nationalist forces. Pressed harshly by the Germans and anticipating at any moment an invasion of their homeland, the British acceded to the Japanese demand, which seriously impaired the Nationalists' ability to resist.

The U.S. embargo of early July was ratcheted up on July 26 when the sale to Japan without license of aviation lubricants and fuel, as well as most types of iron and steel scrap, was flatly prohibited. On September 30, the United

States embargoed shipments of any iron and steel scrap to Japan. (These linked actions were not just about punishing Japan or abating its ability to wage war in China; they had as much to do with closing down the export of the named commodities and goods at a time in which American industry and the military were scrambling to their utmost to meet the growing demands of their vast attempt to bootstrap the war preparations effort.) These moves were wildly popular with the American electorate; 75 percent of poll respondents favored the actions.

On August 30, 1940, Vichy France agreed to permit the Japanese army to occupy the northern half of French Indochina, and on September 22 administrators in Hanoi signed documents ceding airfields and permitting the occupation. Even though the occupation was undertaken with the approval of the Vichy government, and despite Japanese pronouncements that the new base of operations would only support the war in adjacent China, Americans felt this was a raw act of cynicism and deceit against a defeated nation that could not defend its interests.

The emergence of Japan on September 27, 1940, as a Tripartite Pact signatory with Germany and Italy did Japan not one whit of good—the Axis partnership was Darwinian, to say the least—and it both alarmed and alienated those many Americans who were otherwise against U.S. rearmament or even alliances with traditional partners such as Britain. If U.S. policies vis-à-vis Japan had a racist component (they undoubtedly did, at some level), Japan's emergence as a full Axis partner transcended it. The American press openly characterized Japan as a fascist state, which, at a time of total war in Europe, equated to an enemy of the United States. With or without President Roosevelt's arguable hostility toward Japan for its own acts and crimes, American public opinion identified Japan as an enemy in some near-future war.

President Roosevelt responded to Japan's alliance with the Axis with ruthless efficiency. The United States had already abrogated its 1911 trade treaty with Japan, but now Roosevelt severely curtailed the licensing of the remaining trade by American companies with Japanese agencies or firms. When Japan formally protested the embargo of aviation gasoline and scrap metal on October 8, 1940, the U.S. Department of State advised American citizens to leave the Far East. On October 14, three American passenger liners were ordered to Japanese and Chinese ports to repatriate U.S. citizens due to "abnormal conditions." And on November 30, the United States loaned $50 million to China to bring about currency stabilization and granted another $50 million in credits for the purchase of war supplies.

The Americans and Japanese played another tit-for-tat game during the autumn of 1940. On September 29, a U.S. Navy transport anchored at Midway to deliver a detachment of marines and a large number of civilian construction workers who would fortify the base with coastal guns and an improved airfield. In November, the Imperial Navy responded in secret with a massive effort to fortify Japanese possessions in the Caroline and Marshall island groups. On

December 19, Palmyra Island was placed under U.S. Navy jurisdiction, presumably so it could be built up as a satellite base.

In late January 1941, Ambassador Grew passed along to the Department of State the thrust of rumors that indicated the Japanese had begun planning an attack against Pearl Harbor. It is notable that this was the exact time when Imperial Navy planners indeed began to plan such an attack.

In March 1941, Japan agreed to mediate a claim by Thailand for the return of several "lost" provinces along the Thai-Indochina border. In return for their services, which turned some land over to Thailand, the Japanese were paid off with a monopoly on the Indochinese rice crop and basing privileges at Saigon Airport, which was well within bombing range of Singapore.

On April 15, 1941, President Roosevelt agreed to allow American aviators to resign their commissions so they could enlist as mercenaries in the American Volunteer Group of the Chinese air force. The first contingent, drawn from the army, navy, and Marine Corps, was to be equipped with P-40B fighters that would otherwise have gone to the Army Air Corps. Within nine months, this small American contingent would gain fame as the Flying Tigers.

Matsuoka Moves West

The cumulative effect of draconian American measures of late 1940 cast Foreign Minister Matsuoka as a dark cloud in the Konoye cabinet. In March 1941 he set off to Berlin and Moscow in quest of a silver lining.

In Berlin, Matsuoka gained Hitler's permission to make a treaty with the Soviets. In Moscow, he negotiated a five-year neutrality pact, based on Soviet recognition of Japanese sovereignty over Manchuria and Japanese recognition of Soviet sovereignty over Outer Mongolia. The April 13, 1941, pact assured Stalin that the Soviet Union wouldn't be stabbed in the back by Japan, and vice versa.

This is amazing. In the summer of 1938, some diehard Japanese advocates of the go-north strategy had managed to foment a little war with Soviet troops at Kalkhin Gol (also known as Nomanhan), on the ill-defined Manchuria-Outer Mongolia border. In several weeks of all-out ground and air war, the Soviets administered a drubbing that fully ended any notions of Japan's "going north."

Stalin had made a similar nonaggression pact with Hitler a week ahead of the dual invasion of Poland in September 1939. Unbeknown to Stalin, as he spoke with Matsuoka in Moscow, this pact was less than four months away from being traumatically overturned by Operation Barbarossa, the German invasion of the Soviet Union. Indeed, only after the invasion was unleashed, Hitler got around to inviting his new Axis partner to invade the Soviet Far East, something the Nazi lord must have known was not going to happen. Even more amazing was that, at the end of 1941, Moscow would be literally saved from German occupation by troops Stalin withdrew from Outer Mongolia on Matsuoka's word in April 1940 that Japan would not attack the Soviet Far East again. And most amazing of all was that the Soviet troops from Outer Mongolia manned the very same units that had defeated the Japanese go-north strike at

Kalkhin Gol in 1938. (In other words, Hitler had given Matsuoka permission to make a pact with Stalin that ultimately provided Stalin with the troops who would halt the German assault on Moscow.)

To top everything else off, as Stalin saw Matsuoka off on the Trans-Siberian train that would take the Japanese foreign minister to Vladivostok, the Soviet supremo—whose regime would be propped up to a large degree between August 1941 and the end of the war in Europe by American-made war materiel—bellowed these parting words: "Japan can now expand southward."

Countdown to War

Even as Foreign Minister Matsuoka traveled to Berlin and Moscow in the spring of 1941 to nail down Japan's place in the Axis alliance and a nonaggression pact with the Soviet Union, it appears that Emperor Hirohito expressed his reservations with respect to the downward spiral of Japanese-American relations. He ordered the Japanese embassy in Washington to open talks aimed at restoring normal trade.

The Japanese expansion begun in the 1890s was always about commerce. Japan had no natural resources of its own beyond the compliant hard work of its citizens. Raw materials lay to the west and south, in easy reach of a modern industrial state, but it was all in the hands of white people from far, far away.

Americans are often quick to rationalize the "manifest destiny" that drove expansion of their nation from one ocean to the other. So, too, the Japanese felt it was their destiny to rule an Asia of and for Asians. They thought nothing more of moving west into Manchuria and Korea than the young United States had thought of moving west from Pennsylvania to Ohio and Kentucky—both peoples pushing aside or rolling over backward aboriginals as they went. In both cases, a weak power was to be replaced by a manifestly stronger power, better able to exploit god-given resources to the benefit of all.

So, even though President Roosevelt had staked his public good will on halting Japanese expansion, and even though Secretary of State Cordell Hull was as rabidly anti-Japanese as Foreign Minister Matsuoka was anti-American, Ambassador Kichisaburo Nomura, a retired admiral, arranged to open what was, even in the emperor's mind, a last-ditch effort to restore trade and, thus, comity between the United States and Japan. The talks began in March 1941—around the time Imperial Navy strategic planners began to seriously promote the notion of a preemptive strike against the U.S. Pacific Fleet in place of the defense of homeland waters that had been the hallmark of Japanese naval doctrine, planning, and shipbuilding since the end of the Great War.

The U.S. negotiators thought they had an advantage over Nomura and his team. They could read the Japanese "Purple" diplomatic cipher. Underscore that: the *diplomatic* cipher, not the military cipher. If the Japanese diplomats in Washington were dealt out of the war planning—as they indeed were—there was not necessarily a way for American military leaders to learn of and therefore plan against the emerging preemptive naval strategy.

Short of a shooting war, nothing demonstrates one nation's highest degree of disapproval for another nation's behavior than a trade embargo. Trade embargoes cut in two directions; both nations suffer, though not necessarily equally. There was trade between the United States and Japan in the spring of 1941, but it was seriously curtailed on the U.S. side. Japan was suffering, and it was getting the message. It was not processing the message the way the Roosevelt Administration hoped it might, but there was still some room to demonstrate yet more disapproval, or to come off the brake and reward what the United States considered to be good behavior.

Besides, the longer the Nomura-Hull talks continued, the more American intelligence agents thought they could learn of Japanese intentions. Yet in that respect it must be said that the intelligence analyst who attempts to gauge future actions by means of what he perceives an enemy's intentions to be completely misunderstands the workings of intelligence, per se. The only safe bets are those placed on what intelligence agents learn, in aggregate, about an adversary's *capabilities*. Absent a fait accompli—a message reading, in effect, "We will attack at dawn."—a good intelligence estimate based on the best and most accurate data can say only, "Beware! The enemy has the capability to attack at dawn." This is not what American diplomatic and military leaders were getting when their intelligence minions read Nomura's mail. If they had, they would have foreseen the next really stupid move the Japanese made.

For all that Japan is an island nation, dependent upon shipping for the entirety of its trade, it was nonetheless a continental power whose army held the greater power in military councils. Indeed, in Japan, via its rather aggressive program of selective assassination of officials who did not hew to the army's program, the Imperial Army had become the deus ex machina of foreign policy and other important preserves of government.

Japan faces west, across a narrow sea, to the great east Asian land mass. Once it was pulled into the modern world, once it embraced the industrial and imperial models of modern statehood, it became a continental power. True, it ruthlessly drove into the Pacific when the opportunity presented itself in 1914, but its interests lay in the continent to its west. Japan perceived an enemy to the east and prepared itself to take on that enemy in due course, but the Imperial Army was much less interested in seeking redress of an insult over trade than in achieving a position of military and therefore economic hegemony over Korea; Manchuria; at least eastern China; and, in due course, oil- and rubber-rich Southeast Asia and the Netherlands East Indies.

By mid-1941, the go-north strategy had been completely expunged from Imperial Army planning. Kalkhin Gol had seen to that, and the northern flank had been sealed by Matsuoka's authentic nonaggression deal with Stalin. That left plenty of room for actually going south.

The crisis in trade had reached a crescendo with the Imperial Army's occupation of northern French Indochina. At the time, the army and thus the government had claimed that the move had been in the interests of outflanking Chinese land forces in areas north of the Indochina frontier. That was a sop, for whatever it might be worth to whomever chose to listen. The Americans heard it, took it for what it was—then went ahead with ratcheting up their trade embargo.

On July 2, 1941, Japan recalled its merchant fleet from the Atlantic Ocean, and the Imperial Army called up more than a million new conscripts.

On July 6 and 7, Japanese warplanes bombed the Nationalist capital, Chungking. During the attacks, an American church was struck by bombs and the U.S. Navy river gunboat *Tutuila* was struck by shrapnel that holed her hull and turned a light boat to kindling. Japan formally apologized the next day.

On July 18, the Konoye government was dissolved—for one day. When it was reconstituted, the next day, the only change was that Matsuoka, a go-north proponent, had been replaced as foreign minister by a compliant admiral named Teijiro Toyoda.

It must be said that Prince Konoye, by all accounts, personally desired a peaceful outcome to the crisis. But he and the other civilians in his government were so dominated by the military, particularly by the army's fearsome General Tojo, that there was really only one foreseeable outcome.

Far from dialing back the sanctions in the face of Ambassador Nomura's formidable negotiating skills, President Roosevelt ratcheted them up about as far as he possibly could. Together with the United Kingdom and the Royal Netherlands government-in-exile, the United States imposed a *total* oil embargo against Japan on July 26, 1941. Until this embargo, the three oil exporters had supplied 88 percent of Japan's petroleum needs. Also on July 26, the United States froze Japanese—and Chinese—assets in the United States. The very next day, Japan froze American assets in Japan. And as a final insult this July 26—the third July 26 in a row of resolute American action—President Roosevelt federalized the Philippine Army; created the new United States Army Forces in the Far East; and placed all under the command of Lt. Gen. Douglas MacArthur, who had been serving as supreme commander of the prospective Philippine national army since his retirement in 1935 as U.S. Army chief of staff.

Here is the really stupid act: Now that the go-south faction was in complete control, and even with the Hull-Nomura talks ongoing, the army-dominated Konoye regime sent the Imperial Army on July 29, 1941, to occupy the remainder of Indochina. This time, the Japanese did not bother to employ the canard about outflanking the Chinese, for it was plain enough to see that southern Indochina outflanked the largest part of Thailand, a militarily weak, independent monarchy that oversaw yet more vast and underdeveloped natural resources. Thailand then flanked British Malaya to the north and, along with Japanese holdings in China and northern Indochina, most of Burma. At the southern end of Malaya was Singapore, and south of Singapore was Sumatra, in the Netherlands East Indies. Back east of Sumatra was Borneo, where the British colony in North Borneo was the most productive oil-bearing region in Asia.

The Imperial Army's plan, which had been plain enough before the occupation of southern Indochina, was now manifest. The Vichy French had not held off the Japanese, and the Royal Thai Army could not do so in its wildest dreams. The British were fighting for their lives in Europe and North Africa, and they had drawn in most of the Australian and New Zealand armies to help them merely hang in against Japan's European Axis partners. The Netherlands, of course, was under German occupation, so the Royal Netherlands forces in possession of the East Indies were, perforce, both limited and finite. Anyone with a map of Asia and the merest smidgen of deductive powers could see where this was going.

The Nomura-Hull negotiations were allowed to roll on, but the plain fact was that Japan had only 6,450,000 tons of oil in reserve. The most sanguine estimates showed that such a supply could not last beyond four years with even the most draconian regimen of economy. Of course, Japan was involved in a big war in mainland China, so economy was not an option, unless the Imperial Army simply quit the war.

As soon as the total oil embargo was announced, the Konoye government released an all-out domestic press assault against the United States. What it came down to was that a jealous, hostile, and much wealthier United States, which had been allowed to find its destiny in its own West, was now leading the charge to deny Japan its destiny to its west.

Death Spiral

And so it went. On August 8, Ambassador Nomura suggested to Secretary of State Hull that a conference between President Roosevelt and Prince Konoye might alleviate tensions. This led to an August 17 meeting at the White House attended by Roosevelt, Hull, and Nomura to discuss the basis for arranging a conference on the situation in the Pacific. All well and good, but the Japanese could not resist muddying the waters. They filed a protest on August 28 to complain about the shipment of goods to the Soviet Union (a putative Japanese ally that had been under assault by Japan's real ally, Germany, since June 22). The goods were being shipped through Japanese waters to the Far East port of Vladivostok, which was the Soviet Union's biggest warm-water port in the region and which could not be reached except by transiting Japanese waters.

On September 11, in a proclamation aimed chiefly, but not entirely, at Atlantic shipping, President Roosevelt authorized the U.S. Navy to attack any vessel that threatened a U.S.-flag vessel or any vessel sailing under the protection of a U.S. escort.

As the general crisis deepened, the United States began to take overtly defensive measures. On October 17, the U.S. Navy ordered all American merchant ships in Asian waters to put into the nearest friendly port. (On this day, also, the Konoye government resigned and Gen. Hideki Tojo became the new premier.) On November 14, the 4th Marine Regiment, based in Shanghai, and smaller Marine Corps detachments based in Peking and Tientsin were ordered to immediately transfer to the Philippines.

The Japanese made what appeared to be several last-ditch efforts to reconcile with the United States. A special diplomatic envoy, Saburo Kurusu, arrived in Washington on November 15 to confer with Secretary of State Hull. On November 20, Ambassador Nomura presented to Hull Japan's "absolutely final" proposal to maintain peace between their two nations: If the United States provided Japan with one million gallons of aviation fuel from any source, Japan would meet U.S. demands to suspend military operations in China. On November 26, a day after a Japanese transport flotilla under naval escort was spotted off Formosa heading in the direction of British Malaya, the United States made its own "final proposal" via the two senior Japanese envoys in Washington. The next day, Chief of Naval Operations Stark dispatched a "war warning" to the Pacific and Asian fleet commanders. On November 30, Premier Tojo rejected the American proposals set forth via Nomura and Kurusu on November 26.

In nearly the final act of this waltz, Japan for some reason saw an advantage in assuring the United States on December 5, 1941, that massive troop movements in Indochina were merely precautionary.

What If?

As is the case of all modern continental powers, the Imperial Navy took a backseat to the army in political matters. Perhaps Japan was an extreme example of a military dictatorship in the 1920s and 1930s, but at root it was dependent upon its army to take and hold the resource-laden lands it needed to at first modernize and then compete on the world economic stage. Its navy was thus grounded in the traditional role of navies, which is ensuring the unencumbered flow of maritime trade from offshore possessions and, indeed, from trading partners the world around.

The move against German possessions in the Pacific in 1914 had had two purposes: to guard the long Pacific trade routes and to mirror and even outflank the string of American bases already extant in the vast ocean since 1898. Japan's acquisition of Formosa in the last years of the nineteenth century countered from the north the American move into the Philippines, and Japan's acquisition of the Palau Islands in 1914 further outflanked the Philippines to the east. The former German possessions in the Mariana Islands countered the American hold on Guam, also in the Marianas; and possession of the scattered and far-flung Marshall and Caroline island groups provided distant barriers far to the east and south. All that Japan lacked by way of a barrier against a naval advance from Hawaii and the western United States were bases in waters north, northeast, and northwest of the Marianas.

The Imperial Army had absolutely no interest in the far reaches of the Pacific. It occupied Formosa, Korea, Manchuria, and French Indochina; it was massively at work expanding Japanese spheres in China; and it was certainly contemplating moves to and across all of Southeast Asia. To undertake the latter, the army would need lift capacity available from the navy, and the invasion fleets would have to be escorted and supported by warships. That was the sum of the navy's role in the eyes of the dominant army, with a little air support thrown in. But the Imperial Army had never dispatched, nor did it plan to dispatch troops, and had never spent, nor did it plan to spend treasure on the Pacific barrier islands. Inasmuch as the army controlled Japan's military purse, little was done in the post–Great War years to exploit the military aspects of the island mandates that had so attracted the Imperial Navy. Plans were made, but circumstances of budget had forced the Japanese to go along with the provisos in the Versailles Treaty and subsequent agreements that prevented fortification of the central Pacific mandates. The navy hadn't had the funds to fortify any of the Pacific island possessions except the great Truk naval base in the Carolines, and the army hadn't cared to spend any.

Aside from building and planning for the defense of home waters against a foe from the east—certainly the United States—the Imperial Navy took on just two tasks once Japan launched the war in mainland Asia: protecting the narrow western sea's trade routes and sending large parts of its land-based air force to fight in the skies over China. It expected, in due course, to support Imperial Army offensive operations in Southeast Asia in the form of sealift and naval escort, and perhaps air support as well. Its role would be the traditional role of the navy of a continental power.

While waiting and planning for the arrival of an American battle fleet on the doorstep of Japan, a number of influential naval thinkers reconsidered the traditional notion of fighting a grand fleet action so close to home. The Japanese had honed and refined their battle plan—and, perforce, their battle fleet—to the last detail, literally to the last detail. But . . . what if . . . ?

What if the Combined Fleet, as the navy's operational arm was called, sallied east and took on the Americans close to *their* home waters? The Japanese knew the American plan to hold advance bases across the Pacific, and seize new ones—the Americans had published the plan's outline. How did that look in reverse? What American, British, and Dutch bases so threatened Japanese lines of communication that they had to be removed from the board? Or, even if they didn't actually threaten Japanese possessions and lines of communication, which American, British, Dutch, and even French possessions would, in Japanese hands, further protect or enhance the Japanese strategic or tactical stance? And, of course, what American possession just south of Formosa, once in Japanese hands, would yield the greatest treasure in resources and colonial workers? How could the Imperial Navy best hedge its bets in a naval war far from home?

And so the logic became inexorable. And by means of that inexorable logic, the Imperial Navy's best minds forged an action plan of far-reaching scope and breathtaking ambition.

Chapter 32

The Forlorn Hope

The Sands Run Out

THE JAPANESE AIR ATTACK on Pearl Harbor was a means to an end, a logical adjunct to a much, much larger war of aggression aimed at swiftly and definitively delivering the natural wealth of Malaya, Burma, Singapore, the Netherlands East Indies, and the Philippines into the hands of the Japanese industrialists and the Japanese military. Pearl Harbor was attacked because the Pacific Fleet, the most dangerous threat on Earth to Japanese expansionism, was based there. The Japanese never seriously contemplated a land grab so far to the east of what they considered their natural sphere of influence; they attacked the main American regional base because it was the main American regional base, no more and no less. When they had, in an hour's time, reduced Pearl Harbor, Hickam Field, Schofield Barracks, and surrounding bases to shambles, they left with no thought of returning, certain they had given themselves a year of peace from American counterstrokes and certainly enough time to overwhelm the American garrisons and flotillas from Wake Island westward to the East Asian littoral.

American commanders in the Pacific did not see the December 7, 1941, blow at Pearl Harbor coming. They worried about it and even took action against it, but their timing was off and their vision and imagination failed them. They didn't see what was coming before the blow landed; they believed—because they devoutly hoped—they had more time, more space, a little more opportunity to prepare.

What the American commanders saw clearly and worried about the most was the blow they thought would—not might—fall on the Philippines, which was very, very close to securely manned Japanese holdings and way too close to the sea lanes over which Japanese troops would have to be shipped to mount long-expected invasions of Malaya, Singapore, and the Netherlands East Indies. The Philippines were too far from the United States to be relieved. *Not* relieving the Philippines was a cornerstone of Joint War Plan Rainbow No. 5.

The best the American military leaders could promise was to build up the Philippines' defenses so strongly as to hold off an invasion attempt. But there was little to send from home as the weeks and months of 1941 wound down. And there was not enough time to meet all the needs of the defenders. For all the honest effort to build up America's military might, for all the acceleration and ordering of production and manning and integration following the Aircraft Meeting, the fall of France, and the long undeclared war with Germany, the United States was not ready to go to war in December 1941. And nothing short of being in a real war could make her armed forces ready to deliver a balanced offensive within another year's time.

But once having foreseen the reality of the position in which forces in the Philippines would find themselves once Japan moved offensively, a last-minute sense of moral obligation pushed every man and machine that could be spared toward the inevitable showdown there. That much the nation owed its troops and the civilians in its care. The United States recognized the threat, and at the last minute it rushed to pay its dues at the expense of adequately defending other areas, some quite close to home, some far more strategically vital.

Alaska

Until the onset of war in Europe, the navy paid little attention to far-off Alaska, and the army paid none at all. Nevertheless, by November 1939, there was some small concern over the small naval air stations (home to patrol planes only) at Kodiak and Sitka, and the Coast Guard station, naval radio station, and fuel storage on Unalaska Island. The Department of War decided to request funds to build an air base, Elmendorf Field, at Anchorage and dispatch a ground force to defend it. The House Appropriations Committee excised the budget for this construction project in April 1940, but a smaller garrison was approved for Fairbanks. The fall of France in June 1940 saw the Anchorage project reinstated for fiscal 1941. Oddly, in light of the Soviet Union's nonaggression pact with Germany, the army was more concerned about Soviet incursions into Alaska and the Aleutian Islands than it was about Japanese incursions.

Alaska fell within the purview of the Fourth Army, headquartered in San Francisco, but it was too isolated to administer effectively, so the Fourth Army suggested that the region be set up with its own independent command structure. This led to the creation of the Alaska Defense Command.

Actual army troop dispositions by mid-1941 were about 3,500 officers and men at Anchorage, about 1,500 at Unalaska, and about 2,300 divided between Kodiak and Sitka. Also, a composite air group of one pursuit squadron, one medium bombardment squadron, and one heavy bombardment squadron was based at Elmendorf Field. The actual aircraft assigned were twenty P-36s and a total of twelve B-18s. Work was underway to develop eleven emergency airfields around the region, and in due course new major airfield construction was authorized for Umnak Island (to guard Unalaska), Nome, Yakutat (as a waystation on the Gulf of Alaska), and Kodiak Island. A cold-weather experimental air station, Ladd Field, was also approved for a site near Fairbanks. All these bases could support at least rudimentary air operations by the onset of winter weather in 1941, but none was assigned aircraft before the outbreak of war. Four airway communications stations had been set up in the spring, but approval for an early-warning system was not forthcoming until December 3, 1941.

The German invasion of the Soviet Union on June 22, 1941, allayed fears with respect to a Soviet incursion, but by then intelligence had indicated that Japan might be readying a reinforced division to move into Alaska or the Aleutians. The navy was not so moved by this assessment as to beef up its own Alaska-area forces, but it did press for larger army garrisons at its Alaska and Aleutians bases. To this the army complied by requesting funds for expanded facilities to house an aggregate of 11,200 additional troops. But as it seemed more and more likely that the Soviet Union might collapse, fear of Japanese incursions rose, and permission was granted to move nearly twenty-four thousand additional troops to Alaskan bases by October 1941, and then an additional five thousand troops were requested, albeit too late to reach Alaska in 1941. By December 1941, two Regular Army infantry regiments and an Alaska National Guard infantry battalion were the mainstay of the Alaskan ground-defense establishment.

Hawaii

When the United States Fleet had been ordered to remain at Pearl Harbor following its mid-1940 exercises in Hawaiian waters, the fleet's commander-in-chief, Adm. James Richardson, had achieved a terminal level of antipathy from the commander in chief when he complained that, among other things, the facilities at Pearl were not up to taking care of so large a naval force. By the time Richardson was replaced in February 1941, Pearl Harbor was a veritable boom town, with numerous burgeoning navy, army, Air Corps, and Marine Corps subdivisions and suburbs.

Though for more than a week in late November 1941 warnings of a possible Japanese attack were issued from on high in Washington, the various Pearl Harbor–area commanders did not take the stated threat seriously enough to discuss the danger among themselves or independently place their commands on a high state of alert. The closest any of them scored to an accomplishment was the Hawaiian Air Force commander's decision to line up most of the aircraft in his care, wingtip to wingtip and under twenty-four-hour guard, to deter what all the commanders thought to be the greatest and most probable threat, saboteurs.

The Navy

The main naval base was Pearl Harbor, the jewel in the American Pacific crown, a natural harbor whose immense potential as a fleet anchorage was being exploited to the limits of the Pacific Fleet's immense and diverse needs, the center of a defensive ring to rival and perhaps beat out the vaunted defenses at Gibraltar and Singapore. On the one hand, defense-minded commentators on Pearl's positive attributes pointed out that the harbor's long, narrow entrance channel precluded a general surface attack by a hostile battle fleet, but others, including the doomed Admiral Richardson, had carped that the American battle fleet could debouch from its moorings and into open sea at the rate of only one ship at a time, and might thus be picked off, one ship at a time, by an enemy battle fleet waiting offshore. Indeed, the long, narrow channel could be stoppered entirely if any large ship was sunk within its confines. But this rather good argument was countered by a tabulation of the coastal guns and aircraft that stood ready to make it too hot for an enemy fleet to stand and wait outside the narrow harbor entrance.

When the sun rose at 0626 hours on Sunday, December 7, 1941, the U.S. Pacific Fleet counted these ships inside the vast harbor or guarding its narrow entrance: eight battleships, two heavy cruisers, five light cruisers, twenty-nine destroyers, four submarines, one minelayer, eight destroyer minelayers, ten minesweepers, four destroyer minesweepers, one patrol gunboat, two destroyer tenders, four seaplane tenders, two destroyer seaplane tenders, one ammunition ship, two fleet oilers, three repair ships, one submarine tender, one submarine rescue ship, one hospital ship, two store ships, and four ocean tugs.

Naval aviation that early morning was represented by the following operational aircraft: Ford Island Naval Air Station had two utility squadrons with an aggregate of nineteen single-engine utility seaplanes, two PBYs, and one administrative plane; four patrol squadrons with an aggregate of thirty-three PBYs and one scout-observation seaplane; and spare carrier aircraft numbering three SBD scout-bombers, eight F2A fighters, and ten F4F fighters. Kaneohe Naval Air Station had three patrol squadrons of twelve PBYs each plus one wing administrative plane.

One strategic item stored at Pearl rarely comes up for comment, and that is Pearl's huge oil storage tank farm. The supply of bunker fuel for ships that had been built up following transfer of the fleet to Pearl was immense; it was sufficient to supply the Pacific Fleet for months without recharging. Without it, the Pacific Fleet would be incapable of operating from Pearl and would have to disaggregate and fall back on numerous West Coast ports. Ditto the supply of aviation gasoline. And ditto the naval base's repair and maintenance facilities, including machine shops capable of industrial-scale custom fabrications. Without these, the Pacific Fleet would soon be laid up.

The Army

On February 7, 1941, General Marshall had written to the incoming Hawaiian Department commanding general that the army's chief role on Oahu was defense of naval assets at Pearl Harbor. Toward this end, not counting Air Corps personnel, the Hawaiian Department mustered 35,397 officers and men on Oahu by sunup on December 7, 1941.

The major combat units on the island were the triangularized 24th and 25th Infantry divisions, which had been split off from the old four-regiment Hawaiian Division and each filled out with a single Hawaii National Guard regiment, all on October 1, 1941. Neither division was combat-ready. Combat support units on Oahu included a light tank company, two complete and two incomplete coast artillery regiments, and four antiaircraft artillery regiments. Combat support was provided by an engineer battalion and small chemical warfare and aircraft warning detachments. (The latter worked with six functioning mobile air-search radars and was in the midst of a rather long process setting up six permanently emplaced air-search radars. Only one mobile set was actually manned on the morning of December 7.) The coast artillery regiments manned twelve permanent coastal batteries that mounted an aggregate of four 16-inch guns, two 12-inch guns, eight 8-inch guns, twelve 155mm guns, and sixteen 3-inch guns.

Through 1941, the single most feared mode of attack on Pearl Harbor was an air assault by carrier-based bombers. In this the army and navy commands were in complete agreement, and the services established an amicable partnership that gave the development of an adequate antiaircraft defense first priority. For starters, the navy could defend itself up to a point with its immense array of shipborne antiaircraft guns, ranging from 5-inch dual-purpose guns down to .50-caliber machine guns. But the navy felt the army owed it a much better land-based antiaircraft defense than had been laid on, to include antiaircraft weapons guarding the Air Corps airfields. This was true. The army's largest antiaircraft guns in Hawaii were 3-inchers, of which eighty-two of an authorized ninety-eight were emplaced on December 7. Of 120 37mm automatic antiaircraft cannon authorized, all 100 to actually reach Oahu were in place, but only 109 of 308 authorized .50-caliber machine guns on antiaircraft mounts were emplaced. There was also a nearly total paucity of aircraft warning devices, only three barrage balloons of eighty-seven authorized had even reached Oahu, and the navy's request that the army install smoke generators was under study. These shortages, and many more, were not for lack of will, good faith, or misguided priorities; the army in late 1941 was under immense pressure to adequately defend bases from Iceland to Panama and the Aleutians to the Philippines, not to mention cities on all the mainland coasts. Everyone had legitimate claims on equipment that was in short supply or had not even been manufactured yet, and too often there were too few troops to emplace them quickly enough even if they got where they needed to be.

The Army Air Corps

The Army Air Corps, which counted 754 officers and 6,706 enlisted men on Oahu on December 7, fielded a pursuit wing composed of nine pursuit squadrons and a bombardment wing composed of eight bombardment squadrons and an observation squadron. The following aircraft, many of them unfit for combat owing to problems ranging from routine maintenance to lack of spare parts, were distributed around Oahu: Hickam Field—twelve B-17 heavy bombers, thirty-three B-18 medium bombers, thirteen A-20 light attack bombers, and two transports; Wheeler Field—forty P-36 pursuits, ninety-eight P-40 pursuits, thirteen P-26 pursuits, and seven assorted noncombatant aircraft; Bellows Field—eight observation planes. One of the pursuit squadrons based at Wheeler

Field was undergoing gunnery training at Haleiwa in northern Oahu. Auxiliary and emergency airfields outside of Oahu were located on Hawaii, Kauai, Lanai, Maui, and Molokai.

If there was a major shortcoming with respect to the aircraft deployed on Oahu—aside from the large number of obsolete B-18s and P-26s left over from earlier times—it was the small number and thus weak striking power of B-17 heavy bombers. The services agreed that Pearl Harbor's strategic value required that at least seventy-two B-17s be on hand there to help the navy PBYs to undertake armed long-range searches for approaching enemy naval forces. The Air Corps had gone to special trouble and suffered problems elsewhere because of an effort to station at least a full combat-ready group of B-17s at Hickam Field in 1941, and around forty had made the long flight from the West Coast by mid-May. The Air Corps bomber boys knew very well the ship-killing potential of B-17s equipped with the Norden bombsight; they had dined out on this cover story since 1937 and knew it to be quite accurate in its own right. But the nation was short of B-17s throughout 1941, and in the end it was felt that most of the heavy bombers based at Hickam would better serve the nation's strategic needs in the Philippines. So only twelve of these sturdy, long-range ship killers remained in Hawaii at the last peaceful sunrise.

The Marine Corps

Marine defense troops at Pearl Harbor included: 1st Defense Battalion, 261 officers and men; 3d Defense Battalion, 863; 4th Defense Battalion, 818; and 6th Defense Battalion, 21. Though very well trained in the art and science of antiaircraft and coast defense, these nearly two thousand Marines happened to use Pearl Harbor as a depot and staging area from which their units could rotate in and out of far-flung island bases; they had no brief to defend Pearl and, as a result, all of their weapons were in storage or in for maintenance.

The vast bulk of Marine Corps aircraft based outside the continental United States was based at Marine Corps Air Station Ewa: one Marine air group composed of the rear echelon of one fighter squadron equipped with eleven F4F fighters; the rear echelon of one scout-bomber squadron equipped with eight SB2U scout-bombers; one scout-bomber squadron of twenty-three SBD scout-bombers; and one utility squadron of one SBD scout-bomber, two transports, one training plane, one scout seaplane, two single-engine utility seaplanes, and one administrative plane. Marine Air Group 21, to which all these units were attached, had no defensive assignment over Oahu; its combat power was in the process of leaving Hawaii for far-flung island airfields.

In addition to defense battalion troops and aviation assets, such as they were, the Marine garrison on Oahu consisted of the headquarters and two companies of the 2d Engineer Battalion, which were building an amphibious training base on Oahu for their parent 2d Marine Division; 485 infantrymen based at Marine Barracks, Pearl Harbor Navy Yard; 102 infantrymen based at Marine Barracks, Ford Island Naval Air Station; 169 marines guarding the naval ammunition depot north of Honolulu; and 877 officers and men serving aboard battleships and cruisers anchored at Pearl Harbor. The number of marines at Pearl Harbor on the morning of December 7, 1941, totaled more than 4,500, and none but those aboard capital ships had any formal role to play in defense of the base.

Other Islands
Midway

The 6th Defense Battalion deployed 843 officers and men in tiny Midway Atoll. In addition to its infantry weapons, the battalion, composed mainly of artillerymen, had emplaced six 5-inch and twelve 3-inch dual-purpose guns, thirty .50-caliber machine guns, and thirty .30-caliber machine guns. Three 7-inch guns had been delivered (another was still in Hawaii), but they had not yet been mounted.

Seven navy PBY patrol bombers were the only airplanes based at Midway on December 7, but two Royal Netherlands Navy PBYs bound for the East Indies took off at dawn on their way to Wake Island. A detachment of eighteen SB2U scout-bombers from Marine Scout-Bomber Squadron 231 was within flight distance of Midway aboard the carrier *Lexington* and was due to fly off later in the morning.

Wake

Marine Corps troops on Wake included 424 officers and men, nearly all artillerymen, from the 1st Defense Battalion. Defensive weapons emplaced along the beaches included six 5-inch and twelve 3-inch guns, and eighteen .50-caliber and thirty .30-caliber machine guns.

Eighty-six aviation support personnel from Marine Air Group 21 were on Wake, and an advance detachment of twelve Marine Fighter Squadron 211 F4F fighters had been delivered by the carrier *Enterprise* on December 4.

There were no naval aircraft at Wake, but the largest naval contingent on any of the islands that shielded Hawaii was stationed there: ten officers and fifty-eight sailors. An army airways communications detachment of one officer and four enlisted men was also on Wake, and so were 1,146 civilian construction contractors and seventy Pan American employees. A westbound China Clipper that overnighted at Wake took off for Guam at dawn.

Guam

The American navy and marine garrison on Guam was doomed from the start. The American possession was surrounded by Japanese-held islands and yet remained unfortified long after Japan's hostile intentions against the United States had become palpable. Guam would have made a terrific advance fleet base, but the lack of development, much less the lack of meaningful defenses, ultimately was a function of geography. Guam was too small and too isolated to defend in 1940s terms and both too far from Pearl Harbor and too close to

Japanese air bases to relieve. American civilians were evacuated from the island in October 1941.

On December 7, 1941, Guam's naval garrison, located at Piti Navy Yard, consisted of 36 officers and warrant officers, 5 nurse officers, and 230 enlisted men. The island's governor was the senior naval officer, a captain. Marine Barracks, Sumay, was manned by 7 officers, a warrant officer, and 145 enlisted men. The locally recruited Guam Insular Force fielded 246 aggressive but lightly equipped men. There were no heavy guns on the island, just infantry weapons. There were also three small patrol craft incapable of meaningful resistance.

American Samoa

The 7th Defense Battalion, specially organized with an infantry company for the purpose, was dispatched to American Samoa beginning in December 1940. There, on Tutuila Island, it manned four 6-inch naval guns, six 3-inch antiaircraft guns, and a number of lighter antiaircraft weapons. The infantry company, which established combat outposts at likely landing spots, also recruited and trained the 1st Samoan Battalion, Marine Corps Reserve, a unit that never reached authorized strength of five hundred because military-age men were needed to construct defenses, including a major air base at Tutuila. A U.S. Navy officer served as the territory's governor, and a naval detachment ran harbor operations at Pago Pago, where a small naval station had been established.

Johnston

The 1st Marine Defense Battalion deployed 162 officers and men on Johnston Island. The detachment's heavy weapons were two 5-inch guns, four 3-inch guns, eight .50-caliber machine guns, and eight .30-caliber machine guns. The navy deployed a small detachment of PBYs at Johnston, and nearby the atoll on the morning of December 7 were the heavy cruiser *Indianapolis* and five destroyer minesweepers, which happened to be in the area to conduct a simulated bombardment of the place.

Palmyra

The 1st Marine Defense Battalion deployed 158 officers and men on Palmyra, and the navy deployed a small detachment of PBYs. Defensive weapons included four 5-inch and four 3-inch guns, eight .50-caliber machine guns, and eight .30-caliber machine guns.

The Philippines

Joint War Plan Rainbow No. 5 and all the discussion that led to it had explicitly excluded any thought of relieving the Philippines. Strictly speaking, a huge, last-minute effort to rush troops, weapons, equipment, munitions, airplanes, fuel, and everything else a modern army needed to put up a fight was not a relief, per se; it was a reinforcement in advance of a battle.

There were plenty of sound military reasons to reinforce the Philippines, such as interdiction of Japanese lines of supply and communication between the China coast or Formosa and points south such as French Indochina, Malaya, Singapore, and the Netherlands East Indies. Many other arguments could be conjured from the moral realm. But the Philippines defenses had long been neglected mainly because there were no men or machines, or very much of anything, that could be spared for them. Indeed, the decision to not immediately relieve the Philippines garrison rose from this very dilemma. For the longest time, anything or anyone dispatched to the Philippines had to be diverted from service in an equally important strategic setting closer to home (and therefore more defensible). And all but heavy bombers had to be carried across the wide Pacific aboard ships that would be vulnerable to sinking by a prospective enemy who had never begun a modern war with any advance notice whatsoever.

So the reason for neglecting defenses in the Philippines, much less building them up, was a function of supply and demand, with distance thrown in. It simply wasn't wise to stock up the Philippines before Hawaii and even Alaska had received due diligence, and the American coasts, the Panama Canal Zone, and the Atlantic islands. As events transpired, the first time the army chiefs felt comfortable with allotting men and weapons to the Philippines was mid-1941. And then they went as whole-hog as reality permitted. They ended up sending men and planes—especially planes—that they had to rob from other locales. On December 6, 1941, there were just twelve B-17s assigned to the Hawaiian defenses and literally only a handful in operational units assigned to defend the United States. Two light tank battalions, by far the largest American tank force outside the continental United States, were scrounged directly off mock battlefields during the final run of prewar field maneuvers and dispatched to Luzon.

Bottom line: There was a last-minute rush to reinforce and restock the Philippines defenses because it was not until the last minute that the generals in Washington felt they controlled the wherewithal to do so. This last point is critical, for it is prima facie evidence for the very point this entire study sets out to make: that the United States started down the road to rearmament in November 1938 *just in time* to affect the early stage of U.S. involvement in World War II. Absent Lend-Lease—which turned out to be vital to American interests in the Atlantic and Europe—there could well have been earlier and larger reinforcements directed toward Hawaii and the Philippines, and perhaps, remotely, even a massive build-up in Guam. While there is no telling how well much larger, better prepared defense establishments might have fared against the initial Japanese onslaught, they might have been better breakwaters, might have turned into sinkholes to Japanese power, might have delayed or even prevented the juggernaut that did take place, or might have deterred Japan from going to war in the first place.

✳

The Army

Operating under a dizzying array of headquarters structures far too elaborate for the number of troops on hand, the main U.S. Army Forces in the Far East (USAFFE) component on Luzon was the Philippine Division, whose major units were the 31st Infantry Regiment, the 45th Infantry Regiment (Philippine Scouts), the 57th Infantry Regiment (Philippine Scouts), and a 329-man cadre of the 43d Infantry Regiment (Philippine Scouts), which had been reactivated in April 1941. Artillery support was provided by two Philippine Scout artillery regiments aggregating three 75mm gun battalions. Two U.S. Army National Guard light tank battalions, the 194th and 192d, arrived in Manila on September 26 and November 29, 1941, respectively, and both were attached to the Philippine Division. Rounding out the division were Philippine Scout engineer, ordnance, signal, medical, military police, and quartermaster units. Finally, the U.S. Army's horse-mounted 26th Cavalry Regiment (Philippine Scouts) would be the last U.S. cavalry unit ever to ride its horses to war. The 200th Coast Artillery Regiment (Antiaircraft), a repurposed and renumbered New Mexico National Guard cavalry unit, arrived in Manila in September for duty at Clark Field, but the unit had not yet received its weapons or searchlight battery.

The entrance to Manila Bay was guarded by four fortified islands manned by coast artillery batteries as follows: Fort Mills (on Corregidor Island)—eight 12-inch guns, ten 12-inch mortars, two 10-inch guns, two 8-inch guns, five 6-inch guns, nineteen 155mm guns, and twelve 3-inch guns; Fort Hughes—two 14-inch guns, four 12-inch mortars, two 6-inch guns, three 155mm guns, and two 3-inch guns; Fort Drum—four 16-inch guns, four 6-inch guns, and one 3-inch gun; and Fort Frank—two 14-inch guns, eight 12-inch mortars, and four 155mm guns. Beach defenses for the forts, except tiny Drum, included 75mm guns. Antiaircraft defenses for the forts was provided by the 60th Coast Artillery Regiment (Antiaircraft), which deployed forty 3-inch guns, forty-eight .50-caliber machine guns, and seventeen 60-inch searchlights in the southern Bataan peninsula.

In all on December 7, 1941, the headquarters and ground elements of U.S. Army Forces in the Far East stood at a strength of 25,486, counting the Philippine Scouts.

The Air Corps

At sunrise on December 8, the Far East Air Force aircraft deployed with first-line units on Luzon included: at Clark Field—seventeen B-17s and eighteen P-40s; at Del Carmen Field—sixteen B-17s and eighteen P-35s; at Iba Field—eighteen P-40s; at Nichols Field—thirty-six P-40s; and at Batangas Field—twelve Philippine Army Air Corps P-26s. In addition to about thirty spare P-35s, many of which were in need of overhaul, Far East Air Force counted an assortment of obsolete and reasonably defenseless P-26s, B-18s, some observation types, a few light transports, and even a dozen old B-10 bombers.

Command echelons included the Far East Air Force headquarters, the V Bomber Command and V Interceptor Command headquarters, and the Far East Service Command headquarters. Support included communicators, engineers, chemical and weather detachments, a maintenance detachment, and an aircraft warning detachment. Total Far East Air Force personnel strength on December 7 was 5,609 officers and men.

As in Hawaii, the final string of alerts and war warnings caused the Far East Air Force commander to deploy his planes on the ground so as to ward off saboteurs, which is to say in nice, neat rows in the open.

The Navy

U.S. Navy ships based in Manila Bay or Olongapo Naval Base on the morning of December 8 (local time) included four old destroyers, of which two were undergoing repair; thirteen submarines, of which one was undergoing overhaul; six motor torpedo boats; a submarine tender; a seaplane tender; an aircraft transport (the old *Langley*); a repair ship; a former liner undergoing conversion to tender status; five former Yangtze River gunboats; five minesweepers; two fleet tankers; a salvage vessel; an oceangoing tug; and five Philippines Navy patrol craft. The Asiatic Fleet flagship, heavy cruiser *Houston*, was at Iloilo in the central Philippines, and other Asiatic Fleet ships elsewhere in the Philippines included the light cruiser *Boise*, two submarines, and a station ship.

The Asiatic Fleet also had five destroyers based at Tarakan, Borneo, and four destroyers and a destroyer tender at Balikpapan, Borneo. Of these, the ships at Balikpapan were ordered on the evening of December 6 to join Royal Navy forces at Singapore, but they would not be ready to sail for several days. As many as sixteen Asiatic Fleet submarines were at sea, ready to do what submarines do best.

The sum of tender-based U.S. Navy aircraft operating from Manila Bay was twenty-eight PBYs, five single-engine utility floatplanes, and one scout-observation floatplane. Four other PBYs were operating from a tender at Davao, and four tender-based scout-observation floatplanes were at Palawan. Most of the seaborne aircraft were on a schedule of regular patrols, which to the east slightly overlapped patrols undertaken by Royal Netherlands Navy PBYs

The Marine Corps

The 4th Marine Regiment abruptly ended its long service in China when it sailed for Manila from Shanghai aboard two chartered liners on November 27 and November 28, 1941. Both ships had reached Manila safely by December 1, and the regiment was sent to Olongapo Naval Station to conduct field training.

The 4th Marines had been allowed to dwindle down to less than a battalion in strength—44 officers and 728 troops, plus a 32-man navy medical detachment—in the years before the war. Although the regiment fielded two nominal battalions, each had only two infantry companies of two platoons apiece—fewer altogether than the nine rifle platoons of a full-strength infantry battalion. When it arrived at Olongapo, the regiment was bolstered somewhat by addition of the base Marine detachment.

Also by December 7, the Asiatic Fleet commander had, on his own authority, built up a reserve of marines organized as the 1st Separate Marine Battalion, an off-the-books collection of 725 replacements intercepted on their way to China. In October, the battalion had taken over infantry and antiaircraft defense in and around Cavite Navy Yard. The antiaircraft batteries were armed with 3-inch dual-purpose guns, 3-inch antiaircraft guns, and .50-caliber machine guns.

The Philippine Army

The Philippine Scout units serving with the Philippine Division and elsewhere in the commonwealth were U.S. Army troops. The small standing Philippine Army was backed by several hundred thousand reservists organized into ten reserve divisions of varying quality and readiness that were activated on September 1, 1941, and subjected to crash training courses that included a modicum of equipping. The Philippine Army was based throughout the archipelago.

The Final Countdown

November 3, 1941: The Imperial Navy changed all its encryption codes. U.S. Navy intelligence experts warned this probably meant war was imminent.

November 14: Secretary of State Cordell Hull rejected a Japanese proposal that a limited withdrawal from China be met with an American promise to normalize relations.

November 15: Army and navy signals intelligence teams able to read Japanese diplomatic and naval ciphers decoded an order to the Japanese consul in Honolulu to report twice a week on the status of naval warships in Pearl Harbor.

November 16: The Japanese foreign ministry cabled ambassador to the United States Kichisaburo Nomura: "Fate of the Empire hangs by a sheer thread ... please fight harder!"

November 20: Ambassador Nomura presented to Secretary of State Hull an "absolutely final" Japanese proposal asking for the sale of one million gallons of aviation fuel from any source in return for a pledge to suspend military operations in China.

November 22: Army and navy codebreakers deciphered a message from Japan to Ambassador Nomura that he had until November 29 to reach an understanding with the United States. After that, "things are automatically going to happen."

November 24: Chief of Naval Operations Harold Stark warned naval forces in the Pacific to expect "surprise and aggressive movements" by Japan.

November 26: Various intelligence sources noted that a large Japanese convoy, apparently including troopships, had sailed from Formosa in the direction of southern French Indochina. On the basis of these sightings, which clearly indicated a warlike intention, Secretary of State Hull rejected the "absolutely final" Japanese peace proposal.

November 27: Army and navy intelligence teams feverishly working through a backlog of Japanese cable traffic issued an urgent warning to all American commands in the Pacific: "Negotiations with Japan appear terminated." The Pacific Fleet commander-in-chief, Adm. Husband Kimmel, was additionally warned: "This dispatch is to be considered a war warning. . . . Aggressive action expected by Japan in the next few days."

The Forlorn Hope

As a means—a forlorn hope—to deter Japan from sliding all the way into war, the Air Corps had plans to have at least 165 B-17s and 240 P-40s in the Philippines by early 1942. But, while many modern warplanes had reached Luzon airfields in the latter half of 1941, most that had been allotted to the Philippines had not even been built yet or simply could not be transferred from other critical locales. The latest flight of thirteen B-17s left California for Hawaii en route to Luzon on the evening of December 6 (California time), and fifty-two A-24 single-engine attack bombers and eighteen P-40s were on the way by sea with 2,500 Air Corps personnel, fuel, bombs, and machine gun ammunition.

Two thousand ground troops on the way to the Philippines by ocean convoy on the morning of December 8 included two field artillery regiments equipped with forty-eight 75mm guns and forty new 105mm howitzers. Equipment on the way included 340 motor vehicles, and supplies included 3.5 million rounds of ammunition. More troops, equipment, and goods were being marshaled on the West Coast for early shipment and yet more had been ordered to get moving toward West Coast ports. The 34th Infantry Regiment was in motion toward the port of San Francisco for shipment to Manila. . . .

Afterword

A T ALMOST THE LAST MOMENT OF PEACE, after Japan had thrown the dice but before they landed, Adm. Harold Stark is reported to have said to Ambassador Kichisaburo Nomura, himself a retired admiral:

> If you attack us we will break your empire before we are through with you. While you may have initial success due to timing and surprise, the time will come when you too will have your losses, but there will be this great difference. You will not only be unable to make up your losses but will grow weaker as time goes on; while on the other hand we will not only make up our losses but will grow stronger as time goes on. It is inevitable that we shall crush you before we are through with you.

Consider for a moment how low the United States might—would surely—have been laid in December 1941 and well into 1942 had Franklin Delano Roosevelt not called together his brain trust to hear the proposition he set forth on November 14, 1938. For that is the date on which the United States of America set her first true step out on the long and bloody road to save herself and a very large part of the world from the callous hands of Nazi thugs and Japanese mercantile militarists. And not being quite ready in a particular month or year selected by the enemy in no way detracts from the singular and historical accomplishment that came to pass.

If any detractor ever mentions the early failure of timing and the deaths of Britons, Canadians, Chinese, or Soviets while the United States dithered on the sidelines in 1940 and 1941, ask him to imagine what the world might look like had Americans not sacrificed so much of their own blood and treasure in the early months of the Pacific War so that American-made arms and goods—that American soldiers, sailors, airmen, Coast Guardsmen, and Marines could have used in 1942—could be transferred, free of charge, to Britain, Canada, China, the Soviet Union, Free France, and even Turkey, not just in 1939, 1940, and 1941, but in many cases on into the next decade, and then into the next, and the next. . . .

Given the nature of the world after September 1939, and the United States' involvement on the side it naturally fell on, it must be said, it can only be said, that America and Americans did the very best they could possibly have done with what they had in the time they had. And that is a legacy worth honoring.

✳

The title of this book is *How America Saved the World*. This is a bold statement. Is it the truth? Did America *really* save the world?

Through 1940 and 1941, as this book amply covers, a partnership based on true friendship and shared values developed exponentially between the United States and Britain. Before the United States was forcibly enlisted in World War II it provided the Royal Navy with five dozen convoy escorts and dedicated many of its own ships and long-range aircraft to escorting and supporting British-bound convoys between Canada and Iceland. A U.S. Marine brigade freed for better use a division-size British force guarding Iceland. It is quite likely that on December 7, 1941, there were more American-built aircraft in service with British and Commonwealth air forces than there were on U.S. Army Air Forces rosters.

Look beyond the last page of this book. By the end of November 1941, the British army in North Africa—on its only active front in the war against European fascism—was utterly stalemated in a battle of attrition it was bound to eventually lose. The war in the Western Desert ebbed and flowed back and forth across the Egyptian-Libyan frontier until the vast British counterattack at El Alamein was undertaken in mid 1942 with the aid of weapons and equipment made in America, not to mention American-manned combat aircraft. In November 1942, the fate of Axis forces in North Africa was sealed when an army composed mainly of Americans, supplied mainly by American industry, and lifted mainly by American ships invaded French Northwest Africa.

In the Pacific, Japan went to war against the United States as a means to secure Dutch oil in the East Indies and British natural resources in Malaya, then on to Burma, from which eastern India could be threatened. British, Dutch, Australian, and American forces were defeated at every turn through April 1942, yet American fighter aircraft and bombers helped Australian forces to stall Japanese forces in front of Port Moresby, New Guinea. In May, at the Battle of the Coral Sea, American carrier bombers turned back a Japanese invasion convoy bound for Port Moresby. In June, American carrier bombers sank four Japanese fleet carriers at Midway. In August, a U.S. Marine division invaded Guadalcanal, which became a sinkhole for Japanese aircraft and ships in a campaign through which the Pacific War was ultimately decided in America's favor. In September, a former National Guard infantry division went on the offensive near Port Moresby. By the end of 1942, after just one year of American participation, Japan had been turned back in the Pacific and Nazi Germany's war effort in the west was on the brink of decline.

If the Allied victory in World War II literally saved the world from German and Japanese hegemony, and if American industry and American armed forces turned the tide and saved the Allied cause, then, yes, it follows that America saved the world. This assertion in no way dishonors the millions of European and Asian Allied soldiers, sailors, and airmen who died in the mammoth event we call World War II. All it says is that an America well on its way on December 7,

1941, to building a world-class war machine was able to use that machine and share the vast wealth of arms that sprang from it to provide the margin between defeat or stalemate and pure, unadulterated victory. There is no way the United States alone could have defeated both Germany and Japan in a forty-five-month span, but there is also no way the Allies could have defeated Japan and Germany in *any* amount of time without the complete backing of American farms and factories, nor without the direct intervention of millions of America's sons.

Appendix A

Armies, Corps, Divisions, and Independent Infantry Regiments of the U.S. Army

Armies

First Army: Activated on October 1, 1933, at Fort Jay, New York, to oversee army commands and units in the northeastern United States.

Second Army: Activated on October 1, 1933, to oversee army commands and units in the midwestern United States.

Third Army: Activated on October 1, 1933, at Fort Sam Houston, Texas, to oversee army commands and units in the southeastern United States.

Fourth Army: Activated on October 1, 1933, at Omaha, Nebraska, to oversee army commands and units in the western United States. Transferred to the Presidio of San Francisco in 1936.

Corps

I Corps: Reactivated November 1, 1940, in Columbia, South Carolina.

I Armored Corps: Activated July 15, 1940, at Fort Knox, Kentucky.

II Corps: Reactivated August 1, 1940, at Fort Jay, New York.

III Corps: Reactivated December 18, 1940, at the Presidio of Monterey, California.

IV Corps: Reactivated October 20, 1939, at Fort Benning, Georgia.

V Corps: Reactivated October 20, 1940, at Camp Beauregard, Louisiana.

VI Corps: Reactivated August 3, 1940, at Fort Sheridan, Illinois.

VII Corps: Reactivated November 25, 1940, at Fort McClellan, Alabama.

VIII Corps: Reactivated October 15, 1940, at Fort Sam Houston, Texas.

IX Corps: Reactivated October 24, 1940, at Fort Lewis, Washington.

Infantry Divisions

Following is a list of U.S. Army combat divisions in existence, called to national service, or activated between September 1, 1939, and November 30, 1941. The infantry divisions were not labeled as infantry divisions until early 1942.

Regular Army

1st Infantry Division: Stationed at Fort Hamilton, New York, as 1st Division. Moved to Fort Devens, Massachusetts, in February 1941. Composed in 1941 of the 16th, 18th, and 26th Infantry regiments, three 105mm field artillery battalions, one 155mm field artillery battalion, one engineer battalion, one reconnaissance company, and various service and support units attached to the division headquarters.

2d Infantry Division: Stationed at Fort Sam Houston, Texas, as 2d Division. Composed in 1941 of the 9th, 23d, and 38th Infantry regiments, three 105mm field artillery battalions, one 155mm field artillery battalion, one engineer battalion, one cavalry reconnaissance troop, and various service and support units attached to the division headquarters.

3d Infantry Division: Stationed at Fort Lewis, Washington, as 3d Division. Composed in 1941 of the 7th, 15th, and 30th Infantry regiments, three 105mm field artillery battalions, one 155mm field artillery battalion, one provisional antitank battalion, one engineer battalion, one cavalry reconnaissance troop, and various service and support units attached to the division headquarters.

4th Infantry Division: Activated June 1, 1940, at Fort Benning, Georgia, as 4th Division. Reorganized as 4th Division (Motorized) on August 1, 1940, and as 4th Motorized Division on July 11, 1941. Initially composed of the 8th and 22d Infantry regiments (later redesignated motorized), three 105mm field artillery battalions, one 155mm field artillery battalion, one engineer battalion, one cavalry reconnaissance troop, and various service and support units attached to the division headquarters. The 12th Infantry Regiment was assigned from the 8th Division in October 1941 and subsequently motorized.

5th Infantry Division: Activated October 16, 1939, at Fort McClellan, Alabama, as 5th Division. Moved to Fort Benning, Georgia, in April 1940 and to Fort Custer, Michigan, in December 1940. Composed in 1941 of the 2d, 10th, and 11th Infantry regiments, three 105mm field artillery battalions, one 155mm field artillery battalion, one cavalry reconnaissance troop, and various service and support units attached to the division headquarters.

6th Infantry Division: Activated October 10, 1939, at Fort Lewis, Washington, as 6th Division. Moved to Fort Jackson, South Carolina, in November 1939; Fort Benning, Georgia, in April 1940; Alexandria, Louisiana, in May 1940; Fort Snelling, Minnesota, in June 1940; and

Fort Leonard Wood, Kansas, in October 1941. Composed in early 1941 of the 1st and 20th Infantry regiments, three 105mm field artillery battalions, one 155mm field artillery battalion, one engineer battalion, one cavalry reconnaissance troop, and various service and support units attached to the division headquarters. The 63d Infantry regiment was activated at Fort Leonard Wood and assigned in June 1941.

7th Infantry Division: Activated July 1, 1940, at Fort Ord, California, as 7th Division. Composed in 1941 of the 17th, 32d, and 53d Infantry regiments, three 105mm field artillery battalions, one 155mm field artillery battalion, one engineer battalion, one cavalry reconnaissance troop, and various service and support units attached to the division headquarters. The 53d Infantry Regiment was replaced by the 159th Infantry Regiment (California National Guard) in November 1941.

8th Infantry Division: Activated July 1, 1940, at Camp Jackson, South Carolina, as 8th Division and redesignated 8th Infantry Division in July 1941. Composed in 1941 of the 13th, 28th, and 34th Infantry regiments, three 105mm field artillery battalions, one 155mm field artillery battalion, one engineer battalion, one cavalry reconnaissance troop, and various service and support units attached to the division headquarters.

9th Infantry Division: Activated August 1, 1940, at Fort Bragg, North Carolina, as 9th Division. Composed in 1941 of the 39th, 47th, and 60th Infantry regiments, three 105mm field artillery battalions, one 155mm field artillery battalion, one engineer battalion, one cavalry reconnaissance troop, and various service and support units attached to the division headquarters.

24th Infantry Division: Stationed at Schofield Barracks, Hawaii, as the Hawaiian Division until redesignated 24th Infantry Division on October 1, 1941. Composed in 1941 of the 19th, 21st, and 299th Infantry regiments, three 105mm field artillery battalions, one 155mm field artillery battalion, one engineer combat battalion, one cavalry reconnaissance troop, and various service and support units attached to the division headquarters.

25th Infantry Division: Activated October 1, 1941, at Schofield Barracks, Hawaii. Initially composed of the 27th, 35th, and 298th Infantry regiments, three 105mm field artillery battalions, one 155mm field artillery battalion, one engineer battalion, one cavalry reconnaissance troop, and various service and support units attached to the division headquarters.

National Guard

When called to federal service, each National Guard infantry division fielded two infantry brigades of two infantry regiments each. One infantry regiment was transferred from each division, and the brigade headquarters were deactivated in early 1942.

26th Infantry Division: Massachusetts National Guard formation inducted into federal service at Boston, Massachusetts, on January 16, 1941. Based at Fort Edwards, Massachusetts. Initially composed of the 101st, 104th, 181st, and 182d Infantry regiments, two 75mm field artillery regiments, one 155mm artillery regiment, one engineer combat battalion, and various service and support units attached to the division headquarters.

27th Infantry Division: New York National Guard formation inducted into federal service at New York City on October 15, 1940. Based at Fort McClellan, Alabama. Initially composed of the 105th, 106th, 108th, and 165th Infantry regiments, two 75mm field artillery regiments, one 155mm artillery regiment, one engineer combat battalion, and various service and support units attached to the division headquarters.

28th Infantry Division: Pennsylvania National Guard formation inducted into federal service at Philadelphia, Pennsylvania, on February 17, 1941. Based at Indiantown Gap Military Reservation, Pennsylvania. Initially composed of the 109th, 110th, 111th, and 112th Infantry regiments, two 75mm field artillery regiments, one 155mm artillery regiment, one engineer combat battalion, and various service and support units attached to the division headquarters.

29th Infantry Division: Virginia, Maryland, District of Columbia, and Pennsylvania National Guard formation inducted into federal service at Washington, D.C., on February 3, 1941. Based at Fort Meade, Maryland. Initially composed of the 115th, 116th, 175th, and 176th Infantry regiments, two 75mm field artillery regiments, one 155mm artillery regiment, one engineer combat battalion, and various service and support units attached to the division headquarters.

30th Infantry Division: North Carolina, South Carolina, Tennessee, and Georgia National Guard formation inducted into federal service at Fort Jackson, South Carolina, on September 16, 1940. Based at Fort Jackson, South Carolina. Initially composed of the 117th, 118th, 120th, and 121st Infantry regiments, two 75mm field artillery regiments, one 155mm artillery regiment, one engineer combat battalion, and various service and support units attached to the division headquarters.

31st Infantry Division: Alabama, Florida, Louisiana, and Mississippi National Guard formation inducted into federal service at Birmingham, Alabama, on November 25, 1940. Based at Camp Blanding, Florida. Initially composed of the 124th, 155th, 156th, and 167th Infantry regiments, two 75mm field artillery regiments, one 155mm artillery regiment, one engineer combat battalion, and various service and support units attached to the division headquarters.

32d Infantry Division: Michigan and Wisconsin National Guard formation inducted into federal service at Lansing, Michigan, on October 15, 1940.

Based at Camp Beauregard Louisiana, in October 1940, and moved to Camp Livingston, Louisiana, in February 1941. Initially composed of the 125th, 126th, 127th, and 128th Infantry regiments, two 75mm field artillery regiments, one 155mm artillery regiment, one engineer combat battalion, and various service and support units attached to the division headquarters.

33d Infantry Division: Illinois National Guard formation inducted into federal service at Chicago on March 5, 1941. Based at Camp Forrest, Tennessee. Initially composed of the 129th, 130th, 131st, and 132d Infantry regiments, two 75mm field artillery regiments, one 155mm artillery regiment, one engineer combat battalion, and various service and support units attached to the division headquarters.

34th Infantry Division: Iowa, Minnesota, North Dakota, and South Dakota National Guard formation inducted into federal service at Council Bluffs, Iowa, on February 10, 1941. Based at Camp Claiborne, Louisiana. Initially composed of the 133d, 135th, 164th, and 168th Infantry regiments, two 75mm field artillery regiments, one 155mm artillery regiment, one engineer combat battalion, and various service and support units attached to the division headquarters.

35th Infantry Division: Kansas, Missouri, and Nebraska National Guard formation inducted into federal service at Lincoln, Nebraska, on December 23, 1940. Based at Camp Joseph T. Robinson, Arkansas. Initially composed of the 134th, 137th, 138th, and 140th Infantry regiments, two 75mm field artillery regiments, one 155mm artillery regiment, one engineer combat battalion, and various service and support units attached to the division headquarters.

36th Infantry Division: Texas National Guard formation inducted into federal service at San Antonio, Texas, on November 25, 1940. Based at Camp Bowie, Texas. Initially composed of the 141st, 142d, 143d, and 144th Infantry regiments, two 75mm field artillery regiments, one 155mm artillery regiment, one engineer combat battalion, and various service and support units attached to the division headquarters.

37th Infantry Division: Ohio National Guard formation inducted into federal service at Fort Jackson, South Carolina, on October 15, 1940. Based at Camp Shelby, Mississippi. Initially composed of the 145th, 147th, 148th, and 166th Infantry regiments, two 75mm field artillery regiments, one 155mm artillery regiment, one engineer combat battalion, and various service and support units attached to the division headquarters.

38th Infantry Division: Indiana, Kentucky, and West Virginia National Guard formation inducted into federal service at Indianapolis on January 17, 1941. Based at Camp Shelby, Mississippi. Initially composed of the 149th, 150th, 151st, and 152d Infantry regiments, two 75mm field artillery regiments, one 155mm artillery regiment, one engineer combat battalion, and various service and support units attached to the division headquarters.

40th Infantry Division: California, Nevada, and Utah National Guard formation inducted into federal service at Los Angeles on March 3, 1941. Based at Camp San Luis Obispo, California. Initially composed of the 159th, 160th, 184th, and 185th Infantry regiments, two 75mm field artillery regiments, one 155mm artillery regiment, one engineer combat battalion, and various service and support units attached to the division headquarters. The 159th Infantry Regiment was reassigned to the 7th Infantry Division in November 1941.

41st Infantry Division: Idaho, Montana, Oregon, and Washington National Guard formation inducted into federal service at Portland, Oregon, on September 16, 1940. Based at Camp Murray, Washington, until moved to Fort Lewis, Washington, in March 1941. Initially composed of the 161st, 162d, 163d, and 186th Infantry regiments, two 75mm field artillery regiments, one 155mm artillery regiment, one engineer combat battalion, and various service and support units attached to the division headquarters.

43d Infantry Division: Connecticut, Maine, Rhode Island, and Vermont National Guard formation inducted into federal service at Hartford, Connecticut, on February 24, 1941. Based at Camp Blanding, Florida. Initially composed of the 102d, 103d, 169th, and 172d Infantry regiments, two 75mm field artillery regiments, one 155mm artillery regiment, one engineer combat battalion, and various service and support units attached to the division headquarters.

44th Infantry Division: New Jersey and New York National Guard formation inducted into federal service at Trenton, New Jersey, on September 16, 1940. Based at Fort Dix, New Jersey. Initially composed of the 71st, 113th, 114th, and 174th Infantry regiments, two 75mm field artillery regiments, one 155mm artillery regiment, one engineer combat battalion, and various service and support units attached to the division headquarters.

45th Infantry Division: Arizona, Colorado, New Mexico, and Oklahoma National Guard formation inducted into federal service at Oklahoma City on September 16, 1940. Based at Fort Sill, Oklahoma, until moved to Camp Barkley, Texas, in February 1941. Initially composed of the 157th, 158th, 179th, and 180th Infantry regiments, two 75mm field artillery regiments, one 155mm artillery regiment, one engineer combat battalion, and various service and support units attached to the division headquarters.

Philippine Division: Headquartered at Fort McKinley, Luzon. Composed of the 31st Infantry Regiment, the 45th Infantry Regiment (Philippine Scouts), 57th Infantry Regiment (Philippine Scouts), three Philippine Scout artillery battalions, one Philippine Scout engineer battalion, and various Philippine Scouts service and support units attached to the division headquarters.

Armored Divisions

1st Armored Division: Activated July 15, 1940, at Fort Knox, Kentucky, with the redesignation of the 7th Cavalry Brigade. Initially composed of the 1st (Light), 13th (Light), and 69th (Medium) Armored regiments, the 6th Infantry Regiment (Armored), one armored field artillery regiment plus one armored field artillery battalion, one armored cavalry reconnaissance battalion, one armored engineer battalion, and various service and support units attached to the division headquarters.

2d Armored Division: Activated July 15, 1940, at Fort Benning, Georgia. Initially composed of the 66th (Light), 67th (Medium), and 68th (Light) Armored regiments, the 41st Infantry Regiment (Armored), one armored field artillery regiment plus one armored field artillery battalion, one armored cavalry reconnaissance battalion, one armored engineer battalion, and various service and support units attached to the division headquarters.

3d Armored Division: Activated April 15, 1941, at Camp Beauregard, Louisiana. Initially composed of the 3d (Light), 33d (Light), and 40th (Medium) Armored regiments, the 36th Infantry Regiment (Armored), one armored field artillery regiment plus one armored field artillery battalion, one armored cavalry reconnaissance battalion, one armored engineer battalion, and various service and support units attached to the division headquarters.

4th Armored Division: Activated April 15, 1941, at Pine Camp, New York. Initially composed of the 35th (Light), 37th (Light), and 80th (Medium) Armored regiments, the 51st Infantry Regiment (Armored), one armored field artillery regiment plus one armored field artillery battalion, one armored cavalry reconnaissance battalion, one armored engineer battalion, and various service and support units attached to the division headquarters.

5th Armored Division: Activated October 1, 1941, at Fort Knox, Kentucky. Initially composed of the 31st (Light), 34th (Light), and 81st (Medium) Amored regiments, the 46th Infantry Regiment (Armored), one armored field artillery regiment plus one armored field artillery battalion, one armored cavalry reconnaissance battalion, one armored engineer battalion, and various service and support units attached to the division headquarters.

Cavalry Divisions

1st Cavalry Division: Stationed at Fort Bliss, Texas. Initially composed of the 1st and 2d Cavalry Brigade headquarters and the 5th, 7th, 8th, and 12th Cavalry regiments, two horse-drawn 75mm field artillery battalions, one truck-drawn 105mm field artillery battalion, one cavalry reconnaissance squadron, one engineer squadron, and various service and support units attached to the division headquarters.

2d Cavalry Division (Horse): Activated April 1, 1941, at Fort Riley, Kansas. Composed of 3d and 4th (Colored) Cavalry Brigade headquarters and the 2d, 9th (Colored), 10th (Colored), and 14th Cavalry regiments, two 75mm field artillery battalions, one cavalry reconnaissance squadron, one motorized engineer squadron, and various service and support units attached to the division headquarters. This command was never deployed overseas; it was inactivated on July 15, 1942.

Separate and Independent Infantry Regiments

Following is a list of separate and independent U.S. Army regiments in existence, called to federal service, or activated between September 1, 1939, and November 30, 1941.

3d Infantry Regiment: Assigned to the 6th Division between October 1939 and May 1940. 3d Battalion transferred to St. John's, Newfoundland, in January 1941, where it was joined by the rest of the regiment in July 1942.

4th Infantry Regiment: Assigned to the 3d Division until May 1940, and transferred to the Alaskan Defense Command in January 1941.

5th Infantry Regiment: Assigned to the 9th Division until transferred to the Panama Canal Zone in November 1939.

11th Infantry Regiment: Assigned to the 5th Division, but two companies were transferred to Bermuda and Trinidad in April 1941.

13th Infantry Regiment: Assigned to the 9th Division until transferred to the Panama Canal Zone in October 1939. Disbanded in June 1940, and then reactivated as part of the 8th Division.

14th Infantry Regiment: Assigned to the Panama Canal Zone.

19th Infantry Regiment: Assigned to the Hawaiian Division, then to the 24th Infantry Division when it was activated in October 1941.

21st Infantry Regiment: Assigned to the Hawaiian Division, then to the 24th Infantry Division when it was activated in October 1941.

24th Infantry Regiment (Colored): Stationed at Fort Benning, Georgia.

25th Infantry Regiment (Colored): Assigned directly to Third Army and stationed at Fort Huachuca, Arizona.

27th Infantry Regiment: Assigned to the Hawaiian Division until reassigned to the 25th Infantry Division in August 1941.

29th Infantry Regiment: Assigned to the 4th Division until separated in October 1939, and stationed at Fort Benning, Georgia.

31st Infantry Regiment: Assigned to the Philippine Division.

33d Infantry Regiment: Assigned to the Panama Canal Zone.

34th Infantry Regiment: Assigned to the 8th Division until inactivated in June 1940. Reactivated in July 1940, trained with the 8th Division, and reassigned to Schofield Barracks, Hawaii, in December 1941.

35th Infantry Regiment: Assigned to the Hawaiian Division until reassigned to the 25th Infantry Division in August 1941.

37th Infantry Regiment: Activated at Fort Warren, Wyoming, in March 1941 and transferred to Fort Greely, Alaska, in July 1941.

43d Infantry Regiment (Philippine Scouts): Activated on Luzon and Mindanao in April 1941.

53d Infantry Regiment: Activated at Fort Ord, California, in August 1940, and assigned to the 7th Division until separated and transferred to Sacramento, California, in November 1941.

65th Infantry Regiment (Puerto Rican): Stationed in Puerto Rico.

89th Infantry Regiment: Partially activated a few companies at a time at various posts between January 1941 and October 1941. Companies of the 3d Battalion were stationed on Bermuda and Jamaica under the Antilles Command.

295th Infantry Regiment: Puerto Rico National Guard formation inducted into federal service at Camp Tortuguero, Puerto Rico, on October 15, 1940. Assigned to the Caribbean Defense Command on September 26, 1941.

296th Infantry Regiment: Puerto Rico National Guard formation inducted into federal service at Camp Tortuguero, Puerto Rico, on October 15, 1940. Assigned to the Panama Mobile Force but retained in Puerto Rico.

297th Infantry Regiment: Alaska National Guard formation. Its 1st Battalion was inducted into federal service at Juneau, Alaska, on September 15, 1941, and transferred to Fort Richardson, Alaska.

298th Infantry Regiment: Hawaii National Guard formation inducted into federal service at Honolulu, Hawaii, on October 15, 1940. Assigned to the 25th Infantry Division on October 1, 1941.

299th Infantry Regiment: Hawaii National Guard formation inducted into federal service at Honolulu, Hawaii, on October 15, 1940. Assigned to the 24th Infantry Division on October 1, 1941.

367th Infantry Regiment (Colored): Activated at Camp Claiborne, Louisiana, on March 25, 1941.

368th Infantry Regiment (Colored): Activated at Fort Huachuca, Arizona, on March 1, 1941.

372d Infantry Regiment (Colored): District of Columbia, Maryland, Massachusetts, New Jersey, and Ohio National Guard formation inducted into federal service at various locations on March 10, 1941. Based at Fort Dix, New Jersey.

434th Infantry Regiment: Headquarters and three infantry companies activated at Fort Jackson, South Carolina, on June 21, 1941. Transferred to British West Indies.

Appendix B

U.S. Army Air Corps Commands and Units

Following is a list of U.S. Army Air Corps commands and units in existence or activated between September 1, 1939, and November 30, 1941.

Air Forces and Districts

First Air Force: Constituted as Northeast Air District on October 19, 1940, and activated on December 18, 1940, at Mitchel Field, New York. Redesignated First Air Force in early 1941.

Second Air Force: Constituted as Northwest Air District on October 19, 1940. Activated December 18, 1940, at McChord Field, Washington. Redesignated Second Air Force in early 1941. Transferred to Fort George Wright, Washington, on January 9, 1941.

Third Air Force: Constituted as Southeast Air District on October 19, 1940. Activated on December 18, 1940, at MacDill Field, Florida. Redesignated Third Air Force in early 1941. Transferred to Tampa, Florida, in January 1941.

Fourth Air Force: Constituted as Southwest Air District on October 19, 1940. Activated on December 18, 1940, at March Field, California. Transferred to Riverside, California, on January 16, 1941.

Hawaiian Air Force: Constituted on October 19, 1940, and activated on November 1, 1940, at Fort Shafter, Hawaii. (Later redesignated Seventh Air Force.)

Panama Canal Air Force: Constituted on October 19, 1940, and activated on November 20, 1940, at Albrook Field, Panama Canal Zone. Redesignated Caribbean Air Force in August 1941. (Later redesignated Sixth Air Force.)

Philippine Department Air Force: Constituted on August 16, 1941, and activated on September 20, 1941, at Nichols Field, Luzon. Redesignated Far East Air Force in October 1941. (Later redesignated Fifth Air Force.)

Commands

I Bomber Command: Constituted on September 4, 1941, and activated as part of the First Air Force on September 5, 1941, at Langley Field, Virginia.

I Interceptor Command: Constituted on May 26, 1941, and activated as part of the First Air Force on June 5, 1941, at Mitchel Field, New York.

II Air Support Command: Constituted on August 21, 1941, and activated as part of the Second Air Force on September 1, 1941, at Fort Douglas, Utah. Transferred to Will Rogers Field, Oklahoma, in October 1941.

II Bomber Command: Constituted on September 4, 1941, and activated as part of the Second Air Force on September 5, 1941, at Fort George Wright, Washington.

II Interceptor Command: Constituted on May 26, 1941, and activated as part of the Second Air Force on June 4, 1941, at Fort George Wright, Washington. Transferred to Fort Lawton, Washington, on June 19, 1941.

III Air Support Command: Constituted on August 21, 1941, and activated as part of the Third Air Force on September 1, 1941, at Savannah Air Base, Georgia.

III Bomber Command: Constituted on September 4, 1941, and activated as part of the Third Air Force on September 5, 1941, at Drew Field, Florida. Transferred to MacDill Field, Florida, in September 1941.

III Interceptor Command: Constituted on May 26, 1941, and activated as part of the Third Air Force in June or July 1941 at Drew Field, Florida.

III Reconnaissance Command: Constituted on August 21, 1941, and activated on September 1, 1941, at Mitchel Field, New York.

IV Air Support Command: Constituted on August 21, 1941, and activated as part of the Fourth Air Force on September 3, 1941, at Fresno, California. Transferred to Hamilton Field, California, on September 11, 1941.

IV Bomber Command: Constituted on September 4, 1941, and activated as part of the Fourth Air Force on September 19, 1941, at Tucson, Arizona.

IV Interceptor Command: Constituted on May 26, 1941, and activated as part of the Fourth Air Force at March Field, California, on July 8, 1941.

V Bomber Command: Constituted on October 28, 1941, and activated as part of the Philippine Department Air Force on November 14, 1941, at Clark Field, Luzon.

VI Bomber Command: Constituted on October 17, 1941, and activated as part of the Panama Canal Air Force on October 25, 1941, at Albrook Field, Panama Canal Zone.

VI Interceptor Command: Constituted on October 17, 1941, and activated at Borinquen Field, Puerto Rico, on October 25, 1941.

Wings

1st Bombardment Wing: Old-line GHQ Air Force command redesignated 1st Bombardment Wing in 1940 while based at March Field, California. Transferred to Tucson, Arizona, on May 27, 1941.

2d Bombardment Wing: Old-line GHQ Air Force command redesignated 2d Bombardment Wing in 1940 while based at Langley Field, Virginia. Transferred to Detrick Field, Maryland on June 7, 1941. Inactivated September 5, 1941.

3d Bombardment Wing: Old-line GHQ Air Force command redesignated 3d Bombardment Wing in 1940 while based at MacDill Field, Florida. Inactivated September 1941.

4th Bombardment Wing: Constituted on October 19, 1940, and activated on December 18, 1940, at Mitchel Field, New York. Transferred to Westover Field, Massachusetts, on March 20, 1940. Inactivated October 1, 1941.

5th Bombardment Wing: Constituted on October 19, 1940, and activated on December 18, 1940, at McChord Field, Washington. Transferred to Fort George Wright, Washington, on January 9, 1940. Inactivated September 5, 1941.

6th Pursuit Wing: Constituted on October 19, 1940, and activated on December 18, 1940, at Selfridge Field, Michigan. Inactivated December 7, 1941.

7th Pursuit Wing: Constituted on October 19, 1940, and activated on December 18, 1940, at Mitchel Field, New York. Inactivated August 31, 1941.

8th Pursuit Wing: Constituted on October 19, 1940, and activated on November 6, 1940, at Maxwell Field, Alabama. Transferred to Morrison Field, Florida, on May 16, 1940. Inactivated November 1, 1941.

9th Pursuit Wing: Constituted on October 19, 1940, and activated on December 18, 1940, at March Field, California. Inactivated December 7, 1941.

10th Pursuit Wing: Constituted on October 19, 1940, and activated on December 18, 1940, at Hamilton Field, California. Inactivated December 7, 1941.

11th Pursuit Wing: Constituted on October 19, 1940, and activated on December 18, 1940, at Hamilton Field, California. Transferred to Portland, Oregon, on June 1, 1940. Inactivated October 1, 1941.

12th Bombardment Wing: Constituted on October 19, 1940, and activated on November 20, 1940, at Albrook Field, Panama Canal Zone.

13th Composite Wing: Constituted on October 2, 1940, and activated on October 10, 1940, at Langley Field, Virginia. Transferred to Borinquen Field, Puerto Rico, on November 1, 1940; to San Juan, Puerto Rico, in January 1941; and to MacDill Field, Florida, on October 1, 1941. Inactivated October 25, 1941.

14th Bombardment Wing: Constituted on October 19, 1940, and activated on November 1, 1940, at Wheeler Field, Hawaii.

15th Bombardment Wing: Constituted on October 19, 1940, and activated on December 18, 1940, at March Field, California. Transferred to Fresno, California, in August 1941. Inactivated September 3, 1941.

16th Bombardment Wing: Constituted on October 19, 1940, and activated on December 18, 1940, at Langley Field, Virginia. Transferred to Bowman Field, Kentucky, in March 1940. Inactivated September 1, 1941.

17th Bombardment Wing: Constituted on October 3, 1940, and activated on December 18, 1940, at Savannah, Georgia. Inactivated September 1, 1941.

18th Bombardment Wing: Old-line command based at Hickam Field, Hawaii.

19th Bombardment Wing: Old-line command based at Albrook Field, Panama Canal Zone. Inactivated on October 25, 1941.

20th Bombardment Wing: Constituted on October 19, 1940, and activated on December 18, 1940, at Fort Douglas, Utah. Inactivated September 1, 1941.

50th Transport Wing: Constituted on January 8, 1941, and activated on January 14, 1941, at Wright Field, Ohio, under the Office of the Chief of the Air Corps.

Groups

1st Pursuit Group: Old-line unit based at Selfridge Field, Michigan.

1st Photographic Group: Constituted on May 15, 1941, and activated at Bolling Field, District of Columbia, on June 10, 1941.

2d Bombardment Group (Heavy): Old-line unit based at Langley Field, Virginia.

3d Bombardment Group (Light): Old-line unit based at Barksdale Field, Louisiana, and transferred on October 6, 1940, to Savannah, Georgia.

5th Bombardment Group: Old-line unit based at Hickam Field, Hawaii. Designated 5th Bombardment Group (Medium) in December 1939 and 5th Bombardment Group (Heavy) in November 1940.

6th Bombardment Group: Old-line unit based at France Field, Panama Canal Zone. Designated 6th Bombardment Group (Medium) in 1939 and 6th Bombardment Group (Heavy) in 1940.

7th Bombardment Group (Heavy): Old-line unit based at Fort Douglas, Utah, until November 13, 1941. Was in the process of transferring to the Philippines via Hawaii on December 7, 1941.

8th Pursuit Group: Old-line unit based at Langley Field, Virginia. Transferred to Mitchel Field, New York, in November 1940.

9th Bombardment Group: Old-line unit based at Mitchel Field, New York. Transferred to Rio Hato, Panama, on November 12, 1940, and Waller Field, Trinidad, on October 30, 1941. Designated 9th Bombardment Group (Medium) in 1939 and 9th Bombardment Group (Heavy) in 1940.

10th Transport Group: Activated in 1937 under Office of the Chief of the Air Corps and transferred to the Air Service Command in 1941. Based at Wright Field, Ohio, in 1939 and transferred to Patterson Field, Ohio, on January 17, 1941.

11th Bombardment Group: Activated on February 1, 1940, at Hickam Field, Hawaii, as the 11th Bombardment Group (Medium). Redesignated later in 1940 as 11th Bombardment Group (Heavy).

12th Bombardment Group: Constituted at the 12th Bombardment Group (Light) on November 20, 1940, and activated on January 15, 1941, at McChord Field, Washington. Redesignated 12th Bombardment Group (Medium) in December 1941.

13th Bombardment Group (Medium): Constituted on November 20, 1940, and activated on January 15, 1941, at Langley Field, Virginia. Transferred to Orlando, Florida, in June 1941.

14th Pursuit Group: Constituted on November 20, 1940, and activated on January 15, 1941, at Hamilton Field, California. Transferred to March Field, California, in June 1941.

15th Pursuit Group: Constituted on November 20, 1940, and activated on December 1, 1940, at Wheeler Field, Hawaii.

16th Pursuit Group: Old-line unit based at Albrook Field, Panama Canal Zone.

17th Bombardment Group (Medium): Old-line unit based at March Field, California. Transferred to McChord Field, Washington, on June 24, 1940, and Pendleton, Oregon, on June 29, 1941.

18th Pursuit Group: Old-line unit based at Wheeler Field, Hawaii.

19th Bombardment Group (Heavy): Old-line unit based at March Field, California. Transferred to Albuquerque, New Mexico, on July 7, 1941, and to Clark Field, Luzon, on October 23, 1941.

20th Pursuit Group: Old-line unit based at Moffett Field, California. Transferred to Hamilton Field, California, in September 1940.

22d Bombardment Group (Medium): Constituted on December 22, 1939, and activated on February 1, 1940, at Mitchel Field, New York. Transferred to Langley Field, Virginia, on November 14, 1940.

24th Pursuit Group: Constituted on August 16, 1941, and activated at Clark Field, Luzon, on August 16, 1941.

25th Bombardment Group (Heavy): Constituted on December 22, 1939, and activated on February 1, 1940, at Langley Field, Virginia. Transferred to Borinquen Field, Puerto Rico, on November 1, 1940.

26th Observation Group: Constituted on August 21, 1941, and activated on September 1, 1941, at Fort Devens, Massachusetts, and transferred to Providence, Rhode Island.

27th Bombardment Group (Light): Constituted on December 22, 1939, and activated on February 1, 1940, at Barksdale Field, Louisiana. Transferred to Hunter Field, Georgia, on October 7, 1940, and to Manila, Luzon, on November 20, 1941.

28th Composite Group: Constituted on December 22, 1939, and activated on February 1, 1940, at March Field, California. Transferred to Moffett Field, California, on December 10, 1940, and to Elmendorf Field, Alaska, on February 23, 1941.

29th Bombardment Group (Heavy): Constituted on December 22, 1939, and activated on February 1, 1940, at Langley Field, Virginia. Transferred to MacDill Field, Florida, on May 21, 1940.

30th Bombardment Group (Heavy): Constituted on November 20, 1940, and activated on January 15, 1941, at March Field, California. Transferred to New Orleans, Louisiana, in June 1941.

31st Pursuit Group: Constituted on December 2, 1939, and activated on February 1, 1940, at Selfridge Field, Michigan. Transferred to Baer Field, Indiana, on December 6, 1941.

32d Pursuit Group: Constituted on November 22, 1940, and activated on January 1, 1941, at Rio Hato, Panama.

33d Pursuit Group: Constituted on November 20, 1940, and activated on January 15, 1941, at Mitchel Field, New York.

34th Bombardment Group (Heavy): Constituted on November 20, 1940, and activated on January 15, 1941, at Langley Field, Virginia. Transferred to Westover Field, Massachusetts, on May 29, 1941.

35th Pursuit Group: Constituted on December 22, 1939, and activated on February 1, 1940, at Moffett Field, California. Transferred to Hamilton Field, California, on September 10, 1940, and en route to Manila, Luzon, on December 7, 1941.

36th Pursuit Group: Constituted on December 22, 1939, and activated on February 1, 1940, at Langley Field, Virginia. Transferred to Losey Field, Puerto Rico, in January 1941.

37th Pursuit Group: Constituted on December 22, 1939, and activated on February 1, 1940, at Albrook Field, Panama Canal Zone.

38th Bombardment Group (Medium): Constituted on November 20, 1940, and activated on January 15, 1941, at Langley Field, Virginia. Transferred to Jackson Army Air Base, Mississippi, in June 1941.

39th Bombardment Group (Heavy): Constituted on November 20, 1940, and activated on January 15, 1941, at Fort Douglas, Utah. Transferred to Geiger Field, Washington, on July 2, 1941.

40th Bombardment Group (Medium): Constituted on November 22, 1940, and activated on April 1, 1941, at Borinquen Field, Puerto Rico.

41st Bombardment Group (Medium): Constituted on November 20, 1940, and activated on January 15, 1941, at March Field, California. Transferred to Tucson, Arizona, in May 1941.

42d Bombardment Group (Medium): Constituted on November 20, 1940, and activated on January 15, 1941, at Fort Douglas, Utah. Transferred to Boise, Idaho, in June 1941.

43d Bombardment Group (Heavy): Constituted on November 20, 1940, and activated on January 15, 1941, at Langley, Virginia. Transferred to Bangor, Maine, on August 28, 1941.

44th Bombardment Group (Heavy): Constituted on November 20, 1940, and activated on January 15, 1941, at MacDill Field, Florida.

45th Bombardment Group (Light): Constituted on November 20, 1940, and activated on January 15, 1941, at Savannah, Georgia. Transferred to Manchester, New Hampshire, on June 18, 1941.

46th Bombardment Group (Light): Constituted on November 20, 1940, and activated on January 15, 1941, at Savannah, Georgia. Transferred to Barksdale Field, Louisiana, on May 20, 1941.

47th Bombardment Group (Light): Constituted on November 20, 1940, and activated on January 15, 1941, at McChord Field, Washington. Transferred to Fresno, California, on August 14, 1941.

48th Bombardment Group (Light): Constituted on November 20, 1940, and activated on January 15, 1941, at Savannah, Georgia. Transferred to Will Rogers Field, Oklahoma, on May 22, 1941.

49th Pursuit Group: Constituted on November 20, 1940, and activated on January 15, 1941, at Selfridge Field, Michigan. Transferred to Morrison Field, Florida, on May 25, 1941.

50th Pursuit Group: Constituted on November 20, 1940, and activated on January 15, 1941, at Selfridge Field, Michigan. Transferred to Key Field, Mississippi, on October 3, 1941.

51st Pursuit Group: Constituted on November 20, 1940, and activated on January 15, 1941, at Hamilton Field, California. Transferred to March Field, California, on June 20, 1941.

52d Pursuit Group: Constituted on November 20, 1940, and activated on January 15, 1941, at Selfridge Field, Michigan.

53d Pursuit Group: Constituted on November 20, 1940, and activated on January 15, 1941, at MacDill Field, Florida. Transferred to Tallahassee, Florida, on May 8, 1941.

54th Pursuit Group: Constituted on November 20, 1940, and activated on January 15, 1941, at Hamilton Field, California. Transferred to Everett, Washington, on June 26, 1941.

55th Pursuit Group: Constituted on November 20, 1940, and activated on January 15, 1941, at Hamilton Field, California. Transferred to Portland, Oregon, on May 21, 1941.

56th Pursuit Group: Constituted on November 20, 1940, and activated on January 15, 1941, at Savannah, Georgia.

57th Pursuit Group: Constituted on November 20, 1940, and activated on January 15, 1941, at Mitchel Field, New York. Transferred to Windsor Locks, Connecticut, on August 19, 1941.

58th Pursuit Group: Constituted on November 20, 1940, and activated on January 15, 1941, at Selfridge Field, Michigan. Transferred to Baton Rouge, Louisiana, on October 5, 1941.

59th Observation Group: Constituted on August 21, 1941, and activated on September 1, 1941, at Newark, New Jersey. Transferred to Pope Field, North Carolina in October 1941.

60th Transport Group: Constituted on November 20, 1940, and activated on December 1, 1940, at Olmsted Field, Pennsylvania. Transferred to Westover Field, Massachusetts, in May 1941.

61st Transport Group: Constituted on November 20, 1940, and activated on December 1, 1940, at Olmsted Field, Pennsylvania. Transferred to Augusta, Georgia, in July 1941.

62d Transport Group: Constituted on November 20, 1940, and activated on December 11, 1940, at McClellan Field, California.

63d Transport Group: Constituted on November 20, 1940, and activated on December 1, 1940, at Wright Field, Ohio. Transferred to Patterson Field, Ohio, on February 17, 1941.

64th Transport Group: Constituted on November 20, 1940, and activated on December 4, 1940, at Duncan Field, Texas. Transferred to March Field, California, in July 1941.

65th Observation Group: Constituted on August 21, 1941, and activated on September 1, 1941, at Columbia, South Carolina.

66th Observation Group: Constituted on August 21, 1941, and activated on September 1, 1941, at Jacksonville, Florida.

67th Observation Group: Constituted on August 21, 1941, and activated on September 1, 1941, at Esler Field, Louisiana.

68th Observation Group: Constituted on August 21, 1941, and activated on September 1, 1941, at Brownwood, Texas.

69th Observation Group: Constituted on August 21, 1941, and activated on September 3, 1941, at Paso Robles, California. Transferred to Salinas, California, in October 1941.

70th Observation Group: Constituted on August 21, 1941, and activated on September 13, 1941, at Gray Field, Washington.

71st Observation Group: Constituted on August 21, 1941, and activated on October 1, 1941, at Birmingham, Alabama.

72d Observation Group: Constituted on August 21, 1941, and activated on September 26, 1941, at Shreveport, Louisiana. Transferred to Little Rock, Arkansas, in October 1941.

73d Observation Group: Constituted on August 21, 1941, and activated on September 1, 1941, at Harrisburg, Pennsylvania. Transferred to Godman Field, Kentucky, in November 1941

Note: In the U.S. Army command structure of the period, an air force was on a level comparable to a field army, a command to a corps, a wing to a division, and a group to a regiment.

U.S. Navy Capital Ships

Following is a list of U.S. Navy battleships, aircraft carriers, and cruisers in commission on December 6, 1941. (Listings are in numerical order of hull number.)

Battleships

		Commissioned		Main armament
Arkansas	(BB-33)	1912	*Wyoming*-class	twelve 12-inch
New York	(BB-34)	1914	*New York*-class	ten 14-inch
Texas	(BB-35)	1914	*New York*-class	ten 14-inch
Nevada	(BB-36)	1916	*Nevada*-class	ten 14-inch
Oklahoma	(BB-37)	1916	*Nevada*-class	ten 14-inch
Pennsylvania	(BB-38)	1916	*Pennsylvania*-class	twelve 14-inch
Arizona	(BB-39)	1916	*Pennsylvania*-class	twelve 14-inch
New Mexico	(BB-40)	1918	*New Mexico*-class	twelve 14-inch
Mississippi	(BB-41)	1917	*New Mexico*-class	twelve 14-inch
Idaho	(BB-42)	1919	*New Mexico*-class	twelve 14-inch
Tennessee	(BB-43)	1920	*Tennessee*-class	twelve 14-inch
California	(BB-44)	1921	*Tennessee*-class	twelve 14-inch
Colorado	(BB-45)	1923	*Colorado*-class	eight 16-inch
Maryland	(BB-46)	1921	*Colorado*-class	eight 16-inch
West Virginia	(BB-48)	1923	*Colorado*-class	eight 16-inch
North Carolina	(BB-55)	1941	*North Carolina*-class	nine 16-inch
Washington	(BB-56)	1941	*North Carolina*-class	nine 16-inch

Aircraft Carriers

Lexington	(CV-2)	1927	*Lexington*-class
Saratoga	(CV-3)	1927	*Lexington*-class
Ranger	(CV-4)	1934	*Ranger*-class
Yorktown	(CV-5)	1937	*Yorktown*-class
Enterprise	(CV-6)	1938	*Yorktown*-class
Wasp	(CV-7)	1940	*Wasp*-class
Hornet	(CV-8)	1941	*Yorktown*-class

Cruisers

		Commissioned		Main armament
Omaha	(CL-4)	1923	Omaha-class	twelve 6-inch
Milwaukee	(CL-5)	1923	Omaha-class	twelve 6-inch
Cincinnati	(CL-6)	1924	Omaha-class	twelve 6-inch
Raleigh	(CL-7)	1924	Omaha-class	twelve 6-inch
Detroit	(CL-8)	1923	Omaha-class	twelve 6-inch
Richmond	(CL-9)	1923	Omaha-class	twelve 6-inch
Concord	(CL-10)	1923	Omaha-class	twelve 6-inch
Trenton	(CL-11)	1924	Omaha-class	twelve 6-inch
Marblehead	(CL-12)	1924	Omaha-class	twelve 6-inch
Memphis	(CL-13)	1925	Omaha-class	twelve 6-inch
Pensacola	(CA-24)	1930	Pensacola-class	ten 8-inch
Salt Lake City	(CA-25)	1929	Pensacola-class	ten 8-inch
Northampton	(CA-26)	1930	Northampton-class	nine 8-inch
Chester	(CA-27)	1930	Northampton-class	nine 8-inch
Louisville	(CA-28)	1931	Northampton-class	nine 8-inch
Chicago	(CA-29)	1931	Northampton-class	nine 8-inch
Houston	(CA-30)	1930	Northampton-class	nine 8-inch
Augusta	(CA-31)	1931	Northampton-class	nine 8-inch
New Orleans	(CA-32)	1934	New Orleans-class	nine 8-inch
Portland	(CA-33)	1933	Portland-class	nine 8-inch
Astoria	(CA-34)	1934	New Orleans-class	nine 8-inch
Indianapolis	(CA-35)	1932	Portland-class	nine 8-inch
Minneapolis	(CA-36)	1934	New Orleans-class	nine 8-inch
Tuscaloosa	(CA-37)	1934	New Orleans-class	nine 8-inch
San Francisco	(CA-38)	1934	New Orleans-class	nine 8-inch
Quincy	(CA-39)	1936	New Orleans-class	nine 8-inch
Brooklyn	(CL-40)	1937	Brooklyn-class	fifteen 6-inch
Philadelphia	(CL-41)	1937	Brooklyn-class	fifteen 6-inch
Savannah	(CL-42)	1938	Brooklyn-class	fifteen 6-inch
Nashville	(CL-43)	1938	Brooklyn-class	fifteen 6-inch
Vincennes	(CA-44)	1937	New Orleans-class	nine 8-inch
Wichita	(CA-45)	1939	Wichita-class	nine 8-inch
Phoenix	(CL-46)	1938	Brooklyn-class	fifteen 6-inch
Boise	(CL-47)	1938	Brooklyn-class	fifteen 6-inch
Honolulu	(CL-48)	1938	Brooklyn-class	fifteen 6-inch
Saint Louis	(CL-49)	1939	Saint Louis-class	fifteen 6-inch
Helena	(CL-50)	1939	Saint Louis-class	fifteen 6-inch
Atlanta	(CL(AA)-51)	1941	Atlanta-class	sixteen 5-inch dual-purpose

Glossary and Guide to Abbreviations

A-17	Northrop single-engine attack plane
A-20	Douglas twin-engine light attack bomber
A-24	Army Air Corps variant of Douglas SBD dive-bomber
AAF	Army Air Forces
AEF	American Expeditionary Force (World War I)
AFCC	Air Force Combat Command
AT-18	Lockheed advanced navigational trainer variant of Hudson export light bomber
AWPD	Air War Plans Division
B-10	Martin twin-engine all-metal bomber
B-17	Boeing four-engine heavy bomber
B-18	Douglas twin-engine tactical bomber
B-23	Douglas twin-engine tactical bomber
B-24	Consolidated four-engine heavy bomber
Bf 109	German Messerschmitt single-engine fighter
Blitzkrieg	Lightning war
C-46	Curtiss twin-engine cargo/transport plane
C-47	Douglas twin-engine cargo/transport plane
CAA	Civil Aeronautics Agency
CCC	Civilian Conservation Corps
CPTP	Civilian Pilot Training Program
CV	Fleet aircraft carrier
DB-7	Douglas Bomber 7, the export variant of the A-20 light attack bomber
F2A	Brewster Buffalo carrier fighter
F3F	Grumman biplane carrier fighter
F4F	Grumman Wildcat carrier fighter
FMF	Fleet Marine Force
G-1	Staff section or head overseeing personnel and administration
G-3	Staff section or head overseeing operations and training

G-4	Staff section or head overseeing logistics and supply
GHQ	General headquarters
Kriegsmarine	German navy
LB-30	Consolidated British Liberator B-24 variant
LST	Landing Ship, Tank
Lufwaffe	German air force
LST	Landing ship, tank
LVT	Landing vehicle, tracked
M1	U.S. Garand .30-caliber semiautomatic infantry rifle
M2	U.S. light tank
M3	U.S. Stuart light tank or U.S. Lee medium tank
M4	U.S. Sherman medium tank
MOMP	Mid-ocean meeting point
OPM	Office of Production Management
P-26	Boeing fighter
P-35	Seversky fighter
P-36	Curtiss fighter
P-38	Lockheed Lightning twin-engine fighter
P-39	Bell Airacobra fighter
P-40	Curtiss Warhawk fighter
P-43	Republic Lancer fighter
P-44	Republic fighter
P-47	Consolidated Thunderbolt fighter
P-51	North American Mustang fighter
PBM	Martin Mariner twin-engine patrol bomber
PBO	Lockheed twin-engine maritime bomber
PBY	Consolidated Catalina twin-engine patrol bomber
RAF	Royal Air Force
SB2U	U.S. Navy/Marine Corps Vought Vindicator carrier scout-bomber
SBD	Douglas Dauntless carrier dive-bomber
TBD	Douglas carrier torpedo/light bomber
TBF	Grumman Avenger carrier torpedo/light bomber
USAFFE	U.S. Army Forces in the Far East
VMI	Virginia Military Institute
Wehrmacht	The German military as a whole, but often taken to refer to German ground forces.
WPA	Works Progress Administration

Bibliography

Books

Althoff, William F. *Sky Ships: A History of the Airship in the United States Navy*. New York: Crown Publishers, 1990.

Belote, James H., and William M. Belote. *Titans of the Seas: The Development and Operations of Japanese and American Carrier Task Forces during World War II*. New York: Harper & Row, 1975.

Biddle, Wayne. *Barons of the Sky: From Early Flight to Strategic Warfare, The Story of the American Aerospace Industry*. New York: Simon & Schuster, 1991.

Brown, Kenneth T. *Marauder Man: World War II in the Critical But Little Known B-26 Marauder Medium Bomber, A Memoir/History*. Pacifica, CA: Pacifica Press, 1997.

Cardozier, V. R. *The Mobilization of the United States in World War II: How the Government, Military and Industry Prepared for War*. Jefferson, NC: McFarland & Co., 1995.

Carter, Kit C., and Robert Mueller. *The Army Air Forces in World War II: Combat Chronology, 1941–1945*. Washington, DC: Office of Air Force History, 1973.

Carter, Rear Adm. Worrall Reed. *Beans, Bullets, and Black Oil: The Story of Fleet Logistics Afloat in the Pacific during World War II*. Washington, DC: Department of the Navy, 1953.

Copp, DeWitt S. *A Few Great Captains: The Men and Events That Shaped the Development of U.S. Air Power*. New York: Doubleday & Co., 1980.

———. *Forged in Fire: Strategy and Decisions in the Airwar Over Europe, 1940–1945*. New York: Doubleday & Co., 1982.

Craven, Wesley F., and James L. Cate, eds. *The Army Air Forces in World War II*, Vol. I, *Plans and Early Operations, January 1939 to August 1942*. Chicago: University of Chicago Press, 1948.

Cray, Ed. *General of the Army: George C. Marshall, Soldier and Statesman*. New York: Cooper Square Press, 2000.

Dull, Paul S. *The Imperial Japanese Navy (1941–1945)*. Annapolis, MD: Naval Institute Press, 1978.

Eiler, Keith E. *Mobilizing America: Robert P. Patterson and the War Effort, 1940–1945*. Ithaca, NY: Cornell University Press, 1997.

Esposito, Brig. Gen. Vincent J., ed. *The West Point Atlas of American Wars*, Vol. II, *1900–1953*. New York: Frederick A. Praeger, 1959.

Evans, David C., and Mark R. Peattie. *Kaigun: Strategy, Tactics, and Technology in the Imperial Japanese Navy, 1887–1941*. Annapolis, MD: Naval Institute Press, 1997.

Fairchild, Byron, and Jonathan Grossman. *U.S. Army in World War II: The War Department, The Army and Industrial Manpower*. Washington, DC: Office of the Chief of Military History, 1959.

Gabel, Christopher R. *The U.S. Army GHQ Maneuvers of 1941*. Washington, DC: Center of Military History, 1991.

Gole, Henry G. *The Road to Rainbow: Army Planning for Global War, 1934–1940*. Annapolis, MD: Naval Institute Press, 2003.

Hagan, Kenneth J. *This People's Navy: The Making of American Sea Power*. New York: The Free Press, 1991.

Hofmann, George F. *Through Mobility We Conquer: The Mechanization of the U.S. Cavalry*. Lexington, KY: University Press of Kentucky, 2006.

Holley, Irving Brinton, Jr. *U.S. Army in World War II: Special Studies, Buying Aircraft: Materiel Procurement for the Army Air Forces*. Washington, DC: Office of the Chief of Military History, 1964.

Hough, Frank O., Verle E. Ludwig, and Henry I. Shaw Jr. *Pearl Harbor to Guadalcanal*. Vol. I, *History of U.S. Marine Corps Operations in World War II*. Washington, DC: United States Marine Corps, 1958.

Hunnicutt, R. P. *Sherman: A History of the American Medium Tank*. Novato, CA: Presidio Press, 1978.

Johnson, David E. *Fast Tanks and Heavy Bombers: Innovation in the U.S. Army, 1917–1945*. Ithaca, NY: Cornell University Press, 1998.

Kaufmann, J. F., and H. W. Kaufmann. *The Sleeping Giant: American Armed Forces Between the Wars*. Westport, CT: Praeger Publishers, 1996.

Kriloff, Herbert. *Officer of the Deck: A Memoir of the Pacific War and the Sea*. Pacifica, CA: Pacifica Press, 2000.

Larrabee, Eric. *Commander in Chief: Franklin Delano Roosevelt, His Lieutenants, and Their War*. New York: Simon & Schuster, 1987.

Lundstrom, John B. *The First Team: Pacific Naval Air Combat from Pearl Harbor to Midway*. Annapolis, MD: Naval Institute Press, 1984.

Maurer, Maurer (ed.). *Air Force Combat Units of World War II*. Washington, DC: Office of Air Force History, 1983.

McFarland, Stephen L., and Wesley Phillips Newton. *To Command the Sky: The Battle for Air Superirity over Germany, 1942–1944*. Washington, DC: Smithsonian Institution Press, 1991.

Mets, David R. *Master of Air Power: General Carl A. Spaatz*. Novato, CA: Presidio Press, 1988.

Miller, Edward S. *War Plan Orange: The U.S. Strategy to Defeat Japan, 1897–1945*. Annapolis, MD: Naval Institute Press, 1991.

Mondey, David. *Concise Guide to American Aircraft of World War II*. London: Temple Press, 1982.

———. *Concise Guide to British Aircraft of World War II*. London: Temple Press, 1982.

———. *Concise Guide to Axis Aircraft of World War II*. London: Temple Press, 1984.

Morison, Samuel Eliot. *The Battle of the Atlantic, 1939–1943*, Vol. I, *History of United States Naval Operations in World War II*. Boston: Little, Brown and Company, 1947.

———. *The Rising Sun in the Pacific: 1931–April 1942*, Vol. III, *History of United States Naval Operations in World War II*. Boston: Little, Brown and Company, 1948.

Murray, Williamson, and Allan R. Millett, eds. *Military Innovation in the Interwar Period*. Cambridge, U.K.: Cambridge University Press, 1996.

Perett, Geoffrey. *There's A War To Be Won: The United States Army in World War II*. New York: Ballantine Books, 1991.

———. *Winged Victory: The Army Air Forces in World War II*. New York: Random House, 1993.

Potter, E. B. *Nimitz*. Annapolis, MD: Naval Institute Press, 1976.

Reynolds, Clark G. *Command of the Sea: The History and Strategy of Maritime Empires*. New York: William Morrow & Co., 1974.

———. *The Fast Carriers: The Forging of an Air Navy*. New York: McGraw-Hill, 1968.

Rose, Lisle A. *Power at Sea: The Breaking Storm, 1919–1945*. Columbia, MO: University of Missouri Press, 2007.

Ross, Steven T. *U.S. War Plans: 1938–1945*. Boulder, CO: Lynne Rienner Publishers, 2002.

Smith, R. Elberton. *U.S. Army in World War II: The War Department, The Army and Economic Mobilization*. Washington, DC: Office of the Chief of Military History, 1959.

Sherrod, Robert. *History of Marine Corps Aviation in World War II*. San Rafael, CA: Presidio Press, 1980.

Stanton, Shelby L. *Order of Battle: U.S. Army World War II*. Novato, CA: Presidio Press, 1984.

Stille, Mark, and Tony Bryan. *Imperial Japanese Navy Aircraft Carriers, 1921–1945*. Botley, U.K.: Osprey Publishing, 2005.

Tillman, Barrett. *The Dauntless Dive Bomber of World War II*. Annapolis, MD: Naval Institute Press, 1976.

———. *The Wildcat in WWII*. Annapolis, MD: Nautical & Aviation Publishing Company of America, 1983.

Toland, John. *But Not in Shame.* New York: Random House, 1961.

———. *The Rising Sun: The Decline and Fall of the Japanese Empire, 1936–1945.* New York: Random House, 1970.

Turnbull, Archibald D., and Clifford L. Lord. *History of United States Naval Aviation.* New York: Arno Press, 1972.

Watson, Mark Skinner. U.S. Army in World War II: The War Department, Chief of Staff: Prewar Plans and Preparations. Washington, DC: Center of Military History, 1991.

Wildenberg, Thomas. *All the Factors of Victory: Adm. Joseph Mason Reeves and the Origins of Carrier Air Power.* Dulles, VA: Brassey's, 2003.

———. *Gray Steel and Black Oil: Fast Tankers and Replenishment at Sea in the U.S. Navy, 1912–1995.* Annapolis, MD: Naval Institute Press, 1996.

Willoughby, Malcolm F. *The U.S. Coast Guard in World War II.* Annapolis, MD: U. S. Naval Institute, 1957.

Wylie, Adm. Joseph C. *Military Strategy: A General Theory of Power Control.* Annapolis, MD: Naval Institute Press, 1989.

Yeide, Harry. *Steeds of Steel: A History of American Mechanized Cavalry in World War II.* St. Paul. MN: Zenith Press, 2007.

———. *Steel Victory: The Heroic Story of America's Independent Tank Battalions at War in Europe.* New York: Presidio Press, 2005.

———. *Weapons of the Tankers: American Armor in World War II.* St. Paul, MN: Zenith Press, 2006.

Periodicals

Scarborough, William E. "The Neutrality Patrol: To Keep Us Out of War?" Part 1. *Naval Aviation News,* March–April 1990.

———. "The Neutrality Patrol: To Keep Us Out of War?" Part 2. *Naval Aviation News,* March–April 1990.

Unublished Sources

A'Hearn, Francis W. "The Industrial College of the Armed Forces: Contextual Analysis of an Evolving Mission, 1924–1994." Ph.D. dissertation, Virginia Polytechnic Institute and State University, 1997.

Internet

American Presidency Project: www.presidency.ucsb.edu

Arlington National Cemetary: www.arlingtoncemetary.net

Civilian Conservation Corps: www.cccalumni.org/history1.html

History Central: www.historycentral.com

Rainbow 5 Plan: www.ibiblio.org/pha/pha/misc/rainbow5.html
U.S. Naval Historical Center: www.history.navy.mil
Wikipedia: www.wikipedia.com

A note on the Web: Following a long break between narrative histories, this is the first book I have written with fingertip access to the World Wide Web via the wonders of Google and other aids. It is so easy to check facts and draw in details that I am simply floored. That said, and nevertheless, I must point out that an hour's stubborn work on the Web to construct one paragraph in Chapter 27 on the Tuskegee Airmen leaves me at a loss to explain how nine Google sources could be so at variance with one another. Key dates and details differ from one site to another, and two overlapping Wikipedia citations that were drawn up from slightly different search criteria conflict as to details, which is still strange to me even though I perceive that "democratic" Wikipedia data is compiled by hands that don't necessarily know and don't even necessarily seem to care what other hands are doing elsewhere in Wikipedia. In sum, I commend the Web to honest researchers, but, like everything else in the research game (and life), the wise practitioner still needs to consider the source.

Index

Places

Weapons, Aircraft, Ships